William IV entreats Liberty on the throne, 1832

The Republic of Britain

FRANK PROCHASKA

The Republic
of Britain

1760–2000

ALLEN LANE
THE PENGUIN PRESS

ALLEN LANE
THE PENGUIN PRESS

Published by the Penguin Group
Penguin Books Ltd, 27 Wrights Lane, London W8 5TZ, England
Penguin Putnam Inc., 375 Hudson Street, New York, New York 10014, USA
Penguin Books Australia Ltd, Ringwood, Victoria, Australia
Penguin Books Canada Ltd, 10 Alcorn Avenue, Toronto, Ontario, Canada M4V 3B2
Penguin Books (NZ) Ltd, Private Bag 102902, NSMC, Auckland, New Zealand

Penguin Books Ltd, Registered Offices: Harmondsworth, Middlesex, England

First published 2000
1 3 5 7 9 10 8 6 4 2

Picture acknowledgements
British Library: 4, 14; British Museum: frontispiece, 1, 2, 3, 5, 6, 7, 8; Express
Newspapers: 17; Institute of Historical Research: 9, 10; Jamie Reid/ARVO: 18;
Movement against the Monarchy: 20; Punch Limited: 19; Royal Archives ©, Her
Majesty Queen Elizabeth II: 16; University of London Library: 11, 12, 13, 15.

Set in 10.5/14 pt Monotype Sabon
Typeset by Rowland Phototypesetting Ltd, Bury St Edmunds, Suffolk
Printed and Bound in Great Britain by The Bath Press, Bath

A CIP catalogue record for this book is available from the British Library

ISBN 0-713-99454-1

To
Ivon Asquith

Contents

Illustrations

Acknowledgements

It is a pleasure to thank the many people who have helped with the writing of this book. In Britain and America, in seminars and beyond, republicans, supporters of the monarchy and dispassionate observers have contributed generously. I am particularly grateful to All Souls College, Oxford, where I held a Visiting Fellowship in 1997–8, for providing me with such a congenial environment in which to work. When I arrived, I had not written a word and had only a vague notion of the book's architecture in mind. When I left, much of it was in draft and I had a clear conception of where it was going. Part of Chapter 5 was originally a paper delivered to the Visiting Fellows' Colloquium, which appeared in *Twentieth Century British History* in April 1999.

The project would have been impossible without access to royal sources. By gracious permission of Her Majesty the Queen, I have been able to make use of material from the Royal Archives at Windsor. Rarely, if ever, has a Registrar of the Royal Archives been asked to dig out specifically 'republican' material, and I am much indebted to Sheila de Bellaigue and her colleagues for their unstinting attention to my many inquiries and for guiding me through the sources. Other institutions to which I am indebted include the British Library, the British Museum, the Bishopsgate Institute, the Bodleian Library, the King's Fund, the Institute of Historical Research, the Nuffield College Library, the National Library of Wales, Aberystwyth, the Public Record Office and the University of London Library.

My warmest thanks go to John Sainty and Bernard Semmel for their remarks on the manuscript, to Robert Baldock for his publishing advice, to Tanya von Preussen for her computer design skills and to Julia Walworth for help with the photographs. Penguin's expert reader provided just the sort of thoughtful comment needed to bring the book into sharper focus. My editor Stuart Proffitt read the manuscript with discernment and steered it through the press with flair. Richard Duguid, Daniel Hind, Ruth Killick, Richard Marston and Monica Schmoller moved the publishing process along with proficiency. Finally, I must pay a heartfelt tribute to my wife, Alice Prochaska, and to our children Elizabeth and William, for their indulgence and valuable criticism. They support me in dedicating the book to an old friend.

'If Monarchs would behave like republicans,
all their subjects would act as royalists.'
Samuel Taylor Coleridge (1795)

Preface

History is made by misunderstanding. Since the reign of George III, the relationship between republicans and the monarchy has been typified by mutual incomprehension, and dependence. This book is a study of that historic relationship, aiming to shed light on both the modern British monarchy and the various strands of republican opinion. The interaction of royalty and republicans, however they have described their beliefs, is its principal theme. It may be read as a history of radicalism with the monarchy in focus, or a history of the monarchy's reaction to what it perceived to be republican menaces. To royalty, accustomed to obsequious devotion, republicanism was the most hated word in the Palace lexicon, and it was interpreted generously, from mild-mannered complaints about royal expenditure to calls for the sovereign's head. Despite the evidence to the contrary, George V assumed that the Labour movement constituted a republican threat. Republicanism is in the eye of the beholder.

In conception, this book began with a rereading of Thomas Paine's *Rights of Man* (1791–2). There, in an aside, Paine reminds us of the classical meaning of *res publica*, 'the public thing', which did not assume that kingship was inconsistent with republican government. Though he despised the British monarchy, even Paine did not rule out the possibility of a republic with a king, at least in theory. A republic was government in the public interest and so he could hardly rule out every form of administration but the presidential. As he put it: 'What is called a *Republic*, is not any *particular form* of government.' The remark suggests an underlying theme in the history of republican thought, for so many republicans have been less interested in the form of government than in a vision of virtuous citizens creating a higher, risen politics.

In today's common parlance, republicanism is often narrowed to mean little more than opposition to the Crown. This perception, which owes much to royal scrapes in the 1980s and 90s, contributes to a disregard for the varieties and complexities of republicanism, both past and present. The words of the Whig reformer Charles James Fox in the 1790s should make us reflect: 'our Constitution was a republic, in the just sense of the word; it was a Monarchy founded on the good of the people'. For much of the period under discussion here, republicanism had more to do with civic virtue and the expansion of democratic rights than with the monarchy. In its anti-monarchical guise, republicanism has waxed with revolution abroad and royal scandal at home, but it has never enjoyed massive popular support. In its democratic guise, it has been more successful, though it has not led to the transparent, purified politics of the evolving republican imagination.

On one level, this is a study of the battle over what republicanism means. Depending on one's point of view, the title 'The Republic of Britain' may suggest either the constitutional reality or the political aspiration. Today, the *Oxford English Dictionary* defines a republic as any 'state in which the supreme power rests in the people and their elected representatives ... as opposed to one governed by a king'. On this *constitutional* definition, Britain *is* a republic, for Queen Elizabeth II could hardly be said to govern. Over the years, a series of political reforms, capped by the Representation of the People Act of 1918, satisfied the constitutional demands, if not the cultural hopes, of democratic republicans, while retaining what the radical Henry Labouchere called a 'hereditary President'. At the end of the First World War, the republican writer H. G. Wells described the British constitution as a 'Crowned Republic'. The phrase came from Tennyson, who in an epilogue to *Idylls of the King* praised the 'crown'd Republic's crowning common-sense, that saved her many times'.

Such usage suggests the protean nature of republicanism. Individuals often moved from one republican position to another, depending on personal whim or changing political circumstances. But in British history since the eighteenth century at least three types stand out, whose edges often overlapped. First, there were 'classical' or 'civic virtue' republicans, who generally accepted monarchy that was limited and public spirited. Charles James Fox may be seen in this tradition. Second, there were 'theoretical' republicans, who contemplated the end of the monarchy in the abstract, but being practical saw little point in taking it up as a cause. Innumerable reformers fall into this category, including the philosopher Frederic Harrison in the 1870s and a host of current MPs. Third, there were those, known as 'pure' or anti-monarchical republicans, who called explicitly for the abolition of the monarchy, sometimes in violent tones. Thomas Paine may be seen as the embodiment of this tradition.

Pure republican arguments have been fairly consistent since the late eighteenth century, when Paine gave shape to anti-monarchical doctrine. They concentrate on the Crown's political power, undemocratic character, expense and social influence. But in so constitutionalist a nation, pure republicans have been in a minority, typically relegated to the political fringe. Much of the criticism of the Crown turned not on the drastic measure of abolition, but on such issues as the character of individual sovereigns, corruption in Palace administration and the size of the allowances granted to members of the royal family. Crown finance spawned its own republican variant, what was sometimes called 'Civil List' republicanism. Despite the acres of print given over to admonishing the royal family and 'hangers on' at court, such issues were never likely to endanger the throne in a prosperous nation with settled political traditions.

On the face of it, it may seem surprising that the British monarchy is still in existence: 1776, 1789, 1848, 1870–72, 1917–19, 1945–7, 1992–7 could hardly be seen as halcyon days for royalty. Other European nations, of course, turned their backs on monarchy, usually under extreme conditions of war or revolution. But the fact that the British Crown survived while other dynasties toppled was proof to many of its superiority. Former British dominions too have become uncrowned republics, most notably India, that 'Jewel in the Crown', which achieved independence in 1947. The reasons included the need for a visible head of state dedicated to representing that nation alone, and the wish to be unencumbered by historic associations with imperialism. But such arguments did not resonate back in Britain, and thus far the expression of republicanism in the former dominions has done little to enliven opposition to the House of Windsor at home.

The power of custom, as the early nineteenth-century philosopher Jeremy Bentham noted, should not be underestimated when it comes to the Crown's survival. The British public have shown themselves unsus-ceptible to foreign precedents and decidedly resistant to anti-monarchical arguments. The greatest threat to the monarchy in modern history has come not from domestic enemies, but from external ones. Had Britain been defeated by Napoleon or lost wars in 1918 or 1945, the case against the Crown might have seemed more cogent. But in a nation that has not been invaded, nor had a revolution since the seventeenth century, in which the sovereign's power has dwindled to influence, it is perhaps not surprising that the monarchy has been retained. 'Why keep it?' ask the enemies of the Crown. 'Why all the fuss?' reply the general public, who refuse to be reasoned out of monarchy. The issue is not whether the monarchy is reasonable or just, but whether people believe it to be so.

Arguably, the Crown's survival into the age of democracy was not simply a tribute to the power of tradition, or the gradual shift of power from monarchs to popularly elected ministers in a nation that had avoided revolution or invasion. The monarchy has long been more active in its own defence than is commonly assumed. For one thing, the court used its political and social leverage to confound its critics, particularly those in Parliament. For another, the royal family could itself make claims to a hybrid form of republican virtue through its active participation in civic and charitable work. At critical historic moments, such as 1848 and 1918, royalty took out an insurance policy against potential trouble through highly visible, public-spirited social service. This is not to say that the British monarchy has survived only because it turned itself into an agency of welfare or made adjustments to mass politics, but clearly self-help eased the royal road to social democracy.

This is an interpretative book in narrative form. It makes no claims to have exhausted the subject for Britain, let alone to have dealt with the varieties of republicanism in Ireland, the Empire or the Commonwealth, which have their own distinctive traditions. The colonial dimensions of anti-monarchism in particular form an enormous subject in their own right and would require another book. While based extensively on primary sources, this book has benefited from the distinguished writing on British radicalism and from recent work on the history of the monarchy by, among others, Vernon Bogdanor, David Cannadine, Linda Colley, Phillip Hall, William Kuhn, Marilyn Morris and Ben Pimlott. My own *Royal Bounty: The Making of a Welfare Monarchy* (1995) aroused my interest in republican thought. It may seem odd to come to the history of republicanism by way of writing on the monarchy, but it does have advantages, not least the avoidance of tunnel vision.

I

George III and the Rights of Man
1760–1800

'What! What!, if they go on at this rate, in thirty years they will not leave a King in Europe.'   Attributed to George III (1789)

'What is called a *Republic*, is not any *particular form* of government.'   Thomas Paine, *Rights of Man* (1791–2)

What is a republic? In the eighteenth century, republicanism was a shapeless idea, with succeeding generations altering its meaning or shifting its emphasis. The Latin *res publica*, the 'public thing', had been defined variously as the state, the commonwealth, mixed government, limited monarchy, a polity or simply the public domain. Constitutional writers had applied the word 'republic' to both absolute monarchy in France and the Commonwealth under Cromwell, which would suggest that it may signify just about anything, or nothing.[1] Early in the reign of George I, the Whig essayist Joseph Addison accused the Tories of turning republicanism on its head so that it constituted 'Loyalty to our king'.[2] Nearly a century later, President John Adams admired the phrase 'monarchical republic', by which he meant a form of government in which kingship did not descend into despotism. But as the author of a classic work on constitutions, he concluded that the word republic was unintelligible: 'The name republic is given to things, in their nature as different and contradictory as light and darkness.'[3]

The 'classical' republicans or 'commonwealthmen' in eighteenth-century England consisted of a band of well-read men and women, admirers of ancient republics, who wished to carry forward the cause for which Parliament stood in the Civil War.[4] They abhorred despotism, yet few of them were hostile to monarchy or considered it to be unconstitutional.[5] They were less interested in kingship than in ensuring that an élite of independent gentlemen governed the country in a manner conducive to liberty and virtue. Some of them worried that commerce threatened the public good by increasing selfish behaviour. But whatever their views on bourgeois commercial values, classical republicans were typically bookish people with time to devote to public life, which they wished to see purified.[6] Increasingly, they defined their amorphous doctrine in terms of civic virtue or 'public spirit', for a workable republic depended on active citizens placing the good of the community before their own self-interest.[7] Happiness itself was the product of participatory virtue.

The British eighteenth-century mind, still haunted by the Civil War, held fast to monarchy as a fount of social stability, if not eternal order. The Interregnum had unleashed new modes of political thought, but English classical republicans, many of them Dissenters, largely kept faith with the compromises of 1688, which gave them a measure of respectability. They assumed that man's nature was fallen, his reason frail, and thus they emphasized the rule of law and the need for a separation of powers in a mixed government of King, Lords and Commons. (See Plate 1.) Fearing the abuse of power, whether monarchical or ministerial, they put their faith in public spirit, frequent parliaments, administrative reform and economical government. Few of them had any enthusiasm for democracy, which they often equated with anarchy. Their object was not the expansion of political rights but the fragmentation of power, which would provide security, a just measure of liberty and the avoidance of arbitrary rule. If there was a predominant republican belief, it was fear of tyranny.[8]

Eighteenth-century English writings on the duty of kings did not draw their inspiration from the political philosophy of Hobbes. Theories of mixed government had replaced those of divine right and absolutism. Over time, social, religious and political changes had emasculated the atavistic, warrior tradition of princely power, and out of it had emerged a view of constitutional monarchy as described by classical republicans. The ambiguity of the balanced constitution offered the monarch himself scope for testing the limits of royal authority, just as it provided scope for critics of the prevailing political administration. George III's conception of the royal prerogative bore little resemblance to the assumptions of Henry VIII or Charles I. He wished to recover as much control of the executive as possible within the vague parameters of the constitution, but he never sought to repeal the legislation that constituted the Revolutionary Settlement of 1688.[9]

The following is an idealized description of Britain's constitutional monarchy from the mid-eighteenth century, which may be read as a classical republican text:

Thus have we created the noblest constitution the human mind is capable of framing, where the executive power is in the prince, the legislative in the nobility and the representatives of the people, and the judicial in the people and in some cases the nobility, to whom there lies a final appeal from all other courts of judicature, where every man's life, liberty and possessions are secure, where one part of the legislative body checks the other by the privilege of rejecting, both checked by the executive, as that is again by the legislative; all parts moving, and however they may follow the particular interest of their body, yet all uniting at the last for the public good.[10]

In practice, George III, who wrote these lines as a youth under the guidance of Lord Bute, gave rather more weight to the monarch than many classical republicans would have wished.[11] But he had adopted the equivocal language of republicanism to argue the case for the Crown. Ultimately he was a political manager who had to work within the framework established by the Revolution of 1688. As the twists and turns in his relations with ministers suggest, he operated in an ideological context in which kingship was in flux.[12]

In an era of commercial expansion, foreign wars and oligarchic corruption, George III's idealized constitution did not mesh with the political reality. The King lacked tact when conciliation was required, and his obvious enjoyment of power sometimes led to public disquiet. In the 1760s, he was widely suspected, on flimsy evidence, of trying to subvert the constitution. He invited further opprobrium for his generous interpretation of the royal prerogative in the 'Wilkes and Liberty' crisis. His hostility to John Wilkes, who was arrested and thrown into the Tower for his irreverent criticism of government policy, left the politically minded public with the impression that the constitution was being strained to satisfy a royal vendetta.[13] In London, Wilkite rioters reminded the King of the fate of despots by driving a hearse into the grounds of St James's Palace.[14] By a questionable use of his power, the King stirred up a small band of republicans with anti-monarchical leanings.

Several of Wilkes's supporters became outspoken critics of royalty, among them Catherine Macaulay, the historian, and her brother John Sawbridge, an alderman of the City of London.[15] Another was Sylas Neville, a flamboyant radical, who moved easily between the political underworld of public houses and the more fashionable world of West End theatres, where, it has been said, he spent more time with royalty than was consistent with his opinions. Still, he 'abhorred the sight of George and Charlotte', toasted the death of Charles I, and noted in his diary: 'O Lord! May Britain never see another coronation.'[16] Writing in 1771, he denounced the Crown as 'that worst and most dangerous part of our Constitution', which had 'succeeded too well in turning the principles of the People against themselves'.[17]

While Neville's anti-monarchism had an echo in clubs and debating societies, royalty retained a powerful hold on the public imagination. In London, the radical Robin Hood Society held debates on the monarchy in the third quarter of the eighteenth century, with royalists usually winning the vote.[18] But anti-monarchism played little part in the language of conventional politics. It bore little relationship to the known world of courts and oligarchic rule, in which the great mass of mankind toiled offstage. To the majority who accepted a hierarchical view of the universe and looked to Christ as the king of kings, anti-monarchism seemed a perverse conceit.[19] Intellectually, it represented a leap of faith, comparable to atheism in a world of religious convention. The expression of anti-royalist views was seen by polite society in England as scandalous, or treasonable.

The precise form of government Neville wished to see in place is uncertain, though freedom from tyranny, or the advance of 'liberty', would have been its *raison d'être*. Like other republicans with a visceral hatred of royalty, he was more inclined to abuse the monarchy than engage in reasoned discussion. He was the sort of character, it has been said, who would pick a political argument with the person standing next to him in a queue for the theatre.[20] In later life he seems to have disavowed the advanced views of his youth. But when the former stay-maker and exciseman Thomas Paine produced his great polemic *Common Sense* in 1776, Neville was ecstatic, for it treated George III 'as the dog deserves'.[21]

Thomas Paine was not the first to ridicule the King in print, but *Common Sense* may be said to represent the great opening salvo against the modern British Crown. The pamphlet's success as a political document turned on its memorable phrases, mass distribution and a receptive audience willing to be converted to its radical philosophy.[22] Written to liberate America from the shackles of 'tyranny', it introduced a strident anti-monarchism into republicanism. By a fertile combination of invective and passionate argument, Paine began to shift the focus of republican opinion from its classical formulation of the King in Parliament to a democratic polity at odds with monarchy. By widening the meaning of *res publica* to embrace the affairs of the population at large, he fuelled a definition of republic that took it to be synonymous with a state in which supreme power rests in the people, as opposed to one governed by a king.

Paine's America was an arcadia threatened by monarchical tyranny, a land sacrificed to satisfy European dynastic interests. In his view, there was nothing so ridiculous as a king or potentially so wicked, for 'a thirst for absolute power is the natural disease of monarchy'. Kingship was an insult to reason, an 'invention of the devil . . . for the promotion of idolatry'. In another striking phrase, which would have endeared him to American Protestants, he called it 'the Popery of government'. Worse still, monarchy was hereditary, which was 'an imposition on posterity'. Far from producing a race of wise and good men, it 'opens the door to the *foolish*, the *wicked*, and the *improper*'. Men born to rule become self-important. Indifferent to the world, they become despotic. 'In short, monarchy and succession have laid . . . the world in blood and ashes.'[23]

Paine accepted that the British monarchy was less bloodthirsty than elsewhere, but only because of the limitations imposed on it by '*the people*'. At the outbreak of the American Revolution, the English constitution exhibited a treacherous mixture of monarchical and republican elements. He was well aware that others called it a republic. But in his view it was unworthy of the name, for an overbearing monarchy had 'poisoned the republic' by monopolizing the Commons. 'The nearer any government approaches to a republic the less business there is for a king,' he insisted. In England, the King's business was puzzling, for George III had 'little more to do than to make war and give away places'. All the more puzzling was the state of affairs in which the public was expected to worship a man 'allowed eight hundred thousand sterling a year'.[24] The fact that the King did not have all this money at his personal disposal did not cause Paine to pause for thought.[25]

Paine had imbibed much from the classical republican tradition, including the importance of civic virtue in the creation of a just society. But he
departed from republican traditions in jettisoning the historic arguments
for a balanced constitution in favour of citizens' rights as the foundation
of liberty.[26] By defining tyranny so widely, Paine expanded democratic
principles and forged the link between political reform and the future of
the British Crown. By making the monarchy a focus of popular discontent, he began to shift the meaning of republicanism for the common
man. If classical republicanism was an ideology suited to the leisured,
'country' interest, Paine geared his anti-monarchical, democratic republicanism to an artisan culture and the values of an increasingly commercial
society.[27]

From the American perspective, it was much easier to see the King as
a despot heading a tyrannical government, partly because of the absentee
nature of political authority, partly because of the behaviour of the British
Army towards colonial civilians. Americans also blamed George III for
taxation without representation. But outside America, anti-monarchism
was not so easily defined as patriotism. Few in Britain accused the King,
as Paine did, of despotic warmongering. The word 'patriotism', which
came into use in the seventeenth century, tended to be the property of
opponents of the prevailing administration. But the American war put
British radicals and critics of the King's government on the defensive
and challenged their claims to patriotism.[28] As a 'Patriot' pamphleteer
observed in the 1770s: 'a man may hate his King, yet not love his
country'.[29]

Corruption was endemic in British politics, but at home, if not abroad,
the prevailing Whig ideology, which the King shared, was relatively
passive and tolerant. Against the background of civil war between Britain
and her American colonies, challenges to royal authority from rebellious
'petitioning' republicans were widely unpopular. (See Plate 2.) Radical
attacks on the Crown were justified and respectable in America, but they
were much less persuasive in Britain. It could not be assumed in Britain
that George III was a tyrant dominating the Commons, a sovereign
against whom there was no appeal short of revolution.[30] The governing
classes, in introspective mood, rallied behind the monarchy as a source
of political stability. In the climate introduced by the American war,
anti-monarchists had to be even more circumspect. Criticizing King

George was an unlikely ladder for those who wished to get on in their careers.

George III did not take lightly challenges to his authority inside or outside Parliament. The Wilkite Riots, which influenced republican thought and stimulated radical ideas generally, had served as a warning to the Crown. But the American war, which set the terms of the debate on the monarchy, was an altogether more critical experience. George III's refusal to yield when it went badly led to the most serious internal challenge to the monarchy during his reign. If things were not bad enough, the anti-Catholic Gordon Riots broke out in London in the middle of the American crisis. As the King saw it, the American mob rioted in the name of liberty, the British mob in the name of bigotry. Both upheavals confirmed the King's fears and encouraged his resolve.[31]

The American débâcle undermined the King's authority. Frustrated, he considered abdication, but in the end accepted the resignation of Lord North and swallowed the indignity of accepting American independence, which North's successor as Prime Minister, the Marquess of Rocking- ham, pressed on him. It was another milestone in the growth of ministerial power. The episode introduced a modern conception of the relationship between the King and his ministers, in which the sovereign had 'to accept the advice of ministers even if it was unpalatable'.[32] George II once complained that 'ministers are the Kings in this country'.[33] After the American War of Independence, which tilted the balance of the consti- tution towards Parliament and reduced co-operation between King and Commons, George III may well have agreed.[34]

Events in America sparked off a movement for parliamentary reform and, despite the King's resistence, marked a further stage in the decline in the sovereign's power. During the eighteenth century, the growth in ministerial authority had circumscribed the King's room for manoeuvre. The trend had been accelerated by protracted warfare, population growth and prosperity, all of which vastly increased the volume of public business. In such circumstances, it was more and more difficult for the King to keep abreast of public affairs or retain independence of action from his ministers. Increasingly, administration weighed heavily on George III, who did not even have a private secretary until overtaken by blindness in 1805.

The King was not as lavishly financed as Paine and others supposed.

Disputes over royal expenditure had come to a head early in the reign. In 1760, legislation gave George III a fixed Civil List income of £800,000 (increased to £900,000 in 1777), but in exchange for the Crown's hereditary revenues. The change resulted in greater parliamentary control over the King's affairs, which further undermined the Crown's freedom of action.[35] But the Civil List money did not pay simply for the personal support and maintenance of the King, as Paine implied in *Common Sense*. More than half of it was spent on government services, including foreign missions and the salaries of ministers, civil servants and judges.[36] Such an inefficient system of financing government provided a perennial source of complaint to economical reformers, who wanted to eliminate waste, and merriment to anti-monarchists, who pretended that it was a vast royal sinecure.

The incremental reform of royal finance, which was a feature of the reign of George III, was designed to control government spending and prevent the King from falling into debt. It was part of a series of legislative measures which reduced his political influence. But while the King disliked parliamentary challenges to his authority, they were not without benefits for the Crown. The gradual removal of abuses increased the monarchy's stature and moderated suspicions of corruption.[37] Moreover, restrictions on royal authority, as Linda Colley explains, 'made it much easier for the public to distinguish between monarch and minister and to celebrate the former without owing allegiance to the latter'.[38] Given the encroachments on George III's political independence, increasingly noticeable after the American crisis, the anti-monarchical remarks of radicals like Paine looked extreme.

Despite his preoccupation with Parliament and the power of the executive, George III was more directly sensitive to his subjects than his critics, including Paine, imagined. As the monarchy's sanctity and power came under scrutiny, its political and social views became more benign and inclusive. The idea, dear to classical republicans, that privilege entailed responsibility, was not without charm to limited monarchs, who had to persuade in order to rule. Like his grandfather before him, George III was deeply conscious of the constraints on his political freedom and took pains over the way he presented himself in public. Well before the American Revolution, he displayed a popular paternalism and showed himself sensitive to social needs.[39] After the American defeat, it was all the more essential for the Crown to reappraise its practices and presentation and to be seen in a dazzling light. Through tours, processions, military reviews and charitable festivals, the royal family made itself visible in splendid fashion to an expectant public. The expanding press gave its readers the royal news they craved.[40]

Monarchists and monarcho-republicans commonly depicted the king as the first servant of his people. In *The Idea of a Patriot King* (1738), which was frequently reprinted in the second half of the eighteenth century, Henry St John, first Viscount Bolingbroke, argued: 'to govern like the common father of his people, is so essential to the character of a Patriot King that he who does otherwise forfeits the title'. 'Popularity', he added, was the sole foundation of royal authority in a mixed government, and popularity depended on 'appearances'.[41] Bolingbroke imagined a king 'who would himself take the lead in rendering Parliament independent of ministerial and oligarchic control'.[42] While his writing seems not to have influenced George III personally, it was important in shaping public perceptions of royal conduct and reinforcing the idea that people could go over the head of ministers to petition the king.[43]

During George III's reign the vicissitudes of politics and family life brought out the King's resilience and deepened his association with the philosophy of social betterment. To conservatives like Hannah More, the King was to be the focus of national morality. More despised Bolingbroke's doubting theology, but she elaborated his constitutional views in her advice to the monarchy to practise the 'arts of popularity' through benevolence and religious example. As she wrote in 1782, 'A Crown! What is it? It is to bear the miseries of a people! To hear their murmurs, feel their discontents, and sink beneath a load of splendid care!'[44] Thomas Gisborne, a leading divine, also put the case of the philanthropic king: 'streams of happiness flow from a sovereign who regards his subjects as his children and watches over them with charity'.[45]

Evangelical propagandists like More, Gisborne and William Wilberforce were in the ascendancy. Having prepared the royal ground by obsequious flattery, they shamelessly exploited the monarchy's good offices in their crusade to reform the nation's manners and morals. In 1787, they scored a signal triumph when George III issued his 'Proclamation against Vice and Immorality'. It is difficult to measure the success of the Proclamation, but it fuelled the growing exaltation of the monarchy in church circles and brought royalty more closely into the Evangelical orbit. The King and Queen, in response to religious pressures and the ever-greater demands on their charity, did their Christian duty. On a visit to Worcester in 1788, they distributed £550 to the city's needy.[46] The following year they gave away £1,950 to dockyard labourers and the poor of Plymouth.[47] Such beneficent gestures flowed from the King as head of society rather than in his capacity as executive, a distinction that would become increasingly important as the power of the Crown declined.

George III, despite his reputation as a miser, proved to be the most generous monarch in modern British history.[48] He once protested against any reduction of his private income, his Privy Purse (Class I of the Civil List), on the grounds that it was 'the only fund from whence I pay every act of private benevolence'. Charitable distributions, as he lamented, 'alone make the station bearable'.[49] By the 1780s, he was giving away about £14,000, or about a quarter of his Privy Purse, which was set at £60,000 a year in 1777.[50] It might be said that the King was simply redistributing money that could have been put to public benefit more directly. As anti-monarchists like Paine would have it, royal philanthropy was a deceit played on the poor by parasites living in luxurious idleness. Still, the sums George III gave away, which he was not obliged to dispense from his private income, represented benevolence on a grand scale.

Royal patronage was a longstanding tradition, but one which was picking up in the reign of George III, if only because of the growing number of institutions that aspired to it. Enterprising philanthropists, who thrived on advertisement, saw a royal association as the highest accolade. The King, though better known for his support for science and the arts, also served as patron to nine charities, including the Foundling Hospital, St George's Hospital and the Royal Lancasterian Association. Increasingly, the extended royal family took an active interest in the massively proliferating non-governmental institutions – charities, academies and professional bodies – which we now think of as constituting civil society. By the end of the eighteenth century, scores of leading institutions and philanthropists boasted royal support.[51]

For the royal family, charitable patronage was an ideal accompaniment to royal tours and celebrations. It created dependent clients and fostered that acceptance of royalism and hierarchy that so agitated Paine. To charitable organizers, royal associations offered glamour, respectability and increased subscriptions. Those who received the benefits remembered and celebrated royal condescension and example. Quite naturally, the Crown expected all those who came into contact with royal philanthropy to give loyalty in return. As an expert on the 'mystique of monarchy' noted, the Crown was its own best press agent: every time members of the royal family paid a subscription, appeared in public or 'smiled upon a crowd of children', they chalked up 'another notch in the unbounded sentiment'.[52] They also, it must be said, caused good deeds to be done that otherwise would not have been done.

The royal family entered the wide open doors of the nation's voluntary institutions and found it warm inside. No other role offered such rich returns in publicity and deference for so little effort. Most of those who came into contact with royalty at charitable functions believed the King to be a paragon of public spirit. One loyalist went so far as to criticize George III and Queen Charlotte for not giving greater publicity to their beneficence.[53] Such people did not credit Paine's description of the King as an overbearing oligarch, who drained the treasury and corrupted his subjects through titles and placemen. Paine's criticisms persuaded many an alienated radical, but they fell on deaf ears among the many subjects involved in non-political, civic associations. Intriguingly, the monarchy was becoming more closely associated with just the sort of self-governing, civil institutions that Paine thought essential to create a republican society.

In *Common Sense*, Paine made a distinction, unique in the political writing of his day, between government and civil society.[54] The state was an artificial contrivance, 'the badge of lost innocence', whereas voluntary institutions opened up visions of reform based on the citizen's natural sociability. 'Society is produced by our wants, and government by our wickedness; the former promotes our happiness *positively* by uniting our affections, the latter *negatively* by restraining our vices. The one encourages intercourse, the other creates distinctions. The first is a patron, the last a punisher.'[55] Paine, who called for a minimalist state in *Common Sense*, saw the monarchy simply as an expression of state power, or the 'punisher'. Tellingly, he did not make the distinction between the King as executive and the King as head of society. But a growing number of people, who benefited from the non-governmental, civic role of the Crown, thought King George addressed their wants and aspirations through being the nation's first 'patron'.

Paine's ideal republic could only flourish through civic virtue embodied in free associations outside government control.[56] Yet he failed to credit the expanding number of charities, societies and professional bodies in England that expressed the local self-governance that he so admired. Like many radicals, Paine spoke more about rights than duties, and he expressed his own virtue through political association rather than benevolence. Still, the active citizenship valued by all republicans, whatever their stripe, found expression in the array of voluntary associations being set up in the late eighteenth century. Indeed, the royal family, through its support for the intermediary institutions of civil society, was arguably carrying forward a Paineite agenda. Moreover, through its charitable role, which drew on long experience, the Crown mitigated the distress of the very people Paine wished to convert to his particular brand of republicanism.

The royal family's associations outside politics helped to ward off anti-monarchism and compensated for George III's political mistakes. The King's popularity, which had picked up in the late 1780s, turned on a variety of causes. In addition to royal support for a growing number of institutions, a more assertive monarchical image was being created through ceremonial. The Thanksgiving Service for the King's recovery from illness in the spring of 1789 typified such ritual. The celebrations annoyed many a radical – the clergyman Richard Price compared it to 'a herd crawling at the feet of a master'.[57] But George III's return to health came as a great relief to the nation, for it ended a political crisis and restored a semblance of constitutional balance. He recovered just in time to witness the outbreak of the French Revolution. In the following years, he came to be portrayed in less political terms as '*the* uncontentious point of national union'.[58] The Tory radical William Cobbett put it grandly: the sovereign was 'the repository of all that is necessary to the preservation of the national character'.[59]

As the central figure in nationalistic propaganda, George III had much to recommend him. His personal life was blameless, and his behaviour, if sometimes eccentric, was moral and decorous. As John Wesley said of him: 'He believes the Bible . . . he fears God . . . he loves the Queen.'[60] And unlike the Bourbons, he was prudent in financial matters. Contrary to the jibes of Paine and a host of caricaturists, George III was not a corrupt spendthrift, but given to economy in managing his finances.[61] Moreover, he was a man easy to portray, as he was portrayed by loyalists, as a genial, if somewhat pathetic, figure, the epitome of the 'family' monarch. The King kept the revolutionaries at bay by holding himself up as a model of familial virtue and domestic tranquillity. The combination of illness and fallibility made him vulnerable and seemingly accessible to his extended family beyond the court, who felt some affection for him.[62] The expanding press coverage of royal trials and triumphs became part of the nation's conversation about itself and its past.

The King's popularity on the eve of the French Revolution also turned on politics, but perhaps not for reasons that gave him pleasure. An increasingly well-informed public recognized that the political system was slowly undergoing change and generally approved of it. The American war had increased suspicions that the Crown had become overbearing, unbalancing the constitution. Consequently, Parliament introduced the legislation, mentioned earlier, that brought a train of modest economies and reforms which reduced the monarch's capacity to sway political affairs through sinecures and parliamentary placemen. In this sense, the monarchy's recovery in popularity after the American defeat was a function of the King's political weakness, not his strength. It may also have had something to do with George III's physical decline, which made it difficult for him to carry out his duties. In an era marked by ever growing demands for economical and political reform, it might be said that the Crown had more to gain from giving way than from opposing. But would the monarchy survive if it no longer ruled?

In the aftermath of 1789, a more immediate question appeared: would the monarchy survive the momentous events taking place across the Channel? Could it cope with the declaration of the rights of man? The storming of the Bastille was widely welcomed in England. Hannah More's heart exulted at the news.[63] Even George III, it has been said, 'recognized the hand of justice in the enforced limitation of Bourbon power'.[64] But the ensuing events did nothing for the morale of the British royal family. Horrified by the treatment of Louis XVI, Queen Charlotte wrote in August 1789: 'this cannot be the eighteenth century in which we live at present, for antient [*sic*] history can hardly produce anything more barbarous and cruel than our neighbours in France'.[65] Nor was George III amused. 'What! What!', he was reported to have cried, 'if they go on at this rate, in thirty years they will not leave a King in Europe.'[66] In the circumstances, even the Prince of Wales abandoned his Whig friends, some of whom were known to be unsympathetic to the Crown, and rallied to his father's defence.

As the Prince of Wales recognized, the revolution in France was a watershed for king and country in Britain too, an event so significant that it was to affect the lives of a generation. As calls for democratic and social reform rose in a great swell, they resounded at the Palace gates. In a famous sermon 'on the Love of our Country', delivered in praise of the Revolution, the Unitarian radical Richard Price described George III as 'almost the only lawful King in the world'. But he advised him to consider himself 'as more properly the *servant* than the sovereign' of his people. And he concluded his address with a peroration, couched in millennial language, that could only alarm the court: 'I see the ardour for liberty catching and spreading, a general amendment beginning in human affairs, the dominion of kings changed for the dominion of laws, and the dominion of priests giving way to the dominion of reason and conscience.'[67]

To British reformers, the French Revolution created an unexpected opportunity, for it excited a millennial politics in which reason and conscience might carry mankind to a new Jerusalem. Poets and intellectuals fed the radical euphoria. William Blake sported a liberty cap, while the young Wordsworth rejoiced in 'human nature seeming born again'.[68] Gallic 'liberty' revitalized political association in Britain. New clubs and 'corresponding societies' emerged across the country, which proclaimed their solidarity with French revolutionaries and called for greater representation of the people in Parliament. As the revolution deepened in France, it invigorated doctrines and specific political demands that were more egalitarian than anything produced by generations of classical republicans. Not since the seventeenth century had the constitution been subjected to such inquiry or inquisition.

Radical doctrines, including anti-monarchical ones, appealed to alienated intellectuals and large numbers of unrepresented artisans, tradesmen and labourers, whose political views were inchoate.[69] Just as importantly, they appealed to middle-class Dissenters, like Price, who were excluded from full participation in civil government by the restrictions imposed by the Test and Corporation Acts passed in the seventeenth century. Deeply conscious of their disabilities, their 'natural connections', as one of them put it, 'are not with kings and nobles'.[70] The belief that mankind could begin afresh by toppling the social order was potentially attractive to all those outside the political nation. To those in search of political inspiration, it was natural to turn to that turbulent genius of the American Revolution – Thomas Paine.

Loyalists, who believed they had something to lose, saw Paine as the most perfidious radical precisely because he had the greatest following among the disenfranchised. In England, his reputation as a rabble rouser preceded him. Never one to avoid a disturbance, Paine welcomed the events taking place in France. 'A share in two revolutions is living to some purpose,' he told George Washington.[71] His life in America led him to interpret the commotion in France as an extension of the American experience. Back in England, he seized on the madness of George III as symptomatic of a diseased body politic. As events in France unfolded, he took up his pen once again in defence of revolution. The result was the *Rights of Man*, which appeared in two parts in 1791 and 1792. Hugely successful, it did more than any other publication of the day to ignite popular radicalism in Britain.

The *Rights of Man* was a savage indictment of social hierarchy and an appeal for representative government based on natural rights. It was written in response to Edmund Burke's *Reflections on the Revolution in France*. Burke's work took a dim view of human behaviour and represented events in France as the embodiment of evil. 'A good book,' exclaimed George III, 'every gentleman ought to read it.'[72] Paine's work was more sanguine about man as a social animal and depicted the French Revolution, like the American, as another stage in the perfection of mankind. The King is said to have picked up a copy in a Windsor bookshop, but put it down when he came to the passage in which his capacity was likened to that of a parish constable.[73]

No other institution divided Burke and Paine more than the monarchy, which after the French Revolution became something of a touchstone of Left and Right in Britain. To Burke, the choice was stark, between hereditary right and the collapse of civilization. The monarchy was the fount of national stability, which linked subjects to their past and the nation's liberties to the hereditary principle. Burke saw George III as a quasi-religious figure, in law the 'Sovereign Lord the King', and he despised the 'sophisters, economists and calculators' who would tear down 'the decent drapery of life' and expose him as a mere mortal.[74] Taking up the metaphor, Paine likened the monarchy to 'something kept behind a curtain, about which there is a great deal of bustle and fuss . . . but when, by any accident, the curtain happens to be open, and the company see what it is, they burst into laughter'.[75]

Despising hereditary privilege, Paine saw a republic best administered by a democratic system free from aristocratic or monarchical influence. Burke, on the other hand, worked within the classical republican framework of the balanced constitution. Though he had previously criticized the Crown, the French Revolution revived his interest in monarchy as the basis of sound government. He feared what he called 'the tyranny of a multitude' and justified the hereditary system and the existing order on the grounds of convenience.[76] By contrast, Paine believed that subjects once liberated as citizens would promote a commonwealth of liberty and justice. If Paine saw Burke as a reactionary who eloquently defended the indefensible, Burke saw Paine as a utopian theorist who disguised his superficiality by the means of wit and flights of fanciful abstraction.

In the *Rights of Man*, Paine started from the premise that monarchy equalled privilege and privilege equalled evil. Democracy, on the other hand, equalled equality and equality equalled good. This simple logic led him to deduce that once the battle for political rights was won, the monarchy would be exposed as an undemocratic evil and civic virtue would flourish. 'Monarchy would not have continued so many ages in the world', argued Paine, 'had it not been for the abuses it protects.'[77] Remove the abuse, he concluded, and the monarchy would soon wither away. His belief that democracy would spell the demise of royalty and lead to transparent, virtuous government was wishful thinking. His assumption that civic virtue would be awakened by destroying historic institutions was profoundly at odds with those who believed that it was more likely to flourish under the shelter of a balanced constitution in a society in which privilege brought responsibilities.

Paine was a better logician than social psychologist. Having discarded historic precedent in favour of natural rights as a basis for his representative republic, he did not appreciate the power of the Burkean vision of a hierarchical society, in which people saw the monarch as a link with their past, a safeguard against ministerial tyranny, and *the* exemplar of *noblesse oblige*. Nor did Paine anticipate Walter Bagehot's insight into the monarchy's appeal to the imagination. The idea of a democratic nation making a fetish of the royal plumage would have appalled him. Yet for all his talk about the common people of England, Paine's underlying view of them bore similarities with Burke's and Bagehot's, for he portrayed them as boobies, demeaned by the royal 'burlesque' and bamboozled by the display. This 'libel upon the English character' was not lost on his enemies, who used it against him.[78]

Like a legion of political thinkers before him, Paine accepted, at least theoretically, that a republic did not imply 'any *particular form* of government'. He noted the classical formulation of *res publica* as meaning public affairs or the 'public thing'. 'It is a word of a good original, referring to what ought to be the character and business of government.' But his reasoning, deeply influenced by his resentments, made it impossible for him to place any confidence in kings, at least in Britain. By a shift in usage, suited to his prejudices, Paine's *res publica* became 'naturally opposed to the word monarchy'. Monarchy, he added, 'means arbitrary power in an individual person; in the exercise of which, *himself*, and not the *res-publica*, is the object'. The phrase that followed – republican government 'naturally associates with the representative form' – made the link with democracy complete. It was one of the more significant passages in the history of republican thought.[79]

As a republic was government in the public interest, Paine could hardly restrict it to a presidential system. In the case of France, he accepted that the monarch might continue to play a part in the republic, as long as the King obeyed the law. This was a common view among critics of the British monarchy. David Williams, a radical thinker who could rival Paine when it came to savaging George III, stated simply in 1790 that 'every lawful government is necessarily a republic'.[80] It was widely accepted among reformers, whatever their particular beliefs, that rule by law was a crucial consideration in the establishment of a republic. Some, including Paine, had read Rousseau, who had defined a republic as 'any State ruled by law, whatever may be the form of administration'. Every 'legitimate Government' was, in Rousseau's view, republican, with or without a monarch.[81]

Despite Paine's singular influence in shifting the meaning of republicanism to a more avowedly anti-monarchical, and secular, stance, the word
continued to be amorphous, suggesting different things to different
people. Subject to political events and changing fashions, it sometimes
meant different things to the same people at different times. At the
time of his trial for treason in 1794, John Thelwall, a leading light of
working-class radicalism, conceded that he was a republican in his 'private speculations', using the word to mean anti-monarchy. More typically, he saw the 'very soul of the republican system' defined, not by
reference to the Crown, but by the democratic principle. On another
occasion, he noted that republicanism, both ancient and modern, was
often 'made a cloak to conceal the usurpations of the most tyrannical
aristocracy'.[82] Clearly, republicanism remained a shapeless word, despite
Paine's influence. Perhaps a British dislike of abstraction contributed to
the general murkiness.

In the 1790s, some republicans, carrying forward classical formula-
tions, tolerated, even admired, limited monarchy. Others, who came
to be known as 'theoretical' republicans, contemplated the end of the
monarchy in the abstract, but being pragmatists saw no point in promoting it as a cause. Others still, who came to be known as 'pure' republicans,
called explicitly for the monarchy's abolition, which they often coupled
with national renewal.[83] On occasion, they spoke in violent tones about
the end of the House of Hanover, if only for effect. For his part, Paine
would have preferred the exile of George III to covering himself with the
King's blood. Regicide was the 'one crime congenial with republicanism',
said one of his critics, which he is *'not yet up to'*.[84] In a world in which
the monarchy awakened such different thoughts and objects, tensions
often surfaced over the future of the Crown, not least in the radical
associations after the outbreak of war with France.

Pure republicans like Paine, who linked the abolition of the monarchy
to democratic reform, were giving shape to an egalitarian and secular
conception of republicanism. Whereas classical republicans called for
fine tuning the constitution and an end to ministerial corruption, Paine's
republic demanded nothing less than social and political transformation,
what he called the arrival of 'universal civilization'.[85] This was heady
stuff, made all the more heady by the French Revolution. Yet for all his
hostility to monarchy, Paine did not absolutely rule out a republic with

a walk-on part for a king, as long as the king had nothing to say. In this sense, Paine's pure republicanism had its limits. But admirers of the *Rights of Man*, swept along by his impassioned case against the Crown, did not always notice this intriguing qualification. Nor did loyalists, who, for the purposes of reaction, eagerly turned republicans into regicides.

In the 1790s, republicanism remained a protean concept. Like socialism a hundred years later, there was little consensus over what was on the table and some fell out over the entrées. Paine was a formative influence on most republicans of his generation, sometimes distilling, sometimes rejecting longstanding traditions. Though he launched a reasoned attack on hereditary rule, he proved more compelling as a democrat than as an anti-monarchist. Despite his persuasive powers, radicals were reluctant to serve up the King as a course on the republican menu, much less a starter. Before the monarchy was set in front of them they often wished to sample a variety of other dishes. The extension of political rights was centre table, but much else appealed, including land reform, economical government, annual parliaments and the removal of ministerial corruption.

The intellectual traditions out of which such ideas grew were diverse, from Commonwealth ideology to millennial religion, from historic rights to natural rights theory, from American republicanism to French Jacobinism.[86] Irish republicanism, or insurrectionism, was rather outside the radical mainstream, for it was inspired by nationalism rather than a demand for an extension of political rights. While influenced by classical republicanism and the writings of Paine, Irish nationalists eventually rebelled against a Protestant occupying power, which just happened to be a monarchy. With the years, the combination of nationalism and militancy distanced Irish from English republicans.[87] But whatever the intellectual origins or social makeup of republican groupings, whether Irish or English, Welsh or Scots, they all had one thing in common – a hatred of tyranny or what passed for tyranny in the radical imagination.

The love of liberty was a link, though nebulous, with classical republicanism, for which anti-despotism was an obsession. In an era of industrial expansion, religious revival and a rapidly rising population, social and political thought had moved on from classical republicanism. Still, much of that tradition carried over into the era of the French Revolution and beyond. Its emphasis on civic virtue, anti-corruption, annual parliaments and a mixed constitution featured in the political journals of the 1790s and found a powerful echo among commentators, even those who suffered for their political views. John Horne Tooke, the radical philologist, once compared George III to Nero. But at his trial for treason in 1794, his friends testified that he had always been in favour of a balanced polity of King, Lords and Commons.[88]

More often than not, the reform associations took a similar line. The Bristol Constitutional Society for Parliamentary Reform accepted that hereditary monarchy gave dignity and power, but needed the corrective of democracy to prevent its tendency to corruption. Moreover, it decreed that loyalty to the mixed constitution required 'vigilance' and 'civic duty'.[89] In Sheffield, the Society for Constitutional Information opposed 'any attempt that tends to overturn or in any wise injure or disturb the Peace of the People or the laws of the Realm'.[90] Such constitutionalist ideas, though predominant, had to compete with the more strident voices, among them those of so-called 'United Societies' – with their secret oaths and revolutionary addresses – which appeared in parts of Britain where large numbers of Irish had immigrated.[91]

Most radicals indulged in what might be called 'selective' Paineism. Given George III's popularity at the time of the French Revolution, there was little mileage in ritual denunciations of kingship. John Cartwright, a longstanding enthusiast for manhood suffrage and secret ballots, was among those who sought to counteract the influence of Paine's anti-monarchism in radical circles. In May 1792, he carried a motion in favour of 'King, Lords and Commons', with its classical republican overtones, at a meeting of the Friends of the People.[92] Others learned the lesson differently. At the first convention of the Scottish Friends of the People in Edinburgh in December 1792, Thomas Muir called for a declaration against the monarchy, but it was refused.[93] Ultimately, he had to caution his allies against personal attacks on the King. Some 'foolish fellows', he told the meeting, had toasted 'George III and last' and were thrown into jail.[94]

The French Revolution, as it transpired, did not prove to be the Gallic equivalent of 1688, as many people had assumed. As the violence became more extreme in France, most British reformers put Paine's anti-monarchism on the shelf, or treated it 'as an intelligible personal eccentricity'.[95] For reasons of expediency, not a few pure republicans turned into theoretical republicans. After the execution of Louis XVI in January 1793, personal attacks on George III became even riskier. In any case, most reformers were more interested in restoring the purity of the constitution than in storming the Palace. They were anti-absolutist rather than anti-monarchist. For reasons of doctrine, as well as survival, the issue of the future of the House of Hanover played only a small part in radical writings in the 1790s.[96]

The propertied classes did not always distinguish between moderate reformers, who were constitutionalists, and the minority of radicals, who gave the impression of lacking all respect for British institutions. In Paine's absence (he fled to France in September 1792), the so-called English Jacobins, including a few extremists who engaged in conspiracy, dressed up their reformist zeal in extravagant rhetoric and revolutionary symbols. The intemperate Henry Redhead Yorke, who promised to lead the French Army to England, confessed that he and his friends had adopted 'much of the ferocity of the French character', as well as 'much of the bombast of their style'.[97] The Unitarian radical Thomas Cooper, caught up in the general excitement, pronounced 'Te Deum laudamus' when retailing the news of the beheading of members of the French Assembly.[98] Such men may not have been typical of English reformers, but they put the fear of godlessness into the ruling classes, who were increasingly nervous about the demand for rights coming from below. After hearing of the execution of King Louis, the Duke of Sussex was sick for days.[99]

It is difficult to recreate the atmosphere of fear and anticipation aroused in England by affairs in France and the incendiary writings of Paine and his followers. In the mid-1790s, over 12,000 French refugees, many with tales of terrible ordeals, fanned the anxieties of the English propertied classes.[100] Lord Cockburn, the eminent Scottish judge, who was a boy at the time of the Terror, left a telling record of the apprehension created in Britain by the Revolution and how it was transmitted from generation to generation:

Grown up people talked at this time of nothing but the French Revolution, and its supposed consequences . . . I heard a great deal that I did not comprehend; but, even when not fully comprehending, boys are good listeners, and excellent rememberers, and retain through life impressions that were only deepened by their vagueness, and by their not flowing into common occupations. If the ladies and gentlemen, who formed the society of my father's house, believed all they said about the horrors of French bloodshed, and of the anxiety of people here to imitate them, they must have been wretched indeed. Their talk sent me to bed shuddering.[101]

Most British Jacobins preferred satire to violence and rarely spoke of the guillotine and 'King Killing' with 'warm approval'.[102] But as people like the Cockburns knew, not all extremists were so fastidious. Tales of fantastical plots to assassinate the King were rife.[103] One of the more spirited revolutionaries took a robust view and called for that 'humane invention', the guillotine, to be applied in all monarchical states.[104] Another put up a placard for 'the Benefit of John Bull', which promised a performance of 'a new and entertaining Farce, called La Guillotine; or George's head in the Basket!'.[105] Was Thomas Spence, the agrarian reformer, simply making rhetorical gestures when he struck republican medals and pilloried the ruling classes in his penny periodical *Pig's Meat* (1793–5)?[106]

Radicals adopted Burke's notorious reference to 'the swinish multitude' with ironic pride. In a drawing produced by 'Citizen' Richard Lee and his revolutionary friends in Soho, pigs guillotined a Crowned ass – George III – as 'A Cure for National Grievances'. (See Plate 4.) Lee, who loathed kings and 'their cringing creatures', may have had a limited following, but in his pamphlet *The Happy Reign of George the Last* he aimed his provocative message at the labouring poor:

> Do we toil while others reap?
>   Do we starve while others feast?
> Are we sold and shorn, like sheep,
>   By the despot and the priest?
>
> Are we born for them alone?
>   If by divine right they rule,
> Yonder *idiot* on the throne
>   Reigns by divine right a *Fool!*[107]

Many of the well-to-do had welcomed the fall of the Bastille as the just fate of absolutist rule. But when the French Revolution turned vicious, they were horrified by the rumours of conspiracies and writings of extremists which could make the *Rights of Man* look inhibited. In the more feverish and threatening atmosphere, they saw Burke as a sage and Paine as a pariah.[108] Even the Whig politicians who had shown little regard for George III now viewed him with greater sympathy. The government, alarmed by the success of the *Rights of Man* and reports of conspiracy, took fright. The fact that many reform associations contained a plebeian element increased its growing anxiety. When the French declared war on Britain in February 1793, the English closed ranks with their rulers and turned once more against the historic enemy.

But it was not simply the middle and upper classes who rallied to the monarchy and the established Church. The Revolution and the outbreak of war also gave a shot in the arm to the popular conservatism of the lower orders, who could not be said to be enamoured of the French, whatever their principles.[109] Many a humble subject had, after all, lost a relative or loved one to French arms in living memory. About 1,000 loyalist associations against 'republicans and levellers', most of them formed in late 1792 and early 1793, rallied the populace in defence of King and Country.[110] They held mock executions of Paine, shot his effigy and burned his books, often to the tune of 'God Save the King'. Clearly, the extremist wing of the radical movement in Britain failed to convert the workers *en masse*. As an authority on the British reaction to continental affairs argues: 'Fear of anarchy and of invasion in particular succeeded in rallying a majority of the nation behind the protracted campaign against revolutionary principles and French arms.'[111]

In the battle of ideas in the 1790s, there were more loyalist publications than radical ones, and there is no reason to believe that they were without influence.[112] Sometimes sponsored by government, dozens of them targeted the *Rights of Man*. Typically, they equated a republic with constitutional chaos and 'a violent usurpation of all the lands and property of the kingdom'.[113] The more sophisticated propagandists insisted that the British constitution already contained republican elements and was the envy of the world. The *Anti-Jacobin Review* turned Anti-Gallicanism into a patriotic duty and distinguished 'the true-born Englishman from the mongrel cosmopolite'.[114] At the populist end of the market, Hannah More's *Cheap Repository Tracts* simplified Burke in the pragmatic language of Paine.[115] In one of her typical moral tales for the poor, the impressionable Tom, having read of his misery in a radical newspaper, cries out for 'perfect government'; the sagacious Jack retorts: 'You might as well cry for the moon'.[116]

Loyalists, especially the Evangelicals, were quick to exploit the potential in the sense of crisis engendered by the French Revolution. They reminded their followers of man's fallen nature and urged respect for the law and social hierarchy. They depicted George III as the first Christian, the focus of national morality, who was subject only to the workings of providence. As the tract 'One Penny-Worth of Truth from Thomas Bull, to his Brother John' argued:

They tell us that all Kings are bad; that God never made a King; and that all Kings are very expensive. But, that all Kings are bad cannot be true: because God himself is one of them; he calls himself *King of Kings*; which not only shows us he is a King, but that he has other Kings under him: he is never called King of Republics. The Scripture calls Kings, *the Lord's Anointed*; but who ever heard of an anointed Republic?[117]

This particular tract was one of several published by the Association for Preserving Liberty and Property Against Republicans and Levellers founded by John Reeves, who later became George III's printer. The King may even have read it, for the papers of the Association were bound up and presented to His Majesty as a 'Memorial of what Private Persons have done, and may do for preserving our Constitution in Church and State'.[118]

While conservative journalists pumped out a steady stream of propaganda, which was anti-French as often as specifically anti-Jacobin, caricaturists pilloried Paine and drew sharp contrasts between British and French 'liberty'. British liberty was synonymous with law, morality, and prosperity, the French model with anarchy, irreligion and ruin. (See Plate 5.) James Gillray, whose satires had previously targeted royalty, now defended the status quo. His 'Promised Horrors of the French Invasion' may be seen as one of the more fanciful representations of loyalist fears. It turned Burke's horrific vision of Gallic republicanism into a violent tract on domestic English politics. As the French Army marches into the heart of London's clubland, Pitt is being whipped up a liberty tree by Citizen Fox, and Burke is being unseated by the 'Great Bedfordshire Ox' (the Duke of Bedford) whipped on by Thelwall. Meanwhile, the Prince of Wales and the Dukes of Clarence and York are being flung off the balcony of White's Club.[119]

Loyalists accused French and English Jacobins of anything they despised, from king-killing to cannibalism.[120] Mixing theology and political theory, the guardians of religion took particular pleasure in associating them with impiety. Paine played into their hands, for he had turned his back on that strain of puritanism which saw the Bible as a republican handbook.[121] In his deist tract *The Age of Reason*, published in two parts (1794–5), he linked republicanism to a creed based on secular science and hostile to the Bible. Moreover, by attacking priestcraft and 'the adulterous connection of church and state', he made the link between political revolution and the revolution he hoped to bring about in religion.[122] To churchmen, and many Christians, this was convincing proof of the perfidious association of English Jacobinism and apostasy. As Walter Bagehot commented years later: 'when the French Revolution excited the horror of the world, and proved democracy to be "impious", the piety of England concentrated upon him [George III], and gave him tenfold strength'.[123]

Attacks on Church and King were not only heretical and treasonable but an affront to manners and morals. To Christian moralists, and conservatives generally, it was a slippery slope from apostasy to indecency. They were quick to seize on the less reputable prophets of reform, often anti-monarchists and atheists on the radical fringe, who provided evidence of a link between radicalism and licentiousness.[124] In one counter-revolutionary pamphlet, W. H. Reid alluded to the dastardly radical toast (drawn from Diderot): 'May the last King be strangled in the bowels of the last Priest!!!'[125] Loyalists drew a sorry portrait of the radical character. Take W. T. Fitzgerald's 'The Republican's Picture', for example, 'to be sung by every honest Englishman':

> A Republican's picture is easy to draw,
> He can't bear to obey, but will govern the law,
> His manners unsocial, his temper unkind,
> He's a rebel in conduct, a tyrant in mind.[126]

The passive majority must have recognized the portrait on occasion. More of them than not resisted republican entreaties and continued to find consolation in religion, parliamentary monarchy and the force of law.

'Kings will be tyrants from policy when subjects are rebels from principle,' said Burke in the *Reflections*.[127] For a 'tyrant', George III was pretty popular and virtuous. But he was not an innocent bystander, for he was kept informed of radical agitation and stamped his seal of approval on the government's response to it. In 1791, when the Birmingham mob burned down the house of the notable scientist and radical Joseph Priestley, the King wrote to the Home Secretary, Henry Dundas: 'I cannot but feel better pleased that Priestley is the sufferer for the doctrines he and his party have instilled, and that the people see them in their true light.'[128] In keeping with such views, his government, with loyalist mobs in support, sought to rout the radical opposition. Of chief concern was a fear of domestic upheaval fomented by cheap editions of radical publications, most notably the works of Paine.[129]

From the government's point of view in the 1790s, the natural result of freedom of expression was a tendency towards sedition. Booksellers and publishers became an immediate target of the Home Office and the Attorney General. It was soon apparent that attacks on the King were more likely to result in convictions than attacks on ministers. By linking radicalism with regicide, the judges sought to discredit Paine's republicanism in the public mind; but in the process they also attracted sympathy to the King and made him a focus of patriotism. The authorities even treated jokes about royalty as potentially seditious, particularly after the execution of Louis XVI. The radical publisher Daniel Isaac Eaton once spent three months in prison for printing an amusing story of a rooster, beheaded for tyranny, named King Chanticleer.[130] No act of rebellion, however isolated, was too inconsequential to cause alarm. When John Thelwall took a pint of porter and blew off the head with the words 'this is the Way I would serve Kings', a spy reported on it.[131] Wiser heads in the radical camp avoided all references, symbolic or otherwise, to the King.

Fierce for moderation, the government of William Pitt over-reacted, and by the use of spies, state trials, packed juries and oppressive legislation decimated the radical ranks.[132] The machinery of repression, or what might be called war conservatism, was not as ruthless or efficient as is sometimes supposed, but it did leave a number of radicals dead, exiled or imprisoned. For his intemperate behaviour, Redhead Yorke received two years in Dorchester Jail, despite his denial of any association with the doctrines of Paine.[133] Others, including Thomas Cooper, emigrated to America.[134] With his usual matter-of-factness, Doctor Johnson once observed that 'the magistrate has a right to enforce what he thinks; and he who is conscious of the truth has a right to suffer. I am afraid there is no other way of ascertaining the truth, but persecution on the one hand and enduring it on the other'.[135] The historian E. P. Thompson, a less dispassionate observer, saw things differently: the government had simply 'strangled' the revolutionary impulse 'in its infancy'.[136]

Most radicals, of course, never saw the inside of a courtroom on the charge of aiding the King's enemies or compassing the King's death. Indeed, they often distinguished between the Crown in Parliament and the King as a national figurehead and appealed directly to George III for redress. The artisan-dominated corresponding societies founded in London and in the provinces to campaign for a widened franchise were probably more hostile to hereditary institutions than most reform bodies. The London Corresponding Society, established in 1792, was richly endowed with Paineite radicals, many of them critical of the Crown. The radical tailor Francis Place once said that the leading members of the LCS advocated the removal of the sovereign, albeit over time.[137] But sensing the public mood and fearing prosecution, he revised his opinion, arguing that his colleagues were not 'hot headed revolutionists' but simply men who were friendly to representative government.[138] By such means he reconciled George III and the rights of man. It marked his own shift from pure to theoretical republicanism.

At a general meeting of the LCS in June 1792, its leaders drew up a petition, which was to be presented to the King.[139] It was completed only a few weeks after George III's Proclamation against seditious writings, which called on 'loving subjects' to guard against subversion.[140] The address appealed to the King over the heads of his ministers. Harking back to 1688, the LCS accepted the King's constitutional legitimacy and looked to him for support in the campaign for 'free and equal representation'. Contrary to Paine's view that George III was a despot, the petitioners treated him as if he were a sovereign in the ministerial pocket. It warned the King of political betrayal and linked the future of the monarchy with that of the common people: 'The nation stands tottering on the Brink of Ruin, and your existence is coupled with theirs.' We have sought 'to preserve you in the enjoyment of what ought at all times to constitute the chief felicity of a sovereign – the people's love – and to secure you in the happy possession of Peace and universal Tranquillity'.[141]

Such petitions provided a potential defence against the treasonable charge of aiding the King's enemies and were a way of letting off steam. But just how reformers perceived George III is not always clear, for repression led to political posturing and a blurring of boundaries between constitutionalism and anti-monarchism. Depending on one's point of view, petitions to the Palace were either a sensible expedient or exquisite hypocrisy. Earl Stanhope, dubbed 'citizen *sans culotte*' by the cartoonists, presented more than one address to the King calling on him to open negotiations with France.[142] Some radicals meant petitions to imply a threat to the sovereign; to others, they were a recrudescence of an ancient idea that the King and the common people were in an alliance against perfidious oligarchs.

Paine would have dismissed such an alliance out of hand, for to him the Crown was the fount of political corruption, not its solution. But the fact that radicals addressed the King in respectful tones and called on his support is further evidence that they had jettisoned Paine's anti-monarchism. In the end, most of them believed that it was ministerial corruption rather than monarchical obstruction that frustrated their reform agenda. After the government clampdown on political dissent, the tactics of the LCS and other radical associations returned to Boling-broke's idea of the king as the servant of his people. It was a conception driven by political realities, in keeping with Paine's theoretical admission that republicanism was compatible with the retention of a monarch, or Rousseau's view that a king may be needed to provide tranquillity in an era of reform.[143]

There were militant republicans who continued to desire the end of the House of Hanover, not least among the 'United Societies'. But from the mid-1790s, leading radicals who called themselves republicans started to have a rethink about the relationship between the King and his subjects. Few of them saw the monarch as a despot, though the anarchist thinker William Godwin saw him as a despot at heart.[144] Perhaps chastened by his trial for treason, Thelwall made an important distinction between monarchy and a republican idea of 'kingly power'. By monarchy he meant 'government by one man' (Dr Johnson's definition), which was subject to abuse. By 'kingly power' he meant 'a delegated trust, conferred by and held for the acknowledged *benefit of the people*'. It was a concession to classical republicanism, but with a democratic twist. If freedom were alive, Thelwall argued, 'monarchy itself may be attempted with a degree of liberty; without it, republics are but despotism in masquerade'.[145] Here was a hybrid form of democratic republicanism in which the King himself might ennoble the republican project.

George III was not about to don a liberty cap. Any call for 'free and equal representation' antagonized him, for, in his view, it would have opened the floodgates of reform and put the Crown at risk. Petitions, even of the most loyal variety, were apt to pass from his mind when he received news of popular support for radical leaders, among them members of the LCS.[146] His interest in political unrest increased when he ventured out to open Parliament on 29 October 1795. Along the route, a hostile crowd hissed 'No Pitt – No War – Peace Peace, Bread Bread', and a miscreant stoned the royal coach.[147] (See Plate 6.) Loyalists linked this 'daring outrage' to a mass meeting of the LCS in Copenhagen Fields three days earlier, which demanded the dismissal of the King's ministers. As a result, Parliament, which had already suspended Habeas Corpus, put further obstacles in the way of the radical movement by passing Bills on Treasonable Practices and Seditious Meetings. Such measures softened extremist rhetoric and furthered the need for dissimulation in the ranks of reform.

The King was a willing partner in the government's campaign to counter the radical cause. When he received news of a gathering of the LCS in November 1795, he remembered that a similar assembly had led to the Gordon Riots fifteen years earlier. At the time of those riots, he had remarked: 'my attachment is to the laws and security of my country, and to the protection of the lives and properties of all my subjects'.[148] His response to the meeting of the LCS in 1795 was consistent with his earlier pronouncement: 'it seems to require every possible exertion to prevent any future assembly of the kind'.[149] Any hope that royal support might be forthcoming in the radical campaign was a chimera, for neither the King nor his ministers were in a mood to support an extension of the franchise. Eventually the penny dropped among reformers. As a radical ballad of 1800 put it:

Tho' millions of People thro' poverty groan,
The cries of the Nation are shut from the Throne.
Sing ballinamona, &c.
No tricks with Petitions for me.[150]

By the beginning of the nineteenth century, little remained of the radical movement in Britain, much less Paine's brand of republicanism, save a human residue of dashed hopes. The disillusionment of reformers was palpable. The respectable classes generally associated radical ideas with French savagery and European tumult and assumed that they would lead to chaos rather than to a purified politics. The combination of loyalist opposition and repressive legislation left the more persistent radicals with little option but to enter an ineffectual, subterranean world inhabited by revolutionaries pursued by spies. Still, democratic and, to a lesser extent, anti-monarchical doctrines had had a hearing in the years of the American and French Revolutions. They would resurface in the early nineteenth century, propelled by a vision of power and who would wield it, and by a hatred of privilege and who would inherit it.

Just how close Britain came to a dynamic union of all those alienated by the existing political system in the 1790s, and to Paine's republic, is controversial and ultimately unanswerable.[151] But there was never that conjuncture of ideological, economic and political conditions necessary to foment a revolution. The radicals had an ideology. The poor and disenfranchised had a grievance. But in a decentralized country it was difficult to bring together disparate groups of reformers and create a national movement. Moreover, most Britons, including reformers, were constitutionalists and loath to rebel. Even those who had the will to rebel lacked co-ordination. An invasion might have made a difference, but the various French naval expeditions to Ireland between 1796 and 1798 failed to make a serious impact. Meanwhile, the machinery of government and the loyalist reaction to reform effectively suppressed the opposition. The centre held. So did the Crown, which was, among other things, the symbolic centre.

A stone thrown at the King's coach did not constitute a revolution. Nor was a limited monarch, free from scandal and of sober disposition, likely to trigger a revolution in Britain. Shielded by his ministers, George III kept largely above the fray. Yet he was always more than the 'conse-

crated obstruction' of Bagehot's imagination. The very debate and turmoil over the French Revolution, as Linda Colley and Marilyn Morris
have shown, highlighted the monarchy as a focal point of national will
and identity. Constitutional reformers and loyalists alike looked to the
King as a final court of appeal. As hundreds of petitions attested, the
former could see him as a potential ally in the battle against ministerial
corruption, the latter a pillar of Church and State. The 1688 political
settlement was so open to interpretation that Charles James Fox could
pronounce, in the gloom of 1795: 'Our Constitution, maimed and
mangled as it now was, differed less from a Republican than from any
despotic form of Government . . . Our Constitution was a republic, in
the just sense of the word; it was a Monarchy founded on the good of
the people.'[152]

Invigorated by the French Revolution, the Crown served as a resplen-
dent focus for sentiment and opinion, sometimes conflicting, across a
wide social spectrum. In a sense, radicalism served the purposes of the
Crown, for the dialectic of political argument threw up a shapeless model
of 'republican kingship', which brought together aspects of reform and
tradition. They came together in 'an image of paternal authority coupled
with republican devotion to the public good'.[153] Radicals did not have a
monopoly on civic republicanism, and the vibrant voluntary culture of
Protestant loyalism would harden into the bedrock of monarchism in
the nineteenth century. (In Ulster it would harden into Unionism.[154]) The
monarchy itself played a part in the process, for increasingly it had
become allied with patriotic middle England through its civic and
charitable work. As Samuel Taylor Coleridge observed in 1795: 'If
Monarchs would behave like republicans, all their subjects would act as
royalists.'[155]

On the more pressing political front, the portrayal of George III as a
German tyrant laying waste his kingdom was a parody, and therefore
unpersuasive. Though a keen observer of politics, Paine had confused his
countrymen with Americans. He had also failed to recognize the changes
taking place in royal affairs. It was a price he paid for preferring abstract
principles to a study of history. Over the years, the monarchy had come
under increasing constraint. The gradual shift in power from the King to
his ministers, though often disputed by George III, took the sting out of
anti-monarchism. Opposition to the Crown lost its edge when the public

believed abuses of power came more from politicians than from sovereigns. The case against the monarchy, inside and outside Parliament, became increasingly difficult to sustain as it exchanged power for influence.

Paine believed that 'the nearer any government approaches to a republic the less business there is for a king'. But as he recognized, an absolute monarch was more likely to alienate his subjects than would a limited one. In any case, Paine acknowledged that a nation did not become a republic simply by abolishing its monarchy. The sight of George III's head in a basket would not usher in 'universal civilization'. That would require a dramatic shift in human behaviour. Paine spoke in prophetic terms of mankind transformed by reason. In the language of the common man he disguised romance. Sceptics did not need Burke to remind them that national revival might prove elusive, even with a democratic constitution, or to question whether a revolution would lead to the reign of selfless public service. To most Britons, Napoleon was an unlikely engineer of human souls.

Against the background of war and revolution, of inertia and reaction, Paine's republican project fell away in Britain. Its most compelling ingredient had not been anti-monarchism, which had little appeal, but the extension of political rights. Francis Place spoke for many other chastened radicals in the 1790s when he said that republicanism simply meant a commitment to a representative form of government.[156] The democratic republicanism excited by the American and French Revolutions had profound implications. But in the conservative backlash, it came in for a drubbing as 'the stalking horse of the demagogue'.[157] It was a view that Napoleon did little to dispel. Nor did the Emperor serve the anti-monarchical cause by giving rein to dynastic ambitions worthy of the Bourbons. Meanwhile, Paine, back in America and in decline, took comfort in his schemes for a French invasion of England. The British monarchy, meanwhile, had more to fear from the dictator's forces than from republican arguments.

2

The Battered but Unbroken Crown
1800–1837

'It does not argue the necessity of abolishing monarchy to establish a republican government.'

Richard Carlile, *Republican* (1819)

'O, that the free would stamp the impious name of King into
the dust!' Percy Bysshe Shelley, *Ode to Liberty* (1820)

In the 1880s, when H. M. Hyndman, the apostle of Marx and founder of
the Social Democratic Federation, sought an explanation for the survival
of the British monarchy, one of the things he pointed to was the enduring
legacy of the French Revolution. 'To this day,' he observed, 'the French
Revolution and the Reign of Terror are quoted in almost every middle-
class household as standing warnings against any attempt of the people
to organize themselves in earnest.'[1] He might have added that loyalists
so demonized Napoleon that the late Victorians still cautioned their
children with the phrase 'Boney will get you'.[2] The fact that Britain
survived the prolonged and costly war with France without catastrophe
at home was persuasive evidence of the superiority of British institutions.
Whenever the monarchy or the constitution came under attack from
radicals, loyalists waved away the criticism with the smug conclusion
that the political system, whatever its failings, worked better in Britain
than in perfidious France.[3]

In the earliest years of the nineteenth century, a tradition of political
reform was preserved in Britain, but to little effect. Underground conspirators failed to make headway among the working classes, and constitutional radicals failed to arouse the propertied classes from their
conservatism. This last was partly because of government repression but

also because of the powerful reaction to French principles during wartime. The romantic radical William Cobbett bemoaned that reform invariably met with the cry: 'What, you want a REVOLUTION, do you?', followed by a recital of French extremism.[4] The politically articulate were not alone in their reaction, however, for loyalist insularity remained entrenched in the country at large. Whatever their social background, British subjects could see that the Revolution had deteriorated into terror, irreligion, regicide, and a military dictatorship that threatened the independent nations of Europe.

In Britain, all but the disaffected rallied to the monarchy, which had ossified into the ancient constitution of loyalism. As Coleridge wrote in 1809: 'If the Jacobins ran wild with the Rights of Man, and the abstract Sovereignty of the People, their Antagonists flew off as extravagantly from the sober good sense of our Forefathers and idolized as pure an abstraction in the Rights of *Sovereigns*.'[5] Coleridge, who compared his own youthful flirtation with Jacobinism to building castles in the air, spoke for many of his generation whose views had been tempered by war and Napoleon. He now described the revolutionary mentality as a form of hysteria, and, like Burke, took a government based on abstract principles to be inimical to freedom and continuity. In a social contract between a government of pure reason and the citizen, the former had the right to absolute rule, the latter the right to obey.[6]

When British reformers did return to the fray towards the end of the first decade of the nineteenth century, they carried forward aspects of the democratic republican project of the 1790s.[7] But with any taint of Jacobinism still posing a real threat of arrest and imprisonment, they had little enthusiasm for 'metaphysical reasoning' and 'grievances of theory'.[8] Disillusioned and bowing to political reality, some reformers also had lost faith in direct action and manhood suffrage. A few, including Henry Redhead Yorke, had cut their links with radicalism entirely and joined the loyalist ranks.[9] The issues that now beset the country were mundane: the burden of wartime taxation, high inflation and ministerial jobbery. Keeping within the conventional limits of pragmatic English politics, they focused on that perennial bane, 'Old Corruption', and on traditional British liberties. They campaigned for parliamentary reform on a platform of ancient rights and a return to purity of the constitution.

The constituency of Westminster, at the heart of metropolitan London, served as a focus of the reform agitation. With 10,000 electors, many of them artisans and tradesmen, it was particularly suited to the radical campaign. Yet personal rivalries and divisions over objects and tactics bedevilled the movement. Elections there brought together disparate individuals, from Francis Place to the turbulent 'tribune of the people', Sir Francis Burdett. Despite their heterogeneous nature, the respectable radicals of the early nineteenth century reverted to the language of conventional political debate. Pragmatic and flexible, they pursued a host of causes beyond the extension of the franchise, including law reform and schooling. They grafted their agenda on to the time-honoured classical republican emphasis on anti-corruption and civic virtue.

Though many reformers resented the monarchy's cost and influence, the abolition of the Crown was not on their agenda. As in the 1790s, most radicals had accepted a constitutional role for what Thelwall called 'kingly power', or were content to wait upon events. In any case, they commonly defined republicanism by reference to the expansion of political rights not anti-monarchism. George III, after 1805 blind and increasingly debilitated, was not taken to be much of an impediment to the radical programme – his ministers were. To the general public, the King remained widely popular. Periodic British victories against French arms, celebrated by royal festivities, enhanced his popularity. So did his Jubilee in 1809 (three months after the death of Thomas Paine), which Redhead Yorke saw as an expression of political reconciliation and social harmony.[10] Clearly, civic dignitaries and charities exploited the Jubilee for their myriad purposes. With the court linked to national stability, civic culture and good works, the King's subjects felt they had cause to celebrate.[11]

While the public widely revered George III, the behaviour of his offspring sometimes stirred up public indignation. It would have been injudicious to make direct attacks on the Crown, but there was an open season on the extended royal family. A royal scandal was an occasion for reformers to savour and to exploit. In 1809, the Duke of York, Commander-in-Chief of the Army, offered them an opening, in what proved to be a scandal so embarrassing that it perplexed inveterate monarchists.[12] The Duke had been charged with misconduct, for allowing his mistress, Mary Anne Clarke, to sell Army commissions. When the House of Commons rejected the motion to declare him guilty, it excited a great public outcry against corruption in high places.[13] The Duke, though acquitted, resigned. Across the country, reformers saw the scandal as a providential opportunity to widen support for the reform of Parliament, but it did not imperil the Crown.

As long as peaceful reform seemed possible and the war with France persisted, calls for the overthrow of the monarchy rarely surfaced outside the haunts of the far left fringe. Luddite industrial protests periodically disturbed the peace, but they did not represent a co-ordinated revolutionary movement which threatened the government or the Crown.[14] From time to time, the Prince of Wales, who was sworn in as Regent on 5 February 1811, received anonymous death threats, signed 'Vox Populi' or 'An enemy of the damned Royal Family'. In the north, placards appeared which offered a hundred guineas for the Regent's head.[15] On other occasions republicans drank outrageous toasts such as 'May the guillotine be as common as a pawnbroker's shop and every tyrant's head a pledge'.[16] But beyond the rule of General Ludd and the radical underworld, there were few resolute enemies of royalty in evidence, and if they wished to stay out of trouble they kept their pens dry and their mouths shut. The radical poet and essayist Leigh Hunt, later an admirer of Queen Victoria, received two years' imprisonment in 1812 for libelling the Prince Regent.

At the end of the Napoleonic wars it became easier not only to promote radical causes but to criticize the Crown. Among moderate reformers, royal extravagance was a recurring complaint, which the calamitous economy made all the more telling. Even monarchists like Cobbett criticized the junior members of the royal family for their generous allowances and believed they should pay taxes.[17] Inside and outside Parliament, there was disquiet over the cost of the monarchy, which the Prince Regent had exacerbated by his reckless spending. In 1815, he had vast debts, a large staff, voracious relatives, and plans for rebuilding the Marine Pavilion at Brighton that his aides dreaded to contemplate. The expense of the Pavilion caused such alarm in political circles that the Prime Minister, Lord Liverpool, along with senior colleagues, wrote ominously to the Prince that given the 'temper of the times' no more public money would be forthcoming to defray the costs.[18]

In Parliament, royal expenditure aroused sporadic discontent, most notably from Whigs, who continued to regard the reduction of the monarchy's influence as an object of reform. In the debate on the Civil List in April 1815, George Tierney, who once fought a duel with Pitt, accused ministers of keeping the Prince Regent in the dark about the pervasive extravagance in government finance and moved for an inquiry into the Civil List account. Samuel Whitbread, who called for a 'minute examination' of the expenses at Windsor, ridiculed those who thought that the Prince Regent should be allowed to spend £5,000 on a greenhouse without any oversight by the House of Commons.[19] The following March, Henry Brougham went further and made a violent speech, in which he denounced the Regent's profligacy and accused him of an 'utter disregard of the feelings of an oppressed and insulted nation'.[20]

In a debate in the House of Lords in June 1816, another leading Whig reformer, Lord Holland, asked for a comparison between the Civil List in Britain, which had risen to over £1,000,000 a year, and the cost of government in America. At the same time he expressed the necessary pious support for the British form of government: 'God forbid that we, who were not republicans, should compare ourselves with a republican government.' But he went on to say that the 'greatest boast and strength' of the British constitution was the democratic part, which 'bore a stronger affinity to the qualities of a republican government, than our monarchical part did to the absolute sovereignties of Europe.'[21]

A few weeks after Lord Holland's address, there was yet another attack on royalty, this time not for profligacy but for parsimony. In August 1816, Princess Charlotte and her husband, Prince Leopold of Saxe-Coburg, contributed to an appeal to relieve the victims of the economic hardship caused by the post-war slump. Henry Hunt, that 'genius of commotion', attacked them for their paltry donation in a speech at the Guildhall: 'The Prince and the Princess of Coburg had given £400, but they received £120,000. This was the comparative rate at which the great paupers thought it their duty to contribute to the support of the little paupers.'[22] Princess Charlotte, who was playing her small royal part in mitigating the effects of the post-war crisis, recoiled in anger at Hunt's 'horrid' speech, which she believed breathed 'a true spirit of revolution'.[23] She over-reacted. For all the bombast, few radicals expected a meeting in the Guildhall to trigger a revolution, much less topple the monarchy. But the throne was a sitting target, which, when hit, gave publicity to other causes.

There were more threatening challenges to the monarchy and the parliamentary system in the post-war years. Anti-monarchy may not have been a driving force behind them, but it is hard to see how the Crown would have survived had they achieved their revolutionary aims. In response to their conditions, the new working classes, helpless victims of distress, were setting up clubs and societies across the country, complete with mass meetings and military drills. The combination of government policy, unemployment and rising prices made many of these bodies susceptible to radical agitators who preferred direct action to peaceful pressure. Despite the efforts of constitutional reformers to quell disturbances, things sometimes got out of hand, and mass meetings, taken over by ultra radicals, erupted into riot. When the authorities intervened with force, it created further disaffection.

On 15 November 1816, the 'pure' republicans Arthur Thistlewood, Thomas Preston and Dr James Watson, followers of the land reformer Thomas Spence, summoned distressed workers to a mass meeting in Spa Fields, London. The appearance of the tricolour flag and caps of liberty carried on pikes suggested menace. Few moderate radicals appeared, but 'Orator' Hunt turned up, made an incendiary speech, and then supported a petition to be presented to the Prince Regent. The petitioners pointed to the hardship in the country and denounced the unrepresentative character of the House of Commons 'as notorious as the sun at noonday'. The meeting adjourned peacefully, although a splinter group marched through Westminster breaking shop windows. When the petition reached the Prince Regent, he expressed regret at the distress of Londoners and gave £4,000 to relieve the inhabitants of Spitalfields.[24] It was a calculated sign of goodwill, a sum well up on the £400 contributed by his daughter Princess Charlotte three months earlier.

When the adjourned meeting met again in Spa Fields on 2 December 1816, the insurrectionists, led by the former estate agent Thistlewood and the shadowy 'Doctor' Watson, broke away from the main assembly. Parading the tricolour flag of red, white and green to symbolize the incipient British Republic, they marched on the City with the idea of seizing the Bank and the Tower. They looted gun shops along the way. But few of the rioters knew how to use the stolen arms, and the cavalry dispersed the crowd and the authorities subsequently arrested several of the leaders.[25] We shall probably never know the full truth about the riots, or just how close they came to success; but they made an impression on the Crown. A week after they took place, the radical Lord Mayor of London presented the Regent with another petition drawing attention to distress and the need for parliamentary reform. It extracted an exasperated reply:

Deeply as I deplore the prevailing *distress & difficulties* of the country, I derive consolation from the persuasion that the great body of His Majesty's subjects, notwithstanding the various attempts which have been made to *irritate & mislead* them are well convinced that the severe trials which they sustain with such exemplary patience & fortitude are chiefly to be attributed to *unavoidable causes* ... I shall resort with the utmost confidence to the TRIED WISDOM of Parliament.[26]

At the opening of Parliament a few weeks later, the crowd hissed the Prince Regent and threw stones at his coach. The incident was reminiscent of the attack on George III's coach in 1795; and the government, as earlier, used it as an excuse to introduce repressive legislation. The Prince Regent, once booed at the door of Carlton House, shared the government's view that the radical leaders sought revolution rather than reform. Like his father before him, he kept himself informed about radical agitators, and like his family generally he believed that 'firmness' was needed to quell the 'abominable revolutionary spirit now prevalent in England'. In a letter written at the request of the Home Secretary, Lord Sidmouth, he described the action of regular troops at a peaceful gathering of workers in St Peter's Fields, Manchester, as 'forbearance'.[27] The Massacre at Peterloo left eleven dead and over 400 wounded. Later in the year he supported the passage of the 'Six Acts', which restricted radical activity by tightening the libel laws and imposing stamp duties on newspapers.

Radical journalists, disillusioned by the prospects for reform, turned venomous after the Peterloo Massacre. It pushed several of them further down the road to rhetorical extremism and pure republicanism. A strident, short-lived radical paper, the *Cap of Liberty*, called on the people to confront the authorities 'in the most imposing attitude which circumstances will admit of'.[28] The monarchy was not forgotten in the general disenchantment. In the *Black Dwarf*, a leading organ of reform, the journalist and political agitator Thomas Wooler attacked the Prince Regent for making 'murder safe under royal patronage' and called on him to 'reconcile differences' and give way to reform.[29] The editor of the *Democratic Recorder* reminded his readers of the latent power of the people: 'The Masters of Kings! The Creators of Kings!! The Transporters of Kings!!! The Executors of Kings!!!!'[30] After Peterloo, many humane men vented their anger on the royal family:

> An old, mad, blind, despised, and dying king, –
>> Princes, the dregs of their dull race, who flow
> Through public scorn, – mud from a muddy spring, –
>> Rulers who neither see, nor feel, nor know,
> But leechlike to their fainting country cling,
>> Till they drop, blind in blood, without a blow, –[31]

The Prince Regent's love of literature did not extend to Shelley.

On 29 January 1820, George III died, and the Regent became King at last. Within a month, a group of conspirators, led by Arthur Thistlewood, who had recently been released from prison, hatched a bizarre plot to assassinate the entire Cabinet as they dined at Lord Harrowby's house in Grosvenor Square. After a coup and the removal of George IV, the conspirators proposed to proclaim Thistlewood president of the republic. As it turned out, spies discovered the revolutionaries in a Cato Street loft, and Thistlewood turned up on the scaffold rather than in the presidential palace. The Cato Street conspiracy, like the earlier Spa Fields riots, was an isolated example of what may be seen as crazed revolutionism by desperate men. In the unlikely event of success, it would probably have seen off the Hanoverians with extreme prejudice. It represented the last manifestation of a tradition of insurrection, with tenuous links with the 'United Societies', dating to the late 1790s. Having failed, it simply encouraged a backlash.

The violent disturbances of the post-war years left moderate reformers in a quandary, for they had to negotiate the exposed terrain between what later came to be termed 'moral' and 'physical force'.[32] Making political capital out of popular unrest invited government repression. Witness Sir Francis Burdett, the outspoken MP for Westminster, who received three months in prison for censuring the government's actions at Peterloo. Papers such as Cobbett's *Political Register* and Richard Carlile's *Republican*, which disseminated radical ideas and co-ordinated reform, displayed contradictory attitudes. Thomas Wooler, more circumspect than some of his radical colleagues, was a model of equivocation.

He had dedicated the *Black Dwarf* to the Prince Regent, with the hope that 'he will awake to a full knowledge of Himself, his Ministers, and his People, before it is too late'.[33] It was just this sort of remark that led Wooler's critics to dub him a 'poor deluded radical'.[34]

For all its venom and bravado, the post-war radical press was more satirical than insurrectionary. As the journalists recognized, juries were more likely to acquit a humorous constitutional radical than a hardened rioter. Wooler, quoting Pope, declared at the head of each issue of the *Black Dwarf*:

> Satire's my weapon; but I'm too discreet,
> To run a-muck and tilt at all I meet.[35]

Such comment may have disarmed the government prosecutors, but it also disarmed the radicals, for laughter fits ill with the implacability associated with the revolutionary temper.[36] Despite the sporadic hostility to the Crown, the treatment of the monarchy by reformers was ambiguous. When the people failed to rise up and confront the authorities, more strident journalists turned to satire, cajolery and menaces. Meanwhile, petitions and remonstrances continued to arrive at the Palace with their curious mixture of supplication and intimidation, or, as Richard Carlile once said, of 'approbation and complaint'.[37]

If Paine thought George III a 'parasite' living in 'luxurious indolence', one can imagine the revulsion that George IV aroused in the radical camp. At the beginning of the new reign, Shelley famously wrote: 'O, that the free would stamp the impious name of King into the dust!'[38] Lord Byron, more personal, reflected: 'Though Ireland starve, great George weighs twenty stone!'[39] The King provided the press with ample scope for contempt, irony and satire. Many a royal item dwelled on 'royal munificence'. Extravagance was a ready issue on which to attack the Crown without fear of a stay in prison, and it proved particularly appealing to utilitarians who admired cheap government. John Wade, a fact-finding disciple of Jeremy Bentham, castigated a political system governed by men made ridiculous by the attributes of monarchy: pageantry, white wands and black rods, ermine and maces. 'It is a . . . barbaric system, which would maintain these fooleries amidst a famishing population, – amidst debts, and taxes, and pauperism.'[40] Carlile put it more concisely: 'Though useless, kings are very expensive.'[41]

In their different ways, Wade, Wooler and Carlile ruffled the royal plumage but refrained from spilling the royal blood. As the more moderate reformers recognized, inflammatory anti-monarchical rhetoric was unlikely to assist the cause of parliamentary reform. Cobbett could be as impulsive as the most hot-headed Jacobin, but he kept his eye on the ball. He despised what he called 'insolent eulogists of republican governments' who diverted attention from reform by indulging in anti-royal bombast. In 1819, he warned reformers of the risk of making impossible demands: 'If we stick to our *one, legal, reasonable* object, we succeed: if we do not, we fail. The man, who, under the present circumstances, would propose *republicanism* as the ultimate object, must be nearly mad, or must have a desire to prevent any change at all.'[42] His specific use of the word 'republicanism' to mean anti-monarchism, by now a commonplace among defenders of the Crown, was revealing.

No self-proclaimed republican was more public about his beliefs than Carlile, a man of working-class origins who championed, and deserted, more causes than any other journalist of his generation. To him, the expression of anti-monarchical views was a test of free speech, and a way of drawing attention to himself. It was also a way in which he distinguished himself from other reformers, notably Cobbett and Hunt.[43] Though his exaggerated rhetoric sometimes suggested a penchant for violent solutions, in 1819 he disassociated republicanism from the 'horrors of the French Revolution'.[44] This was diplomatic, for at the time he was awaiting trial on the charge of blasphemy for reprinting the works of Paine. It is perhaps relevant to add that he spent six years in Dorchester jail for his views, but none the less managed to edit the *Republican* from his cell. Did a radical paper edited from prison constitute free expression? Carlile's experience is a piquant reminder of the ambiguity of both radicalism and the government reaction to it.

Following Paine's lead, Carlile merged secularism and republican thought. 'There can be no public honesty in a *kingdom*', he pronounced, 'no private honesty in a *church*.'[45] To many secularists, the monarchy embodied traditional religious superstition, served to prop up the aristocracy, and nourished the senseless deference which kept the poor in a state of abject dependence.[46] Abolish God, they assumed, and hereditary monarchy would soon go too. The masthead of the *Republican* declared that 'Religion is vice; knowledge is liberty; ignorance is alone slavery'.

In an issue 'dedicated' to the Bible societies, Carlile pronounced that sectarianism would end if only the public would read the *Republican* instead of the scriptures.[47] Many of those listed as subscribers to the paper described themselves as anti-Christian rather than anti-monarchical, though the two often went together. Carlile himself used rhetorical open letters to the King to drum home his secular doctrine. On occasion, he criticized George IV for his Masonic associations. If you remain with the Masons, he warned, 'you will but rank among the last of royal fools'.[48]

Carlile heaped abuse on the King and the royal family with polished sarcasm, Wade and Wooler with utilitarian thoroughness. But they added little to the anti-monarchical thought contained in *Common Sense* and the *Rights of Man*. Carlile devised an idiosyncratic historical theory designed to embarrass the Hanoverians, by which William III was a usurper and James II the rightful king.[49] More typically, he simply recycled Paine, 'our great and only prototype'.[50] Thus he declared that monarchy equalled war, the republic peace; denounced the principle by which kings could be succeeded by imbeciles and children; ridiculed the cost and privileges of the Crown; and abhorred the servility that monarchy inspired. Kings were useless, as Carlile put it, except to inspire men 'to awe, to make them servile and slavish'.[51]

Royalty provided illustrious scapegoats to reformers, but the radical press gave less space to the monarchy than might be imagined, even in those papers under the title *Republican*. This was not simply because it was impolitic to raise the issue, but because radicals had more important things to consider than the abolition of the Crown. In their view, the emergence of a republican government did not necessitate the abolition of the monarchy in any case. This was a point that Paine's followers had inherited from classical republicanism, or from reading the theoretical definition of *res publica* in the *Rights of Man*. The Paineite radical William Sherwin put it clearly in 1817: all those 'who promote public welfare . . . whether kings, emperors, princes, dukes, earls, barons, commoners, they are still, to all intents and purposes, in the fullest acceptation of the word, decided *Republicans*!'. Despotic monarchy was abhorrent, he added, but democracy and monarchy were not irreconcilable. The issue was not the form of government, but government 'most immediately opposed to arbitrary power'.[52]

Carlile, in a moment of composure, made the same point in the 'Preface' to the first volume of the *Republican*: the word 'republican means nothing more when applied to government, than a government which consults the public interest – the interest of the whole people . . . It does not argue the necessity of abolishing monarchy to establish a republican government'. The principal issue, in his view, was the creation of an equal system of representation: 'Whether the present system of hereditary monarchy could exist under such a change I am quite indifferent.'[53] On balance, Carlile did not expect a monarchy to survive in a republic, if only because of its expense. His republicanism was not so much an expression of anti-monarchism as a reaffirmation of Paine's ideas about popular sovereignty.[54] The future of the monarchy was, if not irrelevant, an issue that could be deferred, even with George IV on the throne.

In the febrile years of plots and riots, of Luddism and economic dislocation, loyalties on both sides of the political divide deepened. There was little enthusiasm for compromise on the finer points of the constitution. Stigmatizing the opposition was more in keeping with the mood. As in the 1790s, loyalists turned Paineite republicanism into anything they despised. Their critique of a democratic republic – that it would lead to war, servility and tyranny (of the multitude) – often mirrored the Paineite critique of kingship and the unreformed constitution. As the Tory MP Sir Roger Gresley remarked: 'he could not help lifting up his voice to warn his countrymen that if they weakened the Monarchy, they would destroy liberty'.[55] Radicals said the expense of American government was a fraction of Britain's.[56] Monarchists retorted that 'the personal expenses of the Crown, so far from being greater, were less than in other countries'.[57]

The conservative backlash fed on riots, left-wing conspiracies and the anti-monarchical flourishes of the radical press. Loyalists eagerly rubbed salt into the wounds that radicals inflicted upon themselves. Ignoring the fine print in republican writing and the moderate tone of mainstream reform, they jumped to the conclusion that any criticism of the monarchy was tantamount to a declaration of war against the British state. Moreover, they took secularist republicans at their word. In an era of religious revival, the violent tone of much anti-clericalism simply confirmed the link between blasphemy, radicalism and sedition. As one loyalist argued, recalling the view of James I, no Church meant no King.[58] Conservative propagandists did more to equate republicanism with anti-monarchism, irreligion – and France – than republicans did themselves.[59] They did so quite consciously, in order to discredit radicalism. As a result, constitutional reformers became more and more reluctant to call themselves republicans.

To members of the royal family, surrounded by fawning retainers, any criticism of royalty was seen as disloyalty and translated into a threat to the Crown. George IV, unaware of the finer points of republican thought, had not taken on board the views of Carlile, Sherwin and others – that a king could be a republican. Uneasy about his political role, he did not assume that he would survive in a democracy. To him, democracy meant Spa Fields or Cato Street writ large, and perhaps his head on the block. Acutely sensitive to ridicule, he had caricatures bought up by the thousand and destroyed in the forlorn hope that it would stifle criticism.[60] But he might have profited from a reading of the radical press, not least when it advised him to serve the working classes or to rein in his spending. In fact, he did serve the working classes through his non-constitutional civic work. But in his political guise, he took a hard line against reform, which simply invited abuse from the radical camp. Few kings of England left themselves so open to ridicule. Despite the size of his wardrobe, his enemies always saw him naked. It was not a pretty sight.

George IV's wife, the unruly Caroline of Brunswick, found him 'très gros' even with his clothes on.[61] The King's treatment of his wife, who, after the birth of Princess Charlotte, spent much of her life running up debts and committing adultery, was a royal scandal of the first magnitude. The attempt to divorce Queen Caroline in 1820 was the *cause célèbre* of the era, comparable to the acrimonious marital breakup of the Prince and Princess of Wales in the 1990s. Like previous royal scandals it provided irresistible political capital to reformers, whatever their views on the monarchy. It provoked the most extensive radical campaign of the post-war years and prompted a theatrical display of emotion that bordered on the saturnalian.

The royal imbroglio was a godsend to anyone with a grievance against an unpopular government, from Whig peers to republican journalists. Carlile spoke on behalf of the latter: 'As men struggling to be free, we feel it an imperative duty to support this injured woman – this victim, first to unbridled lust, and now to despotism.'[62] Fêted by unlikely friends, the brainless Queen found herself the plaything of factions and cynical men, who hoped to use her plight to attack the King and his ministers. Francis Place, among others, had no respect for a woman who received £40,000 a year, 'the plunder of the people', but he took up the Queen's case none the less, partly with a view to bringing the monarchy into disrepute.[63] As the caricaturist George Cruikshank saw it, men like Place were scrambling up the 'Radical Ladder' in an assault on the balanced constitution. (See Plate 7.)

The Queen Caroline case focused attention on the cost of the Crown and excited the anti-monarchism latent in republican thinking. In the background was the issue of the marriage allowances to the King's brothers, who, after the death of Princess Charlotte, the heir to the throne, in 1817, suddenly found a purpose in matrimony. The radical press enjoyed a revival that royal gossip guaranteed. Verse satires sold in the hundreds of thousands and, as one informer noted, 'vast quantities' of seditious and inflammatory material vied for distribution.[64] Some of it, which pointed to continental revolutions, was threatening. 'Depend upon it,' declared the *Black Dwarf*, 'the house is tottering . . . and all the exertions of all the ministerial mob can not prevent it from falling.'[65] But for anti-monarchists, taking the side of the Queen against the King looked rather opportunist. Ironically, Paineite republicans were prominent among those who sought to turn the attempt to remove Queen Caroline's royal title into 'a symbol of the assault upon English liberties'.[66]

Though the case damaged the prestige of the monarchy, it was always more likely to bring down the ministry than the Crown. It did neither. The government prosecuted radical leaders and propagandists, but it found it difficult to proceed against them, for the charge of rallying to a member of the royal family was hard to describe as sedition.[67] When the government gave way and abandoned the intended Divorce Bill in November 1820, support for the Queen faded. And when she accepted an annual pension of £50,000 she could hardly have been counted as a proto-republican. The enthusiasm surrounding that great royal show-down, the coronation, suggested that anti-monarchism was not at issue. On the day, a crowd of unruly radicals in Carlisle cried 'The Queen – the Queen', but when they 'crowned an ass', it was the crown that mattered.[68] The history of the ass is unrecorded, but the Queen died within weeks. Londoners marked her funeral by rioting but soon lost interest in political activity. The government survived; the reformers, in disarray, licked their wounds.

Anti-monarchists in the Queen Caroline affair, in keeping with the tactics of Paine, sought to personalize kingship. They assumed that if George IV could be brought down to the level of common humanity, he would be judged a disaster and the monarchy endangered. But as the coronation showed, the strategy failed to ignite. To be sure, the satires and caricatures belittled the King, but they did not pose a serious threat to kingship. Despite the scandal, the public still tended to distinguish between the ass and the Crown, between the King as a man and the King as a king. Even when unhappy with the former, most people remained loyal to the latter. Still, the respectable had to draw on a deep well of forgiveness in the case of George IV. The reformation in manners and morals taking place during his reign made his errant behaviour look all the more reprehensible.

Compared to his father, George IV *was* an ass. The neglect of his duty gave the King more time to adorn his person, but it did little to protect the Crown's prerogatives, which diminished over his reign. The King was idle and bored by politics and consequently unable to take the measure of his ministers. Moreover, the long period of Tory rule altered the political balance and reduced his political options. In 1824, when the government recognized several South American republics, the King could only demonstrate his objection by refusing to read the royal speech announcing the measure, on the grounds of having gout and losing his false teeth.[69] The most significant political reform in the 1820s, Catholic Emancipation, was carried out against his opposition and despite his threat to retire to Hanover. It was, as the constitutional expert Vernon Bogdanor writes, 'an important watershed in the evolution of constitutional monarchy, by which the sovereign was ceasing to be an independent power in the realm'.[70]

Despite his positive attributes of charm and taste, George IV's personal deficiencies marked another stage in the emergence of Cabinet government and constitutional monarchy.[71] Arguably, George IV did the Crown a service by giving way to his ministers, but he often did so for the wrong reasons. As the Whig leader Lord Grenville remarked, he preferred abusing ministers to changing them: 'For a few hard words cost him nothing; but a great political change could not be made, if at all, without much more trouble, fatigue, and worry to the King than he will like to expose himself to.'[72] His enemies criticized him for laziness, profligacy and waste rather than for any abuse of the royal prerogative. When friends sang his praises, they pointed to his accomplishments in everything but governance.

The message was not lost on leading radicals, whose attacks on the Crown lost their punch with the decline in the King's powers. By 1823, Wooler argued that the royal prerogative in England was a sham: 'With all his vaunted prerogatives a King of England can hardly chuse [*sic*] his own valet.' The principle of monarchy, Wooler concluded, 'puts on an *aristocratic mantle*; and *prerogative* accompanying it in its migration, becomes privilege, as it exists in the cabinet, in the house of lords, and in the house of commons!'. He was right in saying that ministers appointed most of the officers in the royal household, thereby undermining the influence of the King in Parliament. But whether the wider prerogative powers of the Crown had been 'usurped' by a self-serving 'faction', was more doubtful.[73] As reformers had Parliament, not the monarchy, in their sights, it suited them to treat the Crown as an expensive plaything of corrupted ministers.

Paradoxically, as royal politics became less contentious, royal behaviour came under greater scrutiny. In a society which looked increasingly to the sovereign as head of society rather than as political leader, the character of the monarch mattered more than ever. As divergent voices from Bolingbroke to Paine suggested, kingship turned on the appearance of the King. The hereditary system protected members of the royal family from the necessity of making their own way in the world, but it put them under continuous pressure to perform duties in the public gaze. With the gradual emergence of a de-politicized monarchy, royalty was well advised to be seen to be respectable and engaged, if only in a nominal way, as patron. The sovereign as first servant would have to serve or at least be seen to serve. It was no accident that the Hanoverians applied the ancient motto on the badge of the heir apparent, 'Ich Dien' (I serve), to civic purposes.[74] It was an antidote to anti-monarchism in an era of political retreat.

George IV's relations with civic and charitable leaders were far less troubled than his relations with ministers. He carried forward the traditions of eighteenth-century royal philanthropy and stamped his own personality on them. He would not have agreed with his father's remark that charitable distributions 'alone make the station bearable', but he did not have the audacity to ignore the suffering of others. A man given to spontaneous acts of charity, he was generous to artists, writers, widows, orphans, servants and penurious relatives. On the institutional front, he took over his father's patronage list in 1820, and added to it. Over the years, he became the patron of nearly fifty institutions, including seventeen hospitals, eight benefit societies, several schools, trade associations and the Royal National Life-boat Institution.[75] After receiving a contribution from the King, the Secretary of the King's Free School in Kew wrote to the Palace: 'Those excellent fruits of the most noble and generous charity which have sprung from the throne . . . could not fail to make us "love, honour, and obey the King".'[76]

George IV was well aware that the 'sunshine' of royal charity, as one petitioner put it, illuminated the giver as well as warmed the recipient. Even his enemies recognized the power of royal patronage and either ridiculed it or sought to harness it to their own purposes. Carlile despised those Masonic institutions supported by royalty, but he advised the King to promote the working classes, especially through mechanics' institutions. 'Were you to do this, you would become a greater monarch than Alexander; than Frederic; than Bonaparte.'[77] George IV did not extend his patronage to mechanics' institutions (Queen Victoria and Prince Albert were to do so), but he mitigated the criticism of the monarchy by his civic and philanthropic associations, as did every other member of his family. And he complemented his patronage work by munificent donations to charitable institutions while on tour, as in Ireland (1821) and Scotland (1822).[78]

As we have seen, radicals could be contemptuous of the charitable contributions of the Crown. When, in 1818, the Palace had contributed an additional £5,000 to the poor of Spitalfields, there was little gratitude in the radical camp. Wooler compared the sum to the £209,848 received in grants by 'the poor of the royal family'.[79] In that digest of political corruption, *The Black Book*, Wade saw a degraded Civil List turning George IV into the premier beneficiary of the nation's charity.[80] By attacks and innuendo, radicals hoped to foment a desire for reform, but when they cursed the 'titled mendicants' in the Palace they often alienated respectable opinion. Royal voluntary bodies and their beneficiaries saw possibilities in royal benevolence where critics saw abuses; consequently, they forgave George IV's manly vices and forgot his marriage. Hannah More was well aware of the King's failings, but at the time of the coronation preferred to write of his 'royal liberality' and devotion to 'the helpless and homeless'.[81]

By the reign of George IV, the voluntary associations of civil society were at the cutting edge of social and political action, whether they were charities for 'the helpless and homeless' or radical debating societies. Early nineteenth-century reformers were often enthusiastic about voluntary organizations, and not only ones which gave them a political voice; for non-governmental institutions expressed the civic virtue at the heart of an evolving republican vision of society. Moreover, they were a check against bloated, uneconomical government, which so outraged radical campaigners. Democracy comes in different forms, and in the early nineteenth century it did not necessarily mean majority rule or popular sovereignty. Paine had advocated representative democracy for larger political communities; but like Coleridge, he believed democracy to be immanent in local institutions outside central government control.

The 'subscriber' democracies of civil society, in which the members had a voice in the running of their institutions, were a most promising way for diverse social groups, not least the disenfranchised, to forge a relationship with the wider society. And they could achieve their *ad hoc* purposes without being enmeshed, or immobilized, by politics. As Paine had recognized, the fluid, instrumental traditions of civil society would make a rigid, monopolistic political system less likely to emerge in his idealized republic. A high degree of self-government would provide a check on the mechanisms of central government and guarantee peaceful competition and solidarity based on shared interests. Paine had assumed, as his latest biographer puts it, that 'the more perfect civil society is, the more it regulates its own affairs and the less occasion it has for government'.[82]

In the early nineteenth century, both radicalism and the Crown were being marginalized politically, though for different reasons. As a consequence, the energies of radicals and the royal family flowed into civic channels outside conventional politics. Occasionally they joined forces. Clearly, members of the royal family did not seek to promote the extension of working-class rights through their civic work. They were paternalists, who sought to reduce human ills in a way that was compatible with the maintenance of the social order. But whether conservative or radical, driven by paternalism or individualism, voluntarists assumed that free associations gave a voice to civic leaders and a hand up to the needy, while acting as a counterweight to central government. The Duke of Clarence (later William IV) was not a man much associated with civil liberty, but he once remarked on a visit to Portsmouth that 'as an Englishman, he was most warmly a friend to the institutions of the country', which he valued as 'the guardians of the People's civil rights'.[83]

In the early nineteenth century, a collection of royal dukes, dissenters and free-thinking radicals came together in the cause of educational reform. The tradition of royal support for working-class education was given tremendous impetus by George III, who, unlike conservative churchmen, was happy at the prospect of poor children being able to read. In 1805 he had given his patronage to the Quaker Joseph Lancaster, a pioneer of the 'monitorial system' of education, in which the pupils themselves, coached by a master, taught other pupils. The King's patronage and the consequent support given to Lancaster by his sons, the Prince Regent and the Dukes of Sussex and Kent, transformed a local initiative into a national institution. Lancaster himself told the Prince Regent that 'whatever good I have been doing, thy name, thy Father's name, and the names of all the royal family have been my passports to usefulness'.[84]

Royal support for a cause promoted by republicans may seem incongruous. Clearly, the aims and motives of the royal family and the radicals who joined the Royal Lancasterian Association (later the British and Foreign School Society) were often at cross purposes. For the Dukes of Sussex and Kent, the institution was designed, in their words, 'to promote the morals of the people and also to insure the safety of the nation'.[85] To Francis Place, a member of the committee, the education of poor children was the foundation of working-class dignity and independence. The utilitarian James Mill, another member of the Association, linked popular education with the cause of political reform. Free-thinking republicans must have swallowed hard when they drank the Association's toast: 'Fear God and honour the King', but they did it because of the importance of royal patronage to their social and political agenda. Place assuaged his conscience by criticizing others in the charity for bowing and scraping.[86]

From the monarchy's point of view, royal support for Lancaster's experimental schools forged links with advanced opinion, while at the same time promoting wider loyalty to the throne. With its more popular members the Dukes of Kent and Sussex in the spotlight, the monarchy was even able to claim a progressive middle-class constituency. The Manchester radical David Holt, whose own Lancasterian school received royal patronage, wrote to the Duke of Kent in 1819: 'I never see a public charity advertized when the names of thyself and any other Branches of the Royal Family appear but I feel the name of Briton dignified and exalted, and I cannot but exclaim, truly these deserve the people's love.'[87] Holt's experience was an example of a radical cause at once extended and disarmed by royal patronage.

Such popular philanthropic causes served well the monarchy's intention of providing a unifying symbol of the nation. And those who received royal favour returned it with a stream of perfected praise. Recalling the charities of the Duke of Kent, who was chairman or president of no fewer than fifty-three societies, William Wilberforce observed: 'Princes strike out for themselves a road, which has now become well worn with many tracks on it, all in the same direction, and all leading alike to esteem, public benefit, and individual comfort.'[88] Voluntary institutions supported by the royal family had hundreds of thousands of members across the country.[89] Not all of them can be counted as royalists, but in a society obsessed by social hierarchy and riddled with snobbery, it may be assumed that a decision to have one's name published on a subscription list headed by the King or a royal duke did not suggest rabid anti-monarchism.

By publicly identifying the monarchy with popular causes, not least religious ones, charitable patronage reaffirmed the royal family's importance. It even gave respectability to Queen Victoria's 'wicked uncles', who were much more involved in good works than royal biographers have allowed.[90] The Crown's voluntary role was all the more significant at a time when the monarchy's capacity to influence politics through money, contracts and favours remained under attack as costly and corrupt. Unlike the patronage of placemen, the patronage of worthy causes did not foster anti-monarchism, rather the opposite. Moreover, through philanthropy members of the royal family promoted the general good without attaching themselves to political factions. The Crown retained its traditional allegiances to aristocratic society, but, through its support of worthy causes, royalty was becoming a mouthpiece for middle-class values.

The growing royal association with good works was another reason why so few people called for the monarchy's abolition. But the decline in radical agitation after the Queen Caroline affair probably had more to do with improvements in the economy. Several radical papers folded in the mid-1820s, including Carlile's *Republican* and Wooler's *Black Dwarf*. Wooler admitted to having been mistaken in assuming that there was a public in Britain devoted to the cause of parliamentary reform. 'The majority', he declared, 'has decided in its cooler moments, for "things as they are".'[91] The dramatic drop in the number of petitions calling for reform was another sign of the times. One contemporary reported that between the beginning of 1824 and the end of 1829 not one such petition had been presented to Parliament.[92] To conservatives, such circumstances were attributable to the blessings of the balanced consti-tution, which, according to Coleridge, gave the English 'fewer restraints on their free agency, than the citizens of any known Republic'.[93]

Radicalism did not die away in the 1820s so much as divide into strands of opinion that competed for a dwindling audience. In a decade more given to ideology than action, pure republicanism was little in evidence in the streets. Early socialists like the Irish landowner William Thompson, labelled the 'Red Republican' by his neighbours, was said to have decor-ated his walking stick with the tricolour.[94] But his views, disseminated in the radical press, pointed to the economic causes of impoverishment rather than taxation, political corruption or the unreformed constitution. In socialist thinking, the monarchy was a subsidiary issue, a symptom of a deeper malaise, which would be addressed with the removal of the inequitable social system. Such views had sinister implications for the Crown, which were not lost on its defenders. In a letter to the *Poor Man's Guardian*, the constitutional writer and monarchist J. B. Bernard said that if the object of reform was to remove power from moneymongers and commercialists it would be impossible 'without the application of force in a number of quarters'.[95]

The social reformer Robert Owen could not be described as an enemy of the monarchy, though where George IV fitted into his utopian view of society is an open question. He was far less interested in natural rights or Old Corruption than in the development of co-operative communities and philanthropic schemes to aid the poor. Moreover, he was a firm believer in persuading the leaders of society to engage in the schemes his fertile mind devised. Consequently, he came into the orbit of royalty. As a charitable campaigner in the 1810s, he had recruited Queen Victoria's father, the Duke of Kent, as chairman of one of his benevolent societies. It was another example of royal patronage linking with advanced opinion.

The friendship between Owen and the Duke was as peculiar as it was fascinating. Owen, softened up by royal flattery, admired the Duke for the 'power and goodness' of his mind, and once loaned his 'best disciple' £1,000, a sum never repaid. Intriguingly, the Chartist poet John Bedford Leno said that he was shown a letter to the effect that the Duke 'made overtures' for placing his daughter in Owen's charge.[96] (The thought of Queen Victoria being brought up by the 'Father of Socialism' should amuse counterfactual historians.) Clearly, Owen enjoyed the seductive charms of royal favour. His spiritualist communications with the deceased Duke may be seen as symbolic.[97] The royal embrace reached far and wide, in Owen's case beyond the grave. By exciting expectancy, and affection, in unlikely circles, it took the anti-royalist edge off reform.

Jeremy Bentham's mundane philosophical radicalism was potentially more damaging to the monarchy than socialist theory or Paineite republicanism. Bentham dismissed 'natural rights' as an 'anarchical sophism', yet his own doctrine was as pure in its republicanism as Paine's Jacobinism. He gave the impression that he demanded the immediate abolition of the Crown. But safe in his armchair, he was not a man likely to take any direct part in achieving it. In the background, it should be said, he had a grievance against royalty. He believed, wrongly, that George III had been responsible for the rejection of his prison design, the Panopticon.[98]

In Bentham's 'felicific calculus', the Crown was all pain and no pleasure. Only in a pure democracy, free from the trappings of royalty, could general felicity exist. Even a monarchy limited by democratic representation was necessarily evil. Any self-respecting king would simply lay down tools. Reminiscent of Paine, Bentham believed the hereditary principle led to impropriety, lunacy and slavery: 'Every Monarch is a Slave-holder upon the largest scale.'[99] Warming to his theme, he compared the King's view of his subjects to a proprietor surveying his cattle. Perhaps reminded of George III's derangement, he argued that in all monarchical states the great likelihood was that 'at any given period, the fate of all its members will be in the hands of a madman'.[100]

Bentham believed that people only tolerated monarchy from force of custom; but he conceded that custom made the abolition of the British monarchy unlikely. His friends and political allies tended to avoid the issue, recognizing that there were few votes in renouncing the sovereign. His leading disciple, James Mill, who worked with the royal dukes in educational reform, was, according to his illustrious son, largely 'indifferent to monarchical or republican forms'.[101] As the historian Elie Halévy later observed: 'The political party which recognized him [Bentham] as its leader ... was silent on the question of the House of Lords and it accepted the monarchy; it was a Radical without being a Republican party.'[102]

If the life of George IV was not enough to create a republican party in Britain, his death, on 26 June 1830, was unlikely to do so. Out of touch politically, and sensitive about his size, the King had spent his final years in retirement, having rid himself, as Elizabeth Longford put it, 'of all his better qualities except good taste'.[103] Outside his charities, who sang his praises, few lamented the King's passing. Pure republicans, who would miss him, looked back on George IV as 'the incarnation of true vulgarity; a mixture of the butler and the bully'.[104] Years later, the novelist William Thackeray, lecturing in America, called him 'a great simulacrum'.[105] At the time of the funeral, *The Times* described a monarch unregretted by his subjects, who had to pick up the bill for his extravagance: 'Nothing more remains to be said about George IV but to pay, as pay we must, for his profusion.'[106]

The King's death had followed an economic crisis in the industrial and agricultural districts and preceded, by less than a month, the July Revolution in France, which contributed to the political agitation that led to the Great Reform Bill of 1832. The new king, William IV, soon found himself in a country in turmoil. Outbreaks of looting and rioting in the agricultural districts of southern England, the 'Captain Swing' riots, raised the political temperature. So did the government's more vigorous enforcement of the laws against a resurgent unstamped press, which incensed radical journalists and drove their rhetoric further into extremism. Whether or not there was revolutionary intent among rioters or reformers, it was not a moment in which the propertied classes, nervous about disturbances emanating from France, were likely to indulge in a royal reckoning.

At the time of his accession, the affable, if boorish, William IV was widely popular, except in ultra-radical circles, which treated him as just another royal nuisance. In some respects he was an ideal monarch to cope with the pressures of the early 1830s. Princess Lieven, the wife of the Russian ambassador, believed that 'what a nation most appreciates in its sovereign is domestic virtue'.[107] Compared to George IV, King William was a model of dullness, prone to falling asleep after dinner while the dutiful Queen Adelaide embroidered. He was also more economical. His coronation cost £30,000 against £240,000 for George IV's.[108] His admirers would even celebrate his many deficiencies, not least his lack of serious opinions. One early biographer remarked that the King was 'peculiarly fitted to supply the British Empire with a monarch', for he had 'no capacity for public business, and little inclination to interfere in it'.[109]

One area where the King did have views was royal finance. It was an issue, full of ambiguity and contested sums, which remained a sore point to radicals and Whigs. The Civil List debates took place in November 1830 and February 1831, shortly before the introduction of the Reform Bill. There was little in the way of criticism of William IV, though many MPs desired to reduce expenditure and make the monarchy's costs more transparent. The Benthamite Joseph Hume, who had royal associations through educational reform, expressed an opinion that summed up the moderate radical case. He hoped that 'the good sense of the Royal Family would induce them to consider the value of public opinion, and reduce their expenses'.[110]

An important issue at stake, which had repercussions for anti-monarchists, was whether the personal expenses of the Crown should continue to be mixed together with charges for other public services. Some MPs took the view that disguising the cost of royalty among other charges had advantages for the monarchy, for if the public saw the amount the sovereign received for his personal gratification it might damage the reputation of the Crown. Others assumed that a separate account for royal expenditure would clarify a misleading picture, which in the past had, as the Chancellor of the Exchequer noted, led the 'ill-disposed' to exaggerate the monarchy's costs.[111] Brougham put the issue clearly in the Civil List debate of 1830: 'It is well known among us, that the King does not spend nearly the half of the money we are called upon to vote; but out of doors it is generally thought that he consumes every farthing of it.'[112]

Another contentious issue was the pension list. Henry Hunt, returned as MP for Preston in 1830, declared himself a friend of the King but said that 'it was the unanimous demand of the people, that all [Crown] pensions be abolished, except those which had been merited'. William IV took a stern line on pensions. Even though they were granted on ministerial advice (several beneficiaries had slandered the royal family), he saw their reduction as a move towards democracy.[113] In the event, Parliament reduced the pension list in 1831. The King also acquiesced in the cost of various public services being charged on the Consolidated Fund, thereby making separate provision for 'the honour and dignity of the Crown'. The reforms reduced the annual Civil List expenditure to £510,000, less than half that granted to George IV. It was a prudent compromise given the agitation taking place in the country.

If the King thought pension reform raised the spectre of democracy, he deemed the Reform Bill a wild form of republicanism inimical to the balanced constitution. In the debates inside Parliament, no one threatened his security of tenure. But the King took no comfort from the food riots, machine breaking, threatening letters, mass meetings with tricolour flags and the many petitions now turning up in favour of parliamentary reform.[114] On one occasion, Londoners harassed him with obscene threats and threw dirt into his carriage, just the sort of behaviour to feed the conservative backlash to republican principles. Royalty has a long memory for insult, and William IV must have been reminded of the similar treatment meted out to his brother in 1817 and his father in 1795.

The radical press gave the monarchy a battering during the reform agitation. Henry Hetherington's *Poor Man's Guardian*, which had grafted co-operative theory on to the radical agenda, contrasted the poverty of the masses with the 'useless extravagance' of Kensington Palace.[115] So did the *Republican*, published by Hetherington and edited by the middle-class firebrand James Lorymer, who was known as a 'democratic writer of the French Republican school' (some thought him a spy). It advertised its principles as 'the extirpation of the Fiend Aristocracy – Establishment of Republic viz. Democracy by Representatives elected by universal Suffrage. Extinction of hereditary offices, titles and distinctions. Abolition of primogeniture, equal distribution of property among all children'.[116] The King probably never read the works of Lorymer or Hetherington, but he was not insensitive to the alarm the radical press caused to the authorities.

The King's popularity waxed and waned as events unfolded over the reform of Parliament. Haunted by memories of the French Revolution, William IV found any idea of political reform alarming. So did Queen Adelaide, whose uncompromising Tory views made her unpopular – 'a nasty German frow', said one radical.[117] But the monarchy had swallowed so much else over the years that it could by now be made to swallow just about anything. Perhaps it was because of his very weakness that the King's defenders have amplified his role in the Reform Bill. In their view, nothing did more to alter William IV's reputation as a loose cannon than his incapacity for business. Being less obstructive than George IV, the King took refuge in delay, in the hope of encouraging reaction. But ultimately, he accepted that reform was unavoidable and reluctantly promised to create enough peers to carry the Bill through Parliament.

Throughout the crisis, pure republicans portrayed the King as an obstructive buffoon, whose actions would accelerate the demise of the Crown. Lorymer, who founded the shadowy Republican Association, which met in Theobald's Road, London, thanked 'William Guelph' for his delay in creating fifty peers: 'The consequence of which was that he was the cause of making about fifty hundred thousands of additional republicans. The Radical Press might have laboured for many years to come, in converting annually about ten thousand citizens to the good cause; we have a "Patriot King" who made as many in an hour!'[118] Here was an example of republican analysis giving way to fancy. In the end, the King acted wisely over the Reform Bill, if only because he had little choice. Could he be blamed for the abuse of power when he had little power left to abuse? A contemporary cartoon pictures the monarch as a nondescript puppet, in keeping with 'An Excellent *Republican* King'. (See Plate 8.)

Both republicans and Palace officials were unhappy with the result of the Great Reform Bill. It conceded little to working-class demands for the franchise, but exceeded royal wishes. While disillusionment set in in radical circles, royalists predicted the disintegration of deference to the

Crown. The Duke of Wellington believed that the King had profoundly damaged the monarchy by his actions over the Reform Bill.[119] He was mistaken, just as Lorymer was mistaken when he said that the King would be undone by his vacillation. Lord Grey put his case for reform simply: 'The principle . . . is to prevent the necessity for revolution.'[120] Whether the Reform Bill was a necessary antidote to save parliamentary monarchy is debatable, but the ossification of the constitution was a greater threat to the Crown than peaceful political evolution. Francis Place, who thought William IV had lost all credibility, put the case of patient anti-royalism. The Reform Act was so great a change that 'Kings and Lords' would 'in time go quietly out of existence'.[121]

With hindsight, it is clear that the 'bloodless change' wrought by the Reform Bill did not so much endanger the Crown as transform it. As noted, the power of the Crown had been in decline for decades because of the weight of public business, the failings of successive monarchs and administrative reforms which had gradually reduced the sinecures and favours it had at its disposal to sway parliamentary affairs. But when the Reform Act widened the franchise to the middle classes and eliminated rotten and nomination boroughs, it set the seal on the monarchy's political influence through traditional forms of patronage and honours. The 'King's men', so important to the republican case against the Crown, ceased to exist.[122] Moreover, the extension of the franchise meant that public opinion would have to be taken much more seriously and politicians would have to work harder for votes. Thus, constitutional reform stimulated the development of political parties and electoral organization, which severely limited the sovereign's room for manoeuvre.[123]

By 1832, the longstanding and contentious issue of the control of the executive was essentially over. As Bogdanor writes: 'the Reform Act seemed to have made parliament the indisputable victor in its conflict with the king'.[124] To constitutional experts at the time, including members of the royal family, the monarch's role as head of state in a parliamentary system remained ill-defined. For his part, William IV continued to hold a pre-reform view of his constitutional powers and removed a ministry in 1834, but at the price of proving that it could not be repeated.[125] The King had not acted unconstitutionally, but he had failed to appreciate that a parliamentary majority was the key factor necessary for a government to remain in office, not the support of the sovereign. As the formerly radical

MP Sir Francis Burdett noted: 'I fear the King has made a rash move and with no apparent justification, and as by the Reform Bill he cannot in reality appoint his Ministers . . . whoever he appoints must go to large bodies of constituents to be approved.'[126]

Although republicans could take little direct credit for it, the republican aim of stripping the Crown of power had been largely achieved. Leopold, King of the Belgians, once wrote to the young Queen Victoria that the 'trade' of a constitutional sovereign now meant trying 'to keep for the Crown the little influence it still may possess'.[127] '*The very* spirit of the old monarchy has been abolished,' he observed on another occasion.[128] Prince Albert's adviser, Baron Stockmar, who regretted the loss of executive power to the ministry, believed that the Reform Bill perverted the English constitution.[129] From his partisan perspective, based on the precedents of George III, it was difficult to appreciate that the decline of the royal prerogative might be in the best interests of the Crown. The loss of sovereign power and the widening of the franchise were steps in a direction that monarchs feared to tread. But concessions to democracy did not, as royalists often assumed, reinforce anti-monarchical views – rather the reverse.

Although Bagehot would later claim that the Reform Bill created a disguised republic, it did not introduce a democratic one. But in extending political awareness and recognizing social change, it opened up prospects for further reform.[130] One effect of reform was to encourage middle- and upper-class alliances in support of British institutions outside politics. Though little appreciated by historians, it had important implications for the Crown. If the monarchy's capacity to influence parliamentary politics through political patronage was negligible after 1832, its long-standing patronages in civil society were money in the bank. It had lost in the high-political struggle, but it had everything to gain in social esteem and influence through further investment in the nation's charitable and civic institutions.

The monarchy stepped up its patronage and welfare work in the reign of William IV, not least because of the influence of Queen Adelaide, who gave away vast sums of money with studied rectitude.[131] Few members of the royal family were so finely tuned to the pieties of the day, and through social work the Queen quietly redeemed herself in the public mind and overturned an unhappy reputation for political meddling. It was a message not lost on others in the royal household. After 1832, the monarchy's support for popular causes and reputable societies provided a crucial link with middle-class voters, and middle-class respectability. Indeed, the development of the monarchy's non-governmental role as head of society would be the most uncontentious way forward in the changing political and social atmosphere.

If the Reform Bill reshaped the monarchy, it left radicalism in disarray. Middle-class reformers, having been given the vote, largely lost interest in working-class aspirations. The landed classes, given a face lift by the decline of Old Corruption, effectively regrouped and prolonged their hold on power. To working-class radicals, the Reform Bill was a 'Great Betrayal', which left them with little in the way of solid achievement and no immediate prospects. Disaffected journalists, who had nurtured radicalism during the Reform crisis, carried forward the radical campaign, but it had to operate in the context of restrictive libel laws and newspaper duties. Increasingly, it spoke in divergent voices, from socialist critiques of industrial society to traditional radicalism, which carried forward the ancient attacks on oligarchic corruption.[132] But whatever their particular ideological leanings, most reformers looked to a widening suffrage and an infusion of public spirit as a solution. In this sense, they could all be called republicans.

After 1832, republicanism remained an amorphous concept, a variable brew of political ideals and frustrations. In the broadest sense, it carried forward the classical republican vision of politics purified by civic spirit and the rule of law, which was anti-despotic rather than anti-monarchical. But over the years, the impact of the American and French Revolutions, heightened by the writings of Paine, Carlile, Bentham and others, had shifted the meaning of the word republican, so that more and more people took it to mean democracy with anti-monarchical overtones. Ironically, the transformation in usage was taking place at the same time that the Crown itself was undergoing a transformation which enhanced its reputation. In so far as royalty was popular, republicanism as anti-monarchism damaged the campaign for political rights. Here was the rub for agitators like Carlile, Hetherington and Lorymer. Their attacks on kingship, out of tune with respectable radicalism, did little, if anything, to assist the cause of further constitutional change.

Lorymer defined the Republic as 'Democracy by Representatives elected by universal Suffrage'. But he added to the definition the 'Extinction of hereditary offices, titles and distinctions'. The first principle was the means, the second an end, an end which was perhaps best left unstated in a society accepting of hierarchy and enamoured of royalty. When reformers applied the word republican to themselves, it was exploited by their opponents and, on occasion, mocked by their allies. Cobbett used the word 'republican' as a term of abuse, a 'species of calamity and disgrace'.[133] In the event, many constitutional radicals disassociated themselves from a word, tarred by a foreign brush, which had become more useful to reaction than to reform. Increasingly, the public identified the appellation republican with extremists, sometimes dubbed 'Red Republicans', who savoured of blood. The more these people became isolated from mainstream reform, the more they used the tag as a badge of defiance.

Though criticism of the royal family remained a commonplace in radical circles after the Reform Bill, demands for the immediate abolition of the monarchy were rare. With the years, men as various as Carlile, Hetherington and Wade lost their anti-royal edge. In 1832, Wade, that scourge of Crown extravagance, admitted that the monarchy remained popular with the people despite its cost. He also admitted that the Civil List granted to William IV in 1831, which cut royal expenditure and removed anomalies, represented 'a substantial improvement on its predecessors'.[134] Carlile's republican zeal, which was an expression of his endemic rootlessness, declined with his release from jail.[135] In the 1830s, he drifted away from politics and converted to Christianity, which he had previously castigated as an abomination. Compared to the attacks on royalty in the 1790s or the 1810s, the attacks in the mid-1830s sounded stale, academic or comic. The enemies of radicalism had become ritual targets: 'There could be no call to a self-conscious working class in such an all-too-easy language.'[136]

The decline in strident anti-monarchism was partly because William IV was benign, relatively prudent and respectably married. But it was also because reform had defused political agitation, while further eroding the power of the Crown, a point that was not lost on reformers. The argument that the monarchy was the fount of borough-mongering was less persuasive after 1832. Virtually all radicals now assumed that their principal enemy was the oligarchy not the Crown. If the King was little more than a 'puppet' of the aristocracy, as Lorymer and others believed, getting rid of him lost its urgency.[137] For his part, Wade continued to rail against monarchy in the abstract for 'tyranny, expense, military domination; unnecessary warfare to gratify the passions of an individual'. But here he had shifted into automatic pilot. He went on to say that a republic meant simply a democracy, a form of politics that he rejected as utopian.[138]

The dissipation of pure republicanism can be traced in the unstamped papers of the day, which remained under surveillance by the authorities. When Lorymer produced *Le Bonnet Rouge* in 1833, even his printer took fright at 'its horrific name' and refused to print. When it did appear with a second printer, it boasted the red cap of liberty on its masthead, and dedicated itself to 'the rising Republic of France and Fraternization of the Two peoples'. English readers, even radical ones it seems, drew the line at such associations, and the paper expired after ten issues.[139] For his pains, Lorymer later spent three months in jail, a martyr to his French principles.

Hetherington's *Poor Man's Guardian* lasted longer, until the end of 1835. But its coverage of royalty, never prominent, showed increasing signs of desperation, as the anti-royal verse which sometimes appeared in its pages suggested.[140] Just before the paper's closure, it printed a letter, signed by 'William Tell', which called for king-killing by 'dagger, air-gun, or, more properly, the steady rifle, so as to mark them as execrated examples to all other tyrants'.[141] Applied to the constitutional monarchy of William IV, this was pure republicanism reduced to farce, a point conceded by the *Poor Man's Guardian* itself, which argued that since the King was but a 'tool' of the aristocracy his assassination would be pointless.[142]

Anti-monarchists in the 1830s did not expect to topple the throne through poetry, satire or threats. The hectoring and menaces were part of the ritual of ultra radicalism, in which William IV was a symbol of the beast, not the beast itself. Lorymer, recalling Bentham, cursed the sovereign for talking about his people as a landowner talked about his cattle, though he acknowledged that royalty did not own the people.[143] Such bluster, however futile, did serve a purpose. It tested the outer limits of free expression, which, along with representation, was an essential radical principle. It carried forward, in etiolated form, an English republicanism dating from the American and French Revolutions. From time to time there were ghostly reminders of the ever more tenuous links with the anti-monarchism of the 1790s. In 1835, an aged William Godwin passed Buckingham Palace with Lady Blessington in a carriage and declared: 'There's a place worse than useless for a thing worse still.'[144]

3

Queen Victoria and the Republican Challenge

1837–1867

'The more we endear the Constitution to the people by making them feel its benefits – the safer will be the just rights of the Monarch who is its head, and the stronger will be the allegiance of the subject who cheerfully obeys.'

Lord Brougham, Debate on the Civil List (1837)

'Republicanism is simply this, self-government; the right of every individual to govern himself, either in person or by representation.'   George Harding, Chartist, *Republican* (1848)

In 1837, Queen Victoria succeeded 'an imbecile . . . a profligate . . . and a buffoon'.[1] This nicely turned, but misleading, assessment of Hanoverian kingship came not from a contemporary republican, but from the royalist Sir Sidney Lee, Victoria's first serious biographer and editor of *The Dictionary of National Biography*. The Queen's admirers tend to dwell on the shortcomings of her predecessors, particularly the 'wicked uncles', for it presents her reign as a gust of royal fresh air. But for all the limitations of George III, George IV and William IV, arguably *because* of them, the British monarchy was stable. It had survived the turbulent politics of the early 1830s with its power eroded but its social influence enhanced. The shift in attention from high political to civil society, which built links with the public and identified royalty with middle-class respectability, had taken hold, to the Crown's advantage. It was a trend that would continue in the reign of Victoria, despite her own keen interest in politics.

Queen Victoria was a strong personality, obstinate, kindly and impetuous by turns. Given her upbringing, with its emphasis on royal history, she was not content to sit back and nod in compliance with ministerial wishes. She failed to grasp fully that the growth of party politics acted as a brake on the royal prerogative. Inclined to assert her independence, as in the bed-chamber crisis early in the reign, she sought to inflate the power of the Crown in an era when no one knew its precise limits.[2] She was too partisan to see that her reputation as a constitutional monarch depended on giving way to ministers; or to see that the running down of the monarchy's political power might be a blessing in disguise, for it acquitted the Crown of responsibility for unpopular policies. It was fortunate for the Queen that few people outside the highest reaches of politics knew about the royal machinations behind the scenes.

It was to the monarchy's advantage to have a reigning queen, especially one so sympathetic to the prevailing middle-class sentiments of the age. The separate spheres of men and women in the nineteenth century sheltered Victoria from criticism and placed her in a unique political realm.[3] Like women of the middle class, she had taken on board the conventional attitudes about 'woman's nature and mission', as both her political and philanthropic work attests. She often said herself that politics was a male preserve, but she turned the cult of the gentleman to her own purposes. The Queen being a virtuous female not only softened her ministers but disarmed her enemies, who preferred monarchs to be sabre-rattling males. Sidney Lee believed she evoked 'a sentiment of chivalric devotion to the monarchy, which gave it new stability and deprived revolution of all foothold'.[4] This was an exaggeration, but, in the royal lottery, the young Queen, sheltered by her ministers, was a republican losing ticket.

The country customarily rallied to a new sovereign. Indeed, the first year of the reign was an *annus mirabilis* for the Queen: 'The pleasantest summer I EVER passed in *my life*', she wrote in her Journal.[5] Under the protective eye of the Prime Minister, the Whig Lord Melbourne, she took to her office with enthusiasm. At a levée in July, nearly 3,000 well-wishers kissed her hand. Even Quakers and reformers, usually averse to royal ceremony and titles, joined the queue. In her declaration to the Privy Council, she said that she had been brought up to 'respect and to love the Constitution of her native country', and that she would defend individual and religious liberties.[6] It was just the sort of royal pronouncement, however perfunctory, that raised the hopes of constitutional reformers. At the time of the coronation, the *Northern Star*, the official paper of Chartism, paid conditional homage: 'We love the Queen . . . None can desire more ardently than we do the happiness of the Throne; but it can only rest securely on the universal happiness of the people.'[7]

The Queen's immediate priorities, which did not include an extension of the suffrage, were to pay off her father's debts and to increase her mother's annuity. While she accepted that public expenditure must be kept within limits, she was confident that Parliament 'would gladly make adequate provision for the support of the honour and dignity of the Crown'.[8] In the debate on the Civil List at the end of 1837, there was no personal criticism of the Queen. A handful of radicals pressed their case against Crown pensions and the waste of taxpayer's money in supporting royal sinecures, but they pilloried the system not the monarch. Joseph Hume took particular exception to the Governor of Windsor Castle and the Master of the Royal Buckhounds.[9] More preposterous still, he argued, was the cost of keeping the accounts of the Civil List, which ran to nearly £10,000 annually. But his motion to reduce the proposed Civil List by £50,000 was defeated by 199 votes to 19.[10] (When Hume lost his seat in the general election of 1837, the Queen greeted the news by clapping her hands.[11])

Viscount Melbourne, for the government, moved the second reading of the Civil List Bill in the Lords. With his customary worldliness, he presented the conventional parliamentary case for the Crown. There was no 'royal road in public accounts any more than in mathematics', and he rued the day when the country would look at the resources of the monarchy 'for contest'. He asked his Lordships to assent to the Bill, 'not from feelings of loyalty and duty to your present young and amiable Sovereign' but because it preserved 'the laws and liberties of your country'. He refused to enter into 'any frivolous dispute' about whether a monarchy was the wisest form of government, but it would be folly to discard such an ancient institution. 'I call upon your Lordships to support this Bill for the support of the monarchy; for in supporting that monarchy you will support the liberty and laws under which the country has attained an amount of property and a degree of prosperity hitherto unexampled in the history of nations.'[12]

If Melbourne was content with the Bill, Lord Brougham, the former advocate of Queen Caroline, was fierce for retrenchment and reform. On the immediate issue before Parliament, he deemed it essential to reduce the Queen's income in order to ensure her survival. He was quick to disassociate himself from 'revolutionary doctrines' and 'rejoiced' in the widespread affection shown to the Queen at her accession. It 'puts to shame' all who would represent the people 'as disaffected towards Monarchical institutions'. But he neatly turned the people's affection to reform purposes, for such affection demonstrated the wisdom of entrusting them with further political rights. There was a trenchant message for the monarchy in his peroration: 'The more we endear the Constitution to the people by making them feel its benefits – the safer will be the just rights of the Monarch who is its head, and the stronger will be the allegiance of the subject who cheerfully obeys.'[13]

Brougham was that familiar political character – an unstable rationalist – whose independent views rattled his allies and enemies alike. Soon after his impassioned speech on the Civil List, he published an anonymous *Letter to The Queen on the State of the Monarchy* (1838), which combined a call for royal economy with a plea for an extension of the franchise. As 'a Friend' of the sovereign, though an enemy of her government, he laced his advice with complaint. The monarchy was, he observed, 'better suited, at least to our present condition, than a republic'; but he fully expected an increase in 'pure republican doctrines' if further political reform should fail to materialize. 'If these men . . . rule the country in *your* name, and in *your* name to obstruct the progress of general improvement, then Madam, be you well assured that a day of reckoning will soon come.'[14]

Now into his stride, Brougham launched into a diatribe worthy of Bentham or Paine. He compared the British constitution to republics which had freed themselves of those hateful appendages: 'An insolvent aristocracy; an intolerant hierarchy; a vexatious administration of the law; mighty standing armies in peace time; numerous colonies for purposes of patronage and corruption; bad laws, to hamper trade; unjust preferences, to oppress industry; evil customs, to discourage genius.' All of this would be taken into account in that 'fearful reckoning which the enemies of reform would force the people to make'. It was a comprehensive indictment of the political system over which the Queen, whom he now dismissed as 'a child', presided. What followed belied his earlier pronouncements in favour of the Crown: 'After all is told, the heaviest item of the whole will remain; the item most difficult in reason to endure; I mean the heavy price we pay for uncontested succession.'[15]

In his *Letter to The Queen*, Brougham displayed many of the hallmarks of the republicanism he disavowed, a point several critics noted with heavy irony.[16] Firstly, he put himself solidly behind the extension of the franchise to the working classes, which in both radical and royal circles implied republicanism. Second, in his attack on heredity and royal expenditure he cited Paine's jibe about 'an able bodied man' doing the King's job for £500 a year. That he did not join the pure republican camp himself turned on his reluctance to call for the Crown's abolition. While monarchical government did, as he argued, require popular support, it may be doubted that he expected a girlish Queen to achieve it. His phrase that the Crown suited 'our present condition' suggested that Brougham leaned towards theoretical republicanism. To have gone further would have closeted him with extremists, which for a former Lord Chancellor would have been quite extraordinary.

Brougham's views would have been seconded by many in the Chartist movement, which was then attracting support among the disenfranchised. The London Working Men's Association, founded in 1836 by William Lovett to promote political education, carried forward the traditional radical programme of Cartwright and Paine. In its call for annual parliaments and equal electoral districts it carried forward aspects of classical republicanism.[17] In 1837, it drafted a petition containing the six points of the 'People's Charter', headed by universal manhood suffrage. As part of its campaign against that familiar bugbear 'Old Corruption', the LWMA looked to the sovereign for support. Its delegates refused to attend a levée because of the requirement to wear court dress, but they dispatched 'a loyal and outspoken' address to the Queen in September 1837. In content and tone, it was reminiscent of the petitions to George III from the London Corresponding Society, or the remonstrances to George IV.

Like Brougham's *Letter to The Queen*, the address hailed the progress of knowledge among the working classes; it championed the right of the people to govern themselves; it condemned the 'monstrous anomalies' of the constitution; and it denounced the arbitrary political system that compromised the sovereign and made Her Majesty the puppet of despotic faction. In conclusion, the address entreated the Queen to instruct her ministers to prepare a Bill to extend the suffrage 'to all the adult population'. If this were done, 'then will the voice of the millions be raised to bless you, their arms to defend you from factions at home or despots abroad, and then will they transmit your name to posterity, as the first to break through the trammels of courtly prejudice to render them justice'.[18] Among the petitioners were Lovett, a declared enemy of 'king and priest-ridden nations', and Hetherington, the former publisher of the *Republican* and the *Poor Man's Guardian*.

The members of the London Working Men's Association seemed to expect quite a lot from an institution whose political influence they more typically abhorred. Did they really expect the sovereign to enliven the republican project by pressing corrupted ministers to give the common man his natural rights? Had the Queen raised the issue of universal suffrage with her ministers, she would have conformed to what one contemporary called a 'Monarcho-Republic', a state in which the Crown mediated between the people and the executive.[19] Her actual views on suffrage reform, however, were unknown to the Chartists, for she did not express them publicly. Had they known her views, they would have seen her not as the plaything of reaction, but the embodiment of reaction itself.

Just as the Chartists did not know the mind of the sovereign, the Queen's notion of Chartism was ill-informed. Needless to say, universal suffrage, secret ballots and annual elections were not on her agenda. Like her forebears, she did not distinguish between radicalism and anti-monarchism. Not surprisingly, therefore, she ignored reform addresses and refused an audience with those Chartists who wished to present her with a memorial. (It was sent by post.[20]) Here, after all, was a monarch who believed Henry Hallam's *Constitutional History of England* (1827) was 'too Republican' because it argued that the sovereign's power derived from the people and not from God.[21] The Chartists might also have been surprised to learn that the influential royal adviser Baron Stockmar thought the Whig leaders 'unconscious Republicans who stand in the same relation to the Throne as the wolf does to the lamb'.[22]

Few outside Palace circles realized that the Queen spent much of her political energy trying to preserve royal prerogatives against what she saw as ministerial encroachments. She certainly would not have enjoyed being called a puppet, and did not act like one when the issue of democratic reform arose, for on this question she was at one with her ministers. With hindsight, it is easy to accuse Chartists of either innocence or insincerity when they turned their minds to the Crown. As in the case of the 1790s, it is not always easy to tell just how reformers perceived the monarchy, for the popularity of the Queen and the threat of reprisal led to posturing and dissimulation. Robert Lowery, a Chartist from Newcastle, was a constitutionalist who looked to the throne for redress. Was he being sincere, naïve or disingenuous when he spoke of the Queen as the 'mother' of her people?[23] And what compelled the revolutionary Bronterre O'Brien, former firebrand on the *Poor Man's Guardian*, to write in the *Southern Star*: 'You have a sovereign of whom you may be proud; and whose reign will form one of the brightest portions of British History'?[24]

Chartist attitudes to the Crown varied enormously. Some were royalists who adjourned meetings to watch the state opening of Parliament. Others took the wait-and-see attitude of theoretical republicanism. And others still, reviving memories of Cromwell, would have been happy to see the Queen pensioned off, exiled or 'die of grief'.[25] After Parliament rejected the national petition in 1839, the strident were more in evidence. When militants called for 'ulterior measures' and stepped up their arming and drilling, the Crown may not have been a primary target. But to the respectable classes, the Chartist insurrections were reminiscent of the social eruptions of the 1810s, which threatened the ancient constitution. To loyalists, any intimations of anti-monarchism were political capital easily turned to defensive purposes.

If the Chartist insurgents of South Wales who rose in Newport in 1839 under the leadership of John Frost had created a 'people's republic' in the Welsh valleys, there were hopes, and fears, that it would spread to London. When the insurrection failed, Frost and his colleagues declared that they had 'never entertained any feeling or spirit of hostility' towards the constitution or the Queen's 'sacred person'.[26] But this was disingenuous, for, as one of them later admitted, the plan was 'to overthrow the present Government of England, & establish a republican' one.[27] Not surprisingly, the Chartist appeal to the Queen to pardon the men fell on deaf ears, though their death sentences were commuted to transportation.

The association of Chartism and revolution was a staple of antidemocratic literature. John Wade, still a sharp observer of the political scene, was among those who saw the Chartist agitations in 1839 as 'puerile', the 'counterpart of the wild designs' of Spa Fields and Cato Street.[28] He no longer accepted the radical analysis of Old Corruption and doubted the wisdom of further extending the suffrage to the working classes. Chartism, he argued, was 'the legitimate offspring of the natural rights of man, of that beautiful theory of pure republicanism – delightful to contemplate! – but as unreal as the visions of youth or dreams of human perfectibility ... those among its leaders who are not needy adventurers, are the incurable fanatics of Republicanism'.[29] By republicanism, he was referring primarily to the adoption of universal suffrage, which might or might not bring into question the future of the monarchy.

The royal family may not have been an immediate target of Chartist extremists, but the Palace might be forgiven for seeing itself in the firing line. Riots, after all, were a presage to revolution in the European experience. The Queen was kept informed of the Chartist disturbances by the Home Office, but, in the early years of the reign, Lord Melbourne tended to play down social threats and economic distress in his discussions with Her Majesty. In waggish mood, he pretended that the most disgraceful thing about the Newport rising was 'the refusal of the Guards to go and put them down, because their officers would find life in Newport too dull'.[30] But when the government found itself on the defensive over Prince Albert's financial settlement, an issue that coincided with the Chartist trials, Melbourne changed tack and satisfied the Queen that economic and social considerations required royal husbandry. The Chartist riots may not have triggered a revolution, but they did contribute to the reduction of £20,000 in Prince Albert's allowance.

Prince Albert was acutely sensitive to the uneasy historic role of European monarchies and the threat of republican movements. Whether he was the architect of the modern constitutional monarchy or a political meddler intent on resurrecting the royal prerogative is an issue that continues to arouse debate.[31] Clearly, the machinations of Victoria and Albert caused occasional alarm in political circles in an era when there was still some uncertainty about the monarch's political role. But the public, radical or loyalist, had only a vague idea of what was taking place behind the Palace drapery. With their eyes fixed on enlightenment, progress and the removal of aristocratic power, republicans treated the monarchy less as an impediment than as an irrelevance, or even a potential ally.

Prince Albert would not have warmed to republican appraisals of royal authority. He was that rarity among princes, an intellectual with wide sympathies. His adaptive mind, free of burdensome originality, penetrated what other princes often ignored – the obvious. Guided by Baron Stockmar, he took the view that in post-1832 British politics the monarchy would become more influential by keeping aloof from factional manoeuvring, which the British public mistrusted in their rulers. An identification with party politics might provide some temporary leverage, but it would undermine the monarchy's wider intention of providing the unifying symbol of the nation. By shedding party political associations, the Crown would have the independence to see Britain's problems in the round and act as 'a balance wheel on the movement of the social body'.[32] Whether he knew it or not, the Prince's views were in keeping with those of Chartist petitioners who had advised the Queen to avoid despotic factions and represent the wider public interest.

It did not take great insight for Prince Albert to recognize that a most fruitful way of ensuring social equilibrium was to consolidate and to expand the royal family's partnership with respectable society. If in politics he steered the monarchy towards neutrality, in manners and morals he steered it towards social service. Outside politics, there were few barriers to royal attainment or renown. Moreover, no one complained about the monarchy when things went wrong in a voluntary society. An active and visible presence in civil society cemented those links which bound the nation together. In time, Albert came to the view that the purpose of royalty was the 'headship of philanthropy, a guidance and encouragement of the manifold efforts which our age is making towards a higher and purer life'.[33] Here was a royal variant on civic republicanism, which served the monarchy's wider object of representing the nation.

The 1840s was a dangerous decade for European monarchies and, in the context of Chartism at home, the royal family took action in its own defence. Though philanthropy was a duty handed down from reign to reign, the Crown's civic and charitable enthusiasms can often be directly related to a nervousness about political affairs. With the coming of the railway, it was easier to carry the Crown's social message into the regions and to sections of the population which had been little cultivated in the past. Prince Albert took the lead. Factories, building sites, ports and dockyards 'drew him like a magnet', and his visits to them brought the monarchy into greater contact with the common people.[34] Housing charities, schools, libraries and mechanics' institutes also found in the Prince a willing ally and patron. Richard Carlile, it might be recalled, had said in 1825 that the monarchy would ensure its greatness by supporting mechanics' institutes.

Increasingly, Prince Albert patronized the great centres of manufacturing, where the citizenry often felt jealous of the level of royal attention lavished on London. In 1843, he visited Birmingham, a city in the forefront of Chartist organization. He did so against the advice of the Prime Minister, Sir Robert Peel, who felt that the radical sympathies of the municipal authorities might cause disturbance. The stated purpose of the Prince's trip was to inspect factories and a leading charity school in the city. The underlying purpose was to test the political terrain in a part of the country that was little cultivated by the monarchy and subject to republican agitation. Members of the royal family had always been sensitive to the way in which they were received by the public, and the Prince, as his Private Secretary reported, was pleased to be greeted by 280,000 loyal, good-humoured people. Even the Chartist mayor, believed by the Palace 'to hold extreme views', gave the Prince an effusive welcome.[35]

The British press, not untouched by xenophobia, was often less effusive, preferring to report on the size of Prince Albert's allowance than on his good works. The royal wedding and the nine offspring born to the Queen in the 1840s and 1850s provided further opportunities to contrast the luxuries of the court with the privations of the poor. On the birth of the Prince of Wales in 1842, *Punch* noted that the royal infant was suckled by a housemaid from Esher: 'from this very fact, will not the Royal child grow up with the consciousness that he owes his nourishment to the very humblest of people? Will he not suck in the humanising truth with his very milk?'[36] The *Northern Star* published 'A Starvation Anthem for the Royal Christening', in which the 'people's bitter tears' baptized the infant's brow.[37] Not to be outdone, the radical printer William Linton published 'anti-odes' on royal birthdays:

Another Guelph! methought I heard a Poor Law Bishop cry –
God bless our Queen and long increase her progeny
And over-population? My Lord Bishop's very sure
There'll be plenty for the prince, howev'r they starve the poor.[38]

Contrasting the condition of paupers with the condition of the prolifer-ating royal brood had become a staple of the radical critique of the monarchy. But though heartfelt, such comment rarely spilled over into direct calls for the immediate abolition of the Crown. It was by now widely held in radical circles that the payments and allowances made to the royal family were not simply for the personal gratification of the Queen but to sustain the 'antiquated absurdities' of an aristocratic court. Wade, whose own hostility to the Crown continued to be largely on grounds of cost, argued that the Civil List was 'the great perquisite of a ministry – the chief prize of party intrigue . . . It is not so much royalty as the aristocracy that are fed and glorified by this munificent parliamentary appropriation'. And he added that 'a constitutional monarchy has been described to be a republic, with the drawback of a Civil List'.[39]

'True loyalty,' as one Chartist contended, 'no less than a necessary economy, will demand a pruning-knife shall be unsparingly applied' to the Civil List.[40] Yet no one could be certain just how much money could be pruned while maintaining the dignity of the Crown on which such loyalty was thought to depend. Some reformers wanted only modest economies, coupled with a reduction in offices and pensions. Others would have the Queen's income reduced to that of her most humble subjects, a proposal tantamount to abolishing royalty. But according to Wade, even if the Queen herself wished to live less ostentatiously, her ministers would not allow it, for 'reasons of state'. In his view, dismant-ling the Crown was politically impossible as long as the royal household offered a ministry a way of maintaining its influence and rewarding its friends.[41]

The radical press, preoccupied with abuse and privilege, took little notice of royal contributions to the poor. When they did, they were prone to distort them. The Queen was sympathetic to the privations of her Irish subjects and contributed £2,500 to Irish Famine relief, but her enemies turned her into a 'Famine Queen', and reported that she donated a miserly £5.[42] They probably never knew that Queen Adelaide donated up to

£40,000 a year to worthy causes in the 1840s, or that Victoria herself gave away 15 per cent of her Privy Purse income annually.[43] Critics of the monarchy could argue that royal handouts were inadequate to meet the social problem and did not reduce the extravagance of the court. In any case, there was much more capital, and fun, to be had in depicting royalty as grasping and parasitical, or 'fat' in the case of Victoria, than in dealing with the complex issue of Crown benevolence. But those who felt its benefits were growing daily in number. In the early years of the reign the royal family's patronage list grew like Topsy.

For a few Chartists, criticizing royal expenditure became something of an obsession. One of the liveliest anti-monarchists of the 1840s was the controversial preacher Joseph Barker, the printer of Barker's Library of miscellaneous writings for the working classes, a self-confessed 'dabbler' in politics. In the *Reformer's Almanac*, he penned another in the long line of radical open letters to the Crown, in which he called on the Queen to reduce her income and extend the rights of her subjects.[44] With an imagination unimpressed by evidence, he put the overall cost of the monarchy at the astounding figure of 'a hundred millions a year', which, if true, would have depleted much of Britain's national income.[45] (The actual annual sum allotted in 1837 was £385,000, which remained unaltered over the reign, although additional grants amounting to nearly £200,000 a year were later given to the Queen's children.[46])

Barker, like Carlile before him, was a misfit, in perennial religious turmoil, and his hostility to the Crown waxed as he moved from Methodism to secularism. A loss of religious faith often accompanied a loss of faith in authority generally, which helps to explain why irreligion and anti-monarchy so often went together. At one moment, Barker thought the Queen's role could be justified, if only she would cut back on expense and become 'the servant of the People' – the next, she was a 'tyrant' who ruled without consent. He might have been talking about the Church, which he despised, or God, whom he doubted, when he bemoaned: 'Kings do no good. They do much harm . . . They oppress the masses. They corrupt the middle classes. They generate wars. They cause evil incalculable. Then why do we not abolish kingship?'[47] Arrested for seditious libel in 1848, Barker spent much of his later life in America and died in Nebraska in 1875. Having returned to the Christian fold, he

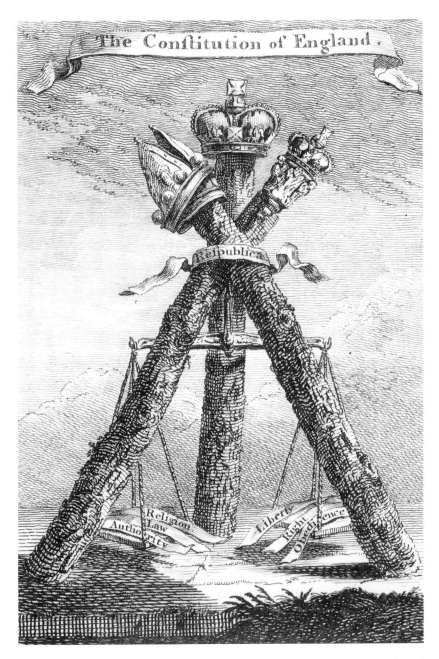

The Constitution of England.

Republica

Religion
Law
Authority

Liberty
Right
Obedience

1. The republic represented by the balanced constitution of King, Lords and Commons, circa 1774. Engraving, unknown artist.

2. A satirical attack on republican petitioners, 1780. Engraving, Richard Sneer (attributed).

3. 'The Rights of Man'. Thomas Paine measuring the crown for a new set of republican breeches. James Gillray, 1791.

CITIZEN GUILLOTINE,
A NEW SHAVING MACHINE.

Tune, " *Bob shave a King.*"

TO the just Guillotine,
Who shaves off Heads so clean,
           I tune my String!
Thy power is so great,
That ev'ry Tool of State,
Dreadeth thy mighty weight,
           Wonderful Thing!
Sweet Billy thee shall hail,
Johnny Reeves at his Tail,
           Pride of our Days!
Placemen, Swan-like shall sing,
Guillotine, mighty King,
Echos from Crowds shall ring,
           With thy juſt Praise.
No, Billy shall not swing,
An Hour upon a String,
           To stop his Breath!
Right Honourable Friend,
The Swine shall ne'er suspend,
Thy Neck from Halters End,
           In ling'ring Death.
No, no, the shining Blade,
Shall hail the *Felon's* Head,
           Fraternal wise,
One blest, but happy stroke,
One soft tho' sudden shock,
Shall roll it from the Block,
           'Midst joyful cries.

4. The 'swinish multitude' take their revenge on the King as 'A Cure for National Grievances', 1793.

5. 'The Contrast' between British and French Liberty, 1793.

6. 'The Republican Attack' on George III in 1795, as interpreted by Gillray.

The RADICAL LADDER

London Pub.^d by G. Humphrey 27 St James's St April 1.st 1821

7. Queen Caroline leads the rabble up 'The Radical Ladder' in an assault on the balanced constitution. George Cruikshank, *The Loyalists' Magazine*, 1819.

8. The proletariat look on as a minister pulls the strings of 'An Excellent *Republican* King'. *McLean's Monthly Sheet of Caricatures*, 1832.

THE REPUBLICAN MEDAL,   AND   ITS REVERSE.

9. An allegory on the republic in the shape of a medal. *Punch*, 1848.

EQUALITY, LIBERTY, FRATERNITY.
EDITED BY G. JULIAN HARNEY,

10. Mast-head of Harney's *The Red Republican*, 1850.

recanted his republican views in his autobiography: 'more extravagant or groundless notions have seldom entered the mind of man'.[48]

Most Chartists were more cautious on the subject of the Crown than Barker. They avoided the anti-royal label even when they felt comfortable with it, partly because they did not wish to encourage reaction and partly because they did not wish to risk following John Frost to Van Diemen's Land. There was a general recognition that the abolition of the Crown was not a practical policy and that anti-monarchical rhetoric was unlikely to win converts to the wider cause. Robert Lowery, nervous about militancy in the ranks, spoke for the moderates when he said that there were a million men willing to protect the Queen 'from every kind of danger' if she would protect the Charter.[49] The weekly organ of teetotal Chartism made a theoretical case for a republic, but it drew back from arguing in favour of one in Britain: '*Firstly*, because it would ill become us living under a monarchy to hold such opinions. *Secondly*, because if we were to hold such arguments our readers would not attend to them.'[50]

Such reserve was all the more explicable in the light of the strong loyalist lobby, which was eager to associate Chartism with hostility to a popular sovereign.[51] Sensitive to such accusations, the Chartist leader Feargus O'Connor wished to keep the hotheads in the ranks under control. What was the point of 'another ten years of reckless prosecutions and persecutions'?[52] He gave 'the palm to a republic', as he wrote in 1841, but if universal suffrage were to prevail and the people recognized as the legitimate source of power, then everything else would follow.[53] Like so many radicals, O'Connor's attitudes to the monarchy were ambivalent, in his case bordering on the incoherent. In 1849, he addressed the Queen as a 'Well-Beloved cousin' and signed himself 'Feargus Rex, by the Grace of the People'.[54]

If Chartists hesitated to call themselves republicans, virtually all those who called themselves republicans in the 1840s were Chartists, if only because they were democrats. Some republicans resorted to direct action, like those who participated in the Newport rising. Others, recalling Rousseau, Paine and Carlile, could theoretically imagine a republic retaining an hereditary monarch in a symbolic capacity. When Lovett and Hetherington signed the petition to the Queen in 1837, did it make them hypocrites? Or were they republicans who could contemplate a republic with a monarch as long as he or she obeyed the law laid down by the people? As in the past, the rule of law defined the republic to many radicals, not the form of government. Just how many republicans of this type petitioned the Queen or signed the People's Charter will never be known, but there were more of them than is commonly imagined. Such considerations should be kept in mind when discussing the relationship of Chartism to republicanism.

Republicanism remained a slippery concept, its boundaries fluid and generous. Defining it by the simple test of anti-monarchism, which has become a commonplace among historians, is not only misleading but has led to an underestimation of its extent. For their part, Chartist historians have largely consigned republicanism to the backwaters of the movement.[55] Republicanism, as the standard interpretation argues, 'played a secondary role in the movement as a warning to the upper classes of what might happen if the demand for the People's Charter was frustrated. Its devotees never succeeded in raising the dethronement of the Queen to the status of a live political issue, nor did they try very hard to do so.'[56] There is something to be said for this analysis, but the assumption that republicans necessarily demanded the dethronement of the Queen is misconceived and present-minded. As in the 1790s or the 1820s, the essential issue remained representation not anti-royalism. The Chartist reluctance to rise up or rail against the Crown did not make them unrepublican. Historians have put the royal tumbril before the democratic horse.

One writer on the constitution in the 1840s, harking back to earlier definitions, described a republic simply as a state in which the will of the majority would be the law, which fitted comfortably with Chartist ideals.[57] George Harding, the Chartist editor of the *Republican*, took a straightforward line in 1848: 'Republicanism is simply this, self-government; the right of every individual to govern himself, either in person or by representation.'[58] Linton was another republican who preferred to define republicanism as 'government by all for all' rather than what he called the 'vague' definition of 'one who objects to a king'.[59] To commentators of quite different persuasions, the Charter was a document squarely in the republican tradition. We have this on no less an authority than Queen Victoria, to whom it implied anti-monarchism.

In the 1840s, as in the past, the word republican sent out mixed signals, including resonant anti-monarchical ones. Its association with the Terror in France remained potent; and loyalists, who saw the guillotine at the end of the republican dream, continued to exploit the word to discredit reform. But a principal meaning of republicanism remained popular sovereignty. The Chartists carried forward that strand of radical opinion, dating to the 1790s, that took a democratic government to be synonymous with a republican one. Students of Paine, or classical thought, knew that *res publica* meant simply the 'public thing' and, more positively, a love of liberty and public spirit. In the Chartist years, criticism of royalty was a recurring feature of journalism, not all of it radical, but it paled into insignificance when compared to the criticism of aristocratic privilege and the undemocratic nature of politics.[60]

The semantics of republicanism were largely lost on members of the royal family, who believed that the 1832 Reform Bill provided quite enough democracy in the constitution. Distinctions between pure and theoretical republicanism, or between moral and physical force, were more arbitrary to those on the receiving end. The Prince of Prussia, a refugee in England, once looked some Chartists in the eye and told Queen Victoria that they were 'horrid looking people' and genuine revolutionaries.[61] Such reports confirmed the Queen's view that Chartist riots and demonstrations threatened not only her prerogatives and security, but the order of society and national well-being. The early years of her reign were those most marked by domestic unrest, and they left her with a deep suspicion of what she called 'advanced' views. Ever after, she assumed that the onset of democracy would herald working-class ascendancy, unravel the ancient constitution and lead to an uncrowned republic.

By the standards of most European monarchs, Queen Victoria was a liberal, but she responded to the word republican rather as the reactionary Tsar Nicholas I responded to the word progress. Royal thinking was clear about republicanism. It spelled democracy and democracy spelled doom. The Queen and her family had taken on board the logic of Paine by way of radical insult and loyalist reaction. Convinced that democrats were inherently anti-monarchical, if not anarchical, they assumed that Chartist petitions, memorials and disavowals of anti-monarchical principles were disingenuous. Moreover, the Chartist usage of the Gallic titles 'National Assembly' and 'the Convention' and the appearance of

French-style republican caps and tricolour flags at mass demonstrations were bound to horrify an historic institution attuned to forms and symbols. (The 'invention of tradition' in British republicanism deserves further study.[62]) The periodic risings and violent language of Chartism confirmed royal fears, as it confirmed the fears of loyalists generally.

Royal reaction to political agitators was at least consistent. When the Rebecca Riots broke out in the vicinity of Newport in 1843, Queen Victoria wrote to the Home Secretary Sir James Graham: 'The Queen trusts that measures of the greatest severity will be taken, as well to suppress the revolutionary spirit as to bring the culprits to immediate trial and punishment.'[63] A Royal Proclamation, described by the *Northern Star* as the 'Queen versus Rebecca', denounced the 'tumultuous assemblages' and offered a reward of £500 for the apprehension of anyone guilty of 'incendiarism'.[64] In the same year, Feargus O'Connor stood trial for seditious conspiracy at Lancaster but escaped imprisonment on legal technicalities and a lack of evidence. Prince Albert wrote to the Prime Minister, Robert Peel: 'I am sorry that Feargus escaped. Still the effect of the trial is satisfactory.'[65]

In certain respects, the Chartist years were a replay of the 1790s or the 1810s, with sporadic violence and extremist rhetoric setting the royal family and respectable society on edge. Chartists may have been happy to work within the framework of existing institutions, but the propertied classes took a grim view of strikes and riots. Nor were they endeared to the Manichaean philosophy of militant Chartism, in which the stark forces of despotism and reaction struggled for ultimate supremacy with liberty and progress.[66] Chartist language often exhibited the fire and brimstone of the pulpit, and even though the public did not always take it at face value, it did not help the wider cause. What were the political classes to make of Joseph Barker, who proclaimed that he would 'have no king, no queen, no House of Lords, and no state church'?[67] The poet John Bedford Leno, who started a Chartist association in Windsor of all places, declared that a 'civil war' was 'fully justifiable'.[68]

Chartist links with anti-monarchism, though limited and curbed by the leadership, were not helpful to the cause in so constitutionalist a nation. 'Do we live under a bloody tyrant, like that of Nero?' asked a contributor to the *Leeds Mercury*. 'Has a despotic monarchy swept away, by an edict, all our liberties?'[69] Inflammatory republicanism was particularly counter-productive in Parliament, where the movement needed party support but failed to find it. Attacks on the monarchy were attacks on the ancient, but recently reformed, constitution; and Members of Parliament were in no mood to risk dismantling it by acceding to working-class demands. They felt obliged to defend the Crown, if only as a symbol of their own legitimacy. They had cause to think about such matters when the French declared a republic in February 1848. The *Northern Star* called the event 'the most glorious in the annals of the human race'. And it added, in a telling juxtaposition, 'let the cry be "the Republic for France, and the Charter for England"'.[70]

The revolutions on the continent in 1848 reminded the British political classes of revolutions past, and deepened their alarm about Chartism. Loyalists now found it easier to attack the movement, especially in its more violent guise. A 'Fellow Labourer', just back from France, wrote that 'Chartism . . . is nothing else but Republicanism', which he defined on the model of French extremism: 'A Republic is a state, in which hundreds of violent, vain, and needy men are struggling together for the executive power . . . A Republic is proclaimed by Utopian patriots, carried on by ferocious brigands, and terminated by a military dictator.' And he reminded his readers that out of 15,413 beheaded by the guillotine during the Terror, 13,000 were artisans! 'What do you think of that for equality?' As to the inutility of the Queen, proclaimed by Chartists, he concluded: 'Be not deceived, the possession of a Queen saves us from cutting each other's throats.'[71]

In 1848, loyalists made more capital out of the continental revolutions than did the Chartists. The reason was familiar. As one pro-Chartist clergyman acknowledged, the French Revolution remained 'hateful to all Englishmen'.[72] *Punch* mimicked a 'Republican Medal' with 'Liberté, Egalité and Fraternité' on one side; on its reverse an armed barbarian trampled on property and religion. (See Plate 9.) Clearly, many Britons still freely associated the word republican with irreligion, conspiracy and blood. When respectable subjects heard the conservative propaganda, so similar to what their parents and grandparents had been told fifty years earlier, they could be forgiven for believing that their institutions, including the monarchy, would not survive the triumph of working-class demands. Whether they were right to believe so in the case of Britain was never put to the test. In the heyday of Chartism, as in the 1790s and the

1810s, the political centre held. So did the monarchy, which had more tools in its survival kit than its enemies imagined.

The Crown's anxiety about social unrest, fuelled by government reports and personal contacts, came to a head in the revolutionary spring of 1848. There is no better illustration of royal worries and how they turned the Palace to charitable solutions than a look at extracts from Prince Albert's diary.

> 6 *March:* Apprehension that they [the Chartists] would come to Buckingham Palace.
>
> 7 *March:* Riots in Glasgow and in Trafalgar Square . . . The property of the French Royal family is sequestered at Paris.
>
> 10 *March:* Riots at Munich.
>
> 17 *March:* Great riots amongst the peasantry in Swabia.
>
> 18 *March:* News of revolution at Berlin.
>
> 24 *March:* King of Prussia in the hands of the Burghers.
>
> 4 *April:* Disquieting views from Ireland.
>
> 11 *April:* Increase of anarchy in Germany.
>
> 18 *April:* A long conversation with him [Lord Shaftesbury] as to what can be done for the working classes.[73]

Despite the sentiments occasionally voiced in the radical press, the English working classes turned out to be less hostile to monarchy than their brethren on the continent. On the night of 6 March, a crowd did turn up at Buckingham Palace, but only managed to shout *Vive la république* and demolish a couple of lamps before being dispersed.[74] But when the Chartists gathered on Kennington Common on 10 April, royal tensions mounted. The day before, the Prince's Private Secretary, Charles Phipps, told the Prince that he expected a few broken windows but that the demonstration 'will be easily suppressed'.[75] The Prince wrote to the Prime Minister, Lord John Russell, that he was confident that good sense would prevail; but he was anxious that a 'commotion' be avoided because 'it would shake that confidence which the whole of Europe reposes in our stability at this moment'.[76] To the great relief of the royal family and the authorities, the mass meeting passed off without incident.

Badly shaken by the Chartists, the Queen remained as nervous as Prince Albert about the political situation. The possibility of disorder spreading from the continent could not be ruled out. 'Revolution' was a word she equated with misery and less favoured nations. She much preferred, as she put it to Russell at the time, 'obedience to the laws & to the Sovereign'. In her view, this meant 'obedience to a higher Power, divinely instituted for the good of the *people*, not of the Sovereign, who has equally duties & obligations'.[77] Here she had elided the Crown with the national interest, just as Prince Albert, Baron Stockmar and others had advised. The Queen persuaded herself that '*Our* revolution', as she called the Kennington Common demonstration, was a model revolution, unlike the tragic fiascos on the continent. In 1849, she praised the 'loyal spirit of my people and their attachment to institutions during a period of political revolution'.[78] But she recognized that if the Crown and the people were to remain faithful to one another, royal 'duties & obligations' must be seen to be done.

At the time of the Kennington Common meeting, Prince Albert had written to the Prime Minister that it was not a time 'for the taxpayers to economise upon the working classes', and he hoped that the government might do something to promote employment, especially in London.[79] The government felt little disposed to heed the Prince's advice. Few ministers, after all, shared his enthusiasm for working-class causes. Still, the propertied classes of London, 'in deep gratitude to Almighty God' for sparing the capital 'from the horrors of anarchy', opened subscription lists to build a free hospital and erect baths, wash-houses and other institutions for the benefit of the poor. Albert received the charitable circular in the middle of April, and he put the Queen's and his own name down for £500.[80] The Chartists failed to achieve universal manhood suffrage, but they did receive a public bath.

Prince Albert could do little to influence continental affairs, but he was determined to step up his labours on behalf of the British working classes. Such activities would serve to stifle criticisms of the royal family, not least the accusations that he received £30,000 a year 'for doing nothing'.[81] When the Queen decided to translate her 'duties' into a ball in aid of Spitalfields weavers and required court ladies to wear only British-made clothes in her drawing-rooms, he remarked: 'there must be some better way of helping the poor'.[82] Thus the Queen invited Lord Shaftesbury to Osborne to discuss what might be done 'to show our interest in the working class'. Shaftesbury, ever the Tory paternalist, advised the Prince to put himself 'at the head of all social movements in art and science, and especially of those movements as they bear upon the poor, and thus show the interest felt by Royalty in the happiness of the Kingdom'.[83] Here he was returning to advice he had given the Prince some years earlier: 'the people of this country, who are sincerely attached to Monarchy as a principle, will love it still more in the person of a Queen, who feels and expresses a real interest in their welfare'.[84]

Lord Shaftesbury always had an improving scheme up his sleeve, and he suggested that Prince Albert visit a slum tenement and then take the chair at a meeting of the Society for Improving the Condition of the Labouring Classes at Exeter Hall. Against the advice of the Prime Minister and the Home Secretary, the Prince duly turned up. His speech, rehearsed with the Queen, reminds us why the Prince was so popular with the manufacturing and commercial classes. 'Depend upon it,' he said, 'the interests of classes too often contrasted are identical, and it is only ignorance, which prevents their uniting for each other's advantage.'[85] Prince Albert simply reminded his audience that acquitting their social obligations was a form of enlightened self-interest, that the philanthropist was the welfare equivalent of the entrepreneur. It was an extension of his view that philanthropy was enlightened royal interest.

The Prince's appearance on behalf of the Society for Improving the Condition of the Labouring Classes was a revealing episode in the emergence of the monarchy's policy of dishing radicalism through good works. Lord Shaftesbury revelled: 'Aye, truly this is the way to stifle Chartism . . . Rank, leisure, station are gifts of God, for which man must give an account. Here is a full proof, a glowing instance!'[86] A disgruntled socialist lamented: 'if the Prince goes on like this he'll upset our apple-cart'.[87] Royal philanthropy remained suspect in radical circles. By mid-century, many of the Crown's enemies believed that it was simply an expedient to disguise rapacity or the tyranny of capitalism. The Glasgow shoemaker and Chartist John McAdam once mocked a royal donation to relieve the victims of a colliery disaster, but failed to ask whether such commonplace acts of benevolence might undermine his own campaign.[88]

In 1848, few people deceived themselves into thinking that Queen Victoria and Prince Albert might be sympathetic to political radicalism. Robert Owen, no stranger to delusion, asked the sovereign for the unthinkable – a royal welcome to revolution. He sent a message to the Queen in June through Lord Brougham. In it he explained to Her Majesty that what was taking place in the world was 'the greatest revolution that has ever occurred in human affairs; revolution not to be dreaded, but one that will be highly beneficial to all, in every country and for ever'. He reminded her that her father was among his 'disciples', and asked for her support, signing off, 'your Majesty's best friend in this period of coming revolutions'.[89] Queen Victoria, who had been putting up the tearful King and Queen of the French in exile, did not reply. Prince Albert wrote to Lord Brougham, dryly: Socialist theories 'could only be tested by their practical adaptation. Unfortunately, such practical experiments have always been found to be *exceedingly expensive* to the Nations in which they have been tried'.[90]

By the time of Owen's letter, Chartism was a spent force, the victim of incoherent strategy, divided leadership, and of a government machine, supported by the propertied classes, which had far too many resources at its disposal to give way to physical or moral pressure. Moreover, economical reform, improved government efficiency and civic leadership had gradually taken the sting out of the radical political analysis. A narrow élite was still in charge, given legitimacy by an ancient and, to some, a despised Crown. But Britain at mid-century was not easily judged an extension of Paine's or Cobbett's polluted land of placemen and pensioners, unpopular taxes and high military expenditure. Thanks to measures taken by successive ministries, the attack on Old Corruption had lost much of its force by the mid-Victorian period, both inside and outside Parliament.[91] In such circumstances, the public looked back on the unrest of the 1830s and 1840s as an aberration. Consequently, a serious rethink was underway in radical circles.

The republican fringe produced some of the most interesting, if impractical, thinking and kept alive a tradition of reform at mid-century. Several publications spread the gospel, or gospels, including George Harding's *Republican*, Ernest Jones's *Notes to the People*, George Julian Harney's *Democratic Review* and *Red Republican*, Joseph Cowen's *Northern Tribune*, and William Linton's *English Republic*. All of them were experiments in political education and expressed, often in memorable language, thinking across the spectrum of one of the liveliest political minorities of the day. But the editors did not carry out market surveys, and their target audience – impressionable working men unhappy with the status quo –

failed to subscribe in any numbers. The law compounded the financial difficulties, for until 1857 unstamped newspapers were prohibited from printing news. Rarely in the British history of the press can so many radical periodicals have been launched in such an unpromising market. Still, the situation in England was better than on the continent, where governments simply silenced the oppositional press.[92]

The inspiration for the resurgence of republican journalism derived partly from radical rivalries in the aftermath of Chartism and partly from the hopes raised by the revolutions on the continent. The ideological inspiration also came from abroad, most notably from the Hungarian revolutionary Lajos Kossuth and the Italian nationalist Giuseppe Mazzini. Not only did the two men raise the morale of British republicanism, at a low ebb at mid-century, but they helped to broaden and internationalize political discussion. Virtually everyone with a political axe to grind, from socialists to anti-socialists, wanted to enlist such charismatic figures. Their most important long-term influence in Britain, it has been argued, was to undermine support for socialism and to provide a consensual form of political radicalism linked with the wider cause of European democracy. Ironically, in addressing foreign issues, they simply pointed up the virtues of Britain's constitutional monarchy over continental despotism.[93] A comparison with political life abroad continued to be one of the British monarchy's strongest suits.

No one worked more tirelessly to spread the creed of romantic republicanism than Linton, the Chartist engraver, poet, journalist, biographer of Paine and self-styled 'political Jeremiah'.[94] Authorized by Mazzini to act for his Republican Party in Britain, he sought to organize small groups to teach republican principles. *John Bull*, the loyalist paper, likened Linton's associational model, the 'family meeting', to the Methodist class meeting and warned the monarchy of the danger: 'forewarned is forearmed'.[95] But Linton lacked Wesley's organizational powers, nor was his message so redemptive. A number of periodicals gave him a column, including Harding's *Republican* and Harney's *Red Republican*. His own *English Republic* (1851–5) may have represented 'the fullest and most venturesome transposition of European republicanism into English', but it was exquisitely obscure.[96] Published in the Lake District, it had a print run of only 300 copies per issue, many of which had to be given away.[97]

Linton's political philosophy was an expression of post-Chartist individualism, an embryonic social democracy halfway between laissez-faire radicalism and state socialism.[98] His catchwords were the familiar liberty, equality and fraternity, which seemed to have an hypnotic effect on republicans, like a mantra that discouraged analysis.[99] But in his case they derived, not from France, but from Mazzini's 'Proclamation to the People', a document dated London, 22 July 1850. Like Mazzini, Linton repudiated class or statist politics, which distanced him from the socialist camp. Like socialists and social Chartists, he thought land should be common property; but, hostile to state planning, he did not want government to organize production or to direct labour, for that would violate individual liberty.[100] Landlordism was anathema to him, which was a reason why he supported Irish republicanism. Yet Linton doubted whether Irish republicans were in tune with 'true' republicanism, which he once described as 'the oneness of humanity, the equality of all peoples and of all people'.[101]

With a mind attuned to such noble sentiment, Linton spent relatively little time decrying the British royal family. This too was in keeping with the loftiness of Mazzini, who, it should be said, hardly placed Queen Victoria in the category of monarchs, owing to the popularity of British institutions.[102] For his part, Linton believed the British monarchy to be a costly form of 'class government', and royalty 'repugnant to common sense'; but the sovereign was 'only a supernumerary in the pageant: the pith of royalty, the real royalty, is perhaps in the Lords and Commons'.[103] He conceded that Queen Victoria, though lacking in taste or talent, was 'our best Monarch for centuries'; but quoting Emerson, he argued that nothing was 'as helpless as a king of England!'.[104] Both the monarchy and the people were weak, content with the restrictions of the royal prerogative. To Linton, such circumstances appeared normal simply because 'men had so long submitted to compromise'.[105]

One of Linton's colleagues on the *English Republic* was W. E. Adams, the president of a republican association, who carried English republicanism to new dreamy heights. He described Mazzini as 'the greatest teacher since Christ', and years later recalled: 'We had found a programme, but we wanted a religion. It came to us from Italy.'[106] Adams wanted something loftier than the simple list of political demands provided by the Charter. Chartism was an expression of republicanism, but not a satisfactory one. The republic 'was not so much a form of government as a system of morals, a law of life, a creed, a faith, a new and benign gospel'.[107] Here, puritanical moral sentiment infused the doctrine of popular sovereignty, giving it a millenarian edge: 'Let it not grieve you that you have been the instruments to break the ice for others: the honour shall be yours to the world's end.'[108]

Adams, who later became editor of the *Newcastle Weekly Chronicle*, drew on traditions of Paine and the English Commonwealthmen, with their high-minded emphasis on civic spirit. But the 'little band' of republican prophets with whom he associated in the 1850s, numbering under a score, looked primarily to Mazzini's conception of 'the Duties of Man', which, as Adams put it, 'were the necessary accompaniment of the Rights of Man'.[109] Linton too had emphasized the holiness of work and social obligation as a form of patriotism.[110] Such ideas, which demanded so much from the citizenry, were far too heady for those hardened Chartists who had suffered years of frustration and abhorred foreign influences. Ernest Jones, for example, a Marxist barrister, thought reform movements based on moral revival were divisive and romantic.[111]

In the late 1840s and early 1850s, the more idealistic republicans paid scant attention to the future of the Crown. Royal behaviour and Crown expenditure hardly mattered in Adams's scheme of things. Still, the tradition of sniping at the monarch as a tyrant in a soul-destroying 'league of kings' was kept alive.[112] In this vein, George Harding's loss-making *Republican*, subtitled 'A Magazine advocating the Sovereignty of the People', occasionally sparkled. In it, contributors castigated the Civil List, by which the people were robbed; they ridiculed divine right theory, still believed in by a few 'relicts of the dark ages'; they denounced the principle of inheritance, by which 'divinity degenerates into idiocy'; and they lavished praise on democracy.[113] But such comments were ritual ejaculations from the political hinterland, which added little to what had been said by Paine, Carlile and so many others in the past.

Chartist poets picked up such themes, extending a long tradition of anti-monarchical verse. Among others, John Leno, Gerald Massey, and Linton, using the name Spartacus, added flavour, and fervour, to the spate of republican periodicals. Indeed, verse filled much of the limited space given over to the British monarchy in such publications. In Harney's *Friend of the People*, Linton penned 'A Glee', in which royalty and its thieving servants, bishops, peers and MPs, are found out and undone by the extension of the suffrage.[114] Massey, who penned the 'Song of the Red Republican' and 'The People's Advent', was a regular contributor to the republican press (he later came to depend on a Civil List pension and grants from royal charities).[115] The opening stanza of 'Kings are but Giants because We Kneel' set the tone of his political poetry in the early 1850s. It was wonderfully over the top in seeing love requited between the English and the French.

> Good People, put no faith in kings, nor merchant-princes trust,
> Who grind your hearts in mammon's press, your faces in the dust,
> Trust to your own stout hearts to break the Tyrants dark dark ban,
> If yet one spark of freedom lives, let man be true to man,
> We'll never fight again boys, with Yankee, Pole, and Russ,
> We love the French as brothers, and Frenchmen too, love us!
> But we'll join to crush those fiends who kill all love and liberty,
> Kings are but giants because we kneel, *one leap and up go we.*[116]

Harney, the *enfant terrible* of Chartism, was happy to provide space to such revealing verse, but to him the Crown was nothing more than a minor impediment in the drive towards human perfectibility. An early English Marxist, he hailed the proletarian republic and proudly wrapped himself in the tricolour. In 1850, he set out his political stall with panache in the *Red Republican*, a title which alienated even fellow republicans like Adams, who thought it 'savoured of blood'.[117] (See Plate 10.) Harney, in fact, disavowed force, but intended the 'infamous' title to aggravate aristocrats, the wealthy and 'professional loyalists', who would equate it with anarchism and savagery: 'We are fully aware of the odium attached to this name in the estimation of all "respectable People". But what of it? . . . Be ours the glorious task to show that the proscribed "Reds" are the reverse of that which they are presented as being by their calumniators.'[118]

Well versed in republican literature, Harney thought there was nothing unorthodox in the title 'Republican'. He quoted Dr Johnson's definition of a republic as 'a state in which the power is lodged in more than one'. According to this definition, 'England then is a Republic – of a sort, and every Englishman may, if he will, term himself a Republican.' But to Harney, England remained a 'sham republic', for while it was 'a state in which the power is lodged in more than one' it was not a state in which power lodged in the people. In equating republicanism with popular sovereignty, he put himself in the tradition of Paine and Carlile, whose interpretations of *res publica* were part of his intellectual baggage. A preoccupation with the abolition of an 'effete sceptre' was hardly the stuff of serious politics. The republic must be about something greater than 'pomps and trappings'.[119] Consequently, the British monarchy rarely received a mention in the *Red Republican*.

As a Chartist, Harney's first commitment was to the expansion of democratic rights. But more than most republican ideologues, his ideal democracy had a utopian socialist edge, more in tune with Marx and Engels than Paine or Mazzini. The 'Charter and something more' became his rallying cry, that 'something more' being 'the cause of the producers' and social revolution.[120] He opened the *Red Republican* with an extended passage from Robespierre's Report of the 18th Pluvoise, year 2 of the French Republic.[121] It was just the sort of thing to taunt his enemies, and Harney adopted it as an expression of his own political testament, which, in common with so much republican thought of the day, had a strong visionary streak. Though full of noble sentiment about mankind's destiny, it was not a message likely to entice the middle classes in England, who had heard so much about Robespierre. Nor was it likely to entice the labouring poor, who were largely indifferent to continental ideas and who had little reason to love the French.

Grafting continental abstractions on to Chartism did not make political propaganda any easier for English republicans. Linton, Harney and others did have a measure of success in setting up associations in places as various as Bethnal Green, Cambridge, Cheltenham, Liverpool, Sunderland and Glasgow.[122] But with the total number of members estimated at about 3,000, few people in Britain would have ever met one.[123] Joseph Cowen, later a Liberal MP, made the breakthrough in Newcastle, where he set up the Republican Brotherhood, with its Mazzinian overtones, in 1855. In such places, the elect read the works of revolutionary leaders, examined candidates for membership and toasted the overthrow of kings and oppressors. They schemed, canvassed and circulated tracts; they lectured on Robespierre and Mazzini, land and freedom, Irish and European politics. In more sober moments, they tempered their visions by reference to the United States.

In the 1850s, republican principles remained diverse, a hybrid of Paine-ite and continental thought, infused by the Chartist political platform and coloured by rhetorical anti-monarchism. If for some, like Linton and Adams, they constituted a 'benign gospel', for others, like Harney and Cowen, they were 'cloaked in the European imagery of barricades, mobs and guillotines'.[124] In so far as these principles were anti-monarchical, they alarmed loyalist opinion. In so far as they were foreign, they alienated British sensibilities. In so far as they were intimidating, they antagonized law-abiding citizens. In so far as they were collectivist, they were at odds with the liberal principles of Mazzini and against the grain of the prevailing economic orthodoxy. Moreover, they had to make their way in an era typified, in Matthew Arnold's words, by English 'invincibility and speculative dullness'.[125]

Republican principles were also against the grain of contemporary Christianity, which in mid-nineteenth-century Britain was rarely associated with speculative freedom. Secularism had taken hold in British republican thought, and it underpinned the tradition of anti-despotism that was central to it. As an article in the *Freethinker* put it: 'Since the time of that great apostle of liberty, Thomas Paine, the questionings of arbitrary authority in all matters political and religious have gone together.'[126] The powerful culture of traditional belief took its revenge by coupling free-thought with the Antichrist and French anti-clericalism. One 'Christian Republican', Washington Wilks, noted that a radical was at a disadvantage in a Christian country, for he was 'compelled to assume a position of egotistical antagonism towards those whom he wishes to convert'. Wilks's own republicanism flowed from his religion, and constituted, as he put it, 'the application of Christian principles to political science'.[127] But his was an isolated voice in a movement which had largely become a 'religion of humanity', however much it lapsed into the language of the pulpit.

Nor did the economy bode well for an expansion of republican thought. The 1850s was not a replay of the 'hungry forties', but a decade of growing prosperity, political tranquillity, quiescent trade unionism and incentives to working-class self-help. In its day, Chartism was always more than a political movement, for it waxed and waned with the trade cycle and the price of bread, declining in years of prosperity.[128] In an era of relative plenty, arguments based on social misery lost their force. Harney's 'Charter and something more' and Linton's nascent social democracy had little appeal to working men and women who were feeling the effects of rising living standards. In 1851, Ernest Jones denounced the Queen's visit to Liverpool as a colossal waste of public money at a time when the people were 'every day sinking lower and lower in poverty and wretchedness'.[129] But to many of the thousands of humble subjects who turned out to see the Queen such comment would have seemed far-fetched.

The post-1848 republicans, inspired by continental influences, carried forward the radical tradition in Britain at a time when it was in disarray. With Chartism exhausted and trade reviving, they unfurled the tricolour only to have to fold it up again. By the late 1850s, little endured save their cackling rhymes, the residue of a creed stillborn. Unacknowledged lines like 'Till Freedom's war-cry, like a dart, shall quiver in the tyrant's heart' or 'Rogues grow fat on her [Britannia's] estate' were never likely to turn Chartist poets into legislators.[130] Republican publications collapsed for want of sales, associations for want of members. The leaders, too, faded away; several of them, including Linton, emigrated to the American republic.

Despite the failure of republicans, the monarchy did not ignore them. Men like Linton, Adams or Harney were not prominent enough to appear in the Palace gallery of rogues, but Queen Victoria and Prince Albert did take notice of leading 'advanced' thinkers, not least the foreigners with British links. Albert had the wider knowledge of European radicalism and once received a letter from the German leftist Arnold Ruge, a member of the National Assembly in Frankfurt, about continental republican-ism.[131] He looked with horror on 'the infamous Mazzini', whom he saw pulling the strings of Italian conspiracy in exile.[132] The Queen disapproved of anyone with a reputation for revolutionary activity, who professed 'objects hostile to their Royal Masters'.[133] This largely explains her aversion to Mazzini and what she called 'the worst refugees' of 1848.[134]

Kossuth, who had led the 1848 rising in Hungary, was another republi-can who appeared in the Palace gallery of rogues. King Leopold, writing to Queen Victoria, referred to the 'Kossuth fever' taking hold on the continent. 'It is caused by *ignorance* of the man in whom they see a second Washington, when the fact is that he is an ambitious and *rapacious* Humbug.'[135] When Kossuth landed in England in 1851 he received a rapturous welcome from liberals and radicals. But the Queen was less than impressed by his pronouncements, in which he denounced two sovereigns with whom Britain was on good relations. When the Foreign Secretary Palmerston proposed to receive him, the Queen took umbrage and, supported by the Prime Minister, demanded that the meeting be cancelled. Palmerston gave way. The episode was an example of the Queen's suspicion of refugees, who, as she saw it, might arouse demands with which the government could not comply.[136] When the Italian revolutionary Giuseppe Garibaldi visited England in 1864 she was furious when the Prince of Wales met him without her permission.[137]

Republicans, foreign or domestic, made little headway in Britain in the mid-nineteenth century, but they shaped the monarchy more than might be imagined. The Queen only dimly understood republican opinion, assuming that universal suffrage would be the death-knell of monarchy. But royal nervousness made the Crown more sensitive to advice on how to combat the enemy, real or imagined, outside the Palace gates. Whenever the monarchy was thought to be in danger, well-wishers encouraged members of the royal family to identify publicly with popular, non-political causes and suggested ways in which they might do so. Charles Phipps had written to the Prince in 1848 of the royal couple's 'well-earned popularity – which in a constitutional monarchy founded upon so broad a basis of democratic power, is the truest safeguard of the throne'.[138] (His reference to democracy confirmed that Palace officials thought there was quite enough of it already.) In times of political uncertainty, as in 1848, the royal family deemed that public service was an effective way of preserving the continuity of British institutions, keeping republicanism at bay, and preventing what Prince Albert called the 'practical adaptation' of socialism.

In the past, the monarchy had concentrated on giving assistance to charitable causes promoted by the privileged classes. But after the troubles and insecurities of 1848, it sought to reach the working classes more directly, especially artisans and mechanics. The 1850s were a golden age of working-class self-help and voluntarism, and Prince Albert, who assumed a tutorial responsibility for the poor, wanted to accelerate the process and share the benefits. As G. M. Young, that most perceptive historian of Victorian England, remarked, Albert 'seized the key positions – morality and industry – behind which the monarchy was safe'.[139] In a letter to Phipps in 1849, the Prince outlined four ways in which the condition of the working classes might be improved: educate children with industrial training, improve dwellings, provide allotments with cottages, and encourage savings banks and benefit societies, preferably managed by the workers themselves.[140] Over the years, more than a few working men noted the Prince's views and approached him for support.[141]

Philanthropy and manufacturing, the gospel of Christ and the gospel of work, were interwoven in the Prince's thinking, whatever the project at hand. When he encouraged charitable education for the poor, he sought to arouse the 'honest industry' of the children but also to make their parents identify with the schools through contributing fees.[142] When he promoted model cottages for the Society for Improving the Condition of the Labouring Classes, it was to create a home environment that would produce industrious, independent men and women. And when he paid to have a pair of cottages put on display at the Great Exhibition in 1851, his object was to persuade developers and manufacturers to translate his ideas into bricks and mortar.[143] The Great Exhibition itself should be seen in the light of the development of Prince Albert's charitable doctrine, which aimed to promote social reconciliation, based on those prime values of a commercial society – prudence and self-reliance.

Against the background of Chartism and continental revolutions, a policy of popularizing the monarchy was in full swing. To show that the Crown was sensitive to public needs and aspirations, Prince Albert reorganized Palace administration, gearing it up for an expansion of civic and charitable business. New guidelines for the Office of the Privy Purse and the Private Secretary to the Prince, endorsed in 1858, provided a coherent policy on royal patronage to deal with increased demand.[144] Audiences, annual charity dinners, balls and banquets, and garden parties (from the 1860s) also played their part in transforming the monarchy into an institution more visibly engaged and seen to be in touch with the issues of the day. Could the middle classes, who were eager to address a myriad causes, resist the royal embrace? The monarchy's capacity to transform public duty into pleasure was enough to make many an aspiring subject feverish – and civic-minded.

Loyalty in the shires, where republicans were few and far between, could be taken for granted; so the Palace focused its attention on centres of culture and manufacturing, where Chartism had been prominent and deference to the throne less entrenched. There were royal tours to Dublin and Belfast (1849), Liverpool (1851), Manchester (1851 and 1857),

Birmingham (1855 and 1858), Glasgow (1859) and Edinburgh (1861). Charitable visits and initiatives punctuated the round of levées and receptions. The royal party fine-tuned each and every detail. Sensitive to Irish disaffection, the Queen and Prince Albert cultivated Roman Catholic loyalty in Dublin. In Belfast, they studiously avoided the Deaf and Dumb Institution because it was overtly sectarian, and they distributed the royal bounty to 'the least divisive bodies'.[145] At the end of the tour, the Prince wrote to Stockmar: 'Of the enthusiasm that greeted us from all quarters you can form no conception.'[146] Not 'all quarters' in fact. In Dublin, a group of rebels conspired to kidnap the Queen and hold her hostage in the Wicklow mountains but failed to assemble a sufficient force to proceed with the attack.[147]

Laying foundation stones, knighting mayors, encouraging charity and industry were by now *de rigueur* on tour. Assisted by Home Office and Palace officials, the royal family monitored the public mood and the size of the crowds. In Salford in 1851, mechanics and working men lined the streets, and in Peel Park 82,000 schoolchildren assembled and sang 'God Save the Queen'. The Prince took a side trip to Bolton to inspect Thomas Bazley's factory and was pleased to discover that the cottages were comfortable, the schools excellent and a co-operative store established, all working in directions that he had encouraged. Between Salford and Manchester, the royal couple were seen by a million people according to one eyewitness, a judgement that delighted the Queen.[148] As she had said some years earlier about Albert's civic work: 'I glory in his being seen and loved.'[149]

Such comment would have made anti-monarchists sick. Lacking any fixed patriotic religion, or insight into social psychology, they could not fathom the veneration of the Crown; and they ridiculed as flunkeys others who sensed a living reality behind what they mocked as malignant royal formulas. But there was much more to monarchism than flunkeyism. In the reign of Victoria, the communion of interest between respectable society and the monarchy had become increasingly evident. In an age in which the word 'duty' resounded like a drumbeat, they discovered that they had a duty to one another. Many people found the monarchy both an enabling institution and a theatre of loyalty, which gave them a sense of belonging, unity and purpose. The reverence for the monarchy, which bordered on religious faith, and was conditioned by it, encouraged people at all social levels to feel they were part of some great, unfolding historical narrative, and not simply dedicating their lives to Mammon. Secular republicans did not appreciate Christianity's capacity to encourage public spirit, much less the monarchy's; and they failed to notice that the deference and social hierarchy which they despised often stimulated the very civic virtue they admired.

The pains taken by the royal family to widen its social appeal through public service complemented those domestic and family values that respectable society admired in the Queen. It may seem incongruous, but the ancient English Crown, once identified with militarism and corruption, was being transformed into an institution in tune with the great Whig historical tradition, at once moral, Protestant and progressive. Through public service, the royal family was itself becoming republican, a monarchical tradition whose origins, as suggested, can be traced to the reign of George III, if not beyond. It was not republican in a democratic sense, but in the classical, pre-Paineite sense, which sought social stability through public spirit, a balance of powers and respect for the rule of law. Arguably, Prince Albert, who did so much to give shape to the modern British monarchy, was the most prominent 'civic republican' in the nineteenth century. When he died in 1861, dignitaries across the country, and the Empire, paid tribute to his memory by erecting monuments and founding charitable institutions.[150]

In familial partnership, the Queen and the Prince Consort encouraged greater public spirit in all classes, and they fully expected it to produce social harmony and improvement. In an age when the demand for state intervention was at a relatively low level, they radiated a religious ethic, at once conservative and ameliorative, that invigorated civic life across the country. In political terms, the development of free, non-governmental institutions was thought indispensable to a liberal society. The Queen's speech to Parliament at mid-century closed with an echo of classical republican sentiment: 'By combining liberty with order, by preserving what is valuable and amending what is defective, you will sustain the fabric of our institutions as the abode and the shelter of a free and happy people.'[151] When assisting the poor or exciting the respectable classes to voluntary association, the monarchy acted as a check on arbitrary government and a counterweight to pure republicanism. This non-political *via media* was an essential ingredient in Monarcho-Republicanism.[152]

In the mid-Victorian years, the Crown remained an enemy of the democratic republicanism of 'one man one vote', but through its voluntary work it encouraged 'subscriber' democracy and local decision-making, self-help and social pluralism. In step with respectable society, which it did much to shape, the Victorian monarchy distrusted notions of majority rule and the trend towards bureaucratic government. Yet, unintentionally, it encouraged democratic-republican aspirations among the disenfranchised by its diffusion of a liberal social vision. Along with a growing army of allies in voluntary institutions, the Crown offered a helping hand to individuals who sought to climb up the slippery social ladder through the steady application of their moral and intellectual faculties. It summoned rich and poor alike to assert greater control over their lives and to adopt a uniform moral code, which helped to erode the distinctions between the 'two nations'. Could independent, self-disciplined working men, who shared the same values as the middle classes, then be denied political rights?

In 1867, the year in which legislation added nearly a million new voters to the electorate, the Queen noted traces of anti-royalism on her journey to open Parliament – the 'hissing', 'groaning' and 'nasty faces' among agitators.[153] Still, she wrote to the Princess Royal: 'The lower classes are becoming so well-informed, are so intelligent and earn their bread and riches so deservedly, that they cannot and ought not to be kept back.'[154] She did not oppose the modest concession to political democracy that the Reform Bill produced, particularly as she believed the middle classes to be largely sympathetic to it. Though hostile to universal suffrage, she identified increasingly with the loyal and respectable working class. She saw the nation, as Elizabeth Longford put it, 'reshaping itself in forms ever more favourable to a benevolent Monarchy'.[155] In the creation of a more 'benevolent Monarchy', indeed a more civic republican monarchy, enemies of the Crown had made a significant, if thankless, contribution. They failed to notice it, but it was arguably their greatest achievement.

4

The Anti-Monarchical Moment
and its Aftermath
1867–1901

'As a matter of fact our Government at the present time is in reality, though not in name, a republic, with an hereditary President.'   *The Bee-Hive*, official trade union paper (1870)

'A true republic cannot exist until the majority of the citizens are both desirous and worthy of political life.'

Charles Bradlaugh, Inaugural Address to the
London Republican Club (1871)

The idea of the republic persisted. If it remained elusive to radicals who defined it by representation, it was well beyond the reach of the prophets of the New Jerusalem, who demanded the Charter and something more. If to others it remained out of mind, or was a word that conjured up unhappy images, to royalty it loomed ominously on the horizon. To the ironic Walter Bagehot, the reality was already in place, albeit in disguise, for a republic had 'insinuated itself beneath the folds of a monarchy'. In his view, the monarchy cloaked the republic's imperfections, enabling 'our real rulers to change without heedless people knowing it'.[1] Bagehot welcomed what Harney despised – a hierarchical society of pomp and trappings. That they both saw the nation as a republic, though in different ways defective, should give pause for thought. We are dealing with a pliable concept, which drove Victorians into the past or the future as their tempers required.

For all their insight and phrase-making, most commentators on the monarchy knew rather less about the institution than they thought they did. In the conduct of affairs, it was not as impotent as Harney imagined nor as neutral as Bagehot prescribed. The widespread belief in Queen

Victoria's political rectitude survived 'the direst proof of the contrary' because her ministers protected her. She meddled and intervened, not least in foreign policy and appointments, more often than an ill-informed public surmised. This is not to say that she took executive decisions, or even exercised her residual prerogative powers; but the prestige of the Crown gave her more discretion as an arbitrator in the political system than outsiders supposed. As Brian Harrison points out, Bagehot's view of the monarchy was 'more appropriate for describing the monarch's domestic role under George V'.[2] But as we shall see, there is reason to suggest that even George V was less impotent or neutral than is widely assumed.

If Victorian commentators did not fully understand the nature of the Crown's political role, they knew even less about its social influence. It was not, as many imagined, to be measured simply by pomp and ceremony, a vaporous progress in antique clothes. Royal popularity rested on more solid foundations than ritual, however attractive that side of its role might be to a public enchanted by the magic theatre of monarchy. Queen Victoria had assumed the leadership of the voluntary movement by endorsing its values. Over the years, the royal family had built up a great fund of strength and credit with the citizenry through its social and religious work. Its support for local sentiments and initiatives symbolized national virtue while empowering the Crown. The reverential public felt grateful for the monarchy's beneficence, even if members of the royal family could not always fathom what it was they were bestowing.

Constitutional writers, preoccupied by high politics, showed little interest in the royal family's points of contact with civil society. Bagehot turned some memorable phrases in the *English Constitution* (1867), but they disguised a lack of curiosity about royal affairs beyond the political and the symbolic. He was not insensitive to the 'salutary influence' of the monarch as the head of society and the 'head of our morality', and he noted that it was 'an accepted secret doctrine that the Crown does more than it seems'.[3] But he failed to delve any deeper into the matter. The English were not as dim as he gave them credit for being, and their reverence for kingship had a foundation in social realities. By the time he was writing, the monarchy's popularity may have had less to do with ornament and symbolism than its penetration of civil institutions and its support for the services supplied by the growing army of volunteers at all levels in society.

Bagehot's emphasis on the monarchy's capacity to satisfy people's emotional longing for splendour and serenity has dazzled successive generations. But his accent on the monarchy as the symbolic, 'dignified' part of the constitution encouraged many people to discount what he himself discounted – the 'efficient' part of monarchy. Ceremonial heightened royal prestige, while suggesting that the Crown was politically harmless.[4] But it often disguised civic purpose. As many nineteenth-century voluntarists would attest, the royal family's social policy was enabling and ameliorative; and while it profited from the mystique that attended royalty, it was implemented with an eye to results. The monarchy's charitable administration was sometimes carried out behind closed doors, but the results could be inversely proportional to the display. When Bagehot conjured up that famous phrase, 'we must not let daylight in on magic', he was in the dark himself.

In the black years after Prince Albert's death, the Queen could be seen visiting hospitals and prisons and overseeing charitable administration at Windsor and Balmoral. The availability of charitable relief in the vicinity of royal residences was so abundant that there was a problem finding deserving applicants.[5] Farther afield, the Queen took a sympathetic interest in a range of voluntary causes, from the cholera epidemic of 1866 in London to Mary Carpenter's work on behalf of schools in India.[6] She acted as patron to about 150 institutions and sent donations to victims of shipwrecks, fires, famines and explosions. To women who gave birth to triplets she offered grants – in 1867, eighty-two mothers requested them.[7] Over her reign, she gave away something in the order of £650,000 to needy individuals and worthy causes.[8] Arguably, she contributed more to the nation's health and happiness through her charitable administration than through her political one.

The Queen seemed happiest when left to her parochial rounds, particularly if there was some connection with Prince Albert's past activities. There were moments when her cult of benevolence drove her into maudlin flights of fancy: 'More than ever', she wrote to Queen Augusta of Prussia in 1865, 'I long to lead a private life, tending the poor & sick.'[9] Good works brought the Queen into communion with the poor, whom she admired for their fortitude, while setting a challenge to the rich, whom she condemned for their frivolity. To be interested in such matters was less eye-catching than dissolving Parliament or forming a ministry, but it had its compensations. She may have weakened her tenuous relationship with government by rarely opening Parliament – only seven times in the last thirty-nine years of her reign – but she rarely failed her constituents in the voluntary sector. When she opened a hospital, which she preferred to opening Parliament, those who were present remembered it.

Despite the Queen's civil engagements, there was mounting criticism of her retreat from state ceremonial. As early as 1864, a handbill appeared on the walls of Buckingham Palace: 'These extensive premises to be let or sold, the late occupant having retired from business.'[10] The Queen defended herself in an anonymous letter to *The Times*, published above the Court Circular, in which she contradicted reports that she was about to resume her place in society. She would appear in public 'whenever any real object is to be attained', but there were higher duties than 'mere representation'.[11] In 1865, *Punch* depicted the Queen as a veiled statue: 'Descend; be stone no more.'[12] The satirical magazine *Tomahawk* draped the throne with a cover to suggest an empty house. (See Plate 11.) And it pictured Buckingham Palace in a state of ruin overrun by rats. More searing criticism was forthcoming, from disgruntled ministers who thought she was malingering at Balmoral, to discontented tradesmen who said she was insane and would never return to the capital.[13]

The Queen's seclusion fed speculation that she had become infatuated with her servant John Brown. In time, stories about 'Mrs Brown' reached the nation's cottages, drawing-rooms and beyond. The *Gazette de Lausanne* said that the Queen had been secretly married and was in 'an interesting condition' – quite an achievement for a woman of forty-seven. *Reynolds's Newspaper*, a weekly with a large artisan readership, repeated the allegation. Such mendacious rumours persisted, partly because the Queen refused to send Brown away. None of her biographers has taken such gossip seriously, for, as one of them says, it 'flew in the face of probability'.[14] Still, it provided ammunition to opponents of the monarchy and a talking point to people besotted by royal affairs, who discussed the Queen and her children with that mixture of tolerance and disapproval reserved for members of the extended family.

The Queen's lack of interest in state ceremonial was a source of complaint, but in the late 1860s there were other reasons for the revival of anti-monarchism, among them Irish discontents and a sharp rise in urban unemployment.[15] There was also some resentment among reformers that the 1867 Reform Act had betrayed the working class and that the pace of political reform had stalled. Resentments found institutional expression in the late 1860s in the Unemployed Poor League, the Land and Labour League, and the International Democratic Association, which has been described as 'the first republican organization in the country since the ineffective republican clubs of the 1850s'.[16] Such bodies usually placed democratic rights, employment or land reform at the top of the political agenda, not the Crown. But on occasion, their meetings, which attracted disaffected artisans, tradesmen and Irish labourers, spilled over into calls for the Queen to be deposed.

Agitation over unemployment and Irish affairs punctuated life in the capital in these years of economic hardship. The Queen remained informed in spite of her seclusion at Balmoral. Her outing to open Parliament in February 1867 had been a painful reminder that her popularity was far from universal. At the end of the year, she received a report from the Home Secretary of a proposed republican rising linked to the Fenians. The minister noted that a revolt might begin in London and that threats 'are undoubtedly made against your Majesty's liberty if not life'.[17] In October 1869, the Prince of Wales wrote to the Queen about a 'tremendous' demonstration in London which brought together Fenians and disparate groups of working men and women. He criticized the government's failure to keep the working classes under control, for it would only increase democratic feelings, and he bemoaned: 'I hear some speakers openly spoke of a Republic!'[18]

The Prince's own reputation did nothing to allay his worries. Rumours that the heir to the throne was a playboy were arguably more damaging to the monarchy than the Queen's isolation, particularly as there was some truth in them. His taste for expensive holidays and the company of married women rather eclipsed his growing reputation as a social campaigner, at least in the press. In 1867, *Reynolds's Newspaper*, published by the former Chartist George Reynolds, lambasted the Prince for idleness and lamented that Parliament would increase his allowance while ignoring the plight of the East End unemployed.[19] It did not mention that in the same year the Prince attended six official functions and raised large sums for the sick poor of East London as Patron of St Bartholomew's Hospital.[20] Such activity, though appreciated by the beneficiaries, counted for little among pundits and political agitators with an eye to press or political advantage.

Early in 1870, the Prince's character came into question when he received a subpoena to appear as a witness at the divorce trial of his acquaintance Sir Charles Mordaunt. The episode not only raised eyebrows in respectable households but came as an unpleasant shock to the Queen, whom the Prince nervously informed. She expressed confidence in her son, but with an eye to the political implications wrote to the Lord Chancellor on 21 February. She feared that the Prince's 'imprudence' in becoming intimate with a married women would damage him in the eyes of the middle and lower classes, 'which is most deeply to be lamented in these days when the higher classes, in their frivolous, selfish and pleasure-seeking lives, do more to increase the spirit of democracy than anything else'.[21] Gladstone wrote to the Prince of Wales two days later. He warned that the throne was secure 'so long as the nation has confidence in the personal character of its Sovereign', adding that a recurrence of the excesses of George IV's reign would 'impair its strength and might bring about its overthrow'.[22]

While the Queen tried to persuade the Prince to drop his less reputable friends, the radical press, with its obsessive interest in royal misdemeanour, revelled in reports of his being booed at the theatre and hissed in the streets. *Reynolds's Newspaper* argued that the middle and lower classes were 'the power of the nation' and that they were making an invidious comparison: 'No more such filthy fellows as George the IV shall ever sit upon the throne of England.'[23] Such comparisons worried Gladstone, who believed that virtue trickled down the social order. He wrote to the Queen: 'I am convinced that Society has suffered fearfully in moral tone from the absence of a pure Court.'[24] The pious Prime Minister dreaded the prospect of serving a rake, and wanted the Prince to reform his behaviour and to undertake suitable employment.

Meanwhile, Charles Bradlaugh, the secularist leader and radical campaigner, began a vendetta against the Prince of Wales in the pages of his journal the *National Reformer*. He carried forward the republican freethought of Paine and Carlile with a righteous indignation characteristic of the Christian culture he disavowed. In his opinion, the heir to the throne was not intelligent, sober or virtuous enough to reign. Bradlaugh did not, however, see the abolition of the Crown as a realistic prospect in the short term and rejected physical force. But 'whereas it is treasonable to talk of dethroning a monarch, there can be no disloyalty in preventing a person not yet a monarch from becoming one'.[25] His tactic was to sink the Prince's reputation and hope for the Queen to sicken or die, thereby precipitating a political crisis. He was always a constitutionalist.

As ever, the French were less squeamish about their constitution. The Franco-Prussian war ended with the fall of Napoleon III and the declaration of a French Republic on 4 September 1870, two days after the battle of Sedan. While it shook the British political élite, the French crisis enlivened their republican opponents, including middle-class intellectuals sympathetic to reform. Edward Beesly, the positivist philosopher, welcomed the French Republic in an address to London working men. In keeping with the battle-cry 'workers of the world, unite', he declared that the ties that bound working men together were 'much stronger and more real than those which kings and diplomatists have invented for them . . . The grand issue is once more before them. The Republic against monarchy and nobles, national independence against foreign domination – it is a simple issue'.[26]

For his part, Algernon Charles Swinburne played Wordsworth for his generation. In old age, he would come to praise Victoria: 'No braver soul drew bright and queenly breath/ Since England wept upon Elizabeth.' But a despiser of kings in his youth, he produced an 'Ode on the Proclamation of the French Republic':

> This shall all years remember;
> For this thing shall September
> Have only name of honour, only sign of white.
> And this year's fearful name,
> France, in thine house of fame
> Above all names of thy triumphs shalt thou write,
> When, seeing thy freedom stand
> Even at despair's right hand,
> The cry thou gavest at heart was only of delight.[27]

In the weeks that followed the declaration of the French Republic, various British reform bodies, along with representatives from Italian and German republican societies, convened a series of mass meetings. In

Trafalgar Square, which was decked out with a red flag beside Nelson's column, an estimated 10,000 demonstrators, donning red caps and ribands and singing 'La Marseillaise', urged the government to recognize the Republican Provisional Government.[28] The speaker who moved the resolution proclaimed that 'with this republic in Europe, and that over the Atlantic, there might be hope for the working men of England'.[29] In Bolton, Oldham, Newcastle and Bristol, demonstrators advanced similar views. In a meeting in Birmingham, the industrialist and municipal radical Joseph Chamberlain was in evidence.

As in the past, events in France brought the anti-monarchical element in British republicanism to the fore (just where the opponents of democratic reform liked to see it). Abroad, the French Emperor was in flight. At home, newspapers with a working-class circulation, from the trade-unionist *Bee-Hive* to the Catholic *Universe*, were running stories about the meanness of the Queen and the impropriety of the Prince of Wales.[30] In the month when the French declared a republic, the propagandists Daniel Chatterton and G. E. Harris launched the *Republican*, a paper in tune with the left-wing views of the proletarian Land and Labour League. 'There can be no republic without love, charity, peace, and a scrupulous respect for the rights of others,' one of its correspondents intoned. But respect for the royal family – 'The English blood, bone, and body consumers' – was little in evidence. Still, the paper's cantankerous pages were more often devoted to the 'natural truth' of democracy, to social revolution and to disparaging its rivals, including Bradlaugh.[31]

Seizing the opportunity provided by French affairs, Bradlaugh himself redoubled his attack on the royal family in the *National Reformer*, which, with a circulation of about 6,000 by 1872, was becoming the standard-bearer of pure republican argument.[32] He was becoming more sanguine. But his attacks on the Prince of Wales had left his many enemies livid, and they were quick to turn him into a revolutionary and call for the pillory. They saw an opportunity when the Paris Commune, with its Jacobin echoes, erupted in March 1871. They knew from long experience that French extremism was the perfect antidote to British republicanism, for it was certain to alienate the respectable classes. One paper observed, 'we should not forget [that] the views publicly propagated by Bradlaugh . . . are the views of these Red Republicans'. Another accused him of teaching the working classes to 'swim . . . in blood'.[33]

In contrast to earlier periods of unrest, the government in the 1870s did not wish to risk creating martyrs to free speech by prosecutions.[34] Thus Bradlaugh filled the role of Paine as pariah for his generation, but without having to emigrate. When the journalistic storm broke over his head, he lamented the attacks from his enemies, which were 'so numerous that I have not space to catalogue them'.[35] In reply, he delivered a series of lectures in which he concocted a potted history of royal ineptitude, which he recycled in his book *The Impeachment of the House of Brunswick* (1873). How had the Crown come to be identified with national greatness when George III was 'stupid', George IV 'licentious' and William IV 'reactionary'? He listed eight reasons to abolish it, from the iniquity of the landed system and imperial taxation to the incapacity and costs of the royal family.[36] But unlike many other anti-monarchist republicans, Bradlaugh did not assume that the advent of democracy or the abolition of the Crown would be an instant panacea. There was a caveat. 'A true republic cannot exist until the majority of the citizens are both desirous and worthy of political life.'[37]

While Bradlaugh delivered his lectures, the Liberal Government gave him more raw material on which to work. A month before the Paris Commune erupted, Gladstone had carried a motion to grant a dowry of £30,000 to Queen Victoria's daughter Princess Louise on her marriage to the Marquis of Lorne. With anti-monarchical feeling running higher than usual in the country, it was provocative. Republicans wanted to know why the royal begging box was being rattled at a time when the Queen showed no interest in opening Parliament? In the debate on the motion, Peter Taylor, the radical MP for Leicester and friend of Mazzini, told the House of Commons that 'some hundreds of thousands out-of-doors' objected to the grant, and he compared the vast expense of the British sovereign with the modest cost of the American President. Disraeli dismissed the comparison, which was a staple of republicanism, as ludicrous, for it did not compare like with like. He joined the Prime Minister in dismissing Taylor's objections to the dowry. So did the House, which voted 350 to 1 in favour of the motion.[38] The vote added another grievance to the republican list.

The proposal in the summer of 1871 to grant the Queen's third son Prince Arthur an allowance of £15,000 added yet another. The Glasgow republican John McAdam took heart, hoping that the Queen would pension 'every whelp in the Royal Kennel', for the more the 'greedy pack' received, the less ceremony would be needed to clear them out.[39] Gladstone, who moved the resolution, recognized that the grant would be 'misunderstood' and 'cause unjust remarks to be made upon the Royal Family and the Sovereign'.[40] But he took the view that Parliament had a 'moral liability' to provide for the junior branches of the royal family. One of his justifications for the size of the allowance was that the Queen's children moved among people who were much richer than they were, 'but above whom they ought somewhat to tower'. He then trotted out a few sums to show that there were 800 persons worth about £15,000 a year and a considerable number who enjoyed over £50,000. 'Under these circumstances, I say that to ask for a child of the Sovereign an income of £15,000 is not unreasonable.'[41]

It was not a persuasive argument to Peter Taylor, or to the Liberal MP for Birmingham, George Dixon, who moved to reduce the size of the Prince's allowance. Dixon commented on the 'large amount of republicanism' among the working classes, which was on the rise. In his view, the poor did not see any disadvantage to the country in the Queen's retirement from public life, but it ought to have resulted in a saving to the country, which could then have been used to maintain the royal offspring. Dixon was not hostile to the sovereign, but he took the scale of royal expenditure more seriously than most MPs: 'If we could convince the people that the Monarchy was less costly . . . we should do more than anything else we can devise to check, and it may be entirely remove, that tendency to Republicanism which exists amongst our people.' Dixon's motion was soundly defeated and the Commons divided 276 to 11 in favour of the grant to the Prince.[42]

The allowances to Princess Louise and Prince Arthur enraged reformers and stimulated the seemingly spontaneous emergence of republican clubs in 1871. The secularist C. Charles Cattell formed a club in Birmingham in February and similar bodies soon appeared in Nottingham, Sheffield, Northampton, Jarrow, Middlesbrough and Newcastle. The London Republican Club, headed by Bradlaugh, formed in March.[43] About seventy-five others appeared between 1871 and 1873, most notably in parts of the country with strong radical traditions such as the West Midlands and the north-east.[44] Their formal membership has been estimated at between 5,000 and 6,000, which was about double the figure for the republican associations at mid-century.[45] The number of people who were sympathetic to republican principles but never signed up is impossible to determine. Most clubs had a mixed membership, though the women were often relegated to 'providing refreshments and stitching banners'.[46] Just how many activists were Irish is unclear, but as Bradlaugh's daughter observed, many adherents joined the bandwagon to promote independence for Ireland not to create a British republic.[47]

In cities across the country, thousands of people attended republican meetings. Some were drab and dingy occasions, with indifferent speeches and cheerless audiences; others became so animated that they ended in scuffles and broken furniture.[48] In sedate Oxford, the students of Wadham College formed a club in 1871, but without undue breakage of glass.[49] One wit called it 'The Society for the Encouragement of the Day after To-morrow'.[50] In Cambridge, the MP Henry Fawcett and some friends set up another club. Its formal definition of republicanism was explicitly anti-monarchical: 'hostility to the hereditary principle as exemplified in monarchical and aristocratic institutions, and to all social and political privileges dependent upon difference of sex'.[51] The inclusion of women's rights was unusual, if not unique, and suggests, yet again, that republicanism was a malleable concept that could incorporate anything that made people feel progressive. But as Leslie Stephen observed, Fawcett and his friends 'were as little likely to proclaim a provisional Government as a meeting of the senior Fellows of Trinity to blow up the chapel with dynamite'.[52]

Nor was Bradlaugh ever likely to proclaim a provisional government, much less be seen in a chapel. His policy was entirely constitutional: to co-ordinate opposition to the monarchy and to strengthen republican links with secularism through the *National Reformer*, which in the spring of 1871 introduced a 'Republican Department'.[53] Secularists offered a ready and willing source of support, as did survivors of the Land and Labour League and other reform bodies. One of Bradlaugh's critics claimed that he created fifty republican clubs overnight by simply adding the word 'republican' to the names of the secular societies of which he was president.[54] This was an exaggeration, but the ability to marshal opposition to the Crown within existing institutions, whether secular societies or working-men's institutions, helps to explain the rapid growth of organized republicanism in 1871. Among other things, such bodies had personnel in place to write letters and prepare petitions.

As in the past, the republican link with secularism had drawbacks in a culture steeped in hierarchy and suffused by religion. To Christians, secularism was simply a polite word for paganism, and, as such, it was seen as just another sect, despite its claims to scientific rationality. At a stroke, republican secularists discomfited both nonconformists and Anglicans, many of whom continued to see the Queen as God's British representative. But republican Christians, for whom there could be no reformation without Christ's doctrine of love and charity, also took offence. One of them denounced Bradlaugh as a 'charlatan and an evil-doer' for his irreligion. Godlessness was as naturally opposed to republicanism 'as the existence of hereditary rule is contrary to justice, and the welfare of the people'. In short, the republicanism of atheists 'is bastard'.[55]

There were more prominent divisions within republicanism than over religion. Apart from those who favoured a British republic simply to further the cause of an independent Ireland, there were two, overlapping strands in the movement, which struggled for supremacy through rival associations.[56] The first, led by Bradlaugh and briefly spurred on by Sir Charles Dilke, was radical, patriotic and legalistic. Supported by artisans and middle-class reformers, it had strong links with secularism. The second was proletarian, socialist and potentially revolutionary. The declaration of a republic abroad and royal embarrassment at home led both strands of opinion to see the Crown as a sitting target, though not necessarily the primary one. If it were damaged or destroyed, republicans hoped to subdue the ruling oligarchs, 'the real kings of the land', who sheltered behind it.[57]

The radical republicans in the early 1870s echoed previous agitations against 'Old Corruption'. Despising the landed élite, they wanted not only an expansion of rights but an end to primogeniture which stood in the way of the more equal distribution of land. They geared their vision of the democratic republic – utilitarian, decentralized and public-spirited – to an urban, industrial society. Its realization would not only rid the nation of idle princes and aristocratic pensioners, but create a low-tax, meritocratic government, with ever-widening opportunities for intellectual and material advancement. The monarchy was objectionable because it was corrupt, costly, irrational and enshrined hereditary privilege in the constitution. But as radicals like Bradlaugh saw it, the creation of a 'true republic' turned less on pensioning off the Queen than on the promotion of civic virtue.

The socialist strand of republicanism in the early 1870s was more interested in class struggle than civic virtue. It had its origins among working men in left-wing societies such as the Poor People's Union and the Land and Labour League. It found expression in the National Republican Brotherhood, an umbrella organization established at the end of 1872, whose leader, the eccentric John de Morgan, was denounced by Bradlaugh as a dishonest conspirator. Harking back to Harney's Charter and something more, anti-monarchical socialists took heart from the Paris Commune and the symbols of direct action. Unlike the bourgeois republicans, they wanted an extension of welfare and the nationalization of land, not simply a career open to talent or the reform of land tenure. When they thought about monarchical privilege they found it objectionable because, like capital, it diminished labour. Moreover, their class analysis led naturally to a loathing of the royal family. If the moneyed classes were on the way out, the monarchy must surely go, for it was the scarecrow that protected the capitalist corn.[58]

Despite the rhetorical fireworks, the heady mix of socialist aims and motives did not lead to a mass movement against the Crown. Indeed, socialists took less notice of the British monarchy than did radicals. With revolution on the horizon, why tinker with the constitution? Friedrich Engels had long despised the social influence of the monarchy, but argued that its power was 'nil' in practice. He did not despair however, for the 'nauseating . . . cult of the crown', as he put it, could be taken as a further sign of impending revolution.[59] To Marx, the British monarchy was a side-show; but like all European monarchies, it was the 'indispensable cloak of class-rule'.[60] Its abolition would come as a consequence of the inevitable triumph of socialist doctrine. Compared to Bradlaugh's reformist creed, this was republicanism as religious faith. (Marx appears to have made no impression on the Queen.[61])

Needless to say, there was no love lost between constitutional radicals and the international socialists. In the sectarian world of reform, personal clashes and mixed motives made unity difficult; and, as in the past, middle-class and plebeian reformers spoke different political languages.

The republic was so open to interpretation that one person's view of it was another's tyranny. Bradlaugh thought socialism a foreign implant, rejected the tenet of class struggle and challenged Marx to hold a meeting at which their respective objects might be discussed. Marx did not reply.[62] In turn, socialists dismissed Bradlaugh as a conservative, who was ignorant of labour issues and frightened of breaking eggs. Splits over ends and means, ideology and tactics, sent out the signal that republicanism was incoherent and tainted by cranks and foreign influences. The Paris Commune, which the French authorities crushed at the cost of 20,000 lives, exacerbated the divisions. It gave socialists a *frisson*, but made Bradlaugh, like Queen Victoria, shudder.

Despite the anti-monarchical rhetoric of the day, few republicans, socialist or radical, revolutionary or constitutional, believed that Britain was a monarchy, in the sense that the Queen ruled. As the secularist writer Austin Holyoake said to the London Dialectical Society in October 1871: 'What we have is the *semblance* of a Monarchical rule without the *reality*.' As no monarch governs, he added, we must adapt 'what we have had in reality for so long a time, – a Republican Government'.[63] In his inaugural address to the London Republican Club in 1871, Bradlaugh admitted that there was much of a 'republican nature' in the post-1688 constitution, and he conceded that for generations 'we have had little or nothing of a monarchy in this country'. Yet the Crown was costly, played no part in social welfare (or so he thought), and had a 'paralysing and vicious influence'.[64] While he tried to disguise his contempt for royalty, particularly the Queen, he came clean in *The Impeachment of the House of Brunswick*: 'I loathe these small German breast-bestarred wanderers, whose only merit is their loving hatred of one another.'[65]

Bradlaugh, Holyoake and others wanted to fill the political vacuum created by the monarchy's decline, but they were less than consistent in their view of royal power. At one moment, they celebrated the Queen's irrelevance, the next they castigated her for not fulfilling the functions of her office. Paradoxically, Bradlaugh rebuked the royal family for failing to initiate 'wise legislation'.[66] Holyoake criticized Victoria for not bringing the Prince of Wales into the political arena, but he would have been appalled if she had.[67] Charles Watts, Bradlaugh's lieutenant on the *National Reformer*, accepted that the monarchy was 'dormant'; and he seemed to agree with monarchists who boasted, as he put it, 'that the value of royalty consists principally of its doing nothing'.[68] It had been some years since the Queen's enemies charged her with political inter-ference. Now they concentrated on the lesser charges of avarice and the behaviour of the Prince of Wales.

The Queen would not have endorsed the view that the Crown survived because it had nothing to do. But her very isolation from the seat of government, about which there was so much complaint, worked to her advantage, for it was hard to square with political interference. So was the fact that she was a woman, better yet, an ageing widow without Prince Albert hovering in the background. The older she became, the more her behaviour could be put down to eccentricity. A high-toned sovereign known to be fond of animals and the middle classes, pictured sitting in a Bath chair at Balmoral bazaars, evoked an endearing image. Few outside the highest political and Palace circles realized that here was a remarkable woman, who in her advancing years was still capable of grieving and meddling at the same time.

Republicans in particular, partly out of lack of interest, had little inkling of what went on behind the scenes at Balmoral or Windsor. They seemed to have accepted, as one of them put it, that the Queen '*never interferes with the course of government*'.[69] But such ill-informed com-ment did not serve the anti-monarchist cause, for the more the people believed the Crown to be neutral or emasculated, the less reason they had to oppose it. And if the Crown was not a political obstruction, would the public rally in support of its abolition? Removing what was seen as an ineffectual institution headed by an ageing sovereign was always likely to be more difficult than removing a transparently vital and meddlesome one. This was the logic behind Bradlaugh's preoccupation with the reputation of the heir to the throne.

If republicans were not well placed to know about the Queen, she was in a better position to know about them. She could take some comfort from the divisions within their burgeoning movement. In April 1871, she received a report from the Home Secretary Henry Bruce about a demonstration in Hyde Park. He observed that it was 'utterly insignifi-cant' – only five or six hundred people turned up – and he concluded that such 'political excitement & extravagance . . . must always be expected when France is undergoing a Revolution'.[70] Henry Ponsonby, the Queen's Private Secretary, happily noted that there was a split in the republican ranks, as Bradlaugh and the trade-union leader George Odger, who failed to attend, were denounced by the 'mob-orators'.[71] But a few weeks later, Sir Thomas Biddulph, the Master of the Royal Household, wrote less reassuringly to the Queen: 'There is no question . . . but that among the Working Classes, Republican feeling has a considerable hold, and even the Upper Class now, in not a few instances talk of the possibility of such a thing occurring after your Majesty's time.'[72]

British monarchs abhorred public expressions of republicanism, but they went with the office. If history was any guide, it was better to ignore such demonstrations and let the government and the conservative press do the over-reacting. Criticism of the Crown by political insiders was harder to ignore. Thus the pamphlet *What does she do with it?*, written under the *nom de plume* 'Solomon Temple', caused a stir when it arrived at Balmoral in the autumn of 1871. It was obviously the work of someone with specialized knowledge – George Otto Trevelyan as it turned out, a former member of the government. In a rare example of a Hanoverian being 'censured for thrift', he totted up the Queen's legacies, inheritances and the transfer of Civil List payments to the Privy Purse, and conjectured that she was hoarding £200,000 a year, clearly enough money to provide for her family. Not counting interest, he estimated that such sums represented an accumulated saving of six million pounds. Why should the nation stump up any more money when the Queen was not performing her public role?[73]

Palace officials spared the Queen the details in 'Temple's' pamphlet, which contained dubious figures and failed to mention the charitable distributions of the royal family.[74] Ponsonby was in a quandary, for he assumed that the working classes disapproved of stinginess in their sovereign, but he was too tactful to thrust his views on the Queen, particularly as she was ill at the time. He thought of asking a reviewer to counter the lies about her legacies and savings. More generally, he fretted about her health and isolation: 'If . . . she is neither the Head of the Executive, nor the fountain of honour, nor the centre of display, the royal dignity will sink to nothing at all.'[75] A year earlier, Ponsonby had joked about a republican meeting in which the royal household had been called 'a pack of Germans'.[76] He was starting to get nervous.

By the autumn of 1871, Gladstone was no less nervous about what he called 'the Royalty question'. Though the Queen and her officials did not appreciate it, he endowed the monarchy with a sacred importance as a focal point of national unity and a bastion of constitutional government.[77] He had complained to Lord Granville some months before that the monarchy's 'fund of credit' was diminishing, and he failed to see how it was to be replenished when 'the Queen is invisible, and the Prince of Wales is not respected'.[78] He now confessed to Ponsonby that the Queen's retirement gave him the 'blue devils'.[79] The Prime Minister had his own reasons for taking fright. He was loath to admit it, but when the Queen was on ceremonial duty, she conferred legitimacy on his government and gave him a return with the electorate. When she appeared as head of state, statesmen were part of the ceremony and a little of the monarchical magic rubbed off on them. As the monarch's fund of credit diminished, so did the government's.

Unlike the Prime Minister, many a metropolitan journalist and some of her advisers, the Queen seems not to have been unduly alarmed by the republican threat in the nation at large. She would have waved away Bagehot's remarks written at the time that 'the showy parts of our Constitution have not been very visible lately, and have not been at all visible on the popular side of any question'.[80] Had she not, after all, carried out more public engagements in 1871 than in previous years? Had not sympathetic crowds cheered her when she opened Parliament in February and the Albert Hall in March? Had she not received a rapturous welcome in June when she and other members of the royal family visited St Thomas's Hospital, across from the Houses of Parliament? Gladstone was also present at the hospital, but the police failed to recognize him and kept him standing out of sight during part of the proceedings.[81]

In September, the Prince of Wales, taking the Prime Minister's view, felt obliged to write to his mother: 'The People are really loyal; but it is feared in these Radical days that, if the Sovereign is not more amongst them, and not more seen in London, the loyalty and attachment to the Crown will decrease, which would be naturally much to be deplored.'[82] The Prince's comments were not unconnected to his own frustrations. Ironically, he was complaining about the weight of his public duties at the time of Gladstone's rebukes and Bradlaugh's vendetta. In April he had written to the Queen: 'You have . . . no conception of the quantity of applications we get in the course of the year to open this place, lay a stone, public dinners, luncheons, fêtes without end; and sometimes people will not take *no* for an answer – and certainly think we must be made of wood or iron if we could go through all they ask – and all these things have increased tenfold since the last 10 years.'[83] In the light of his charitable rounds, criticisms of his idleness must have seemed fanciful to the Prince.

The year 1871 was turning into an *annus horribilis* for both the Queen and the heir to the throne. In early November, the royal family received a particularly nasty jolt when the twenty-eight-year-old Sir Charles Dilke, radical MP for Chelsea, assailed the Crown before a working-class audience in Newcastle. Dilke had inherited republican sympathies from his grandfather, which remained unsullied by the baronetcy that the Queen had conferred on his father. He had opposed the dowry for Princess Louise earlier in the year, which suggested a penchant for lost causes. A frequent visitor to France, he moved among leading republicans and witnessed the dying days of the Commune. As one of his biographers notes, he returned to England full of enthusiasm, 'sporting a red tie, and declaring his theoretical preference for free government unhampered by monarchical and aristocratic restrictions'.[84] The red tie was a conceit, for as Dilke conceded, he had no intention of mounting an English barricade to overthrow what he called a 'cumbersome fiction'.[85]

Dilke's Newcastle speech, 'Representation and Royalty', touched on the redistribution of parliamentary seats, but it was essentially a critique of Crown finance. Dilke's assumption, as Kingsley Martin later observed, 'was that England was already to all intents and purposes a Republic'.[86] But he took exception to the Queen's bloated coffers and particular exception to the sums squandered on sinecures, from court physicians to the grand falconer, the 'Grand Pigeon Shooter in Ordinary'. He affirmed that responsibility for such waste and inefficiency rested with the government, which, in a variant of Old Corruption, continued to make use of royal offices for political purposes. Turning to the Queen, he accused her of neglecting her duties and, wrongly, of not paying income tax. Perhaps carried away by his audience, he ended his speech with words he would live to regret: 'if you can show me a fair chance that a Republic here will be free from the political corruption that hangs about the Monarchy, I say, for my part – and I believe the middle classes in general, will say – let it come!'.[87]

The speech would have received far less attention had it been given a decade earlier, but delivered to a meeting of working men in a radical stronghold at a time of republican revival, it was seen as inflammatory. Predictably, the press and the professions rallied to the Crown. *The Times* rebuked Dilke for vulgarity and 'recklessness bordering on criminality'.[88] The *Lancet* defended those royal sinecures to doctors as 'the highest honours of the profession', which were 'necessary and calculated to benefit the public'.[89] A barrister at the Middle Temple, where Dilke had studied law, called for his exclusion from the dining hall and reminded him of his baronetcy, which was inimical to his republican principles.[90] A clergyman from Kensington called on clerics across the nation to promote loyal addresses from their parishioners to 'the best monarch that ever sat on the throne'.[91] Across the Atlantic the *New York Times* was less unnerved: 'The shires will, we believe, for many years prevent Windsor being let in lodgings or Chatsworth being parcelled into market gardens, let Dilkes, Bradlaughs, and Odgers talk never so wisely.'[92]

One of the more subtle British journalists saw the prospect of avowed republicans like Dilke in the elected House of Commons as potentially beneficial to the monarchy. He predicted that there would henceforth be a small, but formidable, 'extreme Left' Republican Party in Parliament, which would serve the Crown's purposes. 'How often one is indebted to the sharp criticism of opponents for the most valuable indications of the direction in which reform is needed.'[93] He concluded that the monarchy had little to fear as long as the opposition concentrated on the minor matter of royal expense. As a precaution, he called on Her Majesty to institute an inquiry into Civil List expenditure with a view to reform. It was an interesting suggestion, but one that could only be carried through on government advice.

The Queen and her courtiers, who kept a watchful eye on Dilke's reception in the press, failed to see any merit in having republicans in Parliament. Her Majesty's view, as she put it to Ponsonby, was that she did 'not blame people for levelling views, *if that* is their *conviction*, but she does for taking office *under a Crown*'.[94] Biddulph, who reported to the Queen on Dilke's 'indecent and violent attack on the monarchy', suggested that Her Majesty might ask Gladstone to denounce the miscreant.[95] Ponsonby took the view that the MP had 'done himself harm' by 'telling lies all over England', but thought the attack on the Queen's finances might still be damaging. The poor 'will be furious at reading the figures of £3,000 a year spent on foreign cooks while the middle classes who won't object to the expenditure will be furious at the use being made of these cooks'.[96]

On 17 November 1871, Ponsonby wrote to his wife from Balmoral, nervous about the state of the country and suspicious of the Prime Minister's loyalty:

Ten years ago it would have been an unheard of thing to discuss republicanism. It certainly is not now . . . A fight by law or by the sword for Royalty is absurd, though even then, while we should be only too strong as Royalists we should suffer terribly for having no royalty or rather monarchy – actually visible to fight for. But with republican opinion supported and encouraged we should have greatest difficulty in opposing them, having no *raison-d'être* to show against their views.[97]

Two days later he wrote again to his wife, saying he was 'puzzled' about what advice to give to the Queen, who was 'in a low state . . . crying and regularly unhappy over these Dilke insults'.[98] Princess Alice noted with dismay that the Queen appeared apathetic about the future of the dynasty. 'But no one can suggest what should be done and we must sit quietly and let the approaching calamity crush us without an effort.'[99]

The Queen had her fatalistic moments, not least when she thought about the heir apparent. As she saw it, her *raison d'être* was to ensure constitutional and social equilibrium, and her immediate reaction to Dilke's transgression was to look to the Prime Minister for assistance. But, like her Private Secretary, she doubted Gladstone's loyalty if a political crisis were to ensue. She wrote to him on 19 November, chiding him for a speech in which he intimated that the issue of republicanism was 'open to discussion'. At a time when 'revolutionary theories are allowed to produce what effect they may in the minds of the working classes', she was anxious that Dilke's 'fabrications' and 'deliberate false-hoods', such as the accusation that she did not pay income tax, should be contradicted. She pointedly reminded the Prime Minister that it was in the interests of the government as well as the monarchy that such calumnies be countered.[100] Gladstone replied that he did not wish to stir up a discussion of the Civil List or harden republican opinion by over-reaction: 'The best mode is to deal as lightly as may be with the mere signs, but seriously with the causes of the distemper.'[101]

Two days later, the Queen received a telegram from Sandringham saying that the Prince of Wales had contracted a fever. It was diagnosed as typhoid, the disease which it was believed had killed the Prince Consort. At a stroke, the news shattered the royal household and unsettled republicans, who were now cast as insensitive brutes by the loyalist press. Attacks on a dissolute Prince were one thing, attacks on a stricken one another. As the *Annual Register* intoned, all his 'sins' were now forgotten: 'the nation seemed to gather round the throne with a single heart and a single prayer'.[102] While anonymous pamphlets declared that the illness was a diplomatic invention, republican societies sent messages of sympathy to the Queen. Even Bradlaugh, who had been ridiculing the Prince up and down the country, fell silent, if only momentarily.[103] When they heard the news of the Prince's condition, the councillors of Newcastle, where Dilke had launched his assault on the Crown, presented a loyal address, and the mayor described the MP for Chelsea as 'scum'.[104]

In the circumstances, Dilke was tempting fate to carry on, for his appearances now attracted large unruly crowds, both republican and loyalist. At a meeting in Knightsbridge, someone set fire to the platform.[105] In Bolton a man died after a brawl and others were injured by iron bars hurled through the windows.[106] In Bristol, the day before the Prince fell ill, Dilke had declared: 'I make no concealment of the fact that I am a Republican.'[107] Such declarations were music to the ears of his supporters and not a few of his enemies. To the Duke of Cambridge, the Queen's cousin, the 'violent attack' on Her Majesty was 'doing more good than harm'.[108] Joseph Chamberlain took the opposite view and congratulated Dilke: 'The republic must come, and at the rate at which we are moving it will come in our generation.'[109] This was now too sanguine for Dilke, who was so calculating a politician that he even refused an invitation to join the well-behaved Cambridge Republican Club.[110]

Behind the scenes, the Queen sought to bring Dilke to heel. Though distracted by the condition of the Prince of Wales, she wrote again to the Prime Minister in early December. She remained troubled by Dilke's 'disgraceful conduct' but 'perfectly satisfied that the nation is thoroughly loyal and only wants to be well led and for the Government to take a firm stand against revolutionary and extreme views'.[111] Gladstone reassured the Queen that the nation remained loyal and noted that 'Dilke's language has drawn down upon him a vast preponderance of disapproval'. The more independent such disapproval the better, he concluded.[112] From the point of view of many MPs, Dilke had infringed his oath of allegiance to the Queen. He had compounded the offence by doing so to a working-class audience, which, to the dismay of most MPs, linked parliamentary and extra-parliamentary opposition to the Crown. He would be cut dead in the corridors of the House of Commons by all but a handful of radicals.

Sure enough, anti-monarchism was not a stepping stone to a career in politics. Dilke feared that it might even cost him his Chelsea seat.[113] Informed that the Queen did, in fact, pay income tax, he apologized for his mistake. At Leeds, he shifted his focus and now identified the republic with a society based on merit and public spirit. 'To say these things is not to condemn the monarchy,' he concluded.[114] At Chelsea on 19 February 1872, he denied that he had maligned the Queen and failed to see why republicans should be seen as 'dangerous revolutionists', when all they wanted was frugal government and a community 'in which there will be no claim to power but that which merit gives'.[115] Chamberlain, now back-pedalling too, repeated these sentiments in a speech in Birmingham: 'I do not consider the name of the titular ruler of this country a matter of the slightest importance . . . What is important is the spread of a real Republican spirit among the people.'[116] Having put himself in a corner, he was having to get used to the idea that the republic might have to accommodate the Crown.

As Bagehot observed in *The Economist*, the sympathy aroused by the illness of the Prince suggested the 'shallowness and rootlessness of the republican movement'. How could the heir to the throne be so popular 'if the monarchy itself were not equally popular'?[117] When the Prince's fever broke on the anniversary of his father's death, some took it as providential. The Duke of Cambridge rejoiced: 'The Republicans say their chances are up. Heaven has sent this dispensation to save us.'[118] In celebration of the Prince's 'miraculous' recovery, a National Thanksgiving was held on 27 February, which was an occasion reminiscent of the celebrations surrounding the recovery of George III in 1789. It was carefully choreographed to suggest classlessness, to exact loyalist sentiment and to obliterate republicanism.[119] Gladstone, who oversaw the planning, believed it to be a service of moral purification, perhaps even for the Prince himself.

The celebration at St Paul's did not extinguish the republican cause, but it was dispiriting to anti-monarchists to see the sovereign, joined on the day by the exiled Emperor Napoleon of all people, so joyously received by an adoring public. Predictably, the loyalist press, having prepared the ground for the festival's success, was ecstatic, despite the deaths and injuries caused by the unruly crowds. The *Standard* saw it as a 'protest against the cold-blooded theories . . . of English Republicans'. The *Daily Telegraph* called it an 'unparalleled' display 'of unity, loyalty, piety and ideal nationality'.[120] The *Bee-Hive*, the official organ of trade unionism, was also fulsome in its praise: 'Never before did any capital in all the world . . . present such an assemblage, so immense in number, so patient in spirit, so united in sentiment, so one in heart'.[121]

The Queen, who had initially opposed the Thanksgiving, confided in her journal that she was pleased with 'the millions out, the beautiful decorations, the wonderful enthusiasm and astounding affectionate loyalty shown'.[122] The Prince of Wales wrote to the Queen on the day: 'I cannot tell you how gratified and touched I was by the feeling that was displayed in those crowded streets to-day towards you and also to myself.'[123] In the aftermath of the Prince's recovery, and the monarchy's, Alfred Tennyson reinforced the mood with an epilogue to *Idylls of the King*, in which he praised the 'crown'd Republic's crowning common-sense, that saved her many times'. The phrase 'crown'd Republic' would be recalled in the reign of George V.

Dilke's vision of an uncrowned republic was slipping out of sight. His motion to inquire into the Civil List, which had been tabled before the illness of the Prince of Wales, came up for debate at a decidedly inopportune moment. Not only had the country rallied to the Prince, but it was also rallying to the Queen. Two days after the National Thanksgiving at St Paul's, she had been threatened with a pistol (unloaded) in the grounds of Buckingham Palace by the reckless Arthur O'Connor, the nephew of Feargus. As with previous attacks on the Queen, it kindled devotion to the throne. The incident even enhanced the reputation of John Brown, who disarmed the wayward youth. It was against this background that the House of Commons debated Dilke's motion on 19 March. That he persisted with it was a tribute to his sense of honour rather than good sense, for rarely had an aspiring MP been so caught out by the expression of republican sentiments.

Dilke recognized that his motion would suffer because of his opinions and so he concentrated on the minutiae of the Civil List. By his own account, the speech was 'unutterably dull', a tactic designed to disarm a packed and hostile House of Commons.[124] He was careful not to criticize the Queen directly but attacked what he saw as corruption and abuse, among them sinecures and annuities. And why, he asked, should 'four Royal yachts' be kept afloat at vast expense? His wider point was that the possession of a large private fortune by the sovereign in a limited monarchy was 'a constitutional danger of the first magnitude'. Should not Parliament have the right periodically to reassess the Civil List during the reign, not simply at the beginning of it?[125] All in all, it was an unexceptional performance in an exceptional atmosphere, less memorable than the historic speeches of Burke or Brougham on Crown finance.

After a few desultory remarks on the Civil List, Gladstone reminded the House that the motion could not be separated from Dilke's imprudent Newcastle speech which preceded it. To accede to the motion in such circumstances would reinforce the misguided notion that the Queen was 'wastefully consuming the earnings of the people' and that a change in the constitution was needed. 'Such an effect on the public mind we are not prepared to take any share in producing.'[126] Amid cries of 'Divide', catcalls and imitations of crowing cocks, the Liberal MP for Nottingham, Auberon Herbert, who had seconded Dilke's motion, said that the level of royal expenditure was 'hurtful to society' and declared himself a republican.[127] The rest of his speech could scarcely be heard above the din. It was a spirited, if inauspicious, performance. The Prince of Wales later had a word about it with Herbert's brother, Lord Carnarvon, who was embarrassed by the episode.[128]

Dilke had run out of supporters. Anthony Mundella, the radical MP for Sheffield, rose to dissent from the motion but first teased the Conservatives for their antics, which were unconsciously making them 'the most formidable allies of Republicanism'. Some months earlier, Mundella had written to Herbert telling him that Dilke's Newcastle address was a 'political blunder' which would 'only help the work of reaction'.[129] Now he criticized Dilke directly, saying that he was tilting at windmills by quarrelling with the Civil List. There were far more important issues affecting the working classes than the petty cash of royalty. 'True Radicals' were interested in freedom and sound government. Extravagance and abuse could be found in republics too, and 'while our government was Monarchical in form, it was freer in fact, and more Republican in essence than that of any other country in the world'.[130]

Dilke might have hoped to have the support of Henry Fawcett, who had a reputation for being, in Ponsonby's words, 'one of the most extreme radicals'.[131] But like Mundella, Fawcett disapproved of the tone of Dilke's Newcastle speech, believing that it should have been delivered in Parliament and not in public. Republicanism might, he thought, be best for Britain one day, but it should be a question involving the great social and moral issues, 'and not be degraded to a huckstering and quibbling over the cost of the Queen's Household'. In his summary, Dilke, by now as tired of his performance as the House, continued to quibble. The House defeated his motion 276 to 2.[132] The *Manchester Guardian* noted 'that he carried with him into the lobby only just so many followers as he could have carried away with him inside a cab'.[133]

Prince Arthur wrote to the Queen the day after the debate: 'delighted to see how Sir Charles Dilke caught it in the House last night . . . How a man can coolly get up & tell a number of lies like Sir Charles Dilke did, is to me quite astounding'.[134] Queen Victoria felt much the same, and in the future would keep a vengeful eye on the career of the Member for Chelsea. She had followed the Cabinet discussions about his motion with interest. The view of the court, put by Ponsonby, had been that it should never have been allowed to come before the House in the first place, if only because Dilke's access to Treasury documents 'might raise very disagreeable questions' connected to the Privy Purse. The Civil List had been set at the beginning of the reign, and if it was allowed to come up for discussion now, there was the prospect of changes being proposed perennially.[135] There was a collective sigh of relief at court when MPs howled down Dilke's motion.

The humiliation of Dilke and the public elation at the recovery of the Prince of Wales were straws in the wind, evidence that anti-monarchical agitation was waning. There were other signs as well. The *Republican*, which had never had an office staff, ceased publication in the month of the National Thanksgiving for the Prince's recovery, a victim of low sales and what *Reynolds's Newspaper* called 'typhoid loyalty'.[136] The radical newspaper proprietor George Standring lamented that in the commotion over the Prince of Wales people all too often 'became republicans for an hour . . . then, on second thoughts, their republicanism ceased'.[137] Clearly, there was an element of fair-weather republicanism about. The attention given to the Queen's seclusion, royal costs and troubles in the royal family awakened many people to the inconsistencies in their thinking about the monarchy. But their flirtation with republicanism, aroused by press interest in the royalty question, subsided as quickly as it had appeared.

Criticism of the monarchy, of course, did not necessarily mean a wish to be rid of it. The attitude of *The Bee-Hive* was suggestive. It could be severe about the royal family and featured an article applauding Dilke's 'excellent' motion to inquire into the Civil List.[138] But the paper was not in favour of dispensing with the monarchy as an institution, as its effusive remarks on the celebrations at St Paul's marking the Prince's recovery attested. On occasion, it compared Britain's constitutional monarchy favourably with the demoralizing spectacle of presidential contests in America, and with the tragic political history of France. 'As a matter of fact our Government at the present time is in reality, though not in name, a republic, with an hereditary President.' England had, *The Bee-Hive* concluded, 'reason to be proud and thankful for the amount of suffering she has been spared in consequence of being nominally ruled by Heredi-tary Presidents of the Commonwealth'.[139] The notion of the monarch as an 'hereditary President' would persist.

In the world of conventional British politics, the weight of such opinion was not lost on aspiring radicals, including Dilke, who would have further occasion to regret the comments of his youth. Increasingly, they recognized that attacks on the Crown were a distraction. If they wanted preferment, they would be wise to refrain from injudicious remarks about royalty. The great reformer John Bright, who had some sympathy with republicanism in the abstract, showed the way. When informed in April 1872 that republicans would select him as their first President, he replied that anyone who suggested such a thing must be a doubtful friend. He believed that a decision on the monarchy could and should be deferred: 'our ancestors decided the matter a long time since, and I would suggest that you and I should leave any further decision to our posterity'.[140]

The main bout of anti-monarchism was over when one of the most intriguing statements of republican thought appeared in June 1872. Fred-eric Harrison, the prolific author and positivist philosopher, had been invited by the anti-royalist John Morley, a future Liberal MP, to put the republican case in the influential journal, the *Fortnightly Review*.[141] Harrison was an admirer of the Venetian Republic and Rome under the Scipios, and he emphasized the need to cultivate the civic spirit of superior persons, 'the idea that the common good permeates and inspires every public act'. He defined the republic as 'the utmost distribution of function with the greatest social co-operation'. But in a singular departure from his radical contemporaries, he did not equate it with democracy: 'It is an abuse of language to make republic synonymous with democracy . . . The republic is that state, the principle of which is not privilege but merit, where all public power is a free gift, and is freely entrusted to those who seem able to use it best.'[142]

Like so many others, Harrison believed that 'this country is, and had long been, a Republic, though an imperfect Republic, it must be allowed . . . England is now an aristocratic Republic, with a democratic machinery and an hereditary grand master of ceremonies'. Although the monarchy was an otiose remnant of hereditary privilege, it was politically nothing. 'The monarchy is therefore not a political question at all,' he argued, 'but a social question, and since social questions cannot be settled by external revolutions, any violent attack on the monarchy as an institution would fail to secure its object. It would be like attempting to abolish luxury or suppress wealth by Act of Parliament or popular plebiscite.' As a classical republican, revolution from below struck him as unseemly: 'For a formal political change it would risk a critical social convulsion.' But then, he concluded, the monarchy was not in danger in any case, apart from 'being made ridiculous by officious sycophants'.[143]

Harrison's line of argument suggested that only a foreign invasion or an act of God was likely to topple the Crown in the 1870s. The belief, to which he subscribed, that Britain had been a disguised republic since 1688 was certainly an odd way of arousing anti-royalism. But then, as he insisted, attacking the monarchy was a fruitless exercise without the triumph of republican spirit. Nor did his assumption that the essential role of the monarchy was social and ceremonial, which meant unthreatening, augur well for anti-monarchists. Harrison argued that 'for everything that is not mere pageant the country is administered precisely as a republic'.[144] Nor was his preoccupation with creating a meritocracy such a compelling issue as he imagined, at least among the middle classes.

Graduates, clerks and managers felt they were doing quite nicely already, and legislation had recently been passed which opened up the Civil Service to talent.

Harrison thought the monarchy a waste of public money, but wishing to avoid the abuse heaped on Dilke, he did not make a major issue of it. And though egged on by Morley, he spoke of Queen Victoria 'with delicate homage'.[145] (The Queen seems not to have taken any notice of him, though years later George V would consider him for an honour.[146]) Harrison would have agreed with Fawcett that haggling over the Civil List was not exactly high-minded. As such men recognized, the issue of royal expenditure simply lacked the political dynamic to produce constitutional change. Moreover, it had a serious defect – it could be addressed, as it had been in the past. However telling the criticism, most people assumed that a head of state could not be run on a shoestring. Bagehot made this point when he noted that attacks on royal portions and dowries were not necessarily signs of anti-monarchism. They were often 'no more than what they seemed – fits of somewhat vague and ignorant irritation against what was thought a needless and callous tax upon the people'.[147]

The issue of Crown finance came up yet again when Prince Alfred, Duke of Edinburgh, married in 1873 and another Annuity Bill came before Parliament. Peter Taylor opposed it in Parliament. Bradlaugh gathered the faithful in Hyde Park. But Gladstone carried the day, dismissing claims of public opposition to the grant and calling for a better understanding of the royal circumstances. He pointed out, yet again, that by the standards of the nation's wealthiest families, the wealth of the royal family was modest. Moreover, much of it was pledged because of the demands of society and the nature of the establishments that royalty had to maintain. He put the total cost of the monarchy, including annuities and the Civil List, at just over £500,000 a year (Dilke had put the figure at £1,000,000). This, he concluded, was not extravagant for a country with an annual income of over £800,000,000.[148]

What radicals, inside and outside Parliament, had to ask themselves was whether it was worth the effort to invest in a campaign against a sovereign whose political powers they believed to be nil or residual. Was the abolition of the monarchy crucial to democratic reform, as Bradlaugh believed, or was it a distraction, as many radicals had long ago concluded?

Bright thought abolition might prove more than a distraction. As he said in 1873: 'It is easier to uproot a Monarchy than to give a healthy growth to that which is put in its place, and I suspect the price we should have to pay for the change would be greater than the change would be worth.' As so often in the nineteenth century, Gallic history was a touchstone. Like many a loyalist, Bright believed that France had 'endured many calamities and much humiliation' because of its republican past.[149]

Pure republicans, even the most constitutionalist among them, did not provide a blueprint for the monarchy's abolition, or address the question of what would replace it, apart from something democratic and non-hereditary. As Harrison noted, 'amidst masses of republicans there is no republican programme'.[150] Increasingly, they concluded that agitating for the abolition of the Crown was a waste of effort. The Scottish writer James Aytoun, who described himself as a 'theoretical' republican, argued that calls to depose the Queen were injuring the prospects of more practical reforms. In his pamphlet *Constitutional Monarchy and Republicanism* (1873), he wanted the removal of the royal prerogative of nominating and dismissing ministers, but warned that Conservatives were exploiting republicanism for their own ends. 'In short, they are making use of the names Dilke, Odger, and Bradlaugh, as sportsmen sometimes do with red herrings dragged along the ground, in order to turn hounds from following the scent of real game.'[151]

The message that direct attacks on the Crown might be self-defeating was making headway. When a republican conference convened in Birmingham in the spring of 1873, the delegates hardly mentioned the monarchy, preferring to dwell on local self-government, land reform and religious equality. The meeting did launch the National Republican League, a co-ordinating body to rival the National Republican Brotherhood, but it was a lacklustre affair. While Bradlaugh and Odger turned up, it was avoided by radical MPs, including Bright, who was asked to preside. The conference passed a resolution to abolish the House of Lords but not one to abolish the monarchy.[152] Its manifesto declared a republic to be the only form of government 'worthy of a civilized people'. It defined republican government as a state 'in which the sovereign power resides in deputies elected by the people according to equitable principles of representation'.[153] (This is the standard dictionary definition today.) The more strident members of the National Republican Brotherhood, who boycotted the conference, remarked that such a manifesto was 'no better than limited monarchy'.[154]

As the meeting in Birmingham suggested, the republican movement outside Parliament was returning to square one, with anti-monarchism relegated to the periphery of the wider movement for democratic and social reform. Both the National Republican League and the National Republican Brotherhood soon faded, casualties of the contraction in the number of clubs. The personal and doctrinal divisions within republicanism, the fears aroused by the Paris Commune, the recovery of the Prince of Wales and the upturn in employment in 1871 were reasons for the loss of momentum. The minority outside Parliament who expected the Queen to pack her bags for Hanover, because they saw no need for her services, had become detached from reality. When reality dawned, their hopes subsided or diverted into other causes.

As in the past, many a pure republican turned into a theoretical one. This was particularly true of those who hoped to enter politics. Joseph Cowen was a friend of Mazzini and a longstanding anti-monarchist, who had chaired the Newcastle meeting for Dilke in 1871. But when he stood as a Liberal candidate for his father's Newcastle seat at a by-election at the end of 1873, and again at the general election in 1874, the Tories raked over his past and taunted him as a 'regicide'. A chastened man, Cowen denied any active participation in a local republican club, to which he had been elected president, and said that 'the notion that the society was to dethrone the Queen and upset the Constitution of this country is one so utterly ridiculous that I confess I have never failed to smile when I have heard it mentioned'.[155] He narrowly won both elections, although at some cost to his principles. But they were not forgotten. When he appeared at Westminster, 'he found he was not acceptable to the Front Bench Olympians' and Gladstone and Bright 'rudely' insulted him.[156]

By the time of the 1874 general election, which brought in a Conservative government, it was patently clear, even to republicans, that the anti-monarchical moment had passed. One hyperbolical royalist, in triumphant mood, declared: 'you could not have a republic without republicans, and as there are none in England a republic was hopeless'.[157] The 'Republican Department' of the *National Reformer* closed in September 1874; and when George Standring launched the *Republican Chronicle* the following year, he doubted that the journal would last a year. The use of 'Republican' in the title, he later admitted, was a 'stumbling-block in its path'.[158] Not only were anti-monarchists 'steeped' in 'torpor', but many of the republican clubs had collapsed, and with it their propaganda work.[159] Not all opponents of royalty had joined a republican club, of course, but with only 5,000 or 6,000 official members at their peak, the clubs had never signalled a revolution, even had they wanted one. The Rechabite Teetotal Society, not exactly a leader in its field, had a membership of 15,000 in 1870.[160]

The anti-monarchical campaigners were in disarray, but the radical press kept the cause from total eclipse – the weekly circulation of *Reynolds's Newspaper* stood at 300,000 in the 1880s.[161] A few stalwarts sought to expand republican education, or, as Standring put it, to push along 'the less advanced reformers' towards 'the order of things inevitable'.[162] But such certainty, in the face of the immediate defeat, often led republicans to deride everyone who disagreed with them as infantile, which was an unlikely prelude to converting them. Having failed to do so, Bradlaugh blamed 'the people that they have permitted an inefficient and mischief-working family to rule so long'.[163] After the Birmingham conference, he continued to battle in public, but despaired in private. In a moment of dejection, he declared, echoing a popular French song of the 1790s, that 'monarchy is government for children: Republicanism is for men'.[164]

Because Bradlaugh dismissed the electorate as childlike, he rarely asked himself why so many people supported the monarchy. But in Spain, where he travelled in 1873 as an emissary of the National Republican League, he was reported to have said that since the monarchy did not stifle liberty or oppose progress, no one thought of overthrowing it: 'I do not expect, however long I may live, that England will become a Republic in my lifetime.'[165] Was this the same Bradlaugh who only a few days before had expressed 'little doubt that, within twenty years or less, we shall have the Republic in England'?[166] Setbacks had given him cause for confusion. At one moment, he sounded like a theoretical republican, counselling education, patience and slow progress in modest reforms. The next, as on his spirited tour of the United States in late 1873 and early 1874, the old stridency returned.

Unbeknown to Bradlaugh, Palace officials were keeping an eye on him, as they did other prominent republicans. Ponsonby wrote a memorandum to the Queen about Bradlaugh's tour of the United States. He noted that the republican leader had announced to American audiences that his cause was advancing so rapidly in England that the monarchy would be abolished before the Prince of Wales succeeded:

Mr Bradlaugh occasionally attacks Your Majesty but in very cautious and measured terms never saying anything which could be considered personally offensive. But in assailing the Prince of Wales he accuses him of passing a worse than useless life and says he is utterly unfitted to reign. But it is doubtful whether he has said anything which would render him liable to prosecution. He is a clever, cautious and therefore more dangerous man than the wild orators who heedlessly declaim on whatever comes uppermost.[167]

The Queen's advisers preferred the enemies of the Crown to be incendiaries.

Republicans often treated the monarchy as though it were a moribund institution just waiting to be entombed. But the court, as its information gathering suggests, was far from inert. Ponsonby said to his wife that the Crown would have difficulty in opposing republicans because it had 'no *raison-d'être* to show against their views'. But the republican agitation, as in the Chartist years, was not without benefit to the monarchy. As Bagehot noted, inflammatory attacks on the Crown had made the recovery of the Prince of Wales all the more significant.[168] Republican opposition was also a stimulus, something which called for a response. The government and the conservative press could be counted upon, but members of the royal family, aroused from their complacency, became more conscious of the need for better public relations. The outbreak of republicanism was a reminder, if the family of the Prince Consort needed one, that public service was an antidote to hazardous political experiments.[169]

Thanks largely to Prince Albert, the royal outlook was sympathetic to trade and industry, which was an important reason why the commercial and professional classes remained loyal in the early 1870s. (The contrast with France, where the professional classes deserted the Emperor, is illuminating.[170]) Moreover, the patronage work of the royal family had extended the monarchy's tendrils through the institutions of respectable society – from trade associations and freemasonry to the Bible Society and the RSPCA – thereby countering any inclination that the middle classes might have had to become republican. By the 1870s, as a latter day republican laments, the middle-class backbone was 'in chronic and ... complacent curvature'.[171] But a bow to royalty was often a prelude to joining schemes of social usefulness. This was just as the Prince Consort, who believed that subjects should be conservative and princes liberal, would have wished.

Respectable subjects, whatever their beliefs or station, identified with a social hierarchy, linked by numerous, permeable gradations, headed by the sovereign. In an era of extraordinary stability and material progress, they widely believed that progress and royalty, loyalism and patriotism, marched hand in hand, a belief fortified by the Crown's enduring associations with imperial expansion. Meanwhile, royal values continued to metamorphose into a utilitarian philosophy of goodness, which was in tune with a commercial, voluntary society – and republican values. The heroic age of monarchy had given way to the age of princely service. Members of the royal family, however imperious or pleasure seeking, were obliged to be sensitive to social issues. In their fashion they were.[172]

Stripped of those manly pursuits of war and diplomacy, the Prince of Wales collapsed into niceness. He was not always amenable to advice, but after his recovery, he was eager to restore his reputation. Palace officials found it easier to steer him in directions favourable to the monarchy's wider interest. Gladstone's scheme to employ him as the Queen's representative in Ireland aborted, but after the republican scare, the Prince took greater pains to improve his public image. On one front, he made friendly overtures to a few of the monarchy's erstwhile critics, notably Dilke, Chamberlain and later Morley. On another, he forged institutional links with respectable society. Partly because of the influence of Princess Alexandra, who was recklessly charitable, he stepped up his work with voluntary hospitals, extracted millions of pounds from plutocratic friends for medical and other causes and began to visit social blackspots and centres of industry on a regular basis. As Henry Burdett, his adviser on philanthropic issues, remarked in the 1880s: 'the range of the Prince's work is so very wide as to include probably all the most important institutions'.[173]

With the years, the Prince dedicated more and more of his time to bringing the monarchy closer to the concerns of the public. With his social skills and effortless superiority, he effectively combined charity with imperial display. He had his critics in the colonies, as at home; but whenever on tour, he left a trail of schools and hospitals behind, paid for by local dignitaries, which served as a justification of Empire, and the Crown's role in it.[174] Over time, the Prince's work at home and abroad enhanced his reputation as a benevolent patriarch among the patriotic and respectable. Even the odd radical came around to him. In his autobiography, *Sixty Years of an Agitator's Life*, the former Chartist, secularist and champion of Co-operation, George Jacob Holyoake, gave the 'devil his due'. The Prince of Wales had, in his view, done a great deal 'to increase enjoyment of the people'. So had the Queen through her charity and encouragement to the Co-operative movement. 'The power of the Crown' in the promotion of 'social freedom' was, Holyoake concluded, 'greater than is generally known.'[175]

The Queen's social administration was benevolent, but her political administration, unbeknown to most of her critics, could be antagonistic, even vindictive. She might have added the word 'oppose', perhaps even 'obstruct', to Bagehot's dictum that a sovereign had the right to 'consult', 'encourage' and 'warn'. Outspoken anti-monarchists were few and far between in Parliament, for reasons already mentioned; but as Queen Victoria made little distinction between democrats and republicans, she saw rather a lot of political opponents on the radical benches in the House of Commons. Remembering the early 1870s, she was highly sensitive to 'advanced' opinion and jealous of the royal prerogative. Ever watchful, she took great offence at the slightest signs of disloyalty, interpreting words or phrases that might seem innocent to others as a challenge to her authority.

To the Queen, the Liberal landslide in the election of April 1880 was a calamity. After the attentions of Disraeli, the very thought of having to deal again with Gladstone, the *'half mad fire brand'*, made the word *'abdicate'* cross her mind. The 'People's William', the populist of the Midlothian campaign, had in her view confused himself for the sovereign.[176] He reawakened all her partisan instincts. Once she knew the Liberals were to form a government, she summarized her policies to Ponsonby: 'there must be no democratic leaning, no attempt to change the Foreign policy . . . no change in India . . . *no* cutting down of estimates.

In short, *no lowering* of the *high position* this country holds, and *ought always* to hold'.[177] Behind the detail lay her justification for pressing her views on her government, which she put to Gladstone directly: the House of Commons was 'only *one* of the *three* parties in the Constitution'.[178]

The Queen recognized that Gladstone had defended the monarchy's interest in the past. Indeed, he did more to stifle disaffection than Disraeli ever did. But she disliked him personally and assumed that his policies had a tendency to reduce the power of the Crown, which she was determined to protect. Moreover, she detested the republicans, little Englanders, atheists and 'low' revolutionaries who now populated the Liberal Party. She took the election of Charles Bradlaugh as MP for Northampton in 1880 as symptomatic of a disgraceful political decline. His fierce anti-royalism may have faded, but the Queen recoiled at his declaration to the newspapers that the oath of allegiance was 'idle and meaningless words'. Ponsonby commanded Gladstone to disassociate the government from Bradlaugh's revolutionary views.[179]

The Queen could be generous to individual radicals, despite their political opinions, as she was to Bright, Cowen and Fawcett.[180] But she retained a particular animus towards Dilke, whose Newcastle speech still jarred eight years after the event. A month before the election of April 1880, she had written a telling memorandum in which Dilke figured prominently:

It is well known that he is a democrat – a *disguised* Republican – who is in communication with the extreme French Republicans – he has been personally most offensive in his language respecting the Court & the expences etc. and to place him in the Govt not to speak of the Cabinet would be a sign to the whole world that England was sliding down into democracy and a Republic. If the Liberals . . . intend to lean to the extreme Radicals – they can *never* expect *any* support from the Queen . . . These are dangerous times and any attempt to make our Institutions Democratic will be *most* disastrous.[181]

When Gladstone submitted Dilke's name to the Queen as Under Secretary for Foreign Affairs at the end of April, she was 'astonished'.[182] By her own account, it was a sign that the country was sliding into anarchy. She wrote to the Prime Minister that the appointment would be divisive, and she would agree to it only if Dilke would clarify 'his very offensive speeches on the Civil List and Royal Family'.[183] Immediately, Dilke expressed regret to Gladstone and Lord Granville for the foolish comments of youth, and explained that his republican views 'did not affect the old established Monarchies'. His remarks had some effect, and the Queen reluctantly consented to his appointment, on the understanding that he was only an under secretary and she would not need to have anything to do with him.[184] Granville wrote to Ponsonby, comparing Dilke, Chamberlain and Fawcett to 'peppercorns' in the 'bread sauce' of Parliament. They 'give a little flavour, but do not much affect the character of the food'.[185]

When Gladstone sought to bring Dilke into the Cabinet in 1882, the Queen took fresh offence and raised the republican issue again. She had written to the Prince of Wales of her disgust with Gladstone's 'dreadfully radical government which contains many thinly-veiled *Republicans* . . . *All the worst men* who had no respect for Kings and Princes or any of the *landmarks* of the constitution *were put into the Government in spite of me*'.[186] Now she had to swallow the indignity of Dilke's elevation. She wrote in her Journal that 'she should forgive him [Dilke], but others would not forget what he had said'.[187] Ponsonby took soundings and concluded that Dilke was still a republican 'outside the House'; and while he denied making personal attacks on the Queen, most people assumed that his criticism of the Civil List amounted to the same thing.[188] Dilke's stand on the annuity to Prince Leopold, the Duke of Albany, in March 1882 had not gone unnoticed.[189]

The Queen reminded Gladstone that she had accepted Dilke on the condition that he recant or explain 'his former crude opinions'.[190] Dilke's admission that his previous views were an expression of 'political infancy' failed to assuage her. After much negotiation, Dilke joined the Cabinet as President of the Board of Trade in December 1882. Ponsonby continued to press him for further clarification of his views, though a grovelling retraction would have been preferred. The Queen, as he put it, wanted to know 'how can a Minister in a Monarchy . . . be a Republican?'.[191] Dilke replied through one of Gladstone's private secretaries, stating that his republicanism had 'never gone beyond an abstract declaration of an academic kind'. Moreover, he had never joined a republican association.[192]

Despite the flow of correspondence, Dilke's many utterances on the subject never constituted a 'cure' to the Palace. However effusive his recantation, it would have been unlikely to placate the Queen, who assumed that once a republican always a republican. Gladstone, however, was content to take Dilke's 'utterances as "recantation"', for he wanted the services of a talented man.[193] Palace officials, who made little distinction between theoretical and pure republicanism, continued to watch Dilke's pronouncements closely. They consoled themselves with the press coverage. The conservative papers, which had once reviled Dilke, now hailed his apostasy; while the radical press saw him 'rapidly descending to the very deepest depths of political degradation'.[194]

Whether Dilke, whom Gladstone saw as a future leader of the Liberal Party, languished in the political wilderness because of his republicanism is an open question; but it clearly caused him considerable frustration.[195] During the machinations over his appointment to the Cabinet, he told Chamberlain that he thought the Queen might well succeed in keeping him out of office.[196] She did not, but by hounding him she had left an indelible message, which was not lost on Dilke's colleagues. Given his difficulties, it was not surprising that so few leading politicians declared against the Crown. Another effect of her opposition to parliamentary republicanism was to discourage MPs from forging links with anti-monarchists beyond conventional politics, which was a pre-condition of deposing the sovereign by constitutional means. Tellingly, even radicals like Mundella and Fawcett decried Dilke's escapade among the working men of Newcastle.

Joseph Chamberlain was another radical in the Queen's bad books. Though he had made abrasive remarks on the Crown and its costs in 1871, his republicanism had been opportunistic, lightly worn and easily shed. Though hostile to royal privilege, he did not consider the monarchy an impediment to reform. He had higher things to think about, not least his own political ambitions. Like any loyalist worthy, he toasted the Queen's health at public dinners. In 1874, as Mayor of Birmingham, he had received the Prince and Princess of Wales to the city with great courtesy and aplomb.[197] The provincial demagogue, happy to have the royal seal of approval stamped on his municipal reforms, struck just the right note of deference. So much so, that over the next few years the Prince of Wales would assist in the process whereby Chamberlain raised his eyes 'from municipal drains to the imperial horizon'.[198]

But when Gladstone submitted Chamberlain's name as President of the Board of Trade in April 1880, the Queen recoiled, just as she did over Dilke. She wrote to the Prime Minister that she wished 'to feel *sure* that Mr Chamberlain has never spoken disrespectfully of the Throne or expressed openly Republican principles'.[199] Gladstone visited the Queen the following day, saying that Chamberlain, a man of refined feelings, had never criticized the royal family or expressed republican views. He was either ill informed or being economical with the truth. When she mentioned her fears that the government was 'becoming very radical', by which she meant spiralling downwards towards democracy, he assured her that radicals usually became moderate once in office.[200] He misjudged the turbulent Chamberlain, who was rather more than Granville's 'peppercorn' in the 'bread sauce' of Parliament.

The Queen followed Chamberlain's radical pronouncements with growing anxiety. She took particular exception to his speech in June 1883, on the occasion of the twenty-fifth anniversary of John Bright's election as MP for Birmingham. Chamberlain opened his address by comparing the coronation of the Tsar with the festivities for Bright. He commended the Birmingham celebrations, in which the 'representatives of royalty were absent and nobody missed them, for yours was essentially a demonstration of the people and by the people'.[201] The Queen noted the words and told Ponsonby that she was 'shaken & indignant'. That 'horrid Mr Chamberlain' – both he and Bright are 'in fact, Republicans'.[202] She wrote to Gladstone that she wanted steps taken 'to mark her displeasure'.[203]

The Queen's anxieties increased at the end of June when Chamberlain spoke to the Cobden Club, where he called for the widest possible franchise, the compulsory redistribution of landed estates at death and religious equality.[204] Gladstone was compelled to write to Chamberlain to remind him of the balanced constitution and 'the rights of the Crown, guaranteed by the Constitution, and not less sacred in the eyes of the people than are their own liberties'.[205] Chamberlain, who toasted the Queen before every address, replied that he had 'never consciously failed in respect to the Sovereign or the Royal Family' and, unconvincingly, tried to justify his Birmingham speech.[206] Gladstone, who thought Chamberlain had breached the conventions of ministerial public comment, wrote to the Queen that Chamberlain's explanation was about as much of a recantation as could be hoped for in the circumstances.[207] Meanwhile, the republican press mocked Chamberlain for his loyalist display and 'kissing hands'.[208]

The Queen took the greatest offence when Chamberlain peppered his speeches with calls for universal manhood suffrage and attacks on the rich, which she felt excited tensions between the classes. With a controversial new franchise bill in the pipeline, his remarks struck her as all the more incendiary. She took particular exception to his assault on the House of Lords. In keeping with the classical republicanism of George III, she told Gladstone that without a balance of power in the constitution 'the Monarchy would be untenable'.[209] The agitation over the Reform Bill polarized opinion and unsettled the Queen. But comparing the state of affairs in the summer of 1884 with that in 1831–2, she noted with relief: 'The feeling of irritation & of disloyalty to the Throne was great then; but there have been 2 Reform Bills since then.' As she saw it, her role was to conciliate and to warn 'against a general Radical & downward tendency'.[210] While offering to mediate, she continued to complain to Gladstone about Chamberlain. After one of his particularly violent speeches, she concluded: 'He ought *not* to *remain* in the *Cabinet*.'[211]

At the end of 1884, the third Reform Bill received the royal assent. It gave the vote to agricultural labourers and dramatically altered the structure of county politics. In a speech at Ipswich, which Palace officials recorded, Chamberlain declared that the Act 'constituted a transfer of political power unparalleled in the history of political reform. For good or for evil, democracy has established itself in the seat of authority'.[212] The Queen wrote to Earl Granville about Chamberlain's 'outrageous' speeches: 'It *ruins* the Government for it shows great weakness to permit one of its members to hold such democratic not to say Republican opinions.'[213] The third Reform Act, in fact, stopped short of universal manhood suffrage, much less universal suffrage; but after it, and the accompanying Redistribution Act of 1885, the political power of the aristocracy was doomed, the commitment to democracy unstoppable. The republic dreaded by the Crown was getting closer.

The third Reform Act left the impression that the people were gaining the upper hand in the nation's affairs, whether the head of state was hereditary or elective. Far from heralding an uncrowned republic, the widening franchise encouraged a growing sense that Britain had become a crowned one. In the debate on the grants to the children of the Prince of Wales in 1889, Sir Wilfrid Lawson, an advanced Liberal who had consistently called for royal retrenchment, declared: 'I am a Republican.' And he added, to the surprise of the Tories, that 'we are all Republicans. I consider this country is a Republic which chooses to have at its head a hereditary Monarch'.[214] The radical Henry Labouchere seconded Lawson's judgement: 'Although theoretically a Monarchy, this country is practically a Republic with a hereditary President at the head of it.'[215] Making amends earlier in the debate, Chamberlain ridiculed the Crown's detractors as 'Nihilists' and concluded that Britain's constitution was 'more democratic than exists in any Republic of Europe or the world'.[216]

Whether Chamberlain's remarks mollified the Queen is unknown, but the idea of a crowned republic would have alarmed her, especially when articulated by what she saw as dissembling radicals. For a start, it suggested that she had lost all political influence, which she found hard to contemplate and knew to be exaggerated. Moreover, the very word republic still made her quake. Like her forebears, she had taken on board the logic of the Atlantic revolutions and loyalist reaction, seemingly unaware that republicanism to most republicans had more to do with the expansion of rights than the form of government. When she said that democracy was republicanism in 'disguise', she was not contemplating an hereditary presidency. And so when radicals declared for universal suffrage, she saw it as a prelude to the Crown's abolition rather than a platform for its survival. It was the great irony of her reign that she hated most something which was working to the monarchy's advantage – the growth of democracy. But there was also a great irony in the making for those pure republicans who loved democracy and did not wish the Crown to survive it.

The notion that Britain was or was becoming a crowned republic, illustrated, yet again, the elasticity in republican thought. It represented a compromise which had decided advantages for the monarchy. It not only associated the Crown with democratic progress, but shifted criticism away from constitutional issues towards the relatively minor matter of the royal budget. Thirty-eight MPs, among them several Irishmen, voted against the motion to grant Princess Beatrice an annuity in 1885. There was also some bitterness in the lengthy debate over the grants to the children of the Prince of Wales four years later. But the dislike of paying for royalty fell short of calls for the abolition of the monarchy. Morley had denounced the hereditary principle before entering Parliament and opposed the grants to the royal offspring as an MP. But for all his former Jacobin sympathies, he defended Britain's constitutional monarchy as a 'visible symbol of historic continuity' that was wholly in keeping with a democracy.[217] (Edward VII conferred the Order of Merit on him in 1902.[218])

In the parliamentary debate in 1889, there was, it seems, no political capital to be made out of attacking the Crown directly. Most republican MPs accepted the monarchy as a constitutional fixture and contented themselves with protests about the expense of the royal children or the royal buckhounds. Even Bradlaugh conceded that the public had no desire 'to make any change whatever in any of our institutions', but consoled himself that 'they do resent these small burdens'.[219] Handel Cossham, the Liberal MP for East Bristol, opposed 'these petty-fogging demands for more money . . . upon an already heavily burdened people'. But in keeping with Lawson and Labouchere, he declared that he did not much care whether the country became a republic or not, for Britain could pass all the reforms it required with a constitutional monarchy.[220]

Arguably, the Queen could have further undermined the parliamentary republicans by slimming down the monarchy with a few well-chosen and well-advertised economies. Behind the scenes, Palace advisers did in fact consider some cuts in the Civil List in 1888, as a quid pro quo for grants to the children of the Prince of Wales. Ponsonby put various proposals to the Queen, which included the abolition of the royal buckhounds and a sacrifice of some of her income.[221] But Lord Salisbury, the Prime Minister, objected, perhaps, as Labouchere argued, because the proposals would reduce his power of patronage.[222] (The Civil List still paid for whips of the House of Commons![223]) The modest savings suggested by Ponsonby would probably not have been enough to satisfy the critics, but they would have cut some of the ground from under them.

Labouchere, who once suggested that Buckingham Palace be turned into a home for prostitutes, was among the most dogged advocates of royal economy. As a result, the Queen called him 'that horrid wicked Labouchere'.[224] Both in Parliament and in his paper, *Truth*, he censured the 'ridiculous appurtenances' of a constitutional monarchy and the 'fuss and feathers of a court' which created servility in the public. But his essential objection to the Crown, like so many radicals, was on financial grounds; and he claimed that by opposing royal grants he was a 'far stronger friend of the monarchy' than those who supported them.[225] As suggested by his remark that the Queen was an 'hereditary President', he was not a man for the barricades. When once asked why he was always carping about the royal family, he facetiously replied: 'If the love of royalty were not so firmly established in the middle-class English breast, I should not dream of attacking it, for the institution might topple over, and then what should I do? I should have all the trouble of finding something else to tilt against.'[226]

Labouchere nevertheless paid a price for tilting at the royal family, for the Queen objected to his ministerial ambitions in 1892, on the familiar grounds that someone who attacked the monarchy should not serve in the Cabinet.[227] Little did he know it, but Chamberlain, a former ally, advised the Queen that 'immorality' might be grounds for his exclusion.[228] Unlike in the case of Dilke, the Prime Minister did not see fit to come to his rescue. A disappointed man, Labouchere regretted that his own experience might prevent other MPs from censuring the royal family.[229] The remark would have pleased Her Majesty, but her little victory was arguably a hollow one, for as a member of the Cabinet he would have stopped his needling. Rejected, he took his little revenge. In *Truth* and in *The Times*, he questioned the Queen's right as a constitutional sovereign to impose a veto on the Prime Minister's power of appointment, stepped up his attack on royal grants and openly declared a preference for an uncrowned republic, though he did not expect to see it in his lifetime.[230]

Labouchere was prominent among those MPs who argued that the level of royal spending was unpopular in the country. At the time of the annuity to Prince Leopold in 1882, he had presented petitions signed by 14,000 working men to prove the point.[231] It is difficult to judge whether such protests reflected anti-monarchical opinion or simply irritation at an additional tax burden, but, outside Parliament, pure republicans sought to exploit the issue of royal expenditure as a way of opening up wider constitutional issues. In 1879, Standring had written a lively polemic, *Court Flunkeys, their Work and Wages*, in which he had enormous fun outlining the onerous responsibilities of the Keeper of the Swans, the Royal Oculist and the Master of the Tennis Court, which were among the sinecure posts that, in his view, were taken up by aristocratic boot-lickers in 'the first and the worst household in Great Britain'.[232]

Standring would slim down the monarchy to the point of disappear-ance. But he knew only too well that he had little hope of success, for pure republicans, as opposed to those who simply wanted royal economies, were becoming an endangered species in the late Victorian years. They lacked a coherent doctrine, a practical programme or much press support outside the splenetic pages of *Reynolds's Newspaper*. Apart from the issue of costs, they rarely found their views expressed in Parliament, as Bradlaugh's companion, Annie Besant, then going through her secularist phase, confirmed in her pamphlet *English Republicanism* (1878).[233] In 1885, only a single anti-monarchist candidate fought the general election, apart from Bradlaugh, and he came last in the poll in Hull.[234] The same year, Standring confessed that he did not know of 'a single Republican organisation in the United Kingdom'. The next year, he changed the name of his paper the *Republican* to the *Radical*, admitting that eleven years of producing a paper with the word republican in the title had not had any impact.[235]

Clearly, Standring's or Bradlaugh's conception of republicanism dif-fered from Lawson's or Labouchere's. The former two, puritan in their political outlook, found few real republicans about. The latter two, who were trimmers, found them in abundance. Thus the century-old trends continued. Anti-monarchists identified republicanism with a radical over-throw of the tripartite constitution. More moderate republicans saw a monarchical republic being created with the advance of representative government. The reputation of royalty was a variable, which encouraged a situational republicanism, in which individuals swayed with the prevail-ing wind between pure and theoretical positions. But even in the early 1870s, there were probably more trimmers than anti-monarchist puritans. Whatever their particular views, most prominent republicans accepted that Britain was already a republic of sorts.

If one looks for pure republicans towards the end of the century, one can find them. Though isolated and disorganized, they sneered at every royal birth and mocked every royal anniversary.[236] The Queen's jubilees aroused popular expressions of patriotism and public spirit, but they also excited protests, particularly over the money wasted on ceremonial pomp.[237] On the occasion of the Golden Jubilee in 1887, the Metropolitan

Radical Association issued a handbill: 'Royalty is the head and front of a foolish, wicked and costly system.'[238] A Jubilee version of 'God Save the Queen' from Australia, recycled in Britain, opened with 'Lord help our precious Queen/ Noble but rather mean'.[239] Likewise, the Diamond Jubilee in 1897 alienated many a class warrior or radical little Englander, who deplored the military pageantry and the ostentation. The *Labour Leader* celebrated with a mordant 'Jubilee Song':

> Withered slave of the molten steel,
> Lungless wreck of the grinder's wheel,
> Palsied drudge of the pois'nous mine,
> Paupered ghost of a manhood fine,
>   Come, lift your pewters with three times three,
>   And toast Victoria's Jubilee.[240]

The opponents of royal celebrations did little more than let off steam in the late Victorian years. But they were proof that anti-monarchism had a following, which, with greater provocation, might again erupt, as in the early 1870s. As ever, the enemies of the Crown were difficult to pigeon-hole, for they included disparate radicals, communists, socialists, atheists, little Englanders – even anti-Semites who called the Queen an avaricious Jew.[241] Among them was the socialist John Morrison David-son, a Scottish-educated barrister of the Middle Temple, who at the time of the Diamond Jubilee accused the Queen of 'jobbery' and 'robbery'.[242] Elsewhere, he pilloried the sovereign for her 'muddy German blood', and looked to universal suffrage and land reform to rid the country of oligarchic rule. There was, it seems, still some mileage in Old Corruption. 'Kings and aristocrats', jeered Davidson, 'have been tried at the bar of history and reason, and found guilty. They await the inevitable arrival of the executioner – the people.'[243] Strong stuff from a middle-class professional.

More often, anti-royalists were found down the social scale among the poor and inarticulate. Some of them were full of hate, like Daniel Chatterton, the atheist and communist pamphleteer, who had been associated with the *Republican* in the early 1870s. In the 1880s, he wrote an open letter to the Prince of Wales, in which he called for 'the entire gang of royal lurchers' to be 'swept off the face of the earth, like vermin, as you are'.[244] Chatterton was clearly a man of the *idée fixe*, who had 'drunk deep from the cup of human misery' – eight of his ten children had died. In one of the most violent, and obscure, pure republican tracts ever penned, *The Impeachment of the Queen, Cabinet, Parliament, & People*, he pointedly distanced himself from those erstwhile republicans Dilke and the 'blood sucking capitalistic Chamberlain'. What was needed, he railed, was a 'proletaire war' against priestcraft, the 'moneyocrassy' and the 'blood stained Vicious – Victoria'.[245]

After the death of Bradlaugh in 1891, perhaps the best-known republican was the Scottish miner James Keir Hardie, the founder of the Independent Labour Party. Hardie, who 'hated the Palace because he remembered the pit', was a corpse at every royal birth and a bride at every royal funeral.[246] In 1894, he denounced the snobbish press for giving so much attention to the birth of a son to the Duke and Duchess of York (the future King Edward VIII) when a colliery disaster had just taken place in Wales. With characteristic effrontery, he declared that 'the life of one Welsh miner is of greater commercial and moral value to the British nation, than the whole Royal Crowd put together'.[247] The *Standard* called Hardie's attack malicious 'clowning', adding that his 'atrabilious temper' would have vanished had he seen the work done by royalty in the East End.[248] But Hardie was unimpressed by the monarchy's social work, though he had nothing against members of the royal family giving away their wealth. As Palace officials noted, he once thought of presenting a petition to Parliament asking for the Duke of Edinburgh's annuity to be divided among the unemployed.[249]

On a more serious note, Hardie dismissed the idea of a crowned republic as a chimera, for democracy and monarchy were mutually exclusive. He took it for granted that his own brand of republicanism – uncrowned, fraternal and socialist – would shower the land with blessings. But his priority was not to bring down the monarchy, or to promote civic spirit among the working classes. It was to bring down capitalism. This gave his anti-monarchism a theoretical air. As he wrote in the *Labour Leader* in 1897: 'until the system of wealth production be changed it is not worth while exchanging a queen for a president. The robbery of the poor would go on equally under the one as the other. The King fraud will disappear when the exploiting of the people draws to a close'.[250]

Hardie recognized that the abolition of the monarchy might be meaningless without the collapse of capitalism, that 'we might get quit of the royal family without getting rid of our burdens'.[251] Taking up this point, one loyalist argued that one of the reasons for the decline of anti-monarchism was that the public realized that if the royal family disappeared in an age of capital, it would simply enlarge the power of pure wealth and lead to a Gadarene rush for social pre-eminence based on money, connection and intrigue.[252] Frederic Harrison had put a similar view in 1872: 'Without a real republican patriotism, the official disestablishment of monarchy would be no very mighty affair. It would not dethrone wealth, idleness, servility. Lothairs would mount the vacant throne, and scramble for the regalia.'[253] Such thoughts sapped enthusiasm for anti-royal agitation.

The elderly Queen, by now a mother-figure and imperial icon, ignored the vilification from the hinterland, even from Keir Hardie, who entered Parliament in 1892. In her last years, she could take some comfort that she had silenced, or outlived, most of her serious critics. As the Irish writer G. W. E. Russell said years later, it was one of 'the triumphs of her reign that she had lived through, and had lived down Republicanism'.[254] It was never likely that a constitutional monarch, useful to ministers and admired by society, would be seriously threatened. But the Queen, so unsympathetic to the democratic currents of her day, had not seen it that way. Though at times fatalistic about the future of the Crown, she had played a more active part in its defence than members of the public imagined, especially anti-monarchists, who underestimated the very institution they wished to discard.[255]

Over the years, the court and its allies had dashed any hope of a dynamic alliance developing between parliamentary and extra-parliamentary opposition to the throne. With the help of her ministers, who concealed her wayward interventions, the Queen had avoided clashes with Parliament and had discouraged the expression of republican principles in high political circles. With the help of her children, she had endeared the Crown to the wider culture through good works and imperial display. Few monarchs have been so attuned to conventional pieties, which the seclusion and monotony of her life made easier to sustain. Isolation in the Highlands or on the Isle of Wight was clearly not a strategy – many thought it misguided – but it did more good than harm to a widowed matriarch given to meddling. Distance made her a more difficult target and enhanced the monarch as symbol.

At Queen Victoria's death, the tributes were deafening, and sincere enough for Beatrice Webb to write to a friend: 'At last free of the funeral. It has been a true national "wake", a real debauch of sentiment and loyalty – a most impressive demonstration of the whole people in favour of the monarchical principle.'[256] Not quite 'the whole people', for there were dissenting voices, testimony that Her Majesty had failed to beguile the nation entire. *Justice*, the organ of the Marxist Social Democratic Federation, whose objects included the 'abolition of . . . all hereditary authorities', expressed unchivalrous disdain: 'Her late majesty was a very selfish and self-regarding old lady. From the date of her accession to the day of her demise she never took a single step towards improving the lot of the mass of "her" people . . . She preferred to be the idol of the profit-mongering class.'[257] And from the political wilds, a columnist on *Reynolds's Newspaper*, no advocate of a crowned republic, proclaimed: 'Long live the British Republic, Federal, Socialist and Democratic.'[258]

5

The Advent of Socialism and
the Crowned Republic

1901–1936

'Royalty is an anachronism: it is out of date. But so long as our
form of royalty keeps fairly close to the lines of a crowned
Republic any general demand for a Republic in these islands is
unlikely.'

> Robert Blatchford, socialist, 'Of Crowned and Uncrowned
> Republics' (1917)

'I am not concerned at the possible sacrifice of old traditional
ideas and customs regarding Royalty. Some of these have already
been sacrificed. Sovereigns must keep pace with the times.'

> Lord Stamfordham, the King's Private Secretary (1918)

Kings may be made by 'universal hallucination', as George Bernard Shaw
once quipped, but Edward VII's renown at the beginning of his reign
cannot be explained simply by reference to illusion. He seamlessly
inherited a Crown that was identified with material and social progress
and served as the unifying symbol of Empire. In contrast with Queen
Victoria's court, his own was colourful and cosmopolitan, marked by
assured patriotism, lavish hospitality and elaborate ritual. Supercilious
ridicule washed over him – Keir Hardie called him 'a fat, bald-headed
nonentity' – but he could not take his popularity for granted.[1] The
republican models of America and France had lost their charm for
reformers and a specifically anti-monarchical challenge was not in view.[2]
But beneath the surface calm there were surging political and social
currents which threatened to plunge the monarchy into the maelstrom of
materialistic democracy.

It was perhaps just as well that King Edward was less inclined to political interference than his mother. Inexperienced and easily distracted, he gave little ammunition to his enemies, who assumed, like Hardie, that he was a 'nonentity'. He was not, but he disliked administration, a point noted by his ministers, who spared him unnecessary paperwork. As Margot Asquith said of him: 'Our King devotes what time he does not spend upon sport and pleasure ungrudgingly to duty. He subscribes to his cripples, rewards his sailors, reviews his soldiers, and opens bridges, bazaars, hospitals and railway tunnels with enviable sweetness.'[3] Here was a king who was easy to underestimate, if not disregard. Beatrice Webb, who had sat next to him at a school prize-giving ceremony in 1897, dismissed him as a 'well-oiled automaton' who was 'unutterably commonplace'.[4]

Arguably a 'well-oiled automaton', with easy manners and a dignified bearing, was just the ticket when a British monarch no longer ruled, made law or served in war, whose influence turned more on his position as the head of society than as a political leader. Unlike the Tsar or the Kaiser, Edward VII's executive powers were 'a vestigial remnant'. He retained certain prerogatives, which he wished to protect. But as Philip Magnus observed, drawing on Bagehot, the King would have had to sign a bill for his own execution had the government put one before him. Though he was a constitutional rubber stamp, the prestige of his high office gave him a degree of political influence, which he used most forcefully in naval reform and foreign affairs.[5] As a sovereign who did not rule, he was insulated from political discontents. He could hardly be blamed for the failure of his ministers; but it also meant that ministers need not take him very seriously.

'Pure' republicans remained isolated and quiescent early in the century partly because King Edward made so little political noise. There were rumblings of discontent among those who equated the Crown with treachery to working-class interests.[6] In the Civil List settlement of May 1901, the King received a generous £470,000, with little cost to himself apart from the loss of the royal buckhounds. In the debate, Henry Labouchere made his familiar criticisms, and Irish MPs mocked the monarchical system as a violation of Irish liberty. Hardie reaffirmed his anti-royalism with his customary truculence. He 'frankly admitted' that the working classes widely supported the monarchy, but it was 'because they did not understand Royalty or what it meant to them'. An object of a working-class party was to set this omission right and 'to purify the system of government' by removing the reigning royal nonsense.[7]

The King's coronation in the summer of 1902 evoked a predictable mix of satire and fury in the socialist press. H. M. Hyndman's *Justice* dismissed the ceremony as 'so much trouble . . . for so poor a reward' and thought the day would be better marked by a celebration of James II's flight from England.[8] Still, the paper recognized 'that the overwhelming majority of common Englishmen' had no desire to depose the sovereign 'only to set up King Capital, with his horde of greedy sycophants, as President'.[9] For his part, Hardie's *Labour Leader* attacked the ceremony as 'an orgy for the display of wealth and senseless spending' and hoped for a disaster on the day.[10] A stanza from its coronation 'Ode' nicely captures the paper's editorial flavour:

> So let us sing God save the King
> Before his coronation,
> And his nationhood imbrued in blood,
> And fraud and usurpation.[11]

The admission by both Hardie and Hyndman that the working classes supported the monarchy was confirmation of the King's popularity, a popularity which rested on firmer foundations than they imagined. Edward VII had an agenda, little understood by his critics. The monarchy was not only the ritual centre of politics and state; it was, as it was said at the death of Queen Victoria, connected with *'our civic duty'*.[12] Members of the royal family now held well over a thousand patronages, many of them of institutions set up to ameliorate the condition of the poor. The shift in royal endeavour was by now momentous, and led the royal family into the most remote reaches of the country, providing not only a valuable role and favourable publicity, but contributing greatly to the Crown's adjustment to democracy. The Labour left mocked royal philanthropy as an insult to the poor.[13] Yet royal obligation and working-class aspiration merged in countless schemes of public usefulness.

So many applicants, from orphanages to potato growers, requested to use the title 'Royal' or 'King Edward' that in 1903 the Home Secretary became alarmed about the standards of individual societies.[14] The King alone contributed time or money to about 500 institutions each year, which gave a national prominence to voluntary work while marking its local significance.[15] In practice, royal societies carried forward traditions of civic republicanism, which encouraged loyalty to the throne among artisans, skilled workers and the middle classes. Increasingly, they cast their nets to reach the proletariat, who were the primary targets of socialist propaganda. When Edward VII visited a humble dwelling, he wanted to see a picture of himself on the wall, not one of Keir Hardie or Karl Marx. (See Plate 15.)

By the early twentieth century, institutions in need of money were well advised to look to plutocrats rather than to aristocrats, and King Edward was a crucial link, for he was both the impresario of the plutocracy and the nation's premier voluntarist. Aspiring business magnates, if not politicians, took him seriously; and in an unwritten social contract, established when he was Prince of Wales, the King offered good shooting, respectability and honours to the moneyed élite in exchange for support for his favoured causes. With the help of advisers, most notably Sir Henry Burdett, he brought the merchant princes of the City, often German financiers, into fruitful partnership with the voluntary sector. Such a partnership not only enlivened many a charity but offered an alternative to socialism and provided a humanitarian justification for Empire. Such thinking was, for example, behind the Prince of Wales's Hospital Fund for London (later the King's Fund), the great London charity established for the sick poor in Jubilee year 1897.[16]

Voluntary institutions, with their marked local character, felt threatened by the trend towards state intervention; and they looked to the Crown as a counterweight to what many people saw as the 'despotism' of advancing central government.[17] (This was consistent with republican traditions of anti-despotism and local independence.) The ideological battle taking place between voluntarists and the votaries of mass politics in the Edwardian years may be seen as part of the wider debate between proponents of competing political visions of Britain that were often associated with classes or parties.[18] The Crown gave funds, publicity and a more prominent voice to the charitable establishment in the contested fields of health and welfare. But when plutocrats picked up the bills, it alienated those socialist critics of philanthropy who saw capitalism as the cause of distress, not its cure.

For his part, Edward VII did not see far into the future or much beneath the surface, but he viewed the prospect of state intervention with unease. In his view, social progress was most effectively achieved through traditional voluntary means. The notion that it could be delivered by an élite of civil servants was abhorrent to him, just as a regulatory state was abhorrent to a financier. As ministers had taken away the power of the Crown, it would have been masochistic on his part to have wanted to see more authority vested in central government. In the charitable sector, the monarchy was uniquely placed to influence policy and shape administration. Indeed, it could even influence government policy through the lobbying of royal societies, which were institutional expressions of civic democracy. Such agencies comforted royalty, for they radiated age-old Christian values operating within a framework of interdependent classes.

While the King disliked the growth of government responsibility for health and welfare, he recognized that many working people looked favourably on school meals, state pensions and other social benefits, which the Liberal Government brought into existence during his reign. But having built up its welfare role over the centuries, the Crown did not wish to give further encouragement to state intervention. Should government absorb charity's health and welfare functions, it would eliminate the most substantive role remaining to the monarchy. The King's old-Etonian adviser, Lord Esher, who gave shape to the Crown's policies and outlook, declared:

We have lived splendidly and comfortably under an oligarchy and under a voluntary system . . . No man in his senses could desire, in order to square with some theory of government or live up to some political dogma, to change a system so rooted in our habits and so beneficial to the nation in its results . . . No one, in fact, but a dry theorist, would dream of substituting compulsion for voluntary effort so long as the latter could be relied upon to produce average results, whether in education, sanitation, or military service.[19]

Esher, an expert on military affairs and formerly a favourite of Queen Victoria, had a passion for intrigue and back-room politics. A monarchist and a voluntarist to his fingertips, he sought to contain those currents of reform seemingly running against the interests of the Crown. The issue, as he saw it, was 'whether "voluntarism" is compatible with "democracy"' in a modern state.[20] 'The great problem of the future for England and the English race', he wrote, 'lies in the answer to the question whether or no the artisans, the labouring classes, will develop an altruistic ideal.'[21]

It was not surprising, therefore, that the King and his advisers wished to encourage altruism among the poor and to extract working-class contributions to royal charities; they were a demonstration of self-help and class co-operation, ammunition in the propaganda war against social-ism.[22] A working class made healthier and more secure through charitable provision would also be more disposed to imperialism. The imperial ideal went hand in hand with the voluntary ideal. Both entrenched royalty in public affairs.

Challenges to voluntarism and the Empire raised some awkward ques-tions for the King's advisers, for they were seen as challenges to royal authority. Was the monarchy itself compatible with an increasingly powerful executive given to ever-greater intervention and centralization? Was it compatible with majority rule in an industrial economy under strain? Although English democracy, as the jurist Albert Dicey noted, had inherited many of the traditions of aristocratic government, the future of the monarchy was not guaranteed. Historically, the Crown, like the Empire, had shown a capacity to promote unity across class and party boundaries, but could it survive the advent of socialism which set class against class? Few people outside court circles thought in such stark terms. But then they had not lost so much to government already nor had they so much left to lose.

To royalists, the monarchy was the nation's institutional and consti-tutional anchor; and in the reign of King Edward, Palace officials noted disturbing signs of a drift. The political milieu was more volatile than in the 1870s, when republicanism had last erupted. On virtually every front, from social policy to the House of Lords, from industrial issues to female suffrage, the trend of politics gave Buckingham Palace cause for concern. Many trade unionists, distressed by a decline in real wages and politicized by radicals and syndicalists, were rejecting the conventions of deference and respectability. With the aristocracy in decline and labour on the march, was an outbreak of anti-monarchical fervour inevitable? The Crown was popular and seemingly secure, but to advisers like the ubiqui-tous Esher, who had an acute sense of historical vicissitude, the future looked fraught with uncertainty.

The Liberal landslide in the election of 1906 put Buckingham Palace on alert. From the perspective of the Crown, the Liberal Party had been out of power for so long that it had become unaccustomed to dealing with the monarchy. The Tory King and his officials looked in vain for members of the government with strong royalist sympathies, and they soon complained of a failure on the part of ministers to keep the Palace informed of government intentions.[23] The King's Private Secretary, Sir Francis Knollys, once told Esher that Campbell-Bannerman's reports of Cabinet meetings were so perfunctory that they were 'really making an absolute fool of the King'.[24] Palace officials were well aware of the King's failings, not least his reputation for indiscretion, but they believed that if the Cabinet took irrevocable decisions without informing him it weakened the monarchy. Esher wrote to Knollys that the Prime Minister had the 'indolence of senility' upon him.[25]

The royal family, as Margot Asquith said, was apt to confuse Liberals with Socialists.[26] But the election of Labour candidates helped to clarify the differences. At the time of the King's accession in 1901, the infant Labour Party was a modest pressure group. A decade later, it had forty-two MPs and a rapidly expanding party membership composed of about one and a half million trade unionists.[27] In an era of industrial strife and union militancy, the royal family's reaction to the political progress of Labour was predictable. The Prince of Wales, later George V, commented on the rise in Labour fortunes in 1906 in a letter to the King: 'I see that a great number of Labour members have been returned which is rather a dangerous sign, but I hope they are not all socialists.'[28] He was mistaken to think that all socialists were enemies of the Crown, but the belief was deeply ingrained in Palace thinking. The royal family and socialists shadow boxed with mutual incomprehension.

Despite royal assumptions, the Labour Party was not a 'socialist' party, at least not until 1918. Much less was it an anti-monarchical one, though it had a few revolutionaries in its ranks. With their background in nonconformity, socialists did not share the militant rationalism of middle-class radicalism, which took monarchy to be illogical.[29] More importantly, Labour leaders had a streak of English patriotism in their blood, and were content to operate within the conventions of electoral politics as a way of proving their fitness to govern.[30] Since there were few votes in attacking royalty, pure republicanism remained on the Labour Party shelf. To many in the Labour movement, the difference between a capitalist Britain with a king and a capitalist Britain with a president was irrelevant, a point that even Keir Hardie accepted. As the future Labour

Prime Minister Ramsay MacDonald wrote early in the century: 'the political reformer may pass it [the monarchy] by without notice, even though on theoretical grounds he may be a republican'.[31]

Needless to say, the court did not approve of such views. Palace officials collected newspaper articles and monitored speeches touching on the Crown's interest. As in the days of Queen Victoria, they paid particular attention to the views of MPs. Highly sensitive to language, the slightest whiff of republicanism could trigger a reaction from them. Hardie's track record of gratuitous insult was particularly noxious to members of the royal family. Not surprisingly, his name was dropped from the guest list of royal engagements, on the official grounds that he had not turned up in the past. Yet when he saw his name omitted from the King's garden party in 1908, he complained.[32] As Hardie's biographers have not found a morning coat to go with his famous cloth cap, he may have only wanted the opportunity to rebuff future royal engagements. In any case, he launched a series of articles in the *Labour Leader* the following year, condemning the Tsar's official visit to Britain.[33]

Palace officials studied the pronouncements of Liberal ministers as closely as those of the maverick Hardie. When John Burns, a former London labour leader and President of the Local Government Board, made some 'extreme comments' about the House of Lords in 1906, the King complained directly to the newly elected Liberal Prime Minister, Sir Henry Campbell-Bannerman.[34] And when David Lloyd George used the King's name in a speech attacking the House of Lords, Campbell-Bannerman was asked to discipline his colleague for 'breaches of good taste and propriety'. Lloyd George apologized.[35] When the Prime Minister himself used the phrase 'to give effect to the will of the people' in a speech, the King's Private Secretary told him accusingly that such expressions savoured 'more of a republican than a monarchical form of government'.[36]

Nothing in the reign of King Edward savoured more of republicanism than the attack on that pillar of hereditary power, the House of Lords. Its abolition, after all, had been a central plank of republicanism for generations. The last time it had been abolished, in 1649, it had been done by a regicide government, an historic fact that stuck in the royal gullet. In the reign of Edward VII, the institution had become transparently partisan, the willing instrument of Conservatives, now out of government, who wished to block Liberal legislation. The King accepted that some modest reform of the Lords might be justified, but the determination of Asquith's government to reduce its legislative power drastically was anathema to him. As Knollys explained, the King regarded 'the policy of the Government as tantamount to the destruction' of aristocratic power.[37] He might have added that the King regarded the abolition of one hereditary element in the tripartite constitution as a danger to the surviving element.

King Edward readily assumed that the monarchy's fate was bound up with that of the House of Lords. Like Queen Victoria, he lacked the imagination to see that a reduction of aristocratic power might be in the Crown's interest. Still clinging to the vestiges of political influence himself, he failed to appreciate that the monarchy might be made *more* secure, not less, by shedding associations with oligarchy and the partisan politics represented by the Upper House. He failed to do so because he was frightened by republicanism and because his inner social circle consisted largely of aristocrats and plutocrats. Moreover, he retained a view of the constitution that harked back to classical republicanism. It took some getting used to for a British monarch to see power so concentrated in the ministry, and one based on an ever-widening electorate. The idea of a crowned republic, which was gaining currency both among monarchists and theoretical republicans, did not find favour with the King, and not only because of that hated word republic.[38]

King Edward, perplexed by the decline in traditional values, did not live to see the political emasculation of his Conservative friends in the House of Lords. It fell to his son, George V, to give his assent to the Parliament Act of 1911, which reduced the power of the Upper House to legislative amendment and delay. Many contemporaries assumed that the Act would lead to the decline of royal prestige, perhaps even to the collapse of the monarchy. Few, if any, thought that a reduction in the powers of the aristocracy might strengthen the monarchy. But with hindsight, the Act may be seen as another instalment in the incremental rise of democratic republicanism, which brought the crowned republic into sharper focus. To King George, the reform of the Lords was a telling reminder of the delicacy of his constitutional position. Given the drift of legislation and social trends, the new King could be forgiven for thinking his friends were on the run while those he perceived to be his enemies were gaining ground.

*

The sober and dutiful King George, like his forebears, did not make distinctions between pure republicans, for whom the monarchy was a live issue, and theoretical republicans, including many socialists, for whom it was not. With the proletariat on the march, the aristocracy in retreat and troubles in Ireland, he was convinced that the Crown was less secure than it had been in the reign of his grandmother. There were signs of disaffection before his coronation, which attracted the customary insults from the left-wing press.[39] In Parliament, the republican baton had passed from radicals to socialists. In the debate on the Civil List in July 1910, Keir Hardie decried the proposal to provide for the royal offspring an 'income to enable them to live a life of luxury, ease, and idleness', while George Barnes, Labour MP for Glasgow, objected to 'the ever open abyss – the Privy Purse' and the 'nest of parasites' still sheltered by the throne.[40] More worrying to the King were the strikes in the Rhondda and Aberdare valleys and a battle in the East End between anarchists and Scots Guards.

Disputes and strikes punctuated the early years of George V's reign. The King and the ultra-Tory Queen Mary saw them as a presage of a socialist menace to come. Horrified by the disturbances, the Queen blamed the Liberal Government: 'I do think the unrest is due to their extraordinary tactics in encouraging Socialism all these years & in pandering to the Labour Party.'[41] The wily Lord Esher, still a powerful presence behind the throne, wrote to the Queen in 1912: 'The darkest point . . . on the horizon is the growing antagonism between Labour and Capital . . . No outlook has been more gloomy since 1848.'[42] Threats to royal authority, real and imagined, galvanized the King. He did not assume, as Queen Victoria had done in the 1870s, that the nation was 'thoroughly loyal'. He expressed a particular contempt for Keir Hardie, whom he privately mocked as 'that beast'.[43] This was perhaps not surprising since the socialist described the King as 'a street corner loafer' and 'destitute of even ordinary ability'.[44]

The reign of George V did not see a sudden upsurge of specifically republican clubs, as happened in the early 1870s, nor attacks on the Crown by politicians of the stature of Dilke. But to the King, the Labour Party, especially its militant wing, appeared to be republicanism under another label. With anti-royalism latent in socialist ideology and labour militancy on the rise, royal disquiet grew. In a political no man's land,

George V felt obliged to consider a more coherent strategy of self-defence than Palace precedent provided. The strategy that emerged would have more to do with the monarch's influence as head of society, its 'efficient' part, than with the monarch's 'dignified' role as head of state. The King could count on men of property, and clerics, as allies, for they too felt threatened by socialism. He could also count on the voluntary sector and the higher echelons of the armed forces, where devotion to the throne was well entrenched.

Given the delicacy of the King's constitutional role and the Labour Party's growing popularity, it seemed sensible, as a friend of the royal family put it, to try to bring the people and the throne into line.[45] Before the accession, the King and Queen had extended their charitable activities in working-class neighbourhoods. On the advice of Esher, who provided details of deprivation in Scotland, they now stepped up their appearances in the mining and industrial regions with a series of goodwill visits.[46] In June 1912, they penetrated the colliery districts of Glamorgan and the Merthyr Valley, what Queen Mary called the 'the heart of Keir Hardie's constituency'.[47] (The Labour leader had described the trip as a 'ruse' to 'whitewash' the mine owners.[48]) At the end of the tour, Queen Mary wrote to her Aunt Augusta in Strelitz: 'We are assured on all sides that our visit wld do more to bring peace and goodwill into the district than anything else & that we had done the best days work in all our lives.' Keir Hardie, she added, 'will not have liked it'.[49]

The following month the royal couple toured industrial Yorkshire, where they were seen by three million people.[50] Drawing on the philanthropic training imbibed from her mother, Queen Mary mixed easily with the cottage wives. 'We had a most wonderful reception in Yorkshire in the most radical parts,' she wrote to her aunt.[51] Characteristically, the King spoke to groups of miners and factory workers of his interest in their welfare and the need for industrial peace and social cohesion. The last thing he wanted to see was his beloved hierarchical society disintegrating into an embattled nation of 'them' and 'us'. He went down a pit and shook hands with a crippled miner, to whom he had given a pair of artificial limbs some years earlier.[52] In return for such services, which he took to be his duty, he could have assumed that the beneficiaries would reject the slogans of socialist ideologues and accept the traditional order of things.

Welfare visits to the Labour heartlands were a fitting preparation for the cataclysm to come. The outbreak of war did nothing to allay George V's worries about the industrial climate and the deteriorating condition of the poor.[53] The King did not raise 'his baton against a background of fleets and armies', but he and the Queen put on a bravura performance in overseeing charities and visiting hospitals.[54] They instituted food rationing in the royal household and 'took the pledge', acts widely reported in the press.[55] The King toured mines, munitions factories and food centres. On occasion, the Cabinet encouraged him to enter the industrial areas because of fear of disorder.[56] In his *War Memoirs*, Lloyd George paid generous tribute to the King's contributions to tempering discontent: 'In estimating the value of the different factors which conduced to the maintenance of our home front in 1917, a very high place must be given to the affection inspired by the King and the unremitting diligence with which he set himself in those dark days to discharge the function of his high office.'[57]

The course of the war and the government's conduct of it pushed the maintenance of the home front to the top of the King's agenda. The year 1917 was particularly fraught, arguably as perilous in the country's history as 1940.[58] At sea, the unrestricted U-boat campaign had introduced a deadly new form of warfare. In France, the great battles of attrition drained resources and led to war weariness and disillusionment. At home, Labour was growing increasingly restless. The number of working days lost to strikes in 1917 was well up on the previous year, with consequent social dislocation.[59] In the deteriorating economic and social climate, the left-wing press, including the *Daily Herald*, *Justice* and *Forward*, began to see the capitalist social order, and with it the monarchy, as increasingly vulnerable.

No single event personified 'those dark days' in the King's mind more than the Russian Revolution. After 1917, he was always looking over his shoulder for Bolsheviks, whom, by definition, he took to be republicans. He came to believe that there were more Bolsheviks in Britain, or what he deemed to be Bolsheviks, than he could tolerate. The spectre of class war and social revolution on the Russian model preoccupied the King for years. At one time, he seemed to think that Bolshevism might even interrupt the 'cheery contentment' of New Zealand.[60] Ministers, friends and advisers fanned his worries, but they also offered a way round the perceived dangers.

Hereditary rulers are prone to complacency. Not so George V. Though unimaginative, ill-educated and short-tempered, he was better informed and more open to advice than is widely imagined. This was largely due to his sagacious Private Secretary, Sir Arthur Bigge, the son of a Northumberland vicar, who had served as Queen Victoria's last Private Secretary. Bigge, who was created Lord Stamfordham in 1911, was most anxious to keep the King abreast of social and political issues. This was never more true than towards the end of the First World War. Much of his information came from contacts and sources outside mainstream politics, which was valued all the more because Lloyd George was notably lax in providing intelligence to the King.[61] The material provides invaluable evidence of what the monarchy thought to be threats to its survival, and its response. While the royal family abhorred the anti-monarchical rhetoric which surfaced in the socialist camp, the maelstrom of war and politics gave the greatest cause for alarm.

George V may have been politically neutralized and socially isolated, but when, in 1917, someone suggested that the King was kept in ignorance, Stamfordham retorted:

I do not believe that there is any sovereign in the World to whom the truth is more fearlessly told by those in his immediate service, and who receives it with such good will – and even gratitude – as King George. There is no Socialistic newspaper, no libellous rag that is not read and marked and shown to the King if they contain any criticisms friendly or unfriendly of His Majesty and the Royal Family.[62]

In Stamfordham's opinion, the King could only profit from seeing the world unvarnished. As he wrote to Lloyd George towards the end of the war, 'it is only in these ways that Kings can learn what is being said and thought about in worlds with which they are out of touch'.[63] The precise role of George V in the formulation of Palace strategy is unclear, but it would seem that he was happy to be guided by Stamfordham, whose influence suggests just how important the office of Private Secretary had become to the monarchy. In later years, George V remarked: Stamfordham 'taught me how to be a King'.[64]

Nothing concentrates the mind of a dynastic monarch more than trouble in the family. After the storming of the Winter Palace and the abdication of the Tsar in March 1917, Stamfordham was not short of material, including a spate of abusive letters, to put before the King. It is well known that the proposal to offer British asylum to the Tsar, initiated by the Russian Provisional Government, caused George V considerable anxiety. His sympathies for his cousin Tsar Nicholas were at odds with his strong sense of the national interest, and the monarchy's interest, which he assumed to be synonymous with the nation's. His decision to discourage the proposal turned on advice from Stamfordham and a careful appraisal of the reaction of the British Labour movement to events in Russia. In the back of his mind may have been the Tsar's visit to Britain in 1909, which had excited frantic opposition in the Labour press.

On 31 March 1917, the republican Labour leader George Lansbury chaired a meeting at the Albert Hall to celebrate recent events in Russia. The King received an eyewitness report written by a friend of a Palace official. It paid particular attention to the audience's attitude to the monarchy and to 'the state of unrest prevailing in England'. As the gathering expressed no hostility to the Crown, the report contained a measure of reassurance.[65] Less reassuring was an article in *Justice* on 5 April by Hyndman, entitled 'The Need for a British Republic'. Stamfordham marked up the following sentence: 'If the King and Queen have invited their discrowned Russian cousins to come here ... they are misinterpreting entirely the feelings of us common Englishmen.'[66] The remark may have been influential, for Stamfordham pointed it out to the Prime Minister during an important meeting on 10 April, which resulted in the government's U-turn on the offer of British asylum.[67]

Whatever the rights or wrongs of the matter, George V's reluctance to assist his Russian relations did the British monarchy no harm and perhaps a little good. In the circumstances, prudence was advisable. In its impact on British reformers, the Russian Revolution was in some respects a repeat of the American and French Revolutions, for socialists now looked to Russia for inspiration just as nineteenth-century radicals had looked to America and France. As it turned out, the Tsar was to play the part of Louis XVI for his generation, and his assassination reinforced the tendency of the loyalist British public to associate republicanism with regicide. The Bolsheviks – the Jacobins of their generation – excited the British Left; but they frightened the propertied classes and increased their suspicion of socialism.

At the time that the King and his government were considering the future of the Tsar, several people with Palace connections were writing to Stamfordham offering friendly advice. One of the more influential of them was the Bishop of Chelmsford, John Watts-Ditchfield. The Bishop was not a particularly significant churchman, but he had made his reputation among the poor of Bethnal Green, a part of London cultivated by Queen Mary. The King had found him 'very interesting' when they first met at a dinner before the war and came to respect his views.[68] Stamfordham once described the Bishop to the Prime Minister as a man 'thoroughly in touch with the working classes, and as I imagined a strong Liberal in Politics, with even Socialistic tendencies'. And he added that His Majesty had 'profited by information and advice given by the Bishop on questions both social and political'.[69] Ironically, the King liked the 'Liberal' Bishop rather more than did the Liberal Prime Minister, who described him as an 'unconscious tool' of pacifists.[70]

The King and Stamfordham had, in fact, solicited the Bishop's views. His letters, along with a body of other material, have survived in a file in the Royal Archives titled 'Unrest in the Country'. The Bishop wrote to Stamfordham on 5 April 1917, touching on a range of sensitive subjects. On the immediate issue before the King, he retailed the news, which was in keeping with Hyndman's essay, that there was a suspicion among the public that the Tsar was 'backed by this country'. In general, he thought preventive measures were required, since 'anything might happen' at the end of the war. In an intriguing aside, he observed that 'the stability of the Throne would be strengthened if the Prince of Wales married an English lady', and added that 'she must be intelligent and above all full of sympathy'.[71]

The Bishop's main concern, however, was the rise of the Labour Party in a period of social unrest. In his view, it was a failing 'that Labour has not been sufficiently recognised – I think that if His Majesty could *see* the Labour Leaders more the benefit would be enormous'. He suggested inviting them in for talks about their work, and, noting a trip to Russia planned by two Labour MPs, Will Thorne and James O'Grady, he advised the King to 'spike their guns' by seeing them before departure and again upon their return. 'The more the King can be brought into direct touch with these men the better.'[72] Three weeks later, the Bishop visited Windsor where he proposed that the King might address the nation on issues such as health and housing. He should single out munitions workers and women for praise, and end with an appeal for the 'unity of classes'.[73] The government vetoed the proposal as inconsistent with the constitution.

The very day that the Bishop wrote to Stamfordham, Colonel J. Unsworth, a Salvation Army worker from Essex, who had met the King on a visit with General Booth in 1914, sent a similar letter to the Private Secretary. It reinforced the Bishop's fears about the end of the war and demobilization, and the need to involve the King more actively in public life: 'The coming into the war of the United States joined with the change in Russia may give democracy a triumph which in the general reconstruction of society may have effects which the bravest of us may almost dread to contemplate.' Unsworth also noted worrying signs of republicanism in Britain since the Russian Revolution, particularly among the middle classes, and cited a friend, who had overheard a man shouting 'to hell with the King. Down with all royalties'.[74] In his reply, Stamfordham accepted the need to consider the level of the King's public work, as long as it could not be construed to exceed 'the limits of the Royal Prerogative', and lamented that 'the ordinary man in the street has no idea of the amount of work His Majesty does'.[75]

The King's visibility and the issue of his relations with Labour were much in the air in Palace circles in early 1917. In a letter dated 10 April, a former Prime Minister, Lord Rosebery, took up the Bishop of Chelmsford's suggestion that the King should meet the Labour delegates travelling to Russia. He agreed with the Bishop, but advised that it would be wise to do so only when they returned. In the event, Will Thorne did have an audience with the King upon his return from Russia and took great pleasure from it.[76] Rosebery's principal advice was that the King should be seen in public, especially in London. 'It would be a fatal moment when the people of the capital begin to regard their Sovereign as an invisible abstraction. I honestly regard this point as essential to the welfare of the Monarchy.'[77] A letter to Stamfordham from the Home Office, dated 9 April, gave point to Rosebery's advice. It referred to 'anarchical movements', and suggested 'that a considerable and widespread movement was being organized in Labour circles'.[78]

A man so sensitive to criticism and intolerant of dissenting opinion as the King must have been disheartened by the letters and newspaper cuttings in his in-tray. One can only imagine his reaction to Hyndman's piece in *Justice*, mentioned earlier, which called for 'the immediate recognition of a democratic . . . republic for Great Britain'. And what would he have made of the old socialist's comment, marked by a Palace official, that 'apathy is more fatal to Monarchy than enmity'? But Hyndman made two specific points, apart from his warning about offering asylum to the Tsar, that would have attracted the attention of Stamfordham and the King. First, he argued that returning servicemen would 'not be content with the degrading social conditions thought good enough for them three years ago'. Second, Hyndman intimated that the royal family was essentially German and too closely associated with the Kaiser's court.[79]

In the spring of 1917, the royal family's German background was becoming an issue. An article in the *Daily Herald*, for example, entitled 'Republicanism', reported that the 'Jingo Press', with 'its screams of "once a Hun, always a Hun"', had it in for the King.[80] In late April, H. G. Wells stirred things up in *The Times* with letters on republicanism. While he accepted that Britain was a 'Crowned Republic', he insinuated that there might exist such a thing as a 'trade union' of European monarchies. Moreover, he called for the formation of republican clubs, and added, rather disingenuously, that they 'need not conflict with one's free loyalty to the occupant of the Throne'.[81] Wells put his criticisms more directly in an article in the *Penny Pictorial* in May: 'The security of the British monarchy lies in such a courageous severance of its destinies from the inevitable collapse of the Teutonic dynastic system upon the continent of Europe.' And he opined: 'We do not want any German ex-monarchs here.'[82]

Reading such material, Stamfordham could only conclude that hatred of the Kaiser could turn into hostility to King George. But he took what amusement he could from his informants, and the newspaper articles that sometimes complained that he was too old-fashioned and out of touch to be an effective Private Secretary.[83] On one occasion, he received a telegram from the Maharaja of Jaipur, who had been incensed by the views of H. G. Wells. The Maharaja's defence of the King as 'the chosen representative of the Supreme Power' led the laconic Stamfordham to include a copy of the telegram in a letter to Austen Chamberlain, the Secretary of State for India. He observed that 'it is a pity we cannot publish such communications, but I am afraid the Maharaja's belief in the Divine Right would not be quite in harmony with the democratic sentiments of the present moment'.[84]

The press often contrasted Britain's constitutional monarchy with the Kaiser's arbitrary rule. But for a King used to obsequious adoration, any hint of opposition could be unsettling. Monarchs feel secure in proportion to the loyalty of their subjects, and when George V received reports of disaffection in the country it rankled. Towards the end of the war, the issue of the King's German connections became vexed. As Wells had written in his letter to *The Times* in April 1917: 'our spirit is warmly and entirely against the dynastic system that has so long divided, embittered, and wasted the spirit of mankind'.[85] When Wells suggested elsewhere that England had 'an alien and uninspiring Court', the King took umbrage and famously told a visitor: 'I may be uninspiring, but I'll be damned if I'm alien.' Harold Nicolson retailed the story of another occasion, in May 1917, when the King 'grew pale' on being told that people believed he must be pro-German since he had a German name.[86]

Stamfordham received letters from John St Loe Strachey, the editor of the *Spectator*, in late April and early May 1917, which raised the sensitive issue of the King's German connections. Strachey, a former High Sheriff of Surrey, who described himself as an 'old Whig', warned of 'a serious growth of republican feeling' among Derbyshire miners, which turned on their belief that the King was shielding his 'brother monarch', the German Emperor. It was a 'preposterous and ridiculous falsification', he added, but the men believed that 'until there is a Republic all the Kings will stand together'.[87] Stamfordham replied, with his customary equanimity, that 'every sort of charge is being conjured up against the King in regard to other Monarchies. These are the natural outcome of War and the Russian Revolution'. He appreciated the worries but felt inclined to ignore the 'irresponsible talk'.[88]

Strachey agreed that the best policy was 'to ignore all sorts of irresponsible talk about Republics'. But he had to say that the working classes, 'who have never been taught the realities of the Constitution, have got it into their heads that the King could protect the Hohenzollerns if he liked, and that he certainly would, because of the supposed Trades Union among Kings'.[89] He mentioned a letter from a correspondent about a collier who had become a republican on such grounds.[90] It was the sort of intelligence that made the King nervous about the 'visible' German titles borne by members of the royal family who lived in Britain, and eventually encouraged him to make inquiries about his Teutonic background. It was, in fact, the issue of finding British titles for the Tecks and the Battenbergs that triggered an independent search for a new family name for the King.[91]

After protracted discussions, in which Lancaster, York and Plantagenet were mentioned, the King settled on Stamfordham's suggestion of Windsor. Lord Rosebery, who had been involved in the discussions, wrote to Stamfordham in June 1917: 'Do you realize that you have christened a dynasty?'[92] The change of name, announced in the press in July, may have been historic, as Rosebery believed; but its effect on republicanism is difficult to judge. It would certainly not have converted pure republicans, but it probably weakened their campaign to enlist fresh recruits. The case against the Crown on the grounds of German blood, which had been a staple of anti-monarchism since the eighteenth century, may have looked promising, but it lost much of its force in an era when the royal family was seen as public-spirited and patriotic. The public never fully appreciated the strength of the King's anti-German sentiment. Louis Greig, a frequent guest at Sandringham, noted that members of the royal family 'do hate the huns' and were 'dying to bombard' German cities.[93]

In June 1917, over 1,100 labour, socialist and pacifist delegates held a conference at Leeds to mark the Russian Revolution. The King received a lengthy secret War Cabinet report, which provided details of delegates, resolutions and speeches. Philip Snowden, the future Labour Chancellor, endorsed the Russian peace programme. Ramsay MacDonald, who had some years before called the Tsar a 'common murderer', moved the resolution which congratulated the Soviet people on their revolutionary achievements. According to the report, he incited his audience to insurrection: 'Now the war is on, now is your chance.' The most important resolution carried by the conference was the proposal for the setting up of workers' and soldiers' councils, the equivalent of soviets. The War Cabinet's informant concluded that the conference 'intended to lead, if possible, to a revolution in this country', and he recommended that measures should be 'taken as early as possible to counteract the effect of these statements, and to stop the treasonable activities of the persons and societies responsible'.[94]

In the month of the meeting in Leeds, Robert Blatchford published an article in the *Clarion*, titled 'Of Crowned and Uncrowned Republics'. (He had picked up the phrase 'Crowned Republic' from H. G. Wells.) Blatchford had been invited by Wells to take up the republican cause but refused on the grounds that it left him 'cold . . . as cold as the cause of royalty'. As a theoretical republican, he could not work up the energy to oppose a monarchy, however anachronistic, which he believed to have lost its political authority. Though indifferent to Palace affairs, he nevertheless noticed that 'our King and Queen had been bustled and hustled all over the country on a great popularity tour'. He advised against such show, 'for nothing is so likely to irritate our public as the noisy advertisement of the royal family to which we have been treated during the present summer'.[95]

Blatchford put the case, which many other radicals and socialists had also accepted: 'Theoretically, there is nothing to be said for Royalty and there is much to be said for Republicanism. But in practice we do not find Republicanism an improvement upon limited monarchy.' The question was not 'why have a King?' but 'why have a President?'. For Blatchford, the object was to establish a social and economic democracy with a right to land, work and a minimum wage. 'Do we want to side-track all progress and reform for half a century while we fight to change the title of King into the title of President? I cannot see that it matters much what we call our ruler: so long as he does not rule.' What Stamfordham or the King made of such views, which were so out of keeping with their own interpretation of constitutional monarchy, can only be guessed at. But they could take some comfort from Blatchford's conclusion: 'It is a sheer waste of energy to whip up a revolt against a King who is no more a Kaiser than Old King Cole.'[96]

Republicanism may have been irrelevant to Blatchford, but from the King's perspective it was rather more topical. Before the end of the summer of 1917, several other items which touched on social unrest concentrated Palace minds. They included a memo of a meeting that Stamfordham had had with the Prime Minister on republicanism in the country and another memo titled 'Labour in Revolt'. According to Stamfordham, the Prime Minister disapproved of 'too much public talk about Republicanism and Revolution', for it tended to magnify what, in the Prime Minister's view, was 'an insignificant movement. What is wanted is careful watching and silent combating'.[97] The memo 'Labour in Revolt', drawn up by Professor E. V. Arnold of Bangor University, was less reassuring. It referred to 'thousands' of 'narrow-minded Marxist agitators' opposed to the war, who were spreading through South Wales, Clydeside, Manchester and Sheffield. They were generally peaceful and had 'no designs on King George', but they might erupt into violence at any moment.[98]

In a letter to Stamfordham in July, the Bishop of Chelmsford argued that the royal family's recent public engagements had strengthened the monarchy's position. But he worried about a possible 'political landslide after the war'. In his view, a future Labour ministry was now 'probable', and while a socialist administration might not raise the republican banner, it might have it thrust upon it; in which case it would be 'forced in theory to stand for it, and unfortunately large bodies of working men can never separate the theoretic from the practical'.[99] Unsworth too, in a letter of July, thought the position of the throne was now strengthening, in part because of the King's successful visit to France, which had helped to 'remove' the taint of 'German influence and power from the Court'. More generally, he praised the 'wise . . . and well carried out plans of the last few months', which were, in his view, 'slowly but surely' quelling the opposition to the Crown.[100]

By 1918, the policy of making the royal family more visible seemed to be paying off, at least this was the impression of the King's friends. In response to public demand, and anxious to contribute to the home front, the King and Queen had increased the number of their public appearances, particularly hospital visits. According to a Lady of the Bedchamber, the Countess of Airlie, the number of the Queen's engagements trebled during the war. 'Every day there were visits to hospitals – sometimes three or four in an afternoon.'[101] For his part, the King carried out 300 visits to hospitals in 1914–18.[102] George V must have found that decorating his subjects was less onerous than visiting hospitals, for during the war he bestowed 50,000 awards.[103]

In keeping with a suggestion of Lord Esher, the King had created the Order of the British Empire in 1917.[104] It was not accidental that it appeared at the very moment that the extension of the suffrage was under political discussion, nor that trade unionists, including some with syndicalist sympathies, were prominent among the first recipients of the honour.[105] The number of awards rose so rapidly over the next few years that traditionalists thought it debased the honours system.[106] Stamfordham said that he often heard of a recipient 'lost in wonder as to what he has done to merit the decoration bestowed'.[107] As a tool to instil deference and to dish republicanism it was a masterstroke. A. J. P Taylor later observed that 'its holders went over the top for the governing class, just as the officers had done for the generals'.[108]

Palace insiders generally welcomed such innovations. The Archbishop of Canterbury, Randall Davidson, wrote to Stamfordham: 'It would make a huge difference if more of the things which *are* done – giving decorations etc – were done in public. Even those who can't go to such would read about what had happened, and their "cousins and aunts" would go.'[109] He also praised the hospital visits, but he wanted more royal contact with 'genuine working folk' and 'small dinners' for those on whom the King 'would have to rely if trouble came'. Stamfordham noted that the Archbishop's views were similar to those of other of his correspondents, including Lord Rosebery, the Archbishop of York, and the King's Physician in Ordinary, Bertrand Dawson, who had mentioned to him 'how much good would be done if men distinguished in science, art, and literature were asked to Buckingham Palace'.[110] But given the King's aversion to intellectuals, this was perhaps going too far. He was not a man to confuse the intellectual aristocracy with the real thing.

Early in 1918, George V and his family were busy propping up the throne through a mixture of hard work and benevolence. But if the King's advisers were to be believed, the greatest dangers to the monarchy were still on the horizon. No one was more agitated by the prospect of an approaching crisis for the Crown than Lord Esher. He wrote to Stamfordham from France, bitterly attacking 'the Press Combine under Northcliffe', which he believed had usurped the authority of the King and Parliament. By tearing down the British Army leadership, the Northcliffe press was undermining the war effort and creating social division at home. 'Lloyd George', Esher added, 'seems . . . to be standing at an observation post, watching the effect of the artillery bombardment by the Press, ready to let loose the attacking columns at any moment.' He compared the situation of Britain with that of France in 1870, 'when an unlicensed Press destroyed one reputation after another, and left France in the throes of a deadly conflict with a foreign enemy, strangled by the Commune'.[111]

Other warnings were to follow from Esher. In April 1918, he complained to Stamfordham that potential 'centres of disaffection' were
increasing daily in number.[112] In July he wrote again: 'If the Throne, the
Church, the social order of our home life are to survive, there must be
no faltering, and no mean compromises with unwisdom and folly and
crime. If we can keep the flag flying, I believe the monarchy and our
curious form of government, aristocracy and democracy so closely interwoven can be preserved.' Much of the 'reconstruction of our peaceful
habits' was in the King's hands. But he must 'look more to the simple
rules by which his private life is guided, than to the political barometer
that Ministers and others are always thrusting into his hand'.[113] In
October, Esher's fears increased: 'unless tact and sympathy are pronounced features of the demobilization of the vast horde of men and
women now employed under government, Bolshevism is inevitable'.[114]

Stamfordham too worried about the monarchy's future in the autumn
of 1918. He agreed with Esher that demobilization was 'an important'
issue.[115] And he would have agreed with Lord Cromer, the King's Assistant Private Secretary, who took the view that the monarchy was less
stable in 1918 than in 1914.[116] Still, Stamfordham was not a man to be
panicked into hasty action. Even so, from time to time, there were items
that must have tested his sang-froid. An article by the lawyer D. A.
Wilson in the *Nation*, 'England's Easy Road to a Republic', described
how a simple Act of Parliament could transfer the duties of the King to
the Lord Chancellor, thereafter to be called President. Stamfordham had
marked it up, and it was perhaps some consolation that the editor of the
Nation added a note at the bottom of the piece: 'we think we prefer
George V to Lloyd George the First'.[117]

Stamfordham's contacts outside court circles were often helpful and
reassuring. One of the most interesting was Clifford Woodward, Canon
of Southwark, who had his finger on the working-class pulse of South
London.[118] In a letter to Stamfordham of 8 October 1918, he pointed out
that ordinary people were generally indifferent to the monarchy. 'This is
an increasingly practical and utilitarian age, and not unnaturally, men
are not inclined to pay much attention to people and institutions which
do not seem to touch their lives or affect their material welfare.' On the
other hand, antagonism to the Crown, where it existed, was 'theoretical
rather than practical and confined to the comparatively small minority

who devote themselves to active political or socialist propaganda'.[119]

Woodward felt that his diagnosis suggested both a 'possible danger' and a 'possible opportunity' for the monarchy. The danger was that the Crown, like the Church, would be seen as a privileged institution that stood in the way of reform. In an era of Marxist theory, high unemployment and social unrest, it was an easy target for doctrinaire agitators. 'Unless we can seize time by the forelock and adapt ourselves to the new social conditions at home', the monarchy and the church would become 'no more than interesting survivals of a bygone age'. On a more positive note, Woodward believed that the poor, despite their indifference to ancient institutions, still had a vague belief in 'the omnipotence of the Throne'; and he enclosed part of a letter from a friend of 'socialistic tendencies' to illustrate the point. On such grounds, Woodward believed the King might 'save the whole social situation in these coming years by forming . . . the bridge between the two great antagonistic elements in the State . . . It might be possible for His Majesty to . . . go down to history as George the Peacemaker, by establishing an entente between Labour and Capital'.[120]

In Woodward's view, suspicion of political authority was on the rise. This offered the King, who was seen as above politics, a unique opportunity to become a 'mediator of undoubted impartiality'. (Stamfordham underlined the phrase.) But old royal ideas would have to give way to democracy, he added, and this would require His Majesty to be 'far more accessible to the working classes than has ever been the custom'. He advised closer relations with Labour leaders and increased contact with shop stewards and trade unionists. If the King 'could thus form personal and firsthand opinions of the aims that these men are struggling for and the "wants and difficulties" of their lives . . . His Majesty would not only establish himself more firmly than any of his predecessors in the hearts of his people, but would do more than any living person has it in his power [to do] to save England and the Empire from the dangers which very obviously threaten us'.[121]

Stamfordham replied to Canon Woodward at length on 21 October. In the manner of letters from Palace officials, he restated the views presented by his correspondent. But he marshalled his own thoughts with care, and in so doing leaves us a most illuminating expression of Palace thinking on the role of the monarchy at the end of the First

World War. He noted the Canon's remarks that the working classes were largely indifferent to the Crown but retained a residual belief in its 'omnipotence'.

At the same time, the more intellectual politicians of even the extreme school must surely admit that the Crown is the one link that unites those nations – daily becoming more and more *free* nations – of the Empire into one federated whole. Were the King to disappear and be replaced by a President, our Dominions would inevitably break away from the Mother Country.

I conclude, however, from what you say, that the people, while inclined to discount the value of the Throne, still consider or realise that there is a latent and inert power of the Crown.

Then come the questions, do they wish that power to be exerted? Only, I imagine, if in their own judgment its use would be to their benefit.

Anything which they might consider as an interference on the part of the Crown would be resented by them, and in this case they would probably desire to see the power eliminated altogether.

Assuming the existence of a factor which may be usefully turned to account, we are faced with the problem, how can this be done? In some way the power of the Throne must, as your letter suggests, seem to touch the lives of the people, and you recommend that the King might bring about an entente between Labour and Capital, and that in him might be found 'a mediator of undoubted impartiality'.

But, I reply, could the King assume such a role? I am not concerned at the possible sacrifice of old traditional ideas and customs regarding Royalty. Some of these have already been sacrificed. Sovereigns must keep pace with the times.

There would seem to be no reason why the King should not both visit Hospitals and lay foundation stones, and also acting on your suggestion, meet Shop Stewards and Trade Union Secretaries, and form personal and first hand opinions of their grievances, aims and aspirations. I doubt that it would be possible or prudent to go further. A mediator – the agent intervening between parties – the arbitrator who decides between A. and B. – must, in his decision, leave either A. or B. dissatisfied – with whom? The Sovereign.

Thus you would bring the King down into the arena of strife, subject him to criticism, and as constitutionally the King can do no wrong, ministerial responsibility would be necessary to defend such decisions.

Limiting the King's action to personal association with the various representatives of labour, I believe that great scope would be found:

1. By listening with patient and sympathetic interest to the representatives of all parties.
2. By suggestions to A. and B. to meet B's grievances and vice versa, and preparing the way for meetings between the injured parties for amicable discussions.
3. By smoothing acrimonious feelings and discovering possible modus operandi, and communicating impressions and ideas to his ministers.

Curiously enough, since receiving your letter, I have read in a confidential official report of the spread in this country of Bolshevism and 'class consciousness'. To the latter point you yourself refer.

It is reported that there is a peculiar fascination in the term Bolshevism for extreme revolutionaries in this country.

Again, I hear that it is often said at I.L.P Meetings that the Prince of Wales will never reign. This is pushing to an ultimate conclusion the theory you quote that 'the Throne don't count'.

I am grateful for your views, and far from regarding them as 'visionary'! I have only ventured to offer some comments upon them.

In these days we see on all sides monarchical institutions threatened, if not destroyed, and it behoves all who have faith in the Throne to ensure that it does not come to be regarded in the eyes of the proletariat as merely an old-world relic, an institution grown impotent in its influence, and a possible obstruction to their ideals of social and political progress.[122]

Canon Woodward, who became Chaplain to the King in 1919, replied to Stamfordham within the week. He accepted the point about the King's delicate constitutional position, but hoped that he would still be able to enter more fully into personal relations with Labour leaders. The knowledge thus gained 'would inevitably permeate the upper ranks of society to the very great advantage of the community'. He ended with two intriguing proposals. First, the Prince of Wales might, when the war ended, devote himself to social problems. 'It would, I suppose, be far easier for him than for the King and it might lead to very big results. Why should he not live for a time in one of the great industrial centres in the same way that he did in Paris?' Second, Woodward proposed that the Prince marry 'the daughter of one of the great English families – especially if it were a family which had been prominent in the War'.[123] A royal marriage outside the aristocracy would never have occurred to Woodward, or to the King and Queen, who saw their family as a caste apart. But presumably, he thought a union with the daughter of a patriotic grandee would prove popular with the working classes, at least the loyal ones.

Three weeks later Woodward sent Stamfordham some intelligence from Southwark, where a meeting had been held to introduce the local Labour candidate. The working men in attendance 'booed in a thoroughly orthodox way any reference to Capitalists, the Northcliffe Press, etc.', but there was no expression of republicanism. Rather, they 'fully recognized that the Throne in England was entirely compatible with freedom and democracy', or as the candidate put it, 'broad based upon the people's will'. Admittedly, Woodward added, 'South London is not the midlands or the North; we are far tamer folk down here than up there, but still they were typical working men of the political class'. He then returned to his principal theme: 'If Royalty could do something that would capture the imagination to show how much it cared, i.e. by the Prince settling for a year or two in Sheffield, it would have a big influence on the future.' (Stamfordham underlined the words 'year or two in Sheffield'.)[124]

Over the days that Stamfordham and Canon Woodward corresponded, Lord Esher had grown increasingly alarmed. With a melodramatic disposition, his advice was becoming more extreme. A man of old-world certainties, he saw civilian hordes out of work, European monarchies in ruin, oligarchic values in retreat, Bolsheviks on the march and the busybody President Wilson making republicanism 'the Fashion'. He wrote to Stamfordham on 4 November calling for 'imagination and boldness', new unprecedented roles for the King and Queen and 'the abandonment of many old theories of Constitutional Kingship'. Risks must be taken, for 'we stand at the parting of the ways . . . The Monarchy and its cost will have to be justified in the future in the eyes of a war-worn and hungry proletariat, endowed with a huge preponderance of voting power'.[125]

The Bishop of Chelmsford spent part of Armistice Day writing to Stamfordham about his worries for the future. London did not reflect opinion in the North of England or Scotland, he observed. What was needed was political reconciliation and work for the unemployed. In present conditions, anarchy was contagious. 'The vast majority of the working classes are loyal and opposed to anarchy and disorder but their nerves are all on edge. The losses by death, the anxiety, the strain has told upon the masses' nerve, far more than the leaders imagine and they are in such a state that *anything might* happen. Therefore the utmost care must be taken.'[126]

The day after the Armistice, Esher wrote directly to the King. 'No sovereign of Your Majesty's house has had to bear so heavy a burden of anxiety and No Sovereign since Elizabeth has ever witnessed England subjected to so grave a peril.' He only hoped that 'the "leaders" of Democracy in this and other countries do not lose their balance in the midst of this orgy of thankfulness'. Democracy was not Esher's cup of tea, but it would have to be swallowed: 'As Your Majesty well knows, Ambition, Vanity, Tyranny, and a "Swelled Head" are not the characteristics of monarchs only, as it is the fashion of the moment to suppose, but are equally the privilege of Statesmen and Journalists and other leaders of that curious superstition which men called democracy.'[127] Clearly, Esher did not uncork the champagne when the Representation of the People Act enshrined the radical principle 'one man, one vote' in June 1918. Nor, presumably, did the King.[128]

On 14 November, two days after Esher wrote to the King, the Leader of the House of Commons announced the date of the general election. The Labour Party launched its election campaign at the Albert Hall the same evening. The speeches and the atmosphere would have confirmed Esher's worst fears. Bob Williams, the Secretary of the Transport Workers' Union, wanted 'to see the Red flag flying over Buckingham Palace', and demanded redress for the working class, if not by constitutional means then by 'other means'. William Gallacher, a communist firebrand from Glasgow, chimed in with a call for revolution and, if necessary, the use of 'a six inch howitzer gun'. Moderates were shouted down with cries of 'hands off Russia' and cheers for Lenin and Trotsky and, with some laughter, 'The Bloody Revolution'.[129] Clive Wigram, the King's Assistant Private Secretary, wrote to the Assistant Commissioner of the Metropolitan Police: 'there seems to have been some pretty hot stuff let loose at the Albert Hall, let's hope it was all gas!'.[130]

Such revolutionary outbursts helped to recapture the mood in the country that created a state of nervousness among the King's advisers at the end of the First World War. They were not alone in their concern, for many sensible, well-informed members of the governing class who watched events unfold after 1917 believed that class war might erupt at any moment in Britain, and they were anxious to see preventive action taken. This was clearly the view of George V. He may have had little to fear from extremists, but he was not content to sit in the Palace while his enemies sang 'The Red Flag' and toasted Lenin. Drawing on a tradition established at coronations and jubilees, he and the Queen drove through the poorer parts of London in an open carriage on five successive days during Armistice week.[131] As Stamfordham told Margot Asquith, 'the poorest of the poor had clung to their carriage and by special request of the King had not been interfered with by the police'.[132] George V confessed in his Diary that he was touched by the 'waves of cheering crowds' which greeted them.[133]

The royal progress through the East End in Armistice week was a revealing moment in the history of the modern British monarchy. Esher wrote to Stamfordham in late November praising the King's success and applauded what he described as 'the "democratization" of the monarchy', which had by now become Palace policy. He advised the King to shun luxury and waste during the Peace Congress – 'expensive hotels crammed with hangers on, will never do, *if* there is hardship here!'. Above all, the King must avoid 'any relapse into the old "display" . . . until the people begin to settle down, and until they see prosperity reviving. It is the modesty and simplicity of the King that wins hearts'. He ended the letter with a plea for the King to offer clemency to 'a man with much influence with the most *dangerous* sections of the Working Class. He must be let out sooner or later. It would be good policy if he thought that the King had a hand in his release'. The man in question was probably the Scottish communist John Maclean, a member of the British Socialist Party, an avowedly Marxist body which had set up the Leeds Conference in 1917.[134]

Stamfordham took heart from the response to the King's progress among the East End poor, but he recognized that eternal vigilance was the price of monarchy. Only a few days after Armistice week, he had spoken to a large employer of labour, who had confirmed the Bishop of Chelmsford's worries about 'dangerous elements' on the Clyde and in South Wales. He wrote to the Bishop on 25 November that no easy solution to unemployment was in sight, but at least there were signs of devotion to the Crown. On the monarchy's future role, he reminded the Bishop of their meeting at Windsor some two years before when 'you advocated the same line of policy as I have endeavoured to put forward'. He then laid out the policy in some detail:

We must ... endeavour to induce the thinking working classes, Socialists and others, to regard the Crown not as a mere figurehead and as an institution which, as they put it, 'don't count' [Canon Woodward's words], but as a living power for good, with receptive faculties welcoming information affecting the interests and social well-being of all classes, and ready not only to sympathize with those questions, but anxious to further their solutions ... If opportunities are seized, during His Majesty's visits to industrial centres, in conversations with the work-men to show his interest in such problems as employers and employed will have to solve, these men will recognize in the Crown those characteristics – may I say virtues – which I have ventured to enumerate above.[135]

A week after the Armistice, the House of Commons congratulated the King on the prospect of a victorious peace with an address. In seconding the motion, Asquith, who had been Prime Minister for the first two years of the war, paid tribute to George V in language that Stamfordham and the royal family would have appreciated: 'In the crash of thrones ... the Throne of this country stands unshaken, broad-based on the people's will. It has been reinforced to a degree which it is impossible to measure by the living example of our Sovereign and his gracious Consort, who have always felt and shown, by their life and by their conduct, that they are there not to be ministered unto, but to minister.' Monarchies were no longer held by Divine Right, political will or pedigree, Asquith concluded, but 'can only be held, by the highest form of public service, by understanding, by sympathy with the common lot, by devotion to the common weal'.[136]

On the face of it, the portents for the Crown looked less favourable than suggested by the congratulations to the King from the House of Commons. After all, had Germany won the war, the fate of the Kaiser and George V might have been reversed. Where in the post-war world could the monarchy look for the reassurance that Queen Victoria took for granted? Given the disappearance of the German, Russian and Austrian monarchies, a degree of paranoia would have been an understandable reaction in the Palace. George V also had to adjust to post-war scarcity and high unemployment, to a new mass electorate unsettled by war and to the possibility of a Labour government. Still, not all of these changes were as inauspicious as the monarchy imagined. The collapse of the European dynastic system ended the criticism about a trade union of kings. And for all Esher's misgivings about democracy, the Representation of the People Act of 1918 did not have adverse effects on the Crown, rather the reverse.

In the post-war years of pusillanimous politics and economic crisis, Chelmsford, Esher and Stamfordham were prudent to advise vigilance and to keep open their lines of communication. In April 1919, Chelmsford wrote to Stamfordham to say that things were looking up. 'The devotion of the King and Queen to duty is having a great influence on the political situation ... Men cannot challenge the Crown with violent language after a visit such as the Queen made to Bethnal Green. This is the right path to pursue.'[137] He wrote again in August, praising the King and Queen for their efforts. The 'Crisis' was over, and the throne strong, but he advised continued vigilance, for 'the least slip may land us in chaos'.[138]

The distinct possibility of a Labour government, now armed with an explicitly socialist constitution, made matters seem all the more perilous. Clause 4 of the constitution, which called for the 'common ownership of the means of production and the best obtainable system of popular administration and control of each industry or service', was deeply unpopular in Palace circles. Among other things, it threatened those local voluntary traditions so beloved of the Crown. The King hoped that socialists would become more responsible as their power increased and trade improved, but he had persistent doubts, which the intelligence he received often exacerbated. He continued to keep well informed of wage scales, labour conditions and industrial unrest both at home and abroad.[139]

The foundation of the British Communist Party in 1920 put Buckingham Palace on high alert. The King received information on communist activity from the Metropolitan Police, but an important source of intelligence came through the offices of the General Manager of the Great Eastern Railway, Sir Henry Thornton. Thornton was an affable American who knew the King and Queen because they travelled to Sandringham on Great Eastern trains.[140] In 1920 he supplied the Palace with information on unrest in the railways and the coal crisis.[141] Early the following year, he began to send confidential reports on the British Communist Party. These reports were the work of one of his employees, dubbed the 'Bolshevik railwayman', a former communist in the National Union of

Railwaymen, who had turned informant. (His name was kept secret for reasons of security.) Clive Wigram, who handled the files on the King's behalf, wrote to Thornton: 'greatly interested in the reports of your man'.[142]

In the following months, Thornton sent regular dispatches, and, on the advice of the King, kept Scotland Yard informed. (Did the King have better intelligence than the government on communist activities?) Thornton's agent provided detailed information on meetings, names and addresses, speeches, tactics, finances and divisions within the Labour movement. Sinn Fein, which used the Communist Party as its head-quarters in England, was of special interest, though its inner circles proved difficult to penetrate if only because of the agent's accent. In January 1921, he attended a meeting of revolutionaries in the International Socialist Club in the City Road, London, which included delegates from England, Russia, Scotland, Ireland, Japan, India, Italy and Spain. The Italians, he retailed, were the most keen on 'business' and recommended the immediate assassination of 'the present parliamentary leaders in Great Britain'.[143]

The British Communist Party had only 3,000 members in early 1921, and its prospects were comparable, in E. P. Thompson's words, to the prospects for 'winter wheat in Omsk'.[144] But the King, worried about the outbreak of a general strike, did not see it that way at the time. His sleep was not made any easier by reports of extremists touring the industrial districts, of foreign spies freely entering the country, of communist attempts to infiltrate the police, of Russian agents distributing funds from Soviet House or of George Lansbury's *Daily Herald* being used to stir up discontent. Reading the reports, the King was also aware of the remarks of the Scottish communist Mrs Margery Newbold, whose Marxist husband, soon to be elected a Communist MP for Motherwell, had taken part in the Leeds Conference in 1917. A frequent visitor to Russia, she had joined a deputation to meet Lenin. According to her report, Lenin told them 'that they could not bring off a revolution in Britain'.[145]

According to George V's intelligence, British communists adopted Lenin's view. Though unafraid of violence, they favoured a long propaganda campaign centred on unions and schools. Thornton's spy argued that the communists abused British traditions of free speech and assembly and recommended that 'a few deportations might provoke a more healthy atmosphere'.[146] Wigram agreed that 'the doctrine of liberty and freedom' was overdone in Britain and believed that most of those who turned up at revolutionary meetings were aliens.[147] Thornton, who would have deported any alien who slandered royalty, had no immediate fears for the nation, but argued that 'something has got to be done – something vigorous, something effective and something active – otherwise I am afraid we may lose the game by default'.[148]

Armed with his intelligence, George V instructed Stamfordham to write a series of trenchant letters to ministers in September 1921. These graphically illustrated the King's nervousness about communist activity among the jobless, whose numbers now exceeded two million. Stamfordham informed Lloyd George of the King's anxiety about unemployment and his fear of discontent, fomented by agitators, spiralling out of control.[149] He wrote to the Home Secretary, Edward Shortt: 'The King asks whether the Government do not possess powers, statutory or otherwise, with which to combat these evil influences, which are persistently not only opposing all law and order, but doing their utmost to bring about revolution!'[150] And he informed the Secretary of the Cabinet, Sir Maurice Hankey, that the King wanted work, not dole, for the unemployed and appealed to the government to meet the crisis. 'It is impossible', he asserted, 'to expect people to subsist upon the unemployment benefit of 15/- for men and 12/- for women.'[151]

Lloyd George had a greater tolerance for unemployment than the King, but he responded to Stamfordham's letter with suggestions for the alleviation of distress, which he referred to a Cabinet committee.[152] These included the introduction of relief projects and resettling a proportion of the industrial population outside the cities, where workers might cultivate small allotments to supplement their earnings. But the only genuine remedy, according to the Prime Minister, was to rejuvenate those industries for which the unemployed had been trained, which could only be done with the co-operation of business leaders at home and abroad.[153] In his reply to the King, the Home Secretary explained the difficulties of taking legal action against revolutionaries. The police were keeping them under close scrutiny, and the question of introducing legislation to facilitate legal proceedings had already been discussed in the Cabinet. He noted the recent arrest (re-arrest) of the Scottish communist John Maclean.[154]

By the time of this correspondence, the immediate problem of communist agitation, according to the King's information, was subsiding. Police raids and arrests had scattered communist officials, and the Party's organization was in 'a state of chaos'.[155] The reported decline in membership and morale was largely because Russian funds were drying up. Lenin's New Economic Policy, adopted in 1921, made compromises with private enterprise and required adjustments in foreign relations. For a time at least, it damaged the communist cause in Britain. Paid Party activists, according to Thornton's agent, were now pathetic figures who had to go back to work. With less and less to report, Thornton became more sanguine. In his final summary, in March 1922, he argued that recognition of the Soviet state might have advantages, especially if it was willing to meet the financial obligations of the Tsarist government. George V read his analysis 'with greatest interest'.[156] When Thornton left Britain at the end of 1922 to join the Canadian National Railway, the King gave him a reception at Windsor.

Palace officials had little faith in the will of governments to address post-war problems seriously, whether communist agitation or unemployment. And they would have been right to doubt that ministers much considered the interests of the Crown in the determination of policy. Political trends were such that the monarchy was now only of marginal interest to the government. The balanced constitution of King, Lords and Commons, which Queen Victoria tried to sustain, was by now largely a thing of the past. Under the new constitutional arrangements, authority was increasingly concentrated in the office of the Prime Minister.[157] Along with it came the greater centralization of power brought about by the First World War. The King could deal with his boxes all he liked but politicians were under little obligation to take notice, though it sometimes suited them to do so, if only to confer legitimacy on their policies.

As Stamfordham made clear in his correspondence, the Crown did not lack initiative or resolve. Galvanized by the drift of politics and social malaise, it could do something positive to protect itself. In general, royal self-help meant the cultivation of Labour leaders and forging bonds of affection at home and across the Empire. In theory, it was summed up by Esher's phrase 'the "democratization" of the monarchy'. It conformed to the constraints of politics, dovetailed neatly with the Crown's ceremonial role, and drew on the natural human sympathies of the royal family. The Crown would stay true to its traditional middle- and upper-class allies, but it would endeavour to win the hearts and minds of the proletariat, thereby stepping up a trend set in motion by Prince Albert and Edward VII. In practice, it meant royalty visiting slums in dusty motor cars and inviting Labour bumpkins to tea.

Virtually everyone agreed that the King was a model constitutional monarch, but it was as a 'welfare monarch' that he made his greatest contribution to national well-being, and royal popularity.[158] The policy spelled out by Stamfordham provided a role, and reassured the royal family that it could take some action in its own defence. It led, among other things, to the appointment of a full-time Palace Press Secretary in 1918, whose object was to let a little more light in on the Crown, but only light that caught the royal family in a favourable pose. The 'selling' of the image of the family firm to the people who would have to pay for it was to be a major royal preoccupation in the interwar years.[159] But there was more than salesmanship and insubstantial pageant to the monarchy's survival strategy. With its extensive network of patronages, the Crown was well placed to assist the voluntary sector to deliver an array of much-needed social services.

Palace policy prompted the Prince of Wales to initiate his goodwill tours to mining and industrial districts, which were to do so much for his reputation. The Prince was not a social crusader by temperament, but he was susceptible to pressure from his parents. Like them, he feared that pent-up demands for reform might lead to social and political disintegration. The 'provincial forays', as the Prince put it in later life, 'were miniatures of my Imperial tours'.[160] In Britain, he inquired into housing conditions, established youth clubs, playing fields, workshops and canteens, and hammered home the message that he had the interests of ex-servicemen and the poor at heart. The widespread anxiety about Bolshevism had rubbed off on the Prince. After a visit to Glasgow, he reported to his mistress, Freda Dudley Ward: 'I do feel I've been able to do just a little good propaganda up there and given Communism a knock.'[161] He took further pleasure from the fact that after his welfare visits, the public houses in the 'red villages' put up his picture.[162]

In the post-war years, other members of the royal family also increased their public duties and charitable fund-raising. The sums they raised for hospitals and the sick poor in the 1920s were particularly notable.[163]

Queen Mary set a benchmark for the rest of the family. Has a minister of health ever visited more child welfare centres? Sir George Newman, the chief medical officer at the Ministry of Health, said in 1921 that the Queen's philanthropic work was 'invaluable' and her social influence 'sound and statesmanlike'. And he noted, in passing, that her beneficent labours were 'enormously strengthening the influence of the Crown with the people'.[164] Eventually, the King kept a chart in Buckingham Palace which chronicled his family's public work.[165] Labour strongholds, not least the centres of militancy in the industrial districts of Scotland and Wales, were well flagged.

It must have given the King some relief to see the results of the motion put to the Labour Party Conference in 1923: 'Is republicanism the policy of the Labour Party?' The republicans were defeated by a vote of 3,694,000 to 386,000.[166] Still, when MacDonald formed the first Labour Government early in 1924, the revolutionary wing of the Party was not in quiescent mood. On the day MacDonald became Prime Minister, the King wrote in his Diary: 'Today 23 years ago dear Grandmama died. I wonder what she would have thought of a Labour Government!'[167] A degree of apprehension would have been understandable on his part, for he was well aware that Queen Victoria never had to confront a Prime Minister who had called for a revolution in Britain, as he believed MacDonald had done in 1917.

In the first, historic audience between a socialist Prime Minister and a British monarch, the King complained to MacDonald about the singing of 'The Marseillaise' and 'The Red Flag' at a recent meeting at the Albert Hall. And he referred to Lansbury, who, in Cromwellian tones, had spoken about the fate of King Charles when up against the common people. MacDonald, who wished to show the respectable face of Labour, explained his difficulties with extremists and gave assurances that he would try to break down the habit of singing 'The Red Flag'. 'His earnest desire', as he said, 'was to serve his King and Country.'[168] Partly to please the King, he left the talented Lansbury out of the Cabinet.[169] After meeting the new ministers, George V wrote to his mother: they 'have different ideas to ours as they are all socialists, but they ought to be given a chance & ought to be treated fairly'.[170]

Immediately, the issue of court appointments arose. Over the years, the number of sinecure posts had been reduced, but the senior offices of the royal household posed a dilemma for Labour in power. These were, after all, political appointments which socialists had long ridiculed as fit only for flunkeys. The King, in keeping with his wish to cultivate Labour leaders, wanted socialists to serve as court officials. He had one piece of useful intelligence. Sir Frederick Ponsonby, the Keeper of the Privy Purse, had been told by his brother, the Labour MP Arthur Ponsonby, that MacDonald and Sidney Webb, who had to deal with the issue, were 'anxious to play up to the monarchy'.[171] After detailed discussions, a compromise was struck whereby the King was given discretion over the posts of Lord Chamberlain, Lord Steward and Master of the Horse, while the Prime Minister selected and appointed the three political Lords-in-waiting, and the three officers of the House of Commons: the Treasurer of the Household, the Comptroller and the Vice-Chamberlain.[172]

These officers, along with Labour ministers, were soon fitted out with court dress, just the sort of thing to please the King and infuriate the Labour left. Smoothing the rough edges off provincial socialists was the order of the day. The opportunity to meet a duchess, perhaps even Queen Mary, was an experience not be missed for aspiring wives from factory towns. A club, the Half-Circle, was set up to prepare them for such an experience. The Scottish socialist Tom Johnston, who abhorred the bowing and scraping and the housetraining of Labour wives, accused his comrades of toadyism.[173] Another Scot, the revolutionary William Gallacher, complained bitterly about professed socialists grovelling to meet King George. 'Never', he lamented, 'had there been such a rush on court tailors and court dressmakers.'[174]

The King recognized that the cloth-cap image of Keir Hardie's day was becoming an embarrassment to Labour, but he was sensitive to socialist sensibilities over matters of formal dress. Knee breeches might expose ministers to ridicule as well as expense. Consequently, the King required no more than a levée coat at court functions. The ever-helpful Lord Stamfordham, having made inquiries, advised Labour's Chief Whip that such coats might be purchased at reduced prices at Moss Bros.[175] Among those to don their new attire and turn up at a Palace garden party was the 'ferocious' anti-monarchist and Clydeside revolutionary Emanuel Shinwell.[176] Years later, the republican Willie Hamilton could not control his sarcasm: 'Ramsay MacDonald and his motley crew heralded in the revolution, like circus clowns enjoying the paint, powder and ridiculous garb – all symbols of a society they had been elected to destroy.' The royal garden party, he concluded, had become part of the class struggle: 'The revolution could wait. Deportment was all.'[177]

The Labour Party in power proved to be something of a sheep in sheep's clothing, at least as far as the King was concerned, but there remained genuine worries in Palace circles about unrest in the country. Industrial disputes were a feature of MacDonald's brief administration, and the King wanted assurances from the government that it had the Bolsheviks under control. In practice, he wanted the police to be given powers to arrest summarily anyone who openly urged sedition.[178] On one occasion, Stamfordham pressed Arthur Henderson, the Home Secretary, about communist activity in the country. Henderson brushed aside the King's fears with the reply that the authorities did not wish to take action which might be seen as 'persecution', for it might backfire on the government. If the communists broke the law, he would intervene, but 'he was equally averse to doing anything to them merely because they held and advocated different opinions'.[179]

When Stanley Baldwin formed his Conservative Government at the end of 1924, the King did not find any cause to relax his fears about Bolshevism. In February 1925, he noticed a secret police file on communist undergraduates at Cambridge University but hoped that it was simply 'a few precocious young men seeking notoriety and need not be taken seriously'.[180] As Chancellor of the University, the King took particular exception to Maurice Dobb, who, according to Scotland Yard, combined his lecturing duties with 'those of a communist propagandist among undergraduates'.[181] Another report from Scotland Yard in February heightened his fears about Russian money being used to promote communist penetration of the unions.[182] In August, Stamfordham wrote to Baldwin of the King's worries that even the Army might have become infected by the Bolshevik virus: 'His Majesty asks whether in your judgment the time has not come for a more vigorous and drastic policy against these enemies of law and order whose avowed object is the subversion of our whole social and political order.'[183] The government, as usual, proved reluctant to act on the King's views.

George V looked beyond government for reassurance. As ever, he depended on information from outside official political channels. Intriguingly, Ethel Snowden, the wife of the former Labour Chancellor,

Philip Snowden, provided him with useful intelligence. She initiated a correspondence with Stamfordham in 1925, which George V encouraged. It was the fruit of the kindness shown by the King to the Snowdens, dating to the time of the Labour Government, an expression of the usefulness of the advice given to the King to reach out to Labour leaders. It seems unlikely that Mrs Snowden would have written to the Palace without her husband's approval. Had the Labour left known about the correspondence, they would have denounced her as a royal lickspittle.

Mrs Snowden took 'delight' in reporting to Stamfordham on a host of issues, including internal Labour politics, foreign affairs and the General Strike. She seemed as nervous as the King about communist agitators, and she hoped that the government would 'deal seriously with those who seek to pull down the pillars of the state'![184] In November 1925, she described the factions and personal divisions in the Labour Party that made MacDonald's position 'intolerable'. Lansbury, she retailed, was 'very popular with the rank and file . . . but he is totally lacking in judgement, and a real danger to the forces of moderation'. Ellen Wilkinson, the forceful MP for Middlesbrough East, was a vain and bitter communist. Others in the Labour Party were 'violent with hate' for having been passed over by MacDonald.[185] The King agreed with Mrs Snowden that the industrial crisis brought out all MacDonald's indecisiveness.[186]

Unlike Labour, the King had a coherent policy for dealing with the General Strike which broke out in early May 1926. He was well aware that the Communist Party, now with over 5,000 members, was prominent on the propaganda front; and while it paid scant attention to royalty, he never doubted its anti-monarchism.[187] His guiding principle was to work towards the reconciliation of labour and capital, the policy recommended by Woodward and Stamfordham in 1918. He favoured preparedness on the part of the citizenry; but anxious to avoid greater militancy, he was opposed to the government pushing the strikers into a corner by punitive legislation. He urged the arrest of communist agitators and mercy to the suffering families. When St Loe Strachey suggested on 7 May that he intervene in the dispute by setting up a 'Committee of Reconciliation' at Buckingham Palace, the idea was rejected.[188] The King's public call for national unity on 12 May, the day the General Strike ended, was more in keeping with Stamfordham's view that the sovereign should smooth acrimonious feelings rather than be seen to take sides.

The King took heart from the resolution of a crisis which had caused him considerable anxiety. But the refusal of the miners to go back to work took away some of the pleasure. Stamfordham blamed their 'insensate policy' but did not acquit the mine owners of responsibility.[189] When the government protested to Moscow about Soviet funds being sent to the striking miners by the Russian Council of Trades Unions, the King objected. Stamfordham wrote to the Home Secretary that 'it would be disastrous if the Government's action could in any way justify a cry from the Socialist Party that the former were attempting to stop financial aid from Russia ... to save the miners' women and children from starvation'.[190] Moderation not reprisal remained Palace policy. Stamfordham wrote to Mrs Snowden in 1927 that industrial questions should be 'taken out of politics and dealt with by people whose primary interest is not in votes but in the welfare of industry'.[191] It was a further example of the monarchy's view that its interest rose above politics.

A period of industrial calm followed the General Strike and the collapse of the miners' resistance. The King's worries about Bolshevism abated, but he continued to heed Stamfordham's advice to cultivate Labour leaders. In the manner of clever King Magnus in George Bernard Shaw's *The Apple Cart*, he dropped a kind word here and an invitation there. Meetings with the King and Queen tended to be 'lovingly recollected' in the memoirs of Labour politicians and trade unionists, not least those from working-class backgrounds, who were highly susceptible to royal overtures. In 1931, John Hodge, the President of the Iron and Steel Trades Confederation, titled his autobiography *Workman's Cottage to Windsor Castle*. After dining at Windsor, he praised the King and Queen for their intimate knowledge of trade unionism and applauded the Palace aides, who 'made you feel as if you were one of them'.[192] The Snowdens were also frequent visitors at the Palace. In his *Autobiography*, Viscount Snowden skirted over his Leninist outpourings at the Leeds Conference in 1917, preferring to talk about the charm of the King and Queen, who had presented him and his wife with 'gifts we shall always treasure'.[193]

The incorruptible Beatrice Webb lamented: 'This romancing about the royal family is, I fear, only a minor symptom of the softening of the brain of socialists, enervated by affluence, social prestige and political power.'[194]

She had Ramsay MacDonald uppermost in her mind. The Labour leader was highly sensitive to the royal embrace, and by the time of his second administration (1929–31), he had long forgotten his revolutionary utterances of 1917. Whether the King forgot them is another matter, for, like his grandmother, he had a memory for insult. In the dark days of 1931, when economies unpalatable to the proletariat, notably a cut in unemployment benefit, were unavoidable, he refused to accept Mac-Donald's resignation as Prime Minister.[195]

The King's action led to a National Government headed by Mac-Donald, which had disastrous effects on Labour Party unity. The King's decision, taken on advice, may have been what might have been expected of a bewildered monarch in a national crisis, a point made by Herbert Morrison, a member of the Labour Cabinet.[196] But was it consistent with a crowned republic? Bogdanor suggests that it is perhaps a futile question, for a definitive answer is impossible in a country without a written constitution.[197] At the time, several Labour MPs accused the King of meddling in politics.[198] Willie Hamilton, writing in the 1970s, believed that the King 'probably did not act in any overtly partisan way. But . . . he helped by his action to put the British Labour Party into the political wilderness for a generation'.[199]

In the spring of 1935, George V celebrated his Silver Jubilee. It was not a political event, but an awesome demonstration of loyalty to a revered constitutional monarch, a 'Holy Communion' in the words of Mac-Donald.[200] Even Lansbury, who had once described the King as 'a narrow minded, out of date Tory', joined in the celebrations.[201] In seconding the Prime Minister's parliamentary tribute, he noted the advance of democracy and thought the constitution, though 'contradictory', worked. He even had praise for the King and Queen personally. 'Nobody', he said, 'could have been received with more kindness and consideration than myself.'[202]

The King delivered his Jubilee speech, written by the Whig historian G. M. Trevelyan, in Westminster Hall on 9 May. Brilliantly crafted, it included a call for the unity of the Empire, a sympathetic reference to the unemployed and a heartfelt tribute to Britain's 'balanced constitution', in which the monarchy worked in 'perfect harmony' with the parliamentary system. The King remarked upon the unbroken prosperity that marked the time of Queen Victoria's two Jubilees:

Such periods cannot always recur. In looking back over twenty-five years of My Reign, the thankfulness that I feel to-day is chiefly for escape from danger greater than ever before threatened our land. I can never forget how the peril from without at once united all the parties, classes, governments, and races of the Empire; men and women played their parts; the ranks were closed; and, in the issue, strength upheld the free.[203]

This was the King's particular spin on what he described, with relief, as the return to 'our normal ways'.

Jubilee week was an occasion to perplex students of mass psychology, especially as it took place against a background of high unemployment and foreign difficulties. The King and Queen appeared on the balcony of Buckingham Palace every night to rapturous applause. They attended a service at St Paul's, and the King noted that there were 'the greatest number of people in the streets that I have ever seen in my life. The enthusiasm was indeed most touching'.[204] The royal couple drove through Battersea, Kennington and Lambeth. Everywhere the working classes greeted them with jubilation, their houses decorated with flags, streamers and banners bearing loyal messages. George Orwell also noted the expression of loyalty at the Jubilee: 'It was even possible to see in it the survival, or recrudescence, of an idea almost as old as history, the idea of the King and the common people being in a sort of alliance against the upper classes.'[205]

Offstage, there were a few dissenting voices. The Communist Party portrayed the royal family as baleful puppets of monopoly capitalism.[206] The Bristol Socialist League regretted the attitude of the Labour Party Executive to the celebrations and congratulated those local councils which refused to participate in the Jubilee festivities: 'An hereditary Monarchy and the social distinctions inseparable from it were ultimately incompatible with the Socialist conception of society,' it announced.[207] Such views remained common enough among socialists. But as J. R. Clynes, the influential Labour leader and former Home Secretary, asked in Jubilee week, 'how many of them would like the responsibility of electing a president?'. Britain had become, in his phrase, a 'monarchic-democratic country'.[208] 'There is perhaps', he later remarked, 'a little employment for the speculative mind in this singular fact, that as the Labour Party has grown in this country, Republicanism has declined.'[209]

It did not require a speculative genius to appreciate that through its exercise of civic republicanism the royal family contributed to the failure of anti-monarchical republicanism. Just as the Palace intended, the slum visits, the new hospitals and dispensaries, the youth clubs and playing fields, the training schemes and workshops, the consoling words at the pit-heads and in the canteens, were reminders that the monarchy was a living institution that mattered. The Labour left thought that royal good works simply palliated evils which might otherwise be entirely removed. But Labour itself, for a host of reasons, had little success in providing social benefits in the interwar years. Arguably, Labour's greatest achievement was to worry the royal family into stepping up its traditional benevolence. This was no small achievement, although it appears to have been based on the Crown's exaggerated fear of British socialism.

Considering Labour's determination to play by the rules, a Palace strategy to disarm the anti-monarchists in the Labour movement was perhaps unnecessary. But from the perspective of the Palace, the dangers to the throne seemed greater in the reign of George V than in the reign of Queen Victoria, largely because of the war, whose outcome was not a foregone conclusion. The Crown may not have had to contend with an explicitly republican movement as previously, but to the royal family the Labour left served the purpose. Unlike his grandmother, George V also had to deal with the triumph of Paineite, Chartist demands, which the monarchy had consistently opposed. It should be remembered that Queen Victoria assumed that the reform of the House of Lords and universal suffrage would unbalance the constitution. In this, she took her enemies at their word, that in a representative democracy the monarchy would wither and die.

The republican cause of representation had triumphed, but as it transpired, the Crown had little to fear from it. The reform of the House of Lords and the advent of universal suffrage did not signal the monarchy's demise. On the contrary, they further neutralized the political case against the Crown. When power had shifted so decisively to popularly elected governments, the sovereign could share the credit for democratic advance, at least as long as the advance was seen to last. Nations tend to lose interest in constitutional reform once they adopt universal suffrage.[210] This was the case in Britain, at least until the end of the twentieth century.

The Representation of the People Act – the jewel in the crowned republic – cemented the monarchy into the democratic constitution. As Stamfordham put it in 1918, 'constitutionally the King can do no wrong', which was his way of conceding that Britain had become a republic with an hereditary head of state.[211]

By the time of the King's death in January 1936, less than a year after the Silver Jubilee celebrations, very few Labour leaders were overtly hostile to the monarchy. Indeed, some of them, in keeping with much working-class opinion, revered the royal family. Some would say that such attitudes were simply the result of mass idiocy or, in Tom Nairn's phrase, the 'glamour of backwardness'.[212] But royal popularity was partly the result of successful Palace policies and partly the result of Labour's winning 'a stake in things'. As one of the more outspoken Scottish anti-monarchists, John McGovern, admitted: 'Instead of the Throne moving away from the Labour party the Labour party [has moved] nearer and nearer to the Throne.'[213] Another Scottish socialist, P. J. Dollan, put the common view, that George V 'came nearer to the ideal of constitutional monarchy than any previous occupant of the throne'. And he added: 'the abolition of poverty is more important to socialism than the elimination of a constitutional monarchy which in the past 25 years has not interfered with the development of Democracy'.[214]

A little rewriting of socialist history was underway in Labour circles. In the month of the King's death, John Marchbank, General Secretary of the National Union of Railwaymen, concluded that republicanism was 'historically a Radical tradition', and he added that it seemed 'more than a little old-fashioned today, largely because in the last two reigns it has been demonstrated that constitutional monarchy and free citizenship are not antagonistic to each other!'.[215] Arthur Greenwood, the former Labour Minister of Health, regarded republicanism as 'a middle-class creed' and therefore immaterial to socialism.[216] Clement Attlee, the future Prime Minister, airbrushed socialists out of the republican past altogether. The republican movement in the 1870s, he pronounced, 'was not a Socialist movement at all. It was a movement of bourgeois Radicals'.[217]

But while most socialists believed the Crown to be compatible with democracy or a symbolic irrelevance, a few continued to snipe. Leonard Woolf, for one, decried the irrational reverence paid to monarchy, which he thought symptomatic of 'barbarism' and a 'medicine-man frame of mind'.[218] Militant socialism and anti-monarchism were bedfellows, and it was thus not surprising that left-wing Scottish MPs were the most vocal in the Civil List debates at the beginning of Edward VIII's reign. William Gallacher, John McGovern and James Maxton, the eloquent revolutionary of the Independent Labour Party, argued that the Crown was a plaything to distract attention from mass poverty and social decay. They adopted the classic Marxist line, which saw the monarchy as 'simply a dressing for the capitalist State', a 'symbol of a system of exploitation and robbery'.[219] To Gallacher, a classless society and monarchy were irreconcilable. In his view, 'the capitalist class have seen that the monarchy might be used as a centre for reaction and for maintaining their power'.[220]

It may seem surprising that a creed based on class politics did not pose a more serious threat to the continuation of royalism. But for most socialists, the difference between a capitalist society with a monarch and one with a president was 'immaterial'.[221] When Sir Stafford Cripps, who did not always see eye to eye with Buckingham Palace, was asked how he reconciled his left-wing views with monarchy, he replied that royalty, like his title, was not sufficiently important to worry about. And he confessed: 'I believe the alternative to a Constitutional Monarchy is a political President, and I vastly prefer a Constitutional monarch to a political President.'[222] His views were reminiscent of those of Blatchford, who had concluded in 1917: 'Royalty is an anachronism: it is out of date. But so long as our form of royalty keeps fairly close to the lines of a crowned Republic any general demand for a Republic in these islands is unlikely.'[223] As a Labour MP observed in 1936: 'when republicanism ceases to be a heresy, it ceases to be a faith'.[224]

At the time of the abdication in December 1936, Attlee spoke for that large section of the Labour Party that was republican, in the democratic sense, but not anti-monarchical. He wished to see a monarchy free of dated ceremonial and hangers-on, more in tune with the common man. But comparing the power of the House of Commons to the King's, he quoted the dictum of his former colleague, the left-wing John Wheatley: 'I would not raise a finger to turn a capitalist monarchy into a capitalist republic.'[225] 'We have to be realists,' a Labour back-bencher remarked. Calls for the abolition of the monarchy were not only a distraction from more serious issues, but 'might arouse the people of this country against us'.[226] The British left, whether Fabian or revolutionary, would concentrate its energies elsewhere, little distracted by calls for constitutional reform or the elimination of royal privilege. It was a licence for the Crown's survival as long as capitalism survived.

There was little anti-monarchism left in the Labour locker outside Scotland by the time of the abdication. Even Tom Johnston, dubbed 'the uncrowned King of Scotland', had toned down his views. He insisted that Scotland would one day become a republic, but he conceded that the simple election of a president would not, in itself, create a 'socialist commonwealth'. Writing in *Forward*, he no longer saw the Crown as an impediment, but as an enabling institution. 'The monarchy', he remarked, 'might be a useful buffer for a socialist government endeavouring to achieve a transfer to socialism without an insurrection or sabotage by the propertied classes.' So long as 'the King had touched a new law with his sceptre there would be at least some measure of respect paid to the law, and any rebellion against it would be a rebellion against the King'.[227] For a left-wing MP to think of the monarchy as agent and symbol of socialist legitimacy was not only remarkable, it was prophetic.

At the time of the abdication crisis, it was just as well for the monarchy that it had such an extraordinary hold on the public imagination. One reason for the Crown's popularity was that Edward VIII, as Prince of Wales, had played a prominent part in the post-war Palace strategy, though not without prodding. In an era of press restraint, his image had been positive, glamorous and misleading: a forward-looking future king, spreading the gospel of self-help and social service. The patronage work and the visits to industrial and mining areas had been an effective counter to the growth of anti-monarchism among the labouring classes. By the time of his accession, as Philip Ziegler remarks, 'there was a strong emotional attachment to Edward VIII among socialists, because of his stand on poverty and the unemployed'.[228] Miners and East-Enders, however, knew nothing about their monarch's foibles, his pro-Fascist leanings, his calamitous selfishness – or Wallis Simpson.

When the news broke that the King wished to marry the twice divorced Mrs Simpson, his support in the country slipped away. No doubt many people, not least among the unemployed, were indifferent to the royal rigmarole taking place in London.[229] But in the days before the abdication, it became increasingly clear that even the King's working-class followers were turning against him. Attlee told the Prime Minister that Labour voters admired the King for his work in the depressed areas, but, critical of the conduct of royalty, would not accept Mrs Simpson.[230] In London, demonstrators rallied to the King – a lone republican was spotted at Speaker's Corner – but generally there was more gloom than alarm.[231] As the former Conservative minister Leo Amery believed, 'the country as a whole was getting progressively more shocked at the idea that the King could hesitate between his duty to the Throne and his affection for a second-rate woman'.[232]

A monarchy based on middle-class values and public service had created a royal box from which there seemed no easy exit for the King. He paid a high price for his family's reputation for rectitude, and the expectation that he would live up to it. Love, it may be said, vanquished the King of modernity. But he was also undone by a stage-managed public image, which he found impossible to sustain, although he performed one final duty by leaving, as he was told to do. He won back some respect by going quietly and with a touch of pathos redolent of romantic fiction. As he sailed into exile, the gloom receded. His former popularity turned out to be as fleeting as a film star's, and George VI soon restored the monarchy in the dutiful and unglamorous style of George V.[233]

Those who hoped that King Edward's departure would damage the Crown were disappointed.[234] Loyalty to the monarchy as an institution, built up in the reign of George V, transcended the King's failings and transferred to his successor.[235] Anti-monarchists, little in evidence during the crisis, had difficulty exploiting an event which was seen by many people in human as well as political terms. When the Abdication Bill came forward on 11 December, Maxton, Gallacher and a few other Scottish MPs made a gesture of defiance. On hearing the eulogies for the King, George Buchanan, MP for Gorbals, said he had never heard such 'cant and humbug' in his life.[236] Maxton moved a republican amendment, which he hoped would lead to the removal of 'all monarchical institutions and the hereditary principle'. It had the distinction of being the sole occasion in the history of modern Britain when the future of the monarchy has been put to the vote in Parliament. The Commons divided 403 to 5.[237] Partly thanks to the co-operation of the Labour opposition, the abdication did not produce an anti-monarchical movement, but simply a crisis in the royal family.

6

The Crowned Republic and its Enemies

1936–2000

'*Real* democracy will exist only when "every man is, in his own proper self, a king" – when the ordinary has become extraordinary, the humdrum been dissolved in glamour: when mortals step into the enchanted glass or its visions step down to join us.'

Tom Nairn, *The Enchanted Glass. Britain and its Monarchy* (1988)

'The Republican form of Government is the highest form of government; but because of this it requires the highest type of human nature – a type nowhere at present existing.'

Herbert Spencer, *Essays* (1891)

The coronation of George VI in May 1937 was a bleak event for anti-monarchists, though it did provide a footnote in republican history. A man from Walthamstow was sentenced to a month's imprisonment for making slanderous remarks about the King, probably the last person in Britain to be jailed for insulting the sovereign in public.[1] The Civil List debates soon after the coronation likewise left the enemies of royalty despondent. The usual suspects called for the creation of a classless society and, as ever, took the opportunity to mock the reactionary, 'parasitic drones' who surrounded the throne. The desire of Labour members to bring the monarchy more into line with democracy by simplifying the court, led William Gallacher to say that he would simplify it 'out of existence'. But the debate got bogged down over details of state ceremonial and whether MPs were free to wear lounge suits at royal garden parties. This scarcely suggested that a move was underway to turn the monarchy into a '*petit bourgeois* monarchy', much less pack the royal family off to the suburbs as citizens.[2]

George VI himself had many of the characteristics of an ordinary citizen. Though slow and reserved, he was a decent and dutiful family man. Most at ease at home, his excursions into public life brought out his insecurities. Although knowledgeable about youth and industry through his charitable work, he was out of his depth on the world stage, or, for that matter, in the sectarian world of British politics. His traits would have been the ruin of an aspiring politician, but in a sovereign without ambition, bounced into kingship by the Fates, these obstacles could be overcome by that dogged-as-does-it mentality which the British so admire. Had he been imaginative, he would have been censured for meddling. Had he been highbrow, he would have aroused resentment. The public came round to George VI precisely because he was unpretentious, public-spirited, admirably domestic and he battled with his stammer. He was king-as-anti-hero, a constitutional sovereign in tune with a mass democracy, for his subjects could match him in everything but station.[3]

Of all the reigns since George III, the reign of George VI was the least troubled by anti-monarchism. Not only did the unobtrusive King disarm the critics, but his wife, Queen Elizabeth, was hugely popular with the public. She had no constitutional duties as Consort, and, like Queen Mary before her, she recognized that social service constituted her primary work for the monarchy. As Duchess of York, she had carved out a charitable niche for herself, which complemented her husband's interest in industrial welfare and boys' camps. As Queen, she became one of the most effective campaigners the royal family ever produced, with a patronage list that grew to over 300 institutions. In the late 1930s, she worked the hospitals, housing estates and job centres with practised informality. After watching her performance at the opening of some new buildings at Morley College, Harold Nicolson remarked that she had an 'astonishing gift for being sincerely interested in dull people and dull occasions'.[4] Beatrice Webb, who had been looking down her nose at royalty for decades, was more supercilious. She detested the 'worshipful emotion' elicited on such visits and dismissed the King and Queen as 'ideal robots'.[5]

The 'worshipful emotion' increased as the 'shadows of enmity and fear', to use the King's phrase, spread across Europe.[6] With war looming, it would have been very single-minded to make an issue of the British monarchy, and no one of political consequence did. There was no republican party in Britain, and the republics abroad were not exactly models of civic virtue. Socialists had long decried America as a bastion of capitalist greed. Meanwhile, the European republics which emerged at the end of the First World War, with the exception of Czechoslovakia, were hardly advertisements for political progress. Neither the Soviet Union nor Germany looked any more attractive when they signed a non-aggression pact in 1939. A detached British observer might conclude that compared to Stalin and Hitler, even Tsar Nicholas and Kaiser Wilhelm had been relatively innocuous. The virtuous constitutional monarch George VI was, in contrast, a paragon.

The Second World War, like the First, allied the royal family to national purpose. Though the King did not play Henry V, he managed a very good imitation of his father. He carried out troop inspections and toured factories and hospitals with Hanoverian thoroughness. Meanwhile, the Queen, supremely conscious of her public role, was much in evidence at bomb sites, shelters and feeding centres. The visits to the East End and the docks, to Coventry and Plymouth, impressed on the public the steely yet compassionate side of royalty. When the bombs dropped on Buckingham Palace in September 1940, missing the King and Queen by ninety feet, the Ministry of Information, sensitive to complaints by East-Enders that 'it is always the poor that get it', despatched forty journalists to the scene.[7] Their pictures and reports provided priceless propaganda for the monarchy, cementing the bonds of affection between the royal family and the public. George VI's finest hour was not at Churchill's side in the Cabinet war rooms, but surveying the Palace rubble. The Queen's was represented by her famous remark: 'I'm glad we've been bombed. It makes me feel I can look the East End in the face.'

During the war, there remained a disparate body of republicans in the country, mostly socialists, from the politicians James Maxton and Emrys Hughes to the writers Leonard Woolf and H. G. Wells. In 1944, the ageing Wells said that 'I have always regarded and written of monarchy as a profoundly corrupting influence upon our national life, imposing an intricate snobbishness upon our dominant classes'.[8] But outspoken critics were now fewer and farther between than ever, silenced by the blitz and the royal family's contribution to the war effort. The urbane Kingsley

Martin, editor of the *New Statesman*, dug up precious few republican nuggets to polish from the war years when he wrote *The Crown and the Establishment* in 1962. To his dismay, sympathy for the royal family had simply reinvigorated British deference. When the more robust anti-royalist Willie Hamilton dipped into republican history in *My Queen and I* in 1975, he skipped the war entirely.[9]

The monarchy's popularity in 1945 was not in doubt. But if the war was the making of George VI as a king, it exhausted him as a man. No sooner was it over than a fresh set of problems appeared that had serious implications for the Crown. Unlike the end of the First World War, there was little domestic unrest or worry about political problems caused by disillusioned soldiers returning from the front. Nor was there a Russian Revolution, with its attendant fears of Bolshevism at home, to alarm the royal family. Instead, there were discontents in the Empire and an empowered Labour Government in office, which sought to transform industry and social provision. Apart from the monarchy's longstanding suspicions about the anti-royalism and anti-imperialism latent in social-ism, particular trouble loomed in those ringing phrases of Clause 4 of the Labour Party constitution, which called for the common ownership of the means of production and the control of industry and services. What effect would the extension of government controls have on those tra-ditions of civic duty and personal service which had nourished society, and the monarchy, in the past?

The Labour programme of nationalization and central control looked decidedly audacious, if not extremist, to the royal family. (It would also have been unpopular with republicans of previous generations in the radical tradition, who favoured a decentralized politics.) Labour's disre-gard for do-gooders looked likely to subdue and dispirit those voluntary institutions from which the monarchy drew much of its strength. What-ever one thought about the Crown, the expression of civic virtue required more than sitting back, paying one's taxes and leaving the removal of social problems to officialdom. What was the point of civic republicanism if the state, Paine's 'badge of lost innocence', swept all before it? What was the point of royal philanthropy if government provided for all human ills from the cradle to the grave? If the intermediary institutions of civil society collapsed, the implications for the monarchy would be ominous. Presumably, its popularity would depend more and more on mystique, pageantry, and a constitutional role that even monarchists had difficulty defining.

George VI and his family had views on post-war Labour policy, but they kept them largely to themselves, or expressed them obliquely through royal institutions. According to the governess, Marion Crawford, the King and Queen 'never spoke' about the Labour Party's policies in her company: 'In the Palace, discretion and self-control – and I feel I must add genuine self-sacrifice – are carried to lengths quite unbelievable to the world outside.'[10] The King had difficulty concealing his dislike of socialists, as Chips Channon noted, but his relations with Prime Minister Attlee were constitutionally correct.[11] He warned Attlee that the pro-gramme of nationalization was 'going too fast' and that precipitate action threatened British liberties.[12] The royal family clearly had difficulty coming to terms with the nationalization of major industries, the transfor-mation in social policy, the breakup of the Empire and the rise of republicanism in the dominions. One can imagine such trends giving George V a paralytic fit. It left the conscientious George VI discomfited, but outwardly unshaken. If he had to choose between socialism and dismissal, he would opt for the former.

Despite the King's reservations about Labour policies, he served the socialist programme by touching it with his sceptre. As Rousseau had suggested, reforming governments require symbols of legitimacy more than conservative ones, and this was particularly so in post-war Britain under Labour. (In Japan, the American authorities also found the Emperor useful.) It is worth recalling the pre-war views of the left-wing Tom Johnston, who had come around to the monarchy as an enabling institution, or, as he put it, 'a useful buffer for a socialist government endeavouring to achieve a transfer to socialism without an insurrection or sabotage by the propertied classes'.[13] Ben Pimlott, the historian and biographer, takes up this point:

On the one hand the Royal Family could be seen as a typically British piece of camouflage, disguising and making acceptable the Government's radicalism; on the other, its existence stood as a guarantee that pragmatic caution would prevail, and radicalism [be] kept within bounds. Thus when Labour took major industries into public ownership . . . or made adjustments to the powers of the House of Lords . . . both left and right thanked God for the Monarchy.[14]

A similar pattern obtained in medical provision. The creation of the National Health Service was not a measure welcomed by the royal family, for it brought under state control more than a thousand voluntary hospitals, hundreds of them with Crown patronage.[15] The loss of so many friends and allies in the powerful world of hospital charity was bound to dismay the Palace old guard, who preferred voluntary service and pluralism to the corporate and the collective. Queen Mary and Queen Elizabeth must have thought the government's takeover of the hospitals an act of vandalism comparable to the dissolution of the monasteries (but in the case of the monasteries a king had at least had a hand in it). Between the passage of Bevan's Bill in November 1946 and the opening of the new service in July 1948, members of the royal family, including Princess Elizabeth, made a concerted effort to bolster morale in the hospitals by visiting many of them and making symbolic donations. But conscious of the sensitivity of these events, they avoided remarks that might have had a political interpretation put on them.

Hospital voluntarists might have lost the war with the Labour Government, but they fought a rearguard action to have the traditions of personal service and local support for their institutions carried over into the NHS. They considered royal support crucial to their campaign. They wrote to the Palace or spoke to members of the royal family to discover whether royal patronage was compatible with the new hospital regime. Ulick Alexander, the Keeper of the Privy Purse, made inquiries at the Home Office early in 1947. At issue was whether the Crown could patronize an agency of the government, something it had never done before. The reply was crucial to the future role of the royal family in the nation's welfare in an era of the ascendant state.

The Home Office took the casuistical line that a state hospital was not a government department as such, for it was under the control of the Regional Hospital Board. Consequently, neither the Home Secretary nor the Minister of Health had any objection to NHS hospitals enjoying royal patronage. There was a powerful underlying consideration at work in the decision, which became clear in a Home Office letter to the Keeper of the Privy Purse: 'to withdraw Patronage at the time of the transfer from voluntary to State auspices might be construed as indicating that the Royal Family disapproved of the National Health Service'.[16] Not even Bevan, that scourge of social distinction, could bring himself to blackball the royal family from the hospitals. Just as with the nationalization of industry, the government found the monarchy useful in giving respectability to the fledgling NHS. The monarchy, for its part, benefited from becoming closely associated with one of the greatest cultural and social shifts in twentieth-century Britain. In an age of state welfare, the royal family would not be sidelined.

As the Crown stamped contested Labour policies with its symbolic authority, it was not surprising that Attlee and his ministers took a more generous view of the monarchy than some in their party. This was evident when the House of Commons debated the Select Committee report on the Civil List in December 1947, which dealt with annuities for the newly-weds, Princess Elizabeth and the Duke of Edinburgh. Royal costs, as Mass Observation discovered, had led to some grumbling in the country.[17] In the Commons, there was the cry of 'spivs, drones and butterflies' at court and the need for royal economies in keeping with post-war austerity. John McGovern compared the men blinded in the war on 40 shillings a week with the Duke of Edinburgh, who was 'being handed £10,000 a year, in addition to a cushy job at the Admiralty'. The Welsh republican Emrys Hughes, who had married Keir Hardie's daughter, was among those who wished to see British royalty reduced to Scandinavian levels, if not abandoned altogether.

The austere Chancellor, Sir Stafford Cripps, who proposed the royal allowances, had once called the pomp surrounding the throne 'all bunk and bunting'. Now he asserted that the British monarchy was far more economical than the Swedish if cost per head were taken into account, and he reminded critics of the motion that 'the pomp and ceremony' in Moscow was 'vastly greater' than in London.[18] Attlee praised members of the royal family for their hard work and avoidance of luxury during the war.[19] 'It is awfully easy to talk vaguely about a mass of hangers-on doing nothing,' he pointed out. 'I have not observed it myself, and those with whom I come in contact seem fully occupied.' Though he had previously called for a court free of hangers-on and unnecessary pomp, he was now happy to endorse a 'ceremonial' monarchy, whose rituals he compared favourably with those used to shore up dictatorships. Reduce the pomp and there would be complaints, he warned. 'We do want a little light, colour and symbolism in our national life.'[20]

Like Cripps, Attlee had had a change of heart. Here was a political leader who, like others before him, had seen the advantages of the monarchy more clearly once in power, and he was not inclined to be stingy towards the royal family. He seconded the Chancellor's case with his usual matter-of-factness: 'if the thing has to be done it has to be paid for'.[21] While the Conservative benches nodded approval, it left a sour taste in the mouths of Labour republicans and other dissidents who wanted royal economies. The Prime Minister's speech left Emrys Hughes 'absolutely cold'. He chided the Chancellor for marching to the tune of 'Pomp and Circumstance' and accused Arthur Greenwood, the former deputy leader of the Labour Party, of being 'a dehydrated republican'.[22]

Greenwood had made a point earlier in the debate which suggested a further use of royalty to a radical administration. One moment he described himself as a 'convinced republican', albeit of a theoretical kind. The next he confessed to being a 'convinced constitutional monarchist' because of the British overseas dominions. 'I do not believe', he remarked, 'that one could have a sort of presidential republic of the British Commonwealth of Nations . . . Constitutionally the British people and the sister nations overseas must be a monarchy.'[23] Greenwood did not mention it, but when the government had appointed Lord Mountbatten as Viceroy of India earlier in 1947, with a mandate to negotiate Indian independence, it was an advantage that he was a second cousin of George VI and an uncle of the Duke of Edinburgh. There was a presumption that the running down of Empire would be less unnerving to the public if rubber stamped by the House of Windsor, which, as a Labour MP put it, was 'the linchpin of our Imperial Constitution'.[24]

Paradoxically, and happily from Labour's point of view, royalty eased the transition from Empire to Commonwealth. But Greenwood was mistaken in assuming that Britain's 'sister nations overseas must be a monarchy', for twenty-nine of the fifty-one member nations of the Commonwealth eventually became republics, with others considering the possibility.[25] Their status within the organization was achieved by a mixture of subtle diplomacy, a tolerance of differences and the flexibility of the Crown. The desire to throw off memories of subjection and forge a new identity, free from alien symbols of authority, triggered the growth of the republicanism which spread across the Empire from Indian independence onwards. But such matters did not resonate back in Britain and consequently did little to enliven domestic republicanism. Indeed, the shedding of imperial associations, so unpopular on the left, may have undermined the republican cause at home.

By the end of George VI's reign, the post-war and post-imperial social currents – egalitarianism, internationalism and expanding welfare services – had helped to disengage the Crown from the old ruling class in the minds of the public. Through ceremonial and patronage work, the royal family was able to swim with the tide of collectivism, changing social values and imperial decline. Royalty seen opening a hospital ward with a minister, or visiting refugee children with the Red Cross, was in keeping with post-war values. Royal charity received less attention in the press than before the war, but it still served the monarchy's purposes. About 2,000 institutions were now on the Palace patronage list. A glance at the royal family's association with the Save the Children Fund at mid-century is particularly instructive. Rarely have the reciprocal benefits of royal philanthropy been more apparent, as the work of the Princess Royal for the charity continues to illustrate today.[26]

In the years following the Second World War, unlike the First, there was little in the way of a royal strategy for survival. Despite rationing, austerity and Labour's ascendancy, the monarchy had little need to plan. It retained its friends in the voluntary world, who in a period of uneasy transition needed royalty more than ever, while it made new ones in the expanding state services. It was a post-war variant of a theme dating back to the eighteenth century. At mid-century, the Crown nourished, and was nourished by, institutions, old and new, which filled gaps in state provision or served new aspirations. It muddled through by supporting its traditional allies, while mollifying the politicians who needed the monarchy to give respectability to government policies. Meanwhile, the media presented the royal family as a model of domestic virtue and praised the brilliance of Crown ceremonial, which provided a link with the past.

At the accession of Queen Elizabeth II in early 1952, there was nothing to suggest a serious rift between royalty and the British public. The death of a popular King left the nation in grief and gratitude. The dedication of his young, attractive and earnest heir was not in doubt. The Queen had inherited an exceptional sense of public service and a set of values that were interwar, if not Victorian. With a built-in reverence for history and ancestral vocations, she subdued her individuality in the interest of the monarchy's greater good. Like Bagehot's royal magician, she would contrive to efface herself in office, leaving friends and enemies alike to wonder and to fantasize. And like her father and grandfather, she would seek to provide both a unifying symbol of the nation and a caring image that would give the country's disparate elements a sense of common purpose. In the post-war uncertainty, she was widely admired as a beacon of stability and continuity, a model constitutional monarch in keeping with a crowned republic.

If the Civil List debate early in the reign was anything to go by, republicans were few in number and disconcerted. A survey in the *Sunday Pictorial* found that a large number of its readers thought the sum of £475,000 provided in the Bill excessive, but such concern did not equate with anti-monarchism.[27] The Tories were back in power and the wily Chancellor of the Exchequer, R. A. Butler, steered the Civil List Bill through Parliament without mishap, a course made easier by the fact that there were no Scottish Labour MPs on the committee. 'The debate', as one MP put it, 'must be the quietest debate on a Civil List which has ever taken place.'[28] The left-wing Ian Mikardo took the nation's pulse. At the moment, he observed, 'there is virtually no feeling for republicanism at all'. He personally supported the Bill because he preferred the 'hero-worship' of royalty to the 'hero-worship of strange people like film stars'. He was happy 'to further an institution valuable in itself and giving the country a good return for the money'.[29]

There were a host of voices in the debate who wanted a Scandinavian-style monarchy for Britain, though only twenty-five could be found to support a proposal to reduce the Civil List to £250,000.[30] One or two MPs wished to turn Buckingham Palace and Holyrood House into flats. Willie Hamilton, recently elected as the member for West Fife, argued that royalty was less popular in the north than in the south, and he challenged the logic of giving £70,000 to Queen Mary while old age pensioners received only 2 or 3 shillings. Emrys Hughes was among the tiny minority who openly declared against the monarchy, but he observed that republicanism was not an immediate issue, 'having nothing very much to do with poverty'. For his part, Hugh Gaitskell, the former Labour Chancellor, thought it 'enormously important' that the ceremonial should be undertaken not by politicians but by a head of state above the political fray.[31] His colleague Geoffrey Bing gave force to this point when he noted that if Britain had abolished the monarchy at the end of the war, Winston Churchill would probably have been elected President, a proposition far from reassuring to Labour.[32]

At the coronation, Churchill was content to be Prime Minister. The event struck some, including the cartoonist David Low, as a wasteful binge.[33] A few left-wing MPs, followers of Aneurin Bevan, would have preferred the occasion to be a more modest affair, free of any taint of imperialism. (See plate 17.) But to most commentators it was a stunning demonstration of national unity and purpose, a great patriotic display which defined British identity. As the royal family at mid-century signified moral example and family virtue, the coronation could be seen as an extension of the idea of the nation as one large family, with the 'Crown as a moral cord binding the consensus together'.[34] It was, as David Cannadine contends, one of the great moments of royal ceremonial in modern history:

At the time, it seemed as though the threats and challenges of the war and austerity period had been surmounted: the empire was still largely intact; the problem of Indian independence and republican status within the Commonwealth had been triumphantly resolved; Churchill was back at 10 Downing Street; Britain had once more asserted her place as a great power; there was a new Elizabethan age around the corner.[35]

To monarchists, the coronation was convincing proof of the virtue of having a ceremonial as opposed to a slimmed-down monarchy. It was proof too that behind the façade of tradition there was something vital and seemingly contemporary. Herbert Morrison, one of Labour's more pragmatic leaders, called the coronation a 'great national festival' and concluded: 'when the people cheer the Queen and sing her praises, they are also cheering our free democracy'.[36] Clearly, the pageant gave pleasure, or at least a distraction, to a majority of the population; an estimated 27 million people in Britain were glued to the extensive coverage provided by the new medium of television.[37] Television itself was given an enormous boost by the event, and it would change the iconography of royalty for ever. Increasingly, the monarchy would be perceived, and judged, through it. To anti-royalists, who were largely reduced to embarrassed silence on the day, the coronation was just so much grovelling and old-world conservatism dressed up in tinsel, 'a curious mixture of medieval feudalistic ritual and an ancient aristocracy brought out of mothballs for a day of "Moss Bros" magic'.[38]

As the coronation illustrated, there was opposition to the Crown in the 1950s; but as Hamilton admitted, it was 'no more of a threat . . . than a Christmas cracker in Parliament'.[39] The Walton Constituency Labour Party presented a resolution to the Labour Party Conference in 1955 in favour of abolishing the monarchy, but it was quietly dropped.[40] The iconoclastic journalist Malcolm Muggeridge indulged in some gentle sniping at 'The Royal Soap Opera' in the pages of the *New Statesman* in the same year, but it was seen as eccentric.[41] When, in an article for the American weekly the *Saturday Evening Post*, he reported that duchesses thought the Queen a frump, it caused quite a stir.[42] And when the hereditary peer and professed monarchist Lord Altrincham (later John Grigg the historian) described the Queen as favouring a narrow 'tweedy' class, in a special issue of the *National and English Review* in 1957, he was denounced in the press and publicly slapped in the face by an empire loyalist.[43]

In *The Uneasy Heads*, published in 1959, the writer Geoffrey Bocca fired another shot across the royal bows. He feared for the future of an institution conceived to represent a great Empire but which had been reduced to symbolizing a second-rate power that had embarrassed itself in a futile war with Egypt. He detected what he called 'a Cheshire Cat monarchy, consisting of a bright smile surrounded by nothing, a frightened, timorous, monarchy hoping not to be noticed so that the death sentence may be delayed'. In his view, a tendency to half measures and hesitation had taken hold in the running of Palace affairs. Royal advisers, who confused vigorous monarchy with absolutism, were too frightened to take the initiative in areas beyond the ceremonial. He predicted 'a royal crisis of major proportions . . . within the next few years'.[44]

As the memories and memorabilia of the coronation faded, along with any hope of a new Elizabethan age, the monarchy could ill afford to be complacent. The collapse of Empire diminished the Crown's splendour, while the decline of British competitiveness led to disillusionment and political faction. Party dogma, whether from the left or from the right, was potentially damaging to the Crown, for it was more difficult to symbolize a nation that was divided ideologically. In such circumstances, it was a doubtful tactic to defend the monarchy as a treasure house of consolation. Royal ritual may have given a psychological boost to a nation on the slide, but there were limits to the capacity of pageantry and pomp, however accomplished, to compensate for Britain's shaky economic performance, Suez and the loss of Empire.[45]

In the 1960s, royalty continued to enjoy a high degree of popularity, though, as the comments by Muggeridge, Altrincham and Bocca suggested, there were signs that attitudes to the monarchy were changing. Like her father, the Queen was politically unobtrusive and constitutionally correct, though there were moments when her reserve powers caused controversy, as in 1963, when, after consulting the ailing Prime Minister Harold Macmillan in hospital, she summoned Lord Home to the Palace as his successor. (As a result, the Conservative Party set up an electoral procedure for selecting its leader.)[46] Still, a Mass Observation poll conducted the following year confirmed the Queen's standing, though some of those questioned regarded her as cold and aloof. A not insignificant number, 16 per cent, described themselves as republicans. Most of these were socialists. A further 30 per cent, presumably Anglicans, said the Queen was 'especially chosen by God'. Other findings of the survey showed that some respondents worried about the loss of democratic freedoms and saw the Crown as 'a bulwark against danger'.[47]

Intriguingly, the Mass Observation poll found that 60 per cent of the respondents claimed to have seen a member of the royal family. Moreover, it found that they were three times more likely to have done so in a welfare context than in any other. It confirmed that nothing was doing more to bring the monarchy into communion with the public than its social service – the dutiful round of award-givings, variety performances and hospital openings – which had become a staple of royal endeavour. Not a few in the sample wanted philanthropic work expanded and urged the Queen to show more 'intelligent interest in social questions'. Leonard Harris, who initiated this particular survey, concluded: 'The concept of welfare monarch and welfare royalty is thus implicit in much of the current activity of royal people; and it is this aspect of their behaviour which has in total, the biggest *personal* audience.'[48] But evidence that the monarchy's popularity might have more to do with good works than stately ceremonial seems to have made little impression on Palace advisers.

11. 'Where is Britannia?' The satirical magazine *Tomahawk* suggests an empty palace under Queen Victoria, 1867.

WHERE IS BRITANNIA ?

12. Queen Victoria distributing prizes on behalf of one of Prince Albert's charities, Windsor. *Illustrated London News*, 1870.

THE REAL CAP OF LIBERTY.

British Lion. "WHAT CAN THAT *CAP* PROMISE, THAT MY *CROWN* DOESN'T PERFORM? EH, STOOPID?"

13. The Crown as 'The Real Cap of Liberty'. *Punch*, 1871.

14. 'Republicanism by Limelight'. A republican meeting in Trafalgar Square, February 1872. *The Graphic*.

THE ILLUSTRATED
LONDON NEWS.

REGISTERED AT THE GENERAL POST OFFICE AS A NEWSPAPER.

No. 3354.—VOL. CXXIII   SATURDAY, AUGUST 1, 1903.   SIXPENCE.

The Copyright of all the Editorial Matter, both Engravings and Letterpress, is Strictly Reserved.

THE KING'S INTEREST IN THE HOUSING OF THE IRISH POOR: HIS MAJESTY VISITING A TENEMENT DWELLING IN THE POOREST QUARTER OF DUBLIN.

DRAWN BY A. FORESTIER, OUR SPECIAL ARTIST IN DUBLIN.

During his memorable visit to the Dublin tenements, his Majesty was greatly interested in seeing a portrait of himself from an illustrated paper which had been preserved and framed by his humble Hosts.

15. King Edward VII admiring a portrait of himself on a visit to a tenement in Dublin. *Illustrated London News*, 1903.

16. King George V in Sunderland, June 1917.

If the Bevanites ran the Coronation . . .

17. At the Coronation, a mild-mannered call for a scaled-down monarchy. Cummings, *Daily Express*, 1953.

18. By the time of the Jubilee, a more iconoclastic image. Jamie Reid, 1977.

PUNCH

29 JANUARY – 4 FEBRUARY 1992   **£1.20**   US $2.95 DM 8.50

Your P45, Ma'am

Is the royal family on the way out?

OK, YAH BOO SUCKS
We name the Upper Class Twit of the Year

PLUS: THE MASSES
Steve Punt joins the shellsuit set at Center Parcs

19. 'Is the royal family on the way out?' *Punch*, 1992.

M⊙⊙N
at the monarchy
2000

DROP 'EM! IT'S GOING TO BE KECKS AT HALF-MAST FOR BRITAIN'S DOOMED ROYALS IN THE FIRST EVER MASS PUBLIC MOONING!

SATURDAY JUNE 3RD 3PM RIGHT OUTSIDE BUCKINGHAM PALACE

WE WANT 2000 BARE BUTTS TO MAKE THE YEAR 2000 AN ANUS HORRIBILIS FOR THE WINDSORS. GET YOUR ARSE ALONG THERE!

20. Handbill distributed by the 'Movement against the Monarchy' announcing a demonstration at Buckingham Palace, June 2000.

The findings of Harris's poll were pretty consistent with other surveys carried out in the first twenty-five years of the Queen's reign.[49] A survey of Glasgow in 1968, traditionally a republican hotspot, found little evidence of anti-monarchism – only 3 per cent thought the Queen was doing her job badly – but there co-existed a high level of apathy.[50] Taken together, the polls illustrated that the monarchy had accomplished its principal mission, to survive in a political, religious and social environment that had changed dramatically since the 1930s. But over the years, the Queen, as friends and enemies alike noticed, had begun to look increasingly out of touch, a fact which the cultural shift of the 1960s exacerbated. However much attention she gave to modern life – she frequently opened new buildings or inspected innovative technology – she was perceived as a pillar of 1950s values.

The Queen's passivity was to many a reassuring sign of sanity and stability, but it encouraged in others what the polls were suggesting, a growing indifference to the Crown as an institution. Apathy was perhaps most noticeable among the young, to whom the monarchy often seemed dull and withdrawn. Viewing figures for the Queen's Christmas broadcast slipped in the 1960s, while the playing of the national anthem at cinemas and public gatherings died away.[51] Such straws in the wind did not go unnoticed in Palace circles. But the conventional arguments for maintaining the monarchy did not provide an obvious remedy for indifference. They tended to be defensive, often boiling down to Frederic Harrison's point 'that it is there'.[52] Having read little since Bagehot, the Queen's advocates relied on the familiar nostrums of magic and a family on the throne.

Their opponents, who couched their beliefs in the republican language of progress, dwelled on royal backwardness and looked, in Kingsley Martin's words, to 'the new England that waits to be born'. When Martin wrote *The Crown and the Establishment*, a rare, though mild-mannered, republican tract of the 1960s, he castigated royalty as a costly survival of institutionalized privilege, a symbol of the past and 'a vanishing economic order'. But while a republican, Martin believed that 'the monarchy could still be respected and indeed loved, as hereditary presidency of the nation and Commonwealth'.[53] Here was a commentator who, as his assessment of Dilke suggested, was sensitive to the republican elements that already existed in the constitution. He was yet another in the long line of royal critics who could imagine a republic with an hereditary president.

One critic who could not was the Christian Socialist Willie Hamilton, the 'self-appointed scourge of the monarchy', as Harold Wilson called him. Over the years, he had adopted the proletarian mantle of Keir Hardie, with opinions which echoed Harney and Gallacher. 'The Monarchy is the shining, glittering mask that conceals, so far successfully, the ugly face of a class system that is based on avarice, social injustice and inequity. It is hard to see how it could hope to survive the forces which must eventually destroy that system.' As such sentiments suggested, there was little fresh in Hamilton's critique, which treated the Crown as an 'irrelevant ornament' destined for the historical dustbin. Nor was there much new about his Civil List republicanism, which had failed to bring down the monarchy in the past. What Hamilton did bring to the republican tradition was a nice turn of phrase and a gift for the absurd, as when he advised the Queen to attend the Durham Miners' Gala rather than Ascot.[54]

Like others before him, Hamilton believed that the Achilles' heel of royalty was cost. He revelled in contrasting the luxuries of the court with working-class privation, but he failed to see that such grumbling was never likely to bring forth a fraternal republic in a capitalist society tolerant of extremes of wealth and poverty. In *My Queen and I*, Hamilton banged on about the Queen's private wealth. The book appeared at the beginning of 1975, just before Parliament was to consider a rise in the Civil List to meet inflation. It opened with a charge: 'You are known to be among the wealthiest women, if not the wealthiest woman in the world . . . Whatever many of your people believe, you pay no income tax . . . You pay no capital gains tax. You pay no death duty.' The passage ended with a question, which recalled the title of that famous pamphlet on Queen Victoria's finances published in 1871: 'What do you do with it all?'[55]

When in February Parliament debated the request for a rise in the Civil List, Hamilton dismissed the argument that a head of state should be excluded from personal taxation because taxation emanated from the head of state. (Royal immunity from income tax had been acquired incrementally, and quietly, in the reigns of George V and George VI.[56]) 'There is no magic about the Royal Family,' he scoffed. 'They are no more than glorified civil servants, one of them with a crown on her head.

They open things, close things and eat things – and that is about it.' He added that his post-bag was full of letters from constituents who were hostile to 'hangers-on' at court.[57] Harold Wilson, another Labour Prime Minister who, to Hamilton's disgust, had warmed to royalty once in office, picked up the usage: 'I doubt whether there is anyone better rewarded or who is a greater beneficiary from the existence of the monarchy – I would not wish to be so offensive as to refer to a "hanger-on" – through his writings than my Honourable Friend.'[58]

The *Times Literary Supplement* dismissed *My Queen and I* as 'a monstrous irrelevancy', while MPs heckled Hamilton as a crank.[59] But his call for an investigation into royal expenditure and greater public accountability of Civil List expenditure received some support in the Commons, where a motion was tabled opposing the increase in the Queen's allowance. The respected Labour MP for Fulham, Michael Stewart, urged greater clarity on the issue of royal immunity from taxation, which he believed was causing concern in the country. Like a growing band of Labour MPs, he wanted the Queen's private fortune, then said to be no more than £50 million (Hamilton put it at over £100 million), to be subject to tax. Stewart's views signalled that criticism of royal finance, and by implication royal behaviour, was becoming respectable. Ninety MPs, including Neil Kinnock and Dennis Skinner, voted in favour of the motion to annul the increase in the Queen's Civil List. Tony Benn, who was to become the leading exponent of republicanism in the House of Commons, joined the 427 in the monarchical lobby.[60]

Criticism of royal expenditure, inside and outside Parliament, expressed a change in the public attitude towards the monarchy. But in turn, in keeping with post-war culture, the royal family itself was becoming less hidebound. Arguably, the Queen's Jubilee in 1977, which some advisers thought might be a damp squib, was less an expression of ardent royalism than merriment under the pretence of flying the flag. Unlike George V's Jubilee in 1935, there was no longer an Empire to celebrate, nor a recovery from depression. Like the Jubilees of Queen Victoria and George V, there was some colourful opposition. The *New Statesman* produced an irreverent 'Anti-Jubilee Number', but it attacked the monarchical trappings, not the substance. This was in keeping with the view expressed in an article by the historian Kenneth Morgan:

'a republican platform would doom the Labour Party to eternal defeat'.[61]

On the far left, the Communist Party organized a 'People's Jubilee' at Alexandra Palace, and the Socialist Workers' Party distributed anti-monarchist badges and 'Roll out the Red Republic' stickers. Over at the Middle Temple, a graffito appeared in the lavatory, which read, 'Sod the Jubilee, the Ersatz Orgasm of the Silent Majority'.[62] Spotting an opportunity, the Sex Pistols declared their genius with the best-selling singles 'God Save the Queen' and 'Anarchy in the UK', which contained acrid lyrics taunting the Queen as a heartless stooge of a fascist state. In keeping with such abuse, the punk designer Jamie Reid produced an iconoclastic image of the Queen for the record sleeve.[63] (See Plate 18.) Such antics mocked deferential attitudes, but hardly triggered a constitutional debate. Whether they turned many teenagers into committed anti-royalists seems unlikely. To respectable society, they confirmed a link between indecency and radicalism, which had damaged the prospects of British anti-monarchism in the past. Constitutional republicans blanched at the prospect of being associated with boorishness.

Despite the anti-monarchical effusions, the Jubilee was undoubtedly a success, widely heralded as a triumph of monarchy. Once again, it showed that nothing did more to invigorate public spirit in Britain than a royal anniversary. Some critics thought the event celebrated an institution set in aspic. But while other national institutions were undergoing a crisis in public confidence, the monarchy remained relatively unscathed, its critics marginalized as eccentrics, or simply vulgar. An opinion poll in 1978 showed that 97 per cent of the sample were happy with the way the Queen performed her duties.[64] This suited Palace advisers down to the ground. Their policy, if it could be called a policy, was essentially protective, to present the Queen as a unique example of dignified public service and her family as a model of domestic virtue and middle-class respectability. But the selling of the monarchy as the nation's first family, as in the BBC film *Royal Family* (1969), only fuelled an insatiable appetite. In an era of declining deference, the growing press and television interest put ever more flesh and blood on royalty. In hereditary institutions, relatives are hostages to fortune.

As Hamilton noted, relations between the Palace and the media had deteriorated over the years, despite attempts to strike a balance between the right to royal privacy and the commercial demands of the press. The monarchy had, of course, been the subject of cartoons, gibes and abuse for centuries, much of it turning on royal indiscretion. But as a younger generation of writers and journalists entered the scene, a tug of war ensued, which has yet to be resolved, between an intrusive media, and the royal family's demand for privacy. Perhaps, as Pimlott suggests, the tension had less to do with the policies of courtiers or editors than with changes in the technology and economics of mass communication, which encouraged editors to switch 'from craven adulation to prurient derision in order to boost sales'.[65]

The monarchy had adjusted successfully to the rise of democracy, relative economic decline and the shift from Empire to Commonwealth. But intrusion into the private lives of members of the royal family had taken hold, a development which Palace advisers had encouraged by letting down the drawbridge. Turning the romance of Prince Charles and Lady Diana Spencer into a fairy tale could work only so long as the fairy tale lasted. Royal behaviour – the television show *It's a Royal Knockout* in 1987 was a portent – was becoming a threat, compounded by the press. The monarchy was no longer able to mask or to cushion shocks to the system. The *Sunday Times* warned that the 'grotesque appetite of the media for all things royal' would herald a republic.[66] In an era of circulation wars and royal exposure, the monarchy had moved from being dull or irrelevant to being a target of knowing journalists and the disaffected.

It may be that a growing disenchantment with national politics also contributed to the new concentration on royalty. From the mid-1980s, a period of high unemployment and challenges to established institutions, a spate of articles and books appeared which sought to dent the royal mystique in the hope of fomenting radical change. In the tradition of John Davidson and Willie Hamilton, they linked royal ineptitude with national decay, and conjured up idealized worlds against which the monarchy looked archaic. Others, harking back to Bradlaugh's secularism, decried the monarchy as the fount of irrationality.[67] In 1983, a small band of reformers opposed to hereditary privilege formed 'Republic', a London-based pressure group dedicated to the peaceful implementation of pure republicanism. Reminiscent of those obscure republican clubs of the 1850s and 1870s, its 'working party' on the constitution agonized over an alternative to the Queen, while its magazine provided a rare outlet for the expression of anti-monarchical views. Tony Benn contributed an amusing article titled 'Privatization of the Monarchy and the Church of England'.[68]

Though anti-monarchists stepped up their campaign, they made little impression beyond the faithful. Isolation led to frustration, and their sometimes virulent writings were more likely to alienate than to convert those in the political mainstream. The academic Piers Brendon, in the radical tradition, looked to republicanism to trigger a renaissance of public spirit. A republic, he declared in *Our Own Dear Queen* (1986), 'could wash Britain free of the feudal accretions which hamper her progress. It could sluice out the aristocratic privilege enshrined at the heart of Britain's national life'.[69] Edgar Wilson, a leading member of 'Republic', denounced the royal family as an instrument of class oppression in his book *The Myth of the British Monarchy* (1989). In *The Monarchy* (1990), the provocative journalist Christopher Hitchens saw royalty as the fount of credulity, and the Crown in Parliament as 'rubbing in . . . the fact that we have no rights, properly understood, but rather traditions that depend on the caprice of a political compromise made in 1688'.[70]

Along these lines, Tom Nairn's *The Enchanted Glass* (1988) dazzled. But lifting the veil on royal mystique was easier said than done, for whatever criticisms could be levelled against it, the monarchy retained a hold on the public imagination, a state of affairs which Nairn called 'appalling'. Royalism was not, in his analysis, simply mindless twaddle imbibed by passive idiots. It gave the public a positive 'electric charge'. Unlike some Marxist critics, who trivialized the monarchy as a symptom of class oppression, he saw it as central to the British malaise. The House of Windsor was 'a farce', but members of the royal family were pillars of Britain's fossilized conservatism, 'real icons of community and power, of national identity and State authority'. The idea that the monarchy might be removed by 'peevish grousing' over the Civil List was a chimera. What was needed was a major shift in British self-perception.[71]

Nairn accepted that Britain was already a republic of sorts, but it '*was not a Republic in the modern sense*', for its features, backward and patrician, were inimical 'to mass democracy and popular sovereignty (never mind socialism)'.[72] Yet he saw little prospect of shaking the British public out of their conservative culture, for there was no republican movement nor a language of anti-monarchism in everyday debate. Exasperation brought out his utopianism. 'Genuine republicanism' – that is, socialist transformation – would require a revolution in human behaviour: '*Real* democracy', he wrote, 'will exist only when "every man is, in his own proper self, a king" – when the ordinary has become extraordinary, the humdrum been dissolved in glamour: when mortals step into the enchanted glass or its visions step down to join us.'[73] In *The Enchanted Glass*, the republic of the imagination had come a long way from its ancient core of anti-despotism.

Nairn's sociological critique contributed to making anti-monarchism intellectually respectable on the left, but it might have had a wider impact had it first appeared at the time of the public collapse of the marriage of the Prince and Princess of Wales. Royal misadventure gave fresh virulence to the anti-monarchical element in republican thought, particularly when the heir to the throne was involved. The public spectacle of royal confession and recrimination was arguably the biggest boost to anti-royalism since the troubles of a former Prince of Wales in the 1870s. It brought out the latent contradictions in people's thinking about the monarchy, reminding them that the hereditary principle is undemocratic and capable of producing unpopular sovereigns. Unhappily for the Crown, royal reverses mounted up just as the campaign for constitutional reform, led by Charter 88, a pressure group described by Nairn as 'closet' republican, was gaining momentum.[74] Ironically, the collapse of communism in Europe provided another fillip, for after 1989 socialists had to focus on secondary enemies. Compared to capitalism, the monarchy was a soft target.

The saga of royal troubles in the early and mid-1990s, which emboldened anti-monarchists, is so familiar that it hardly needs repeating.[75] But with a stalwart royalist in the Prime Minister, John Major, republicans made no headway in the House of Commons. Tony Benn's Bill (1992) to create a socialist commonwealth and replace the Queen with a president elected by MPs, a unique document in the history of modern British politics, failed to engage his colleagues and never came to a vote.[76] As in the late nineteenth century, aspiring MPs with republican leanings were chary of jeopardizing their careers over an institution which they thought to be of marginal political importance. They consoled themselves with the view that the office of head of state was essentially symbolic; thus the need for an election was questionable. When their thoughts turned to a president, they were reminded that Mrs Thatcher might top the poll. An essential problem for republicans was to produce a convincing alternative to a system which already was a republic in constitutional essentials, albeit with an hereditary head of state.

The republican campaign was kept alive in the press, from *Red Pepper* to the *Independent on Sunday. Punch* ran a cover story: 'Is the royal family on the way out?'[77] (See Plate 19.) Meanwhile, a host of programmes, conferences and staged 'debates' on the monarchy, the equivalent of the public meetings in the 1870s, expressed the sometimes frenzied media interest, if not always the public mood. Such events, with their instant polls and whipped-up audiences, turned politics into entertainment. They rarely got beneath the surface of the important constitutional issues at stake and sometimes deteriorated into farce.[78] Caricatures of the Queen as 'divine' or 'a tyrant' were hardly instructive. The truism that you can have a republic with a monarchy, accepted by a host of political philosophers in the past and once a commonplace among the educated in Britain, was lost in the din.

Writers and academics, lawyers and clerics, many of whom avowedly had never thought seriously about the monarchy before, began to express opinions, for and against. Royal embarrassment invigorated republican derision and loyalist truculence. Reminiscent of the tactics of Bradlaugh in the 1870s, enemies of the Crown sought to sink the reputation of the heir to the throne. The left-wing playwright David Hare encapsulated republican venom in a speech at the 'Monarchy Debate' at the Queen Elizabeth Centre in 1993: 'We shall mock them [the royal family] till they wish they had never been born.'[79] He is now Sir David. The novelist Martin Amis, while claiming not to care about the monarchy, declared on the same occasion that 'this soap is clearly falling apart . . . It whines to be put out of its misery'.[80] It had become respectable, indeed fashionable, to call oneself a republican, at least outside government circles. But as so much opposition to the monarchy at the time was media driven, and often careless with facts, it is difficult to assess its underlying seriousness.

Without access to royal records, it is equally difficult to judge just how seriously the monarchy took the threat to be. Palace officials, ruffled by the personal abuse levelled at the royal family, monitored the media, pressed their allies into service, and held strategy meetings with a range of advisers. In 1995, senior members of the royal family and their private secretaries formed the Way Ahead Group to discuss matters of policy and to co-ordinate the royal programme. But were these measures a reaction, indeed an over-reaction, to a phantom? Unlike earlier outbreaks of anti-monarchism, there was no trade depression, social unrest or revolution abroad. At no time during the 1990s did the polls suggest that more than 20 per cent of the population favoured deposing the sovereign.[81] But the Queen's seeming aloofness, the troubles of the heir to the throne and the appearance of republican clubs invited comparisons with the 1870s.[82] So too did the re-emergence of the republican stand-by, the issue of the monarchy's cost, which was raised in the media and by Phillip Hall's critical study *Royal Fortune: Tax, Money and the Monarchy* (1992).

As it had turned out in the past, Civil List republicanism did not have the dynamic to advance the pure republican cause. The monarchy simply disarmed the critics by introducing a few reforms. On advice, the Queen began to pay tax on her private income, reimbursed the government for the parliamentary annuities to members of the royal family, opened Buckingham Palace to pay for the repair of Windsor Castle following the fire, decommissioned the Royal Yacht and accepted greater parliamentary scrutiny of royal accounts.[83] Such actions confirmed what a host of republicans, from Fawcett to Nairn, had argued, that denunciations of the monarchy's costs were a 'futile sidetrack'.[84] Most people, it seemed, accepted the argument put by Bagehot, Gladstone and Attlee, that a head of state had to be paid for. While they might complain about the expense of royalty – just over £1 per person a year in the mid-1990s – it seldom translated into a wish to see the monarchy abolished.[85]

If the criticism of royal expenditure did not pose a serious threat to the Crown, there were potential problems on the horizon. Constitutionalist republicans, while privately praying for royal self-destruction, argued that devolution in Scotland and ever-closer European Union would embarrass the Crown and attenuate its role. They also assumed that opposition to the monarchy in Britain would be enlivened by Australia's declaration as a republic; but this seemed open to question since many other Commonwealth nations had became republics without doing so. Most put their faith in the reform of the House of Lords, for they expected that that would trigger a demand for further reforms, including a written constitution, which would leave the monarch's role in doubt. At the least, they believed the reform of the upper house would leave the monarchy cruelly exposed as the last element of hereditary privilege in the constitution. They did not consider the possibility that the removal of hereditary peers might represent a final stage in the perfection of the crowned republic.

In the longer term, republicans, among them Thatcherites hostile to the hereditary principle, believed that the global economy, the demands for institutional efficiency and the acceleration of cultural change would leave the monarchy looking like an expensive white elephant.[86] But it was unclear whether a vacuous global culture would make the British more or less protective of their own traditions. In frivolous mood, the Young Conservatives, at an annual conference in 1989, tabled a resolution to privatize the royal family, but decided the notion would make risible the arguments for privatizing anything else. One radical libertarian, only half in jest, took up the idea and foresaw a time when the monarchy would be subjected to the same scrutiny as the money supply and hospital cleaning services.[87]

In the short term, republican theorists concentrated on the constitution. They had become disillusioned with the very democracy their nineteenth-century forebears had helped to create. They pointed to the obvious imperfections of political democracy in Britain, and the need to make government more accountable. Disaffected from representative government that had not led to popular sovereignty, they sought to turn passive *subjects* into active *citizens* by uprooting what they saw as a retarded political culture, propped up by an unelected sovereign. Supreme power rested, as many of them saw it, in an 'elective dictatorship' manipulated by a self-serving élite, which governed quasi-regally and sheltered behind the royal prerogative. According to the journalist Jonathan Freedland, a fervent admirer of Paine and the American Constitution, it was imperative 'to wrest control from the combined force now in charge: the crown-in-parliament'.[88]

While their arguments rested on the abuse of the royal prerogative by the executive, they piled the blame for national infirmity on the Crown. Stephen Haseler, another Paineite republican, bemoaned that Britain suffered from a 'feudal' constitution and that its people would not enjoy the twenty-first century with an hereditary sovereign.[89] Freedland, who accused the monarchy of instilling 'fresh generations of Britons with a feudal history of inequality', insisted that the Queen was politically potent. He singled out her reserve power to appoint a Prime Minister in a hung parliament as a breach of democracy.[90] Such variations on the theme of 'Old Corruption' – anachronistically described as 'feudal' – were a departure from those republican traditions which saw the monarchy as politically irrelevant, or even as an ally in the battle against a perfidious oligarchy.[91] It may be recalled that diverse republicans, from the radical John Thelwall in the 1790s to the socialist Tom Johnston in the 1930s, had said that the Crown might be instrumental in promoting the advance of liberty.

Republicanism retained links with its tradition of anti-despotism and public spirit, but beyond that, it remained a slippery and contentious concept among contemporary theorists. At its most basic, it could simply be a tag for anti-authoritarianism. In America, a parallel school of political commentary had mutated republicanism into a host of modish interpretations.[92] A study in 1997 of Anglo-American political thought included multi-culturalism, environmentalism and women's rights as republican causes.[93] In Britain, however, republicans increasingly focused on the monarchy, which had suddenly become vulnerable. However much they dressed it up in radical or socialist ideals, they had turned the abolition of the Crown into the *sine qua non* of republicanism. In the free-for-all over republican usage, the anti-monarchists had triumphed. But had they driven the republican tradition in Britain into a cul-de-sac of ritualized protest, which distracted attention from more pressing issues?

Given the degree of republicanism already in the constitution, widely acknowledged by republicans themselves in the past, the monarchy was less obstructive to democratic reform than anti-royalists in the 1990s assumed. Britain, of course, retained a vestige of ancient privilege in an unelected head of state. Though the Queen normally exercises her prerogative powers on ministerial advice, the strongest argument against the monarchy remained its lack of direct sanction from the electorate. The hereditary principle is indefensible on democratic grounds, though many argue, harking back to classical republicanism, that the sovereign serves the nation by acting as a check on executive power. Judging from the experience of other countries, there is no reason to believe that uncrowned republics are more democratic than constitutional monarchies. A survey of western democracies published in the journal of the American Political Science Association in 1998 argued that while monarchy 'had no direct effect on democratic performance in the 1980s, it consistently bolstered the conditions that, themselves, promoted democracy'.[94]

Whatever the relationship between monarchy and democracy, an hereditary element in the constitution was something the British electorate was willing to tolerate even at the nadir of royal popularity in the mid-1990s. Anti-monarchists could not escape this fact. Without popular consent, they would either have to foment a revolution or persuade the royal family to join their campaign. Monarchies may be removed by various means: revolution, parliamentary legislation, a vote for a republic or the sovereign simply giving up. None of the above seemed likely in Britain. With a touch of innocence or desperation, anti-royalists sometimes did ask the Queen to resign voluntarily, or entreated Prince Charles to stand down when the Queen died.[95] More often, they put their faith in a referendum on the monarchy, to be held, if not immediately, at the close of the Queen's reign.

Doubters, from constitutional experts to the editor of the *Sunday Telegraph*, questioned just how the abolition of the monarchy would bring about a transformation in Britain's fortunes.[96] How would it lead to the transparent politics, whatever was meant by the phrase, of the republican imagination? More specifically, how would it check or decentralize the power concentrated in the Prime Minister's office? The removal of the sovereign's personal prerogatives might lead to greater democratic accountability – it would certainly shelter the Queen from accusations of political interference.[97] But the abolition of the monarchy altogether threatened to be a political Armageddon. Was it worth the effort or the risk? Would it improve schools or cut hospital waiting lists? Though theoretical republicans had argued in the past that attacking the Crown was a distraction from more serious political business, the new generation of pure republicans argued that serious politics could only begin with its removal. Engaging with this view in his book on the constitution, Ferdinand Mount argued that reformers were simply looking for 'a scapegoat for their own dissatisfactions, without being able to define exactly' what was wrong.[98]

To the sceptical mind, a campaign that promised national renewal through changes to the constitution, and assumed that government edict would trigger a social transformation, was politics in the language of faith.[99] People did not need to be inert conservatives, or even monarchists, to suspect that a revival of Britain might prove elusive even with a new model constitution, or to question whether the abolition of the Crown would transform them into active citizens. More thoughtful anti-monarchists recognized that the creation of an uncrowned republic worthy of the name would require more than removing the sovereign. Caroline Ellis, Charter 88's Political Officer, argued that a republic which did not encourage participatory democracy 'would be just as empty a shell as monarchy'.[100] Such issues had, of course, been addressed by republicans in the past. Harrison, who waved away the political importance of the monarchy, had said that a violent attack on the Crown would simply risk a 'critical social convulsion' in the cause of 'a formal political change'.[101] As Bradlaugh recognized, one could become a citizen without becoming sovereign.[102]

Matthew Arnold once wrote how in France the citizen 'feels that the power which represses him is the State', whereas in England, the subject feels that 'the power which represses him is the Tories, the upper class, the aristocracy and so on'.[103] Would the abolition of the monarchy lead to a shift in perceptions about the British state? Conceivably, an uncrowned republic might simply mark a further stage in the perfection of state power, the triumph of the Prime Minister as 'an elected monarch', or, to use Lord Hailsham's phrase, the triumph of 'elective dictatorship'.[104] The Crown's enemies have always been more absorbed in tearing down than building up, better at theory than on the practicalities of what would fill the void left by the departed sovereign. In the 1990s, they tended to dismiss the monarch's ceremonial role, which diverts the prestige and moderates the delusions of grandeur that can so easily accompany Prime Ministerial power.[105] Yet they assumed that in an uncrowned republic executive ambition would be moderated by an elected president. But why would the executive accept such a rival in the first place? The continuing debate over an elected replacement for the House of Lords makes this point. Prime Ministers are well aware that elected presidents are more likely to be politically potent than unelected sovereigns.

Republicans had a case when they said that royalty was a powerful symbol of class, which encouraged notions of social hierarchy. But the belief that the monarchy's abolition would herald the end of class and privilege was sanguine in a capitalist economy. One need only dip into Proust to see that social divisions and ambitions persisted in the Third Republic. Without the royal family as a focal point of society, would the British be able to avoid an indecorous scramble for social pre-eminence? Republicans in the past thought it unlikely without the triumph of republican spirit or the collapse of 'King Capital'. 'Title', as Keir Hardie put it, 'is not indispensable to toadyism.'[106] In some respects, republics mimicked former monarchies, and presidential administrations re-created many of the trappings and offices of former royal courts, as the political dynasties of the United States might suggest. The abolition of the Crown would take away the privileges of the Windsors and their intimates, but would it not simply pass them on to others in a different guise? Privilege is something always enjoyed by others.

In the 1990s, republicans argued that Britain's social system was more oppressive than elsewhere, that the monarchy blighted not only the national character but the country's economic prospects. According to the constitutional writer Anthony Barnett, Britain's undemocratic 'Empire State' was incompatible with a return to prosperity.[107] The argument ran: 'Britain can never become a truly modern state while the trappings of feudalism remain.'[108] (How did the Japanese or the Dutch manage it? asked the doubters, who detected no correlation between republicanism and modernization.[109]) Just how the removal of an hereditary sovereign would turn Britain, invariably described as a backwater by republicans, into a world-beating meritocratic society of free and equal citizens, remained a mystery. It would require millions of subjects, who according to republican arguments have been cowed by centuries of royal mystification and class oppression, to become spontaneously endowed with participatory virtue.

Many of the academics, journalists and poets who have driven the republican movement forward have been frustrated rationalists, or visionaries in the socialist tradition, prone to deride the very people they seek to liberate. Since the French Revolution, enemies of the Crown have ridiculed loyal subjects as infantile or idiotic. Bradlaugh, it may be remembered, accused his countrymen of subservience and declared that 'monarchy is government for children: Republicanism is for men'. Republicans in the 1990s carried forward the tradition. Haseler and Freedland, like Bradlaugh, argued that monarchy induced 'childish sensibility' or imprisoned the nation in 'political infancy'.[110] The writer Richard Hoggart stated as 'a major fact: that most British people are not ready intellectually or, more importantly, imaginatively to have done with the monarchy'.[111] Christopher Hitchens admitted to being disconcerted to find himself 'slightly despising my fellow citizens for their repetitiveness, their credulity, their deference, I would say almost their servility'.[112] A dislike of being associated with this stance may have discouraged other reflective republicans from actively joining the campaign.

Since Paine's day, republicans have put their faith in democracy's capacity to transform society, and the more dreamy their visions the more inadequate the citizenry appeared. But what were the prospects for their ideal of popular sovereignty if the electorate were so debilitated and credulous? A disregard for their potential recruits brought into question the democratic credentials of some republicans in the 1990s. 'It is true that a majority is in favour of keeping the monarchy,' one of them argued, 'but this is an inadequate justification.'[113] The arbitrary rule of a new oligarchy under the pretence of democratic social transformation could not be ruled out. Given the electorate's royalist sympathies, conceded by Nairn and others, a long propaganda campaign seemed necessary to move the case against the Crown forward. Some republicans, however, favoured by-passing the electorate. One means was to give MPs a free vote on the monarchy, rather like a free vote on abortion or blood sports.[114] Publications by the Fabian Society and the think-tank Demos proposed a more piecemeal approach, to 'modernize' the monarchy into oblivion.[115]

In the 1990s, republican arguments, however powerfully expressed, made little impact on the general public. Royal behaviour rather than disenchantment with the constitution fuelled the *popular* expression of anti-monarchical republicanism. Barnett, the co-ordinator of Charter 88, ruefully admitted in 1994 that 'few people in Britain express the slightest interest in the constitution – at the moment'.[116] It is doubtful that calls for the abolition of the monarchy would have made any impression on the public without the collapse of the marriage of the Prince and Princess of Wales. The Crown's enemies had their heyday between the serialization of Andrew Morton's *Diana, Her True Story* in the summer of 1992, which confirmed the rumours about the marriage, and the death of the Princess of Wales five years later. The fact that the Conservative Party's support disintegrated over the same period is a coincidence that might repay further study.

Though it was not immediately obvious, the tragedy of the Princess's death was a turning-point in the monarchy's fortunes. It created a momentary surge of anti-royalist murmuring, which republicans sought to exploit.[117] In response, the monarchy made symbolic concessions and the Queen addressed the nation in an extraordinary broadcast. Ironically, republicans had been prominent among those who sought to turn the removal of Princess Diana's royal title into political capital. But the ploy to turn the Princess into a proto-republican, like a latter-day Queen Caroline, failed. Not only was the Princess an unlikely radical heroine, but her many admirers knew that she wanted Prince William to become king. Anthony Holden, the anti-monarchist author of several books on royalty, was prescient in saying that compassion for the young princes 'could set the republican cause back a generation'.[118]

With the rival court at Kensington Palace removed, the focus on royalty softened and shifted to Prince Charles as a single parent and a charitable campaigner in his own right. The popularity of Blair's new Labour Government, with its comforting language of national renewal, also provided a distraction from royal troubles. Gradually, the public standing of the heir apparent began to pick up.[119] A year after the death of the Princess of Wales, only 15 per cent of those sampled in a Mori poll thought Britain would be better off without a monarchy, a figure in keeping with surveys in the 1960s.[120] In October 1998, a 'March on Buckingham Palace' by the far left Movement against the Monarchy, which featured a guillotine on its handbills – along with the Queen's head on a toilet roll – made no impression on the general public.[121] Meanwhile, the lobbying of MPs by anti-royal pressure groups failed to sway the new Labour administration, despite a plethora of theoretical republicans on the Labour front and back benches.[122] In the government's inquiry into constitutional reform, the monarchy was not on the agenda.

Tony Blair's interventions in the days following the death of the Princess of Wales suggested that he handled the royal tragedy with purpose. No one should be surprised by this, for he inherited a political system and a civil service disposed to constitutional monarchy, backed by voters with little enthusiasm for political upheaval. With a dislike of the hereditary principle, he might be described as a theoretical republican. But so long as the Queen eclipsed him in the polls, she could count on his support. From his unique perspective, dispensing with an institution that had provided political continuity for hundreds of years would be hazardous without the guarantee that it could be easily replaced by something obviously superior. (Presumably, the House of Lords was more expendable.) The royal family, for its part, knew that in a time of troubles it needed to placate the executive. The result was a *modus vivendi* between the monarchy and Labour in power, which, as in the reign of George V, was enough to turn republican stomachs.

Like former Labour Prime Ministers, Blair assumed that the Crown was a fixture; as such, it should be relevant. Where republicans saw royal obstruction, he saw royal potential. Most reforming Prime Ministers, including Gladstone, Attlee and Wilson, had had strong royalist sympathies, if only because they understood that popular rule required symbols of legitimacy to smooth the path of reform. The monarchy, as Bogdanor observes, 'offers fixed constitutional landmarks and a degree of institutional continuity in a changing world, so that the costs of change come to appear easier to bear'.[123] Moreover, the royal family has long been an agency of social empowerment, as the charitable work of the Princess of Wales so richly demonstrated. On issues such as education and youth unemployment, Blair and the Prince of Wales had mutual interests, and the Prince's Trust would play a part in the government's Welfare to Work programme.

By the end of the 1990s, anti-monarchism was beginning to have an historical ring. Once again, the pragmatic British public proved unwilling to risk political or social convulsion without guarantees. The Crown's opponents might call this infantile, but was it childish to favour one form of imperfection over others, or to wish to avoid the turmoil and uncertainty that deposing a popular sovereign would entail? Public caution was unsurprising in a prosperous country with a long tradition of political stability and a constitution which, for all its vagaries, was not held in as much contempt in the country at large as in the metropolitan think-tanks. In a nation that preferred to reform its institutions rather than destroy them, there was simply not enough pressure from below to move the anti-monarchical argument forward in Parliament. Nor did the prospects for linking parliamentary and extra-parliamentary opposition to the Crown look any more promising than in the past, if only because of the diffuse and disorderly nature of the republican campaign. The polls, though putting a question mark over the monarchy in the long-term, suggested that the House of Windsor had a future.

While fair-weather republicans moved on to other issues, fervent anti-monarchists continued to abuse the royal family in the press.[124] A few extremists, with a penchant for political gestures, threw eggs and screamed obscenities at the Queen during her public outings. The Movement against the Monarchy, with 400 members, planned to mark the millennium celebrations by rubbishing the Queen Mother's 100th birthday. With a taste for the scatological, they also planned a 'mass public mooning' at Buckingham Palace, 'to make the year 2000 an Anus [*sic*] Horribilis for the Windsors'.[125] (See Plate 20.) These pranksters, anarchists and class warriors were part of a subterranean culture that barely impinged on the public consciousness but alienated respectable opinion when it did. Were they the modern counterparts of those radicals who stoned the coach of George III in the 1790s, or the Red Republicans who rioted in the 1870s? Their behaviour, which discomfits constitutional republicans – presumably to the delight of Palace officials – may help to explain the loyalist reaction to outbursts of anti-monarchism in the past. Will historians fifty years on praise them as post-modern levellers or dismiss them as political morons?

At the end of the last millennium, more conventional republicans avoided incendiary language and personal attacks on the royal family. If they had heard of the Movement against the Monarchy, they were unlikely to join a 'mass public mooning' at the Palace gates. As constitutionalists, they still held out hope that the monarchy would vanish in the wake of House of Lords reform, European Union, Scottish devolution and the declaration of an Australian republic.[126] But there was little to suggest a falling off in royal popularity at the opening of the Scottish Parliament in July 1999.[127] And the failure of the referendum in Australia the following November was seen as a setback, though the country was arguably a republic already. Still, with constitutional change on the horizon in Britain and abroad, the issue of the monarchy's place at home, in Europe and in the Commonwealth seemed destined to re-emerge. The contemporary obsession with symbols of authority, which marked the

Australian referendum debate, also suggested that the monarchy would remain controversial.

As their priorities suggested, the Crown's enemies had an atavistic preoccupation with the political role of the monarchy (which royalists shared), and a belief in a written constitution and a referendum as a way around what they saw as the royal impasse. Because they were so antipathetic, republicans rarely considered any explanation for the monarchy's continuing existence, apart from tradition, mass delusion or plutocratic convenience. As radicals, they had little patience with the Burkean notion of an organic society in which people identified with historic institutions. They did not understand the pleasure people took from the foibles of the most glamorous branch of the national family. Nor did they ask themselves how royalty had coped with democratic change. A lack of interest in the monarchy's evolution had led them to misunderstand, and consequently misrepresent, the institution they sought to destroy. In the manner of Paine, they exaggerated the Queen's political importance and cursed the establishment without coming to terms with the substantive reasons for royal popularity. They mocked loyal subjects as deluded but ignored the monarchy's claims to public esteem beyond the ceremonial side-show.

One of the striking things about republican thought, at least in the radical tradition of Paine, Bradlaugh, Harrison and Freedland, has been its emphasis on public spirit.[128] Yet with their tendency to opposition and scorn, republicans rarely credited the expression of public spirit all around them. Preoccupied with high politics, most took little notice of the army of voluntarists involved in civic causes. But as A. J. P. Taylor put it, voluntarists were 'the active people of England', who 'provided the ground swell of her history'.[129] Over the centuries, British society has nurtured a rich array of voluntary organizations, which have served as a buffer between the individual and the state. Civic and charitable institutions, professional and trade associations, self-help and mutual aid societies, social clubs and religious agencies, were free expressions of the public spirit consistent with republican thought. Such institutions operated within a society of class and privilege. With the years, increasing numbers of them enjoyed Crown patronage. This did not recommend them to socialists, for whom the very idea of *noblesse oblige* was an insult.

The monarchy has always fortified royal popularity by nurturing the belief that individuals, however humble, have a claim on its services. Cannadine observes that in civic and charitable association 'the royal culture of hierarchical condescension, and the popular culture of social aspiration . . . completely and successfully merged'.[130] But because they despise privilege and deference, anti-royalists have failed to notice just how much the monarchy has stimulated the advance of public spirit, both practically and symbolically. Royal jubilees alone confirm the point. Over the last 200 years, the monarchy reaffirmed its importance by forging a popular role for itself outside politics as patron, promoter and fund-raiser for the deserving and underprivileged. It was not surprising that the Mass Observation survey in the 1960s discovered that the monarchy's humdrum social work had become as important in its survival as its 'dignified' duties. In the 1990s, the royal family had well over 3,000 institutional patronages, among them a majority of Britain's leading fund-raising societies, and carried out about 4,000 official engagements each year, nearly half of them charitable.[131]

If the rise of socialism stimulated royal benevolence in the reign of George V, the decline of socialism presents the monarchy with fresh opportunities to expand it in the present reign. In a utilitarian society shedding its collectivist zeal and coming around to pluralism in social policy, the scope for royal intervention, and partnership with government, becomes all the greater. The work of the Prince's Youth Business Trust, the largest business agency in the country outside government, is instructive. How many ministers can claim to have created 39,000 companies and 52,000 jobs?[132] The message that Prince Charles seeks to promote is that social problems are best remedied by public spirit, local initiative and self-help, which is in tune with the regeneration of civil society that many republicans, disenchanted with overbearing government, now desire.[133] His civic republican credentials, like those of Prince Albert, are not inconsiderable. They will, his advisers believe, persuade the public that Prince Charles is a conscientious king (or hereditary president?) in waiting.

Despite the monarchy's opposition to universal suffrage throughout the nineteenth century, it has been a consistent supporter of pluralism and participation in local spheres. One of the arguments in favour of retaining a monarchy in the nineteenth century was that by propping up so many voluntary societies it acted as a defender of institutional democracy.[134] In so doing, it served as a buffer between the state and society and acted as a counterweight to the dictatorial tendencies of central government. The present Queen endorsed such views in 1991 in her Christmas broadcast on charitable service and a free society. As she saw it, a healthy voluntary sector, independent of government control, was the foundation of an open society. In a revealing sentence, which could have been written by Paine, she remarked: 'democracy depends, not on political structures, but on the goodwill and the sense of responsibility of each and every citizen'.[135] Unspoken in her address was the corollary that, through its promotion of voluntary bodies, the monarchy was itself part of the bedrock of civil society and a check on the arbitrary power of the state.

As so much of the Crown's mystery has been dissipated by royal scrapes and tabloid intrusion, it is likely that the monarchy will be judged increasingly on the practical benefits it brings to society. 'It is . . . in the practical employment of its symbolic influence, that the monarchy will find its future,' concluded Bogdanor in his book *The Monarchy and the Constitution* (1995).[136] The point is understood by members of the royal family and their officials, who in a time of trouble have cause to remember the motto 'Ich Dien'. As a senior adviser to Prince Charles declared in 1997: 'The monarchy is moving from being an institution principally famous for ceremonial occasions to being an institution principally of value for what it can add to the country through public service.'[137] Even political journalists began to notice the royal family's commitment to charity in the late 1990s, if only because Princess Diana raised its profile. But the public remained ahead of the pundits. Witness the readers of *The Big Issue*, the voice of the homeless and dispossessed, who elected Prince Charles their 'Hero of the Year' in 1999.[138]

A reputation for social service would not save the monarchy in revolutionary circumstances, such as those in France in 1793 or Germany in 1918. But in more settled times, the royal expression of republican spirit, as Coleridge prophesied, is a form of insurance against oblivion. A royal strategy for survival which builds on the Crown's longstanding civic traditions seems more obvious now that collectivist principles have waned, the Empire has vanished and Bagehot's model family on the throne is a memory. Over the years, the monarchy has reaped enormous benefits from its public service and its promotion of social pluralism and associational democracy. But in the contest over the language of reform, it has largely failed, leaving anti-monarchists and other republicans to define the meaning of republicanism to suit themselves. Whether the monarchy could co-opt, or reclaim, a republican tradition so endowed with revolutionary symbolism is an open question. But members of the royal family could make greater capital out of their social and civic work if they couched it in a progressive vocabulary more often. They appear not to appreciate it, but when they encourage public spirit and democratic values, they are expressing republican sentiments.[139]

As Harney conceded in 1850, England was already a republic of sorts, and 'every Englishman may, if he will, term himself a Republican'.[140] Yet the monarchy has long been on the defensive, unable, or unwilling, to take advantage of the possibilities in the meaning of *res publica*. The political language in which Britain was seen as a 'crowned republic', a 'monarcho-republic' or a 'monarchic-democracy', so useful to the Crown in the past, has faded. Apart from the promotion of public spirit, the most enduring aim of republicanism since the late eighteenth century has been democratic reform. Despite longstanding royal conservatism, fuelled by anti-monarchists and reinforced by loyalists, the advance of democracy posed a less serious threat to the monarchy than imagined by George III and his successors. The Way Ahead Group might wish to consider Lord Brougham's remark, made at the beginning of Victoria's reign, that the best way to ensure the future of the Crown was to 'strengthen the people's hands by confirming their liberties and extending their rights'.[141]

No one can predict with any precision what would happen if the British monarchy, an institution so embedded in the nation's past and consciousness, were to be abolished. Prophecies vary from national regeneration to a nightmare of reaction. Fracturing the country's distinctive historical narrative would certainly bring surprises. But to abolish the institution without overwhelming public approval would trigger more than a little local disturbance and open up ideological divisions between monarchists and republicans in Britain, such as those which once bedevilled French and American politics. Compared to republican clubs, the Constitutional Monarchy Association and the Monarchist League are long lived. And if history is any guide, pure monarchists are, if anything, more inflexible and belligerent than pure republicans, and they might not go quietly. (Consider the examples of British monarchists' reactions to European events in 1789, 1848 and 1917.)

Few people would opt for a system which turns on an accident of birth if they were devising a constitution from scratch. Yet few monarchies have come to an end because they were thought irrational. As Harold Nicolson noted, the First World War and its aftermath 'witnessed the disappearance of five Emperors, eight Kings and eighteen more dynasties'.[142] None of them disappeared because of logic. Arguably, the greatest danger to the British monarchy in modern history erupted in the reign of George V, but the threat came less from republican argument than from the German armed forces. Should the British monarchy collapse in the future, it would be unlikely to be the result of anti-monarchical reasoning, which has failed to persuade the public in the past. Monarchy persists, as republicans have insisted, partly because of custom. But custom underpins the political stability that people desire. As long as stability is valued so highly, royal self-destruction or war would be the most likely cause of the British monarchy's demise. A republican case against the Crown would then come into view as justification.

Throughout history, *res publica* has been a malleable and contradictory concept, its frontier always on the move, in keeping with whatever its proponents deemed liberating or progressive. The 'invention of tradition', an idea widely associated with monarchy, is in fact more applicable to republicanism.[143] Should the British monarchy come to an end and the promised national revival fail to materialize, it is probable that republicanism itself would be reinvented as a critique of the uncrowned republic. Should the Crown endure, no one should assume that anti-monarchy marks the end of republican permutations. One can even imagine a reinvigoration of those classical norms, in which crowned republics figured prominently in political thought. There is, after all, nothing paradoxical in the idea that a nation can be self-governing and a people free under a monarchy.[144] Constitutional monarchists and anti-monarchists agree on at least one issue: they oppose tyranny. This was the thinking behind Sir Wilfrid Lawson's remark in the House of Commons in 1889 that 'we are all Republicans'.

In modern history, republicanism has had greater success in its democratic guise than its anti-monarchical one. Nevertheless, the occasional threat to the Crown, whether real or imagined, has had an impact, though not of the sort anti-royalists might wish. The relationship of republicans and the monarchy has been one of mutual dependence. Clearly, the royal family has found opposition invigorating, rather like an inoculation that prevents the onset of a terminal affliction. With a republican shot in the arm, the monarchy became more sensitive to respectable opinion and responsive to social issues. When the Chartist throngs converged on Kennington Common in 1848, Prince Albert turned his mind to housing, schools and factories. When British socialists on 'Red' Clydeside and in South Wales expressed sympathy for the Russian Revolution, George V dispatched his family to the nation's blackspots. In recent years, the monarchy has once again been startled by its adversaries. In consequence, the royal family is on alert and on parade.

In her memorable '*annus horribilis*' speech in November 1992, the Queen acknowledged the republican opposition and the need to use criticism 'as an effective engine for change'.[145] It was reminiscent of Lord Stamfordham's remark in 1918, that the monarchy could only survive by 'keeping pace with the times'. If the House of Windsor can continue to claw back public respect, the anti-monarchical cause will sink further into the political sands. It will eventually resurface, if only because an hereditary system cannot furnish a popular head of state for ever. But no one should assume that if the monarchy were to self-destruct or be abolished, it would lead to that elusive *res publica* of the radical imagination. To those driven by a vision of mankind perfected, the green light of the pure republic will forever flash on the horizon. The down-to-earth nineteenth-century philosopher Herbert Spencer put it squarely: 'The Republican form of Government is the highest form of government; but because of this it requires the highest type of human nature – a type nowhere at present existing.'[146]

Notes

1. George III and the Rights of Man

1. See David Wootton, 'Introduction', *Republicanism, Liberty, and Commercial Society, 1649–1776*, ed. David Wootton (Stanford, 1994), pp. 1–7.

2. Joseph Addison, *Freeholder*, no. 29 (30 March 1716).

3. John Adams, *A Defence of the Constitutions of Government of the United States of America*, 3 vols. (Philadelphia, 1797), vol. 1, p. 87; vol. 3, p. 159. See also Wootton, 'Introduction', *Republicanism, Liberty, and Commercial Society, 1649–1776*, pp. 1, 6.

4. On classical republicanism see J. G. A. Pocock, *The Machiavellian Moment: Florentine Political Thought and the Atlantic Republican Tradition* (Princeton, 1975); Caroline Robbins, *The Eighteenth-Century Commonwealthman* (Cambridge, Mass., 1959); Steve Pincus, 'Neither Machiavellian Moment nor Possessive Individualism: Commercial Society and the Defenders of the English Commonwealth', *American Historical Review*, vol. 103, no. 3 (June 1998), p. 710; Wootton, 'Introduction', *Republicanism, Liberty, and Commercial Society, 1649–1776*, pp. 8–9.

5. Blair Worden, 'English republicanism', *The Cambridge History of Political Thought 1450–1700*, ed. J. H. Burns (Cambridge, 1991), pp. 446–7. Gregory Claeys, *Citizens and Saints: Politics and Anti-Politics in Early British Socialism* (Cambridge, 1989), p. 27. See also Quentin Skinner, *Liberty before Liberalism* (Cambridge, 1998), chapter 1.

6. Isaac Kramnick, *Republicanism and Bourgeois Radicalism: Political Ideology in late Eighteenth-Century England and America* (Ithaca, NY, and London, 1990), p. 1.

7. Blair Worden, 'The Revolution of 1688–9 and the English republican tradition', *The Anglo-Dutch Moment: Essays on the Glorious Revolution and its World Impact*, ed. Jonathan I. Israel (Cambridge, 1991), p. 269.

8. 'Introduction', *Two English Republican Tracts*, ed. Caroline Robbins (Cambridge, 1969), p. 43. Fear of tyranny, or love of liberty, remains a preoccupation of republican thought. See, for example, Philip Pettit, *Republicanism: A Theory of Freedom and Government* (Oxford, 1997).

9. Richard Pares, 'Limited Monarchy in Great Britain in the Eighteenth Century' (Historical Association, 1957), p. 21.

10. Quoted in John Brooke, *King George III* (London, 1985), pp. 56–7.

11. See, for example, the views of the Dissenting minister Richard Price on the balanced constitution in the 1770s. *Richard Price, Political Writings*, ed. E. O. Thomas (Cambridge, 1991), pp. 26–7.

12. Marilyn Morris, *The British Monarchy and the French Revolution* (New Haven, 1998), p. 26. For the view that the Revolution of 1688 did not result in a dramatic decline in the royal prerogative see J. C. D. Clark, *Revolution and Rebellion: State and Society in England in the Seventeeth and Eighteenth Centuries* (Cambridge, 1986), chapter 5.

13. Pares, 'Limited Monarchy in Great Britain in the Eighteenth Century', pp. 21–3.

14. Linda Colley, *Britons: Forging the Nation 1707–1837* (New Haven and London, 1992), p. 208.

15. On these early republicans see Robbins, *The Eighteenth-Century Commonwealthman*, pp. 357–63.

16. *The Diary of Sylas Neville, 1767–1788*, ed. Basil Cozens-Hardy (Oxford, 1950), pp. 43, 91.

17. *Ibid.*, p. 97.

18. Mary Thale, 'The Robin Hood Society: Debating in Eighteenth-Century London', *London Journal*, vol. 22, no. 1 (1997), pp. 33–50.

19. H. G. Koenigsberger, 'Republicanism, monarchism and liberty', *Royal and Republican Sovereignty in Early Modern Europe*, eds. Robert Oresko, G. C. Gibbs and H. M. Scott (Cambridge, 1997), p. 64.

20. Wootton, 'Introduction', *Republicanism, Liberty, and Commercial Society, 1649–1776*, p. 3.

21. *The Diary of Sylas Neville*, p. xv; Robbins, *The Eighteenth-Century Commonwealthman*, p. 362.

22. John Keane, *Tom Paine: A Political Life* (London, 1996), pp. 110, 113.

23. Thomas Paine, *Rights of Man, Common Sense, and other Political Writings*, ed. Mark Philp (Oxford, 1995), pp. 15–18.

24. *Ibid.*, p. 19.

25. In the *Rights of Man* (1791–2), Paine also argued that the Civil List was

'for the support of one man'. See his more detailed analysis of the Civil List in *Letter Addressed to the Addressers on the late Proclamation* (1792).

26. Bernard Bailyn, *The Ideological Origins of the American Revolution* (Cambridge, Mass., 1967), p. 285. For introductions to Paine's thought see Mark Philp, *Paine* (Oxford, 1989) and Gregory Claeys, *Thomas Paine. Social and Political Thought* (London, 1989).

27. Claeys, *Thomas Paine. Social and Political Thought*, pp. 5, 48.

28. Colley, *Britons: Forging the Nation 1707–1837*, pp. 142, 145.

29. *The Patriot. Addressed to the Electors of Great Britain* (London, 1775), p. 4.

30. See Archibald S. Foord, 'The Waning of "The Influence of the Crown"', *English Historical Review*, lxii (1947), pp. 484–507. Pares, 'Limited Monarchy in Great Britain in the Eighteenth Century', p. 27.

31. Brooke, *King George III*, p. 218.

32. Vernon Bogdanor, *The Monarchy and the Constitution* (Oxford, 1995), p. 11; see also Richard Pares, *King George III and the Politicians* (Oxford, 1953), pp. 119–20.

33. Quoted in Bogdanor, *The Monarchy and the Constitution*, p. 11.

34. Betty Kemp, *King and Commons, 1660–1832* (London, 1957), p. 103.

35. E. A. Reitan, 'The Civil List in Eighteenth-Century British Politics: Parliamentary Supremacy versus the Independence of the Crown', *Historical Journal*, ix, no. 3 (1966), p. 318. On the separation of government finance from royal control see Phillip Hall, *Royal Fortune: Tax, Money and the Monarchy* (London, 1992), chapter 1.

36. Brooke, *King George III*, p. 206. *Parliamentary Debates*, vol. 34 (6 June 1816), pp. 998–1002. See also *A Protest against T. Paine's "Rights of Man": Addressed to the Members of a Book Society* (Canterbury, 1793), pp. 13–14.

37. Brooke, *King George III*, p. 231.

38. Linda Colley, 'The Apotheosis of George III: Loyalty, Royalty and the British Nation 1760–1820', *Past and Present*, 102 (February, 1984), pp. 104, 126.

39. Colley sees the 1780s as a turning-point in the monarchy's image. See Colley, *Britons: Forging the Nation 1707–1837*, chapter 5. Matthew Kilburn, 'Royalty and Public in Britain: 1714–1789', D.Phil. thesis, Oxford University (1998), detects the growth of the monarchy as the embodiment of national virtue earlier, in the reigns of George I and George II.

40. Colley, *Britons: Forging the Nation 1707–1837*, chapter 5; Kilburn, 'Royalty and Public in Britain: 1714–1789', passim.

41. *The Works of the Late Right Honourable Henry St. John, Lord Viscount Bolingbroke*, 8 vols. (1809), vol. 4, pp. 281, 324.

42. J. G. A. Pocock, *Virtue, Commerce, and History: Essays on Political Thought and History, Chiefly in the Eighteenth Century* (Cambridge, 1985), p. 241.

43. For a discussion of Bolingbroke's legacy see David Armitage, 'A Patriot for Whom? The Afterlives of Bolingbroke's Patriot King', *Journal of British Studies*, 36 (October 1997), pp. 397–418.

44. Hannah More, 'Daniel', *Sacred Dramas* (1782), p. 241.

45. Thomas Gisborne, *An Enquiry into the Duties of Men in the Higher and Middle Classes of Society in Great Britain* (1794), p. 53.

46. William Henry MacMenemey, *A History of the Worcester Royal Infirmary* (1947), pp. 119–20.

47. John Watkins, *Memoirs of Her Most Excellent Majesty Sophia-Charlotte, Queen of Great Britain* (1819), pp. 390–91. See also *A Diary of the Royal Tour, in June, July, August, and September, 1789* (1789).

48. Frank Prochaska, *Royal Bounty: The Making of a Welfare Monarchy* (New Haven and London, 1995), p. 12.

49. Brooke, *King George III*, p. 215.

50. The figure of £14,000 was widely cited at the time. See, for example, Thomas Biddulph, *National Affliction Improved: In Three Sermons* (1820), p. 57. See also Brooke, *King George III*, p. 215.

51. Prochaska, *Royal Bounty: The Making of a Welfare Monarchy*, chapter 1. The list of leading philanthropists who received royal support in the reign of George III included Thomas Coram, John Howard, Edward Jenner, Sarah Trimmer, Joseph Lancaster, Thomas Bernard, Elizabeth Fry and Robert Owen.

52. Percy Black, *The Mystique of Modern Monarchy* (London, 1953), p. 59.

53. *London Chronicle* (8 September 1768), vol. 24, p. 239.

54. On Paine and civil society see Keane, *Tom Paine*, pp. 116–19.

55. Paine, *Rights of Man*, ed. Philp, p. 5.

56. When classical republicans discussed the expression of civic liberty, they thought of it in political terms. See Skinner, *Liberty before Liberalism*, p. 17. Paine's views on civil society extended the meaning of civic virtue and gave shape to our present view that it includes participation in non-governmental institutions that occupy the moral ground between the individual and the state. See Keane, *Tom Paine*, pp. 116–19.

57. 'A Discourse on the Love of our Country', *Richard Price, Political Writings*, p. 185.

58. Colley, *Britons: Forging the Nation 1707–1837*, pp. 207, 212.

59. Quoted in George Spater, *William Cobbett: The Poor Man's Friend* (Cambridge, 1982), p. 302.

60. *The Works of John Wesley*, 14 vols. (1872), vol. 11, p. 16.

61. Brooke, *King George III*, p. 205.

62. Morris, *The British Monarchy and the French Revolution*, pp. 159, 161.

63. *The Debate on the French Revolution, 1789–1800*, ed. Alfred Cobban (London, 1950), p. 44. For a discussion of the reaction to the Revolution by three young English radicals see *Youth and Revolution in the 1790s: Letters of William Pattison, Thomas Amyot and Henry Crabb Robinson*, eds. Penelope J. Corfield and Chris Evans (Stroud, 1996).

64. Asa Briggs, *The Age of Improvement 1783–1867* (London, 1974), p. 130.

65. *The Later Correspondence of George III*, ed. A. Aspinall, 5 vols. (London, 1962–70), vol. 1, p. 440.

66. Quoted in [David Williams] *Lessons to a Young Prince* (London, 1790), p. 20.

67. 'A Discourse on the Love of our Country', *Richard Price, Political Writings*, pp. 186, 195. On Price as a millennial republican see Jack Fruchtman, Jr, *The Apocalyptic Politics of Richard Price and Joseph Priestley. A Study of Late Eighteenth Century English Republican Millennialism* (American Philosophical Society, Philadelphia, 1983).

68. Quoted in Briggs, *The Age of Improvement 1783–1867*, p. 131.

69. *Political Writings of the 1790s*, ed. Gregory Claeys, 8 vols. (London, 1995), vol. 1, pp. xix–xx.

70. John Aitken, *Address to the Dissenters of England on their Late Defeat* (London, 1790), p. 18.

71. Quoted in Keane, *Tom Paine*, p. 283.

72. Quoted in Brooke, *King George III*, p. 345.

73. Ingram Cobbin, *Georgiana, or, Anecdotes of George the Third* (London, 1820), pp. 11–12. Paine's *Letter Addressed to the Addressers on the late Proclamation* (1792) also likens the King to a parish constable.

74. Edmund Burke, *Reflections on the Revolution in France* (New York, 1955), pp. 37, 87.

75. Paine, *Rights of Man*, ed. Philp, p. 234.

76. *The Correspondence of Edmund Burke*, ed. Thomas Copeland, 10 vols. (Cambridge, 1958–78), vol. 6, p. 96.

77. Paine, *Rights of Man*, ed. Philp, p. 257.

78. John Jones, *The Reason of Man: with strictures on Rights of Man, and other of Mr. Paine's Writings* (Canterbury, 1792), p. 18.

79. Paine, *Rights of Man*, ed. Philp, p. 230.

80. [David Williams] *Lessons to a Young Prince*, p. 23. For more on Williams see *Biographical Dictionary of Modern British Radicals*, eds. Joseph O. Baylen and Norbert J. Gossman, 3 vols. (Hassocks, Sussex, 1979–88), vol. 1, pp. 534–9.

81. *Rousseau: The Social Contract and other later Political Writings*, edited and translated by Victor Gourevitch (Cambridge, 1997), p. 67. John Adams agreed. See *A Defence of the Constitutions of Government of the United States of America*, vol. 3, pp. 159–60.

82. *The Politics of English Jacobinism. Writings of John Thelwall*, ed. Gregory Claeys (Pennsylvania State Press, 1995), pp. xxxviii–xxxix, 54, 288.

83. For an early use of the term 'pure republicanism' see *Life and Correspondence of Major Cartwright*, ed. F. D. Cartwright, 2 vols. (London, 1826), vol. 1, p. 192.

84. John Jones, *The Reason of Man part Second. Containing Strictures on Rights of Man* (Canterbury, 1793), p. 19. See also Morris, *The British Monarchy and the French Revolution*, p. 53.

85. Paine, *Rights of Man*, ed. Philp, p. 271.

86. For an introduction to conceptions of revolution in 1790s England see J. R. Dinwiddy, *Radicalism and Reform in Britain, 1780–1850* (London, 1992), chapter 9.

87. Marianne Elliott, 'Ireland and the French Revolution', *Britain and the French Revolution, 1789–1815*, ed. H. T. Dickinson (London, 1989), pp. 83–101.

88. Christina and David Bewley, *Gentleman Radical: A Life of John Horne Tooke, 1736–1812* (London, 1998), p. 133.

89. *Address of the Bristol Constitutional Society for a Parliamentary Reform, to the People in Great Britain* (1794), pp. 4–5.

90. John Stevenson, *Popular Disturbances in England, 1700–1832* (London, 1992), p. 180.

91. On the 'United Societies' see R. Wells, *Insurrection: The British Experience 1795–1803* (Gloucester, 1983). See also Dinwiddy, *Radicalism and Reform in Britain, 1780–1850*, pp. 185–7.

92. *Life and Correspondence of Major Cartwright*, ed. Cartwright, vol. 1, p. 192.

93. Malcolm I. Thomas and Peter Holt, *Threats of Revolution in Britain* (London, 1977), p. 10.

94. Christian Bewley, *Muir of Huntershill* (Oxford, 1981), p. 45.

95. John Belchem, 'Republicanism, popular constitutionalism and the radical platform in early nineteenth-century England', *Social History* (1981), p. 3. See

also Albert Goodwin, *The Friends of Liberty* (London, 1979), chapter 6.

96. See, for example, *The Political Writings of the 1790s: The French Revolution Debate in Britain*, ed. Gregory Claeys (London, 1995), passim.

97. Dinwiddy, *Radicalism and Reform in Britain, 1780–1850*, pp. 174–5.

98. Thomas Walker, *The Original*, ed. Blanchard Jerrold, 2 vols. (London, 1874), vol. 1, p. 86.

99. *The Later Correspondence of George III*, ed. Aspinall, vol. 1, p. 641; vol. 2, p. 3.

100. See Kirsty Carpenter, *Refugees of the French Revolution: Émigrés in London, 1789–1802* (London, 1999).

101. Lord Cockburn, *Memorials of His Time* (Edinburgh, 1856), p. 45.

102. E. P. Thompson, *The Making of the English Working Class* (London, 1963), p. 141.

103. Morris, *The British Monarchy and the French Revolution*, p. 125.

104. *The Rights of Princes*, extracts from Piggot's Political Dictionary [no date], p. 5.

105. Included in *The Debate on the French Revolution, 1789–1800*, ed. Cobban, p. 285.

106. On Spence see Malcolm Chase, *'The People's Farm': English Radical Agrarianism 1775–1840* (Oxford, 1988). See also the article on Spence by T. M. Parssinen in the *Biographical Dictionary of Modern British Radicals*, eds. Baylen and Gossman, vol. 1, pp. 454–8.

107. *The Happy Reign of George the Last* [1795], p. 3.

108. See John Dinwiddy, 'Interpretations of anti-Jacobinism', *The French Revolution and British Popular Politics*, ed. Mark Philp (Cambridge, 1991), p. 49.

109. On English Francophobia see Gerald Newman, *The Rise of English Nationalism: A Cultural History 1740–1830* (London, 1987). See also Colley, *Britons: Forging the Nation 1707–1837*, passim.

110. Robert Dozier, *For King, Constitution, and Country: The English Loyalists and the French Revolution* (Lexington, Ky., 1983), pp. 61–2. See also David Eastwood, 'Patriotism and the English state in the 1790s', *The French Revolution and British Popular Politics*, ed. Philp, pp. 146–68.

111. H. T. Dickinson, 'Popular Conservatism and Militant Loyalism 1789–1815', *Britain and the French Revolution, 1789–1815*, ed. Dickinson, p. 120.

112. *Political Writings of the 1790s*, ed. Claeys, vol. 1, p. liv. For a statistical analysis of reformist literature see Gayle Trusdel Pendelton, 'Radicalism and the English "Reign of Terror": The Evidence of the Pamphlet literature', *The Consortium on Revolutionary Europe, 1750–1850: Proceedings 1979* (Athens,

Ga., 1980), pp. 195–205. See also Morris, *The British Monarchy and the French Revolution*, chapter 3. For a study of anti-Jacobin fiction see M. O. Grenby, 'The Anti-Jacobin Novel: British Fiction, British Conservatism and the Revolution in France', *History*, vol. 83 (July 1998), pp. 445–71.

113. *Liberty and Property preserved against Republicans and Levellers, a collection of tracts*, no. x (1793).

114. *The Anti-Jacobin Review and Magazine*, I (July–December 1799), p. 107. Quoted in Edward Royle and James Walvin, *English Radicals and Reformers 1760–1848* (Brighton, 1982), p. 91.

115. Dickinson, 'Popular Conservatism and Militant Loyalism 1789–1815', *Britain and the French Revolution, 1789–1815*, ed. Dickinson, passim.

116. Hannah More, *Modern Politicians: a word to the working classes of Great Britain, by Will Chip, a Country Carpenter* [1797?].

117. 'One Penny-Worth of Truth from Thomas Bull, to his Brother John', *Association Papers* (London, 1793), pp. 3–4.

118. This hand-written dedication found in the King's Library copy of the *Association Papers*, now in the British Library, is presumably from Reeves.

119. For a more detailed analysis of this elaborate print see Nicholas K. Robinson, *Edmund Burke: A Life in Caricature* (New Haven and London, 1996), pp. 183–4. For a list and description of the vast number of satires in the 1790s see Mary Dorothy George, *Catalogue of Political and Personal Satires preserved in the Department of Prints and Drawings in the British Museum* (London, 1938, 1942), vols. vi and vii.

120. Grenby, 'The Anti-Jacobin Novel: British Fiction, British Conservatism and the Revolution in France', pp. 456–7.

121. Edward Royle, *Chartism* (London, 1980), p. 8.

122. Philp, *Paine*, p. 95. For a discussion of the reception of Paine's *The Age of Reason* in England, see F. K. Prochaska, 'Thomas Paine's *The Age of Reason* Revisited', *Journal of the History of Ideas*, vol. xxxiii, no. 4 (1972).

123. 'The English Constitution', *The Collected Works of Walter Bagehot*, ed. Norman St John Stevas, 15 vols. (London, 1974–86), vol. 5, p. 233.

124. For a stimulating discussion of the radical fringe see Iain McCalman, *Radical Underworld: Prophets, Revolutionaries, and Pornographers in London, 1795–1840* (Cambridge, 1988).

125. Quoted in *The Infidel Tradition from Paine to Bradlaugh*, ed. Edward Royle (London, 1976), p. 15. In his *Testament*, Jean Le Curé Meslier (1664–1729) noted that an ignorant man once told him 'that all great men in the world and all the nobility could be hanged, and strangled in the guts of priests'.

126. See miscellaneous broadsides and leaflets, BL 648. c.26, nos. 27, 61 and passim.

127. Burke, *Reflections on the Revolution in France*, p. 89.

128. *The Letters of King George III*, ed. Bonamy Dobrée (London, 1935), p. 212.

129. Stevenson, *Popular Disturbances in England, 1700–1832*, pp. 179–80.

130. *The Politics of English Jacobinism. Writings of John Thelwall*, ed. Claeys, p. xix.

131. Mary Thale, *Selections from the Papers of the London Corresponding Society, 1792–1799* (Cambridge, 1983), p. 140.

132. For an introduction to the state trials see Clive Emsley, 'Repression, "terror" and the rule of law in England during the decade of the French Revolution', *English Historical Review*, vol. c (1985), pp. 801–25; F. K. Prochaska, 'English State Trials in the 1790s: A Case Study', *The Journal of British Studies*, vol. xiii (November 1973), pp. 63–82.

133. Thompson, *The Making of the English Working Class*, p. 87.

134. For more on Cooper see Dumas Malone, *Public Life of Thomas Cooper* (New Haven, 1926).

135. *Boswell's Life of Johnson*, ed. George Birkbeck Hill, 6 vols. (Oxford, 1934), vol. 2, p. 250.

136. Thompson, *The Making of the English Working Class*, p. 177.

137. BL, Add. MSS 27808, fol. 113.

138. *The Autobiography of Francis Place (1771–1854)*, ed. Mary Thale (Cambridge, 1972), p. 196.

139. *Account of the Proceedings at a General Meeting of the London Corresponding Society . . . 29 of June, 1792*. See also Dinwiddy, *Radicalism and Reform in Britain, 1780–1850*, pp. 175–6.

140. The King's Proclamation was delivered at the Queen's House on 21 May 1792. It was reprinted by the Association for Preserving Liberty and Property against Republicans and Levellers. See *Political Writings of the 1790s*, ed. Claeys, vol. 7, pp. 121–2.

141. *Account of the Proceedings at a General Meeting of the London Corresponding Society*, p. 9.

142. Ghita Stanhope and G. P. Gooch, *The Life of Charles Third Earl Stanhope* (London, 1914), pp. 152, 155–6.

143. *Rousseau: The Social Contract and other later Political Writings*, ed. Gourevitch, p. 258. Rousseau was thinking specifically of Poland.

144. William Godwin, *An Enquiry Concerning the Principles of Political Justice*, ed. Isaac Kramnick (Harmondsworth, 1976), p. 421. See also Peter H. Marshall, *William Godwin* (New Haven, 1984), p. 105.

145. John Thelwall, *The Rights of Nature against the Usurpation of Establishments* (London, 1796), pp. 6–7, quoted in Morris, *The British Monarchy and the French Revolution*, p. 93.

146. See, for example, *The Later Correspondence of George III*, ed. Aspinall, vol. 2, pp. 458–9.

147. For an eyewitness account see *The Autobiography of Francis Place*, ed. Thale, pp. 145–7. See also Stevenson, *Popular Disturbances in England, 1700–1832*, pp. 215–17.

148. Quoted in Brooke, *King George III*, p. 218.

149. *The Later Correspondence of George III*, ed. Aspinall, vol. 2, p. 420.

150. *Mr. Fox's Celebrated Speech, with the Proceedings at the Shakespeare Tavern, on Friday, October 10, 1800, being the anniversary of his first election for the City of Westminster* (London, 1800), p. 23.

151. For a discussion of this issue see Stevenson, *Popular Disturbances in England, 1700–1832*, pp. 326–30; see also D. G. Wright, *Popular Radicalism: The Working-Class Experience, 1780–1880* (London, 1988), pp. 52–8; *The French Revolution and British Popular Politics*, ed. Philp, passim.

152. *The Parliamentary Register*, vol. 40 (5 January 1795), p. 164.

153. Morris, *The British Monarchy and the French Revolution*, pp. 190, 193.

154. See Ian McBride, *Scripture Politics: Ulster Presbyterians and Irish radicalism in late eighteenth-century Ireland* (Oxford, 1998). See also the *Times Literary Supplement* (4 December 1998), p. 12.

155. Samuel Taylor Coleridge, *The Plot Discovered; Or, An Address to the People against Ministerial Treason* (Bristol, 1795), p. 15, quoted in Morris, *The Monarchy and the French Revolution*, p. 99.

156. *The Autobiography of Francis Place*, ed. Thale, p. 196.

157. *Political Essays on Popular Subjects* (London, 1801), p. 53.

2. The Battered but Unbroken Crown

1. Henry Hyndman, *The Coming Revolution in England* (London [1884]), p. 9.

2. I am grateful to Penelope Lively for this information, handed on from her grandmother.

3. Clive Emsley, 'Revolution, war and the nation state', *The French Revolution and British Popular Politics*, ed. Mark Philp (Cambridge, 1991), pp. 116–17.

4. *Political Register* (May 1809), p. 225.

5. *Friend*, no. 10 (19 October 1809), p. 155.

6. Richard Holmes, *Coleridge: Darker Reflections* (London, 1998), pp. 166–9.

7. For a discussion of the reform movement during the Napoleonic period see Ann Hone, *For the Cause of Truth: Radicalism in London 1796–1821* (Oxford, 1982).

8. J. R. Dinwiddy, *Radicalism and Reform in Britain, 1780–1850* (London, 1992), pp. 208–9; Peter Spence, *The Birth of Romantic Radicalism: War, popular politics and English radical reformism, 1800–1815* (Aldershot, 1996), pp. 1–2.

9. On Yorke's conversion to loyalism see *Weekly Political Review of Henry Redhead Yorke*, 11 vols. (1805–11). See also *France in Eighteen Hundred and Two described in a Series of Contemporary Letters by Henry Redhead Yorke*, ed. J. A. C. Sykes (London, 1906).

10. *Weekly Political Review of Henry Redhead Yorke*, vol. viii (4 November 1809), pp. 311–12.

11. Linda Colley, 'The Apotheosis of George III: Loyalty, Royalty and the British Nation 1760–1820', *Past and Present*, 102 (1984), pp. 94–129; Linda Colley, *Britons: Forging the Nation 1707–1837* (New Haven and London, 1992), p. 224; Frank Prochaska, *Royal Bounty: The Making of a Welfare Monarchy* (New Haven and London, 1995), p. 16.

12. See *Weekly Political Review of Henry Redhead Yorke*, vol. vi (January–June 1809), pp. 65–8, passim.

13. Spence, *The Birth of Romantic Radicalism: War, popular politics and English radical reformism, 1800–1815*, chapter 6.

14. D. G. Wright, *Popular Radicalism: The Working-Class Experience, 1780–1880* (London, 1988), pp. 60–62. M. I. Thomas, *The Luddites: Machine-Breaking in Regency England* (Newton Abbot, 1970) argues that Luddism was a purely industrial protest without wider revolutionary intent.

15. Christopher Hibbert, *George IV: Regent and King 1811–1830* (London, 1973), p. 21.

16. Iain McCalman, *Radical Underworld: Prophets, Revolutionaries, and Pornographers in London, 1795–1840* (Cambridge, 1988), p. 122.

17. George Spater, *William Cobbett: The Poor Man's Friend* (Cambridge, 1982), pp. 241–2.

18. Hibbert, *George IV: Regent and King 1811–1830*, pp. 81, 123–4.

19. *Parliamentary Debates*, vol. 30 (14 April 1815), cols. 627, 640–43.

20. *Ibid.*, vol. 33 (20 March 1816), col. 497. See also Arthur Aspinall, *Lord Brougham and the Whig Party* (Manchester, 1927), pp. 61–2.

21. *Parliamentary Debates*, vol. 34 (6 June 1816), cols. 1002–3.

22. *The Times* (22 August 1816), p. 3. See also John Belcham, *'Orator Hunt': Henry Hunt and English Working-Class Radicalism* (London, 1995), pp. 36, 51.

23. *Letters of Princess Charlotte, 1811–1817*, ed. A. Aspinall (London, 1949), p. 245.

24. M. W. Patterson, *Sir Francis Burdett and His Times (1770–1844)*, 2 vols. (London, 1931), vol. 2, pp. 414–15; John Stevenson, *Popular Disturbances in England, 1700–1832* (London, 1992), pp. 239–43.

25. Wright, *Popular Radicalism: The Working-Class Experience, 1780–1880*, pp. 66–8; Stevenson, *Popular Disturbances in England, 1700–1832*, pp. 240–43.

26. Quoted in Patterson, *Sir Francis Burdett and His Times*, vol. 2, p. 416.

27. Hibbert, *George IV: Regent and King 1811–1830*, p. 130.

28. Quoted in John Belchem, 'Republicanism, popular constitutionalism and the radical platform in early nineteenth-century England', *Social History*, vol. 6 (1981), p. 15.

29. *Black Dwarf*, vol. 3 (22 September 1819), pp. 627–8.

30. Quoted in Belchem, 'Republicanism, popular constitutionalism and the radical platform in early nineteenth-century England', p. 15.

31. From Shelley's sonnet 'England in 1819'.

32. Stevenson, *Popular Disturbances in England, 1700–1832*, p. 235.

33. *Black Dwarf*, vol. 1 (1817), dedication page.

34. *Remarks on Wooler and his Dwarf* (Newcastle, 1820), p. 4.

35. *Black Dwarf*, vol. 2 (26 August 1818), p. 529.

36. John Dinwiddy, *From Luddism to the First Reform Bill: Reform in England 1810–1832* (Oxford, 1986), p. 37.

37. *Lion*, vol. 1, no. 3 (1828), p. 73.

38. From Shelley, *Ode to Liberty*.

39. Quoted in the *Red Republican* (10 August 1850), p. 62.

40. John Wade, *The Black Book; or Corruption Unmasked!* (London, 1820), p. 110.

41. *Republican*, vol. 2 (4 February 1820), p. 107.

42. *Political Register* (13 November 1819), quoted in Dinwiddy, *From Luddism to the First Reform Bill: Reform in England 1810–1832*, p. 39.

43. Richard Carlile, *An Effort to set at rest some little Disputes and Misunderstandings between the Reformers of Leeds upon the Subject of some late Deputy Meetings and a Declaration of Sentiments arising therefrom* (London, 1821), pp. 8–13.

44. 'An Address to the Public', *Republican*, vol. 1 (27 August 1819–7 January 1820), p. viii.

45. *Prompter*, no. 29 (28 May 1831), p. 468.

46. F. B. Smith, 'The Atheist Mission, 1840–1900', *Ideas and Institutions of Victorian Britain*, ed. Robert Robson (New York, 1967), p. 221.

47. *Republican*, vol. 9 (2 January 1824), pp. iv–v.

48. *Ibid.*, vol. 12 (8 July–30 December 1825), dedication page.

49. Joel H. Wiener, *Radicalism and Freethought in Nineteenth-Century Britain. The Life of Richard Carlile* (Westport, Conn., 1983), p. 104.

50. Carlile, *Republican*, vol. 1 (27 August 1819), p. 1.

51. *Republican*, vol. 2 (4 February 1820), p. 107.

52. W. T. Sherwin, *Republican*, no. 1 (1 March 1817), pp. 4–5.

53. 'Address to the Public', *Republican*, vol. 1 (27 August 1819–7 January 1820), pp. ix–x.

54. Wiener, *Radicalism and Freethought in Nineteenth-Century Britain. The Life of Richard Carlile*, p. 103.

55. *Parliamentary Debates*, vol. 2 (4 February 1831), cols. 178–9.

56. *Black Dwarf*, vol. 12 (7 January 1824), p. 8; Wade, *The Black Book; or Corruption Unmasked!*, pp. 129–31.

57. *Parliamentary Debates*, vol. 34 (6 June 1816), col. 999.

58. See, for example, W. H. Reid, *The Rise and Dissolution of the Infidel Societies in this Metropolis* (London, 1800).

59. For a discussion of loyalism see H. T. Dickinson, 'Popular Conservatism and Militant Loyalism 1789–1815', *Britain and the French Revolution, 1789–1815*, ed. H. T. Dickinson (London, 1989).

60. McCalman, *Radical Underworld: Prophets, Revolutionaries, and Pornographers in London, 1795–1840*, p. 176.

61. Flora Fraser, *The Unruly Queen: The Life of Queen Caroline* (London, 1996), p. 54.

62. *Republican*, vol. 4 (24 November 1820), p. 436.

63. Dudley Miles, *Francis Place 1771–1854: The Life of a Remarkable Radical* (Brighton, 1988), p. 158.

64. Hone, *For the Cause of Truth: Radicalism in London 1796–1821*, p. 313.

65. *Black Dwarf*, vol. 4 (14 June 1820), p. 808. Quoted in John Stevenson, 'The Queen Caroline Affair', *London in the Age of Reform*, ed. John Stevenson (Oxford, 1977), p. 126.

66. Stevenson, *Popular Disturbances in Britain 1700–1832*, p. 245.

67. Dinwiddy, *From Luddism to the First Reform Bill: Reform in England 1810–1832*, p. 38.

68. *The Times* (24 July 1821), p. 3 contains a lively description of this coronation 'celebration', which deteriorated into riot.

69. E. L. Woodward, *The Age of Reform* (Oxford, 1962), p. 211. See also Vernon Bogdanor, *The Monarchy and the Constitution* (Oxford, 1995), p. 15.

70. Bogdanor, *ibid.*

71. E. A. Smith, *George IV* (New Haven and London, 1999) argues, not entirely convincingly, that the King played a decisive role in the creation of Britain's constitutional monarchy.

72. Quoted in Hibbert, *George IV: Regent and King 1811–1830*, p. 310.

73. *Black Dwarf*, vol. 11 (10 September 1823), pp. 359–62. On the growth of parliamentary control over appointments to the royal household see *Officials of the Royal Household*, part 1, compiled by J. C. Sainty and R. O. Bucholz (London, 1997), pp. xxxiv–xxxix.

74. Today the motto appears on the Prince of Wales's feathers. Its origin, though fourteenth century, is disputed. See Olwen Hedley, *The Princes of Wales* (London, 1975), pp. 6–7.

75. Prochaska, *Royal Bounty: The Making of a Welfare Monarchy*, pp. 41–2.

76. Royal Archives 30161.

77. *Republican*, vol. 12 (8 July–30 December 1825), dedication page.

78. Prochaska, *Royal Bounty: The Making of a Welfare Monarchy*, p. 43.

79. *Black Dwarf*, vol. 2 (26 August 1818), p. 541.

80. Wade, *The Black Book; or Corruption Unmasked!*, pp. 110–16.

81. Hannah More, *Moral Sketches of Prevailing Opinions and Manners* (1821), p. xvi.

82. John Keane, *Tom Paine: A Political Life* (London, 1996), pp. 117–18.

83. Henry Moses, *Visit of William the Fourth when Duke of Clarence, as Lord High Admiral To Portsmouth, in the Year 1827* (1840), p. 7.

84. *Philanthropist*, vol. 1 (1833), p. 384. For more information on Lancaster's educational experiment see Alice Prochaska, 'The Practice of Radicalism: Educational Reform in Westminster', *London in the Age of Reform*, ed. Stevenson, pp. 102–16; Prochaska, *Royal Bounty: The Making of a Welfare Monarchy*, pp. 14, 32–5.

85. *Philanthropist*, vol. 1 (1811), p. 376.

86. British Library, Add. MSS 27823, fol. 36.

87. RA Add. 7/27.

88. *The Life of William Wilberforce*, ed. Robert Isaac Wilberforce and Samuel Wilberforce, 5 vols. (London, 1838), vol. 2, p. 461.

89. The Bible Society alone, whose patronage lists boasted Queen Caroline, the Duchess of Kent and the Dukes of York, Cumberland, Sussex and Cambridge, had a vast nationwide membership through its 630 or so branches in the 1820s. See *The Twenty-First Report of the British and Foreign Bible Society* (1825), appendix 1, p. 11. See also Revd George Browne, *The History of the British and Foreign Bible Society*, 2 vols. (London, 1859), vol. 1, pp. 83–4.

90. Prochaska, *Royal Bounty: The Making of a Welfare Monarchy*, pp. 24–37.

91. *Black Dwarf*, vol. 12 (7 January 1824), pp. v–vi.

92. Michael Brock, *The Great Reform Act* (London, 1973), p. 15.

93. Samuel Taylor Coleridge, *Collected Works*, ed. Kathleen Coburn (London, 1976), vol. 10, p. 96.

94. *Biographical Dictionary of Modern British Radicals*, eds. Joseph O. Baylen and Norbert J. Gossman (Hassocks, Sussex, 1979–88), vol. 1, p. 480.

95. 19 September 1835, *The Poor Man's Guardian, 1831–1835*, 4 vols. (London, 1969), vol. 4, p. 677.

96. *The Aftermath: With Autobiography of the Author John Bedford Leno* (London, 1892), p. 73.

97. *The Life of Robert Owen Written by Himself*, 2 vols. (London, 1971), vol. 1, pp. 193–4, 197–9, 229.

98. Elie Halévy, *The Growth of Philosophic Radicalism* (London, 1952), p. 415. On George III, Bentham and the Panopticon see Janet Semple, *Bentham's Prison: A Study of the Panopticon Penitentiary* (Oxford, 1993), pp. 324–6.

99. *The Collected Works of Jeremy Bentham. First Principles Preparatory to Constitutional Code*, ed. Philip Schofield (Oxford, 1989), p. 171.

100. *Ibid.*, pp. 161, 171 and passim. See also H. A. L. Fisher, *The Republican Tradition in Europe* (London, 1911), pp. 161–2.

101. John Stuart Mill, *Autobiography* (London, 1873), p. 107.

102. Halévy, *The Growth of Philosophic Radicalism*, p. 415.

103. Elizabeth Longford, *Victoria R.I.* (London, 1964), p. 26.

104. *Republican and Radical Reformer*, vol. 3, no. xv (17 November 1832), p. 119.

105. W. M. Thackeray, *The Four Georges* (London, 1861), p. 169.

106. *The Times* (16 July 1830), p. 2.

107. *Letters of Dorothea, Princess Lieven, during her Residence in London, 1812–1834*, ed. Lionel G. Robinson (London, 1902), p. 225.

108. Philip Ziegler, *King William IV* (London, 1971), p. 193.

109. A. J. Maley, *Historical Recollections of the Reign of William IV*, 2 vols. (1860), vol. 1, p. 5.

110. *Parliamentary Debates*, vol. 2 (4 February 1831), cols. 176, 190.

111. *Ibid.*, vol. 1 (15 November 1830), col. 539.

112. *Ibid.*, col. 455.

113. *The Correspondence of the Late Earl Grey with His Majesty King William IV*, ed. Henry Earl Grey, 2 vols. (1867), vol. 1, pp. 126–7.

114. Wright, *Popular Radicalism: The Working-Class Experience, 1780–1880*, p. 87.

115. 10 December 1831, *The Poor Man's Guardian 1831–1835*, vol. 1, p. 199.

116. *Biographical Dictionary of Modern British Radicals*, eds. Baylen and Gossman, vol. 2, pp. 295–9.

117. W. N. Molesworth, *The History of the Reform Bill of 1832* (London, 1865), p. 332.

118. *Republican*, no. 5, vol. 2, 26 May 1832, p. 83; Patricia Hollis, *The Pauper Press: A Study in Working-Class Radicalism of the 1830s* (Oxford, 1970), pp. 262–3.

119. Frank Hardie, *The Political Influence of Queen Victoria 1861–1901* (London, 1963), p. 230.

120. *Parliamentary Debates*, vol. 1 (22 November 1830), col. 613.

121. BL, Add. MSS 27,795, fols. 27–30.

122. See, for example, Richard Carlile's attack on the 'boroughmonger constitution' in the *Prompter*, no. 4 (4 December 1830), p. 51.

123. John P. Mackintosh, *The British Cabinet* (London, 1977), pp. 72, 76; Bogdanor, *The Monarchy and the Constitution*, pp. 16–17; Ziegler, *King William IV*, p. 149.

124. Bogdanor, *The Monarchy and the Constitution*, p. 16.

125. Hardie, *The Political Influence of Queen Victoria 1861–1901*, p. 234. For a discussion of this episode see Norman Gash, *Reaction and Reconstruction in English Politics, 1832–1852* (Oxford, 1965), chapter 1.

126. Quoted in Gash, *ibid.*, p. 4. See also Bogdanor, *The Monarchy and the Constitution*, pp. 18–19.

127. *The Letters of Queen Victoria*, ed. Viscount Esher, 1st series, 3 vols. (London, 1907), vol. 1, p. 134.

128. *Ibid.*, vol. 2, p. 138.

129. Theodore Martin, *The Life of the Prince Consort*, 5 vols. (1875–80), vol. 1, pp. 313–15.

130. Brock, *The Great Reform Act*, p. 335.

131. Prochaska, *Royal Bounty: The Making of a Welfare Monarchy*, pp. 50–66.

132. For a discussion of the ideology of the unstamped press see Hollis, *The Pauper Press*, chapters 6 and 7. See also Wright, *Popular Radicalism: The Working-Class Experience, 1780–1880*, pp. 95–9.

133. Quoted in S. Maccoby, *English Radicalism, 1786–1832* (London, 1955), p. 198.

134. John Wade, *The Extraordinary Black Book: An Exposition of Abuses in*

Church and State, pp. 219–21. The saving was largely the result of putting several classes of expenditure under parliamentary control.

135. *The Infidel Tradition from Paine to Bradlaugh*, ed. Edward Royle (London, 1976), p. 18.

136. Hollis, *The Pauper Press*, p. 289.

137. *Republican*, no. 4, vol. 2 (May 1832), p. 68.

138. John Wade, *Glances at the Times, and Reform Government* (London, 1840), pp. 10, 22–3.

139. *Biographical Dictionary of Modern British Radicals*, eds. Baylen and Gossman, vol. 2, p. 297.

140. See, for example, 30 June 1832, *The Poor Man's Guardian*, vol. 1, p. 445; 1 June 1833, vol. 2, p. 176.

141. 21 November 1835, *ibid.*, vol. 4, p. 747.

142. 12 December 1835, *ibid.*, vol. 4, pp. 777–8.

143. F. Lamennais, *The Book of the People* (London, 1838), p. 93, note.

144. Peter H. Marshall, *William Godwin* (New Haven and London, 1984), p. 382.

3. Queen Victoria and the Republican Challenge

1. Sidney Lee, 'Queen Victoria', *Dictionary of National Biography*.

2. See Frank Hardie, *The Political Influence of Queen Victoria 1861–1901* (London, 1963).

3. For a discussion of this issue see Dorothy Thompson, *Queen Victoria: Gender and Power* (London, 1990). See also the review of this book by David Cannadine in the *London Review of Books* (16 August 1990).

4. Sidney Lee, *Queen Victoria: A Biography* (London, 1902), p. 53. For a discussion of Queen Victoria and chivalry see Mark Girouard, *The Return to Camelot: Chivalry and the English Gentleman* (New Haven and London, 1981), pp. 112–28 and passim.

5. Elizabeth Longford, *Victoria R.I.* (London, 1964), p. 74.

6. Giles St Aubyn, *Queen Victoria. A Portrait* (London, 1991), pp. 65–6.

7. Quoted in Richard Williams, *The Contentious Crown: Public Discussion of the British Monarchy in the Reign of Queen Victoria* (Aldershot, 1997), pp. 16–17.

8. *Parliamentary Debates*, vol. 39 (23 November 1837), col. 137.

9. For information on the offices and salaries of the royal household see *Officials of the Royal Household 1660–1837*, 2 parts, compiled by J. C. Sainty

and R. O. Bucholz (London, 1997, 1998). See also *Sketches of Her Majesty's Household* (London, 1848).

10. *Parliamentary Debates*, vol. 39 (15 December 1837), cols. 1162–3, 1173, 1181.

11. Longford, *Victoria R.I.*, p. 70.

12. *Parliamentary Debates*, vol. 39 (20 December 1837), cols. 1337–43.

13. *Ibid.*, cols. 1347, 1369.

14. A Friend of the People, *Letter to The Queen on the State of the Monarchy* (London, 1838), pp. 12, 22.

15. *Ibid.*, p. 44.

16. See, for example, *An Answer to 'The Friend of the People's' Letter to The Queen* (London, 1839).

17. Quentin Skinner, *Liberty before Liberalism* (Cambridge, 1998), p. ix.

18. *Life and Struggles of William Lovett* (London, 1967), pp. 102–6.

19. *Monarcho-Republicanism* (London, 1848), pp. 5, 13.

20. *Northern Star* (20 May 1848), p. 1; (3 June 1848), p. 1. See also R. G. Gammage, *History of the Chartist Movement, 1837–1854* (London, 1969), p. 334; J. T. Ward, *Chartism* (London, 1973), p. 211.

21. Longford, *Victoria R.I.*, pp. 565–6.

22. St Aubyn, *Queen Victoria. A Portrait*, p. 217.

23. *Robert Lowery, Radical and Chartist*, eds. Brian Harrison and Patricia Hollis (London, 1979), pp. 239, 250.

24. *Southern Star* (12 July 1840), quoted in *Chartism and Society: An Anthology of Documents*, ed. F. C. Mather (London, 1980), p. 23.

25. *Friend of the People* (8 February 1851), p. 70.

26. Quoted in Ward, *Chartism*, p. 138.

27. Zephaniah Williams to A. McKechnie, 25 May 1840, National Library of Wales, Box 40/2. On the Newport rising, see David J. V. Jones, *The Last Rising: The Newport Insurrection* (Oxford, 1985).

28. John Wade, *Glances at the Times, and Reform Government* (London, 1840), pp. 10, 22.

29. *Ibid.*, pp. 22–4.

30. Longford, *Victoria R.I.*, p. 137.

31. See, for example, Williams, *The Contentious Crown*, p. 146.

32. Pierre Crabites, *Victoria's Guardian Angel: A Study of Baron Stockmar* (London, 1937), p. 148.

33. F. H. Myers, *Personal Recollections of Leopold, Duke of Albany*, p. 8, Myers Papers, 28/64, Trinity College, Cambridge.

34. Daphne Bennett, *King without a Crown: Albert, Prince Consort of England 1819–1861* (London, 1983), pp. 154–5.

35. Theodore Martin, *The Life of His Royal Highness The Prince Consort*, 5 vols. (1875–80), vol. 1, p. 194.

36. *Punch*, vol. 1 (1842), p. 222.

37. *Northern Star* (29 January 1842), p. 4.

38. Quoted in F. B. Smith, *Radical Artisan: William James Linton 1815–97* (Manchester, 1973), p. 33.

39. John Wade, *Unreformed Abuses in Church and State* (London, 1849), pp. 62, 67.

40. *The Reformer's Almanac and Political Year-Book, 1849*, p. 45.

41. Wade, *Unreformed Abuses in Church and State*, pp. 67–8.

42. Cecil Woodham-Smith, *The Great Hunger: Ireland 1845–9* (London, 1962), pp. 170, 382.

43. Frank Prochaska, *Royal Bounty: The Making of a Welfare Monarchy* (New Haven and London, 1995), pp. 57–8, 77.

44. *The Reformer's Almanac, and Companion to the Almanacs, for 1848*, p. 4.

45. *Ibid.*, p. 183. Wade put the total cost of the monarchy, from the accession of George III to 1848, at £101,957,807. He neglects to add that much of this money was spent on government business. See *Unreformed Abuses in Church and State*, p. 66.

46. Lee, *Queen Victoria: A Biography*, p. 81.

47. *The Reformer's Almanac, and Companion to the Almanacs, for 1848*, p. 183.

48. Joseph Barker, *The Life of Joseph Barker* (London, 1880), p. 287. See also Joseph Barker, *Teachings of Experience* (London, 1869); Edward Royle, 'Joseph Barker', *Biographical Dictionary of Modern British Radicals*, eds. Baylen and Gossman (Hassocks, Sussex, 1984), vol. 2, pp. 38–41.

49. Quoted in *Robert Lowery, Radical and Chartist*, eds. Harrison and Hollis, p. 239.

50. *English Chartist Circular*, vol. 1, no. 3. (February 1841). See *Chartism and Society: An Anthology of Documents*, ed. Mather, p. 67.

51. See, for example, A Fellow Labourer, *What the Chartists are. A Letter to English working-men* (London, 1848).

52. Quoted in *Chartism and Society: An Anthology of Documents*, ed. Mather, p. 68.

53. *Northern Star* (2 January 1841), quoted in *ibid.*, p. 50.

54. Ward, *Chartism*, p. 230.

55. Early writings on Chartism set the tone. See, for example, Mark Hovell, *The Chartist Movement* (Manchester, 1925); R. G. Gammage, *History of the Chartist Movement, 1837–1854* (London, 1969). More recent books also treat

the movement as non-republican. See, for example, Dorothy Thompson, *The Chartists: Popular Politics in the Industrial Revolution* (Aldershot, 1984); Ward, *Chartism*. See also Williams, *The Contentious Crown*, p. 16. For a recent challenge to this received wisdom, from a different perspective, see Antony Taylor, 'Republicanism reappraised: anti-monarchism and the English radical tradition, 1850–1872', *Re-reading the constitution. New narratives in the political history of England's long nineteenth century*, ed. James Vernon (Cambridge, 1996), pp. 154–78.

56. *Chartism and Society: An Anthology of Documents*, ed. Mather, pp. 23–4.

57. *Monarcho-Republicanism*, pp. 4–5.

58. *Republican*, vol. 1 (1848), p. 141.

59. *English Republic*, vol. 2 (1851–2), quoted in Smith, *Radical Artisan: William James Linton 1815–97*, p. 223.

60. For a more detailed discussion of anti-royalist journalism see Williams, *The Contentious Crown*.

61. Longford, *Victoria R.I.*, p. 197.

62. See James Epstein, 'Understanding the Cap of Liberty: Symbolic Conflict in Early Nineteenth-Century England', *Past and Present*, no. 122, February 1989, pp. 75–118.

63. *The Letters of Queen Victoria*, ed. Viscount Esher, 1st series, 3 vols. (London, 1907), vol. 1, p. 605.

64. *Northern Star* (7 October 1843), p. 8.

65. British Library, Add. MSS 40436, fol. 93 (10 March 1843), quoted in James Epstein, *The Lion of Freedom: Feargus O'Connor and the Chartist Movement, 1832–1842* (London, 1982), p. 301.

66. See, for example, *Friend of the People* (15 February 1851), p. 74.

67. Barker, *The Life of Joseph Barker*, p. 286; *Reformer's Almanack and Political Year-Book, 1849*, pp. 42, 45.

68. *The Aftermath: With Autobiography of the Author John Bedford Leno* (London, 1892), p. 28.

69. 'The Designs of the Chartists, and their probable Consequences. A Letter', *Leeds Mercury* (3 August 1839).

70. *Northern Star* (4 March 1848), p. 4.

71. A Fellow Labourer, *What the Chartists Are. A Letter to English Working-Men* (London, 1848), pp. 4–5, 9.

72. Revd Humphry Price, *A Glance at the Present Times, chiefly with reference to the working-men* (London [no date]), p. 16.

73. Royal Archives VIC/Y 204.

74. David Goodway, *London Chartism 1838–1848* (Cambridge, 1982), p. 113.

75. RA VIC/C 56/11.

76. RA VIC/C 56/12.

77. Quoted in Longford, *Victoria R.I.*, pp. 197–8.

78. Quoted in *The Times* (2 February 1849), p. 2.

79. RA VIC/C 56/12.

80. RA VIC/C 56/47 and 47a.

81. See, for example, *Northern Star* (15 April 1848), p. 2; (6 May 1848), p. 2.

82. Bennett, *King without a Crown*, p. 101.

83. Quoted in Edwin Hodder, *The Life and Work of the Seventh Earl of Shaftesbury* (London, 1892), p. 395.

84. RA VIC/M 51/75.

85. *The Principal Speeches and Addresses of His Royal Highness The Prince Consort* (1862), pp. 88–9.

86. Quoted in Geoffrey Finlayson, *The Seventh Earl of Shaftesbury 1801–1885* (London, 1981), p. 273.

87. Quoted in Roger Fulford, *The Prince Consort* (London, 1949), p. 144.

88. *Autobiography of John McAdam (1806–1883)*, ed. Janet Fyfe (Edinburgh, 1980), p. 157.

89. RA VIC/C 56/100.

90. RA VIC/C 56/101.

91. Philip Harling, *The Waning of 'Old Corruption': The Politics of Economical Reform in Britain, 1779–1846* (Oxford, 1996), p. 4.

92. Rosemary Ashton, *Little Germany: Exile and Asylum in Victorian England* (Oxford, 1986), p. 45.

93. Gregory Claeys, 'Mazzini, Kossuth, and British Radicalism, 1848–1854', *Journal of British Studies*, vol. 28 (July 1989), pp. 231, 259–61. See also Gregory Claeys, *Citizens and Saints: Politics and Anti-Politics in Early British Socialism* (Cambridge, 1989), pp. 306–9.

94. For a rounded portrait see Smith, *Radical Artisan: William James Linton 1815–97*.

95. Quoted in *Friend of the People* (15 March 1851), pp. 109–10.

96. Smith, *Radical Artisan: William James Linton 1815–97*, p. 105.

97. *English Republic*, ed. Kineton Parkes (London, 1891), p. x.

98. Claeys, *Citizens and Saints: Politics and Anti-Politics in Early British Socialism*, pp. 306–9. See also Smith, *Radical Artisan: William James Linton 1815–97*, pp. 102–5.

99. *English Republic*, vol. 1 (1851), p. 149.

100. *Ibid.*, vol. 2 (1852–3), pp. 69–70. Claeys, *Citizens and Saints: Politics and Anti-Politics in Early British Socialism*, pp. 308–9.

101. W. J. Linton, *Ireland for the Irish* (New York, 1867), pp. 15–16, 25.

102. On Mazzini in England see Denis Mack Smith, *Mazzini* (New Haven and London, 1994), chapter 2. See also Edyth Hinkley, *Mazzini: The Story of a Great Italian* (London, 1924), p. 276.

103. *English Republic*, vol. 1 (1851), p. 356.

104. *Ibid.*, pp. 357–8.

105. *English Republic*, ed. Parkes, pp. 111–13.

106. W. E. Adams, *Memoirs of a Social Atom*, 2 vols. (London, 1903), vol. 1, pp. 262–3. See also Aaron Watson, *A Newspaper Man's Memories* (London, 1925), pp. 51–2.

107. Adams, *Memoirs of a Social Atom*, vol. 1, p. 266.

108. *Ibid.*

109. *Ibid.*, p. 265.

110. *English Republic*, vol. 3 (1854), pp. 1–2.

111. Adams, *Memoirs of a Social Atom*, vol. 1, p. 268.

112. *Democratic Review* (June 1849–September 1850), p. 72; *Red Republican* (10 August 1850), p. 61.

113. *Republican*, vol. 1 (1848), pp. 121, 131–4, 224.

114. *Friend of the People* (8 February 1851), p. 70.

115. David Shaw, *Gerald Massey: Chartist, Poet, Radical and Freethinker* (London, 1995), pp. 99, 117, 202.

116. *Friend of the People* (8 March 1851), p. 104. See also *The Poetical Works of Gerald Massey* (London, 1861), p. 311. *Rhymes by a Republican* (Burton-upon-Trent, 1856) also pays homage to the French.

117. Adams, *Memoirs of a Social Atom*, vol. 1, p. 262.

118. *Red Republican* (22 June 1850), pp. 4–5.

119. *Ibid.*

120. *Ibid.* (13 July 1850), p. 27.

121. *Ibid.* (22 June 1850), pp. 4–5.

122. Williams, *The Contentious Crown*, pp. 24–5.

123. Norbert J. Gossman, 'Republicanism in Nineteenth Century England', *International Review of Social History*, vol. vii (1962), p. 59.

124. Nigel Todd, *'The Militant Democracy': Joseph Cowen and Victorian Radicalism* (Whitley Bay, 1991), pp. 38–9.

125. *The Letters of Matthew Arnold*, vol. 1: 1829–1859, ed. Cecil Y. Lang (Charlottesville and London, 1996), p. 148.

126. Quoted in Edward Royle, *Radicals, Secularists and Republicans: Popular Freethought in Britain, 1866–1915* (Manchester, 1980), p. 192.

127. *Republican*, vol. 1 (1848), pp. 7–8.

128. Edward Royle, *Chartism* (Harlow, 1980), pp. 3, 86–7.

129. *Notes to the People*, vol. 1 (May 1851–May 1852; reprinted London, 1967), p. 512.

130. *Rhymes by a Republican*, pp. 7, 75.

131. Arnold Ruge to Prince Albert, 10 November 1851, RA VIC/I 26/105.

132. Prince Albert to William, Prince of Prussia, 23 February 1853, RA VIC/I 29/3. See also Martin, *The Life of His Royal Highness The Prince Consort*, vol. 2, p. 491.

133. *The Letters of Queen Victoria*, ed. George Earle Buckle, 2nd series, 3 vols. (London, 1926–8), vol. 1, pp. 174–5.

134. *Dearest Mama: Correspondence between Queen Victoria and the Crown Princess of Prussia 1861–1864*, ed. Roger Fulford (London, 1968), p. 324. On the influx of refugees after 1848 see Ashton, *Little Germany: Exile and Asylum in Victorian England*.

135. RA VIC/Y 77/26.

136. RA VIC/A 79/77, 95. Longford, *Victoria R.I.*, p. 205.

137. RA VIC/I 36/139.

138. RA VIC/C 56/11.

139. G. M. Young, *Portrait of an Age: Victorian England* (London, 1977), p. 89.

140. *Letters of the Prince Consort, 1831–1861*, ed. Kurt Jagow (London, 1938), p. 154.

141. RA VIC/PP, Prince Albert's Accounts.

142. *The Principal Speeches and Addresses of His Royal Highness The Prince Consort* (1862), p. 175.

143. See John Nelson Tarn, *Five Per Cent Philanthropy: An Account of Housing in Urban Areas between 1840 and 1914* (London, 1973), p. 20. For more detail on Prince Albert's role in the Great Exhibition see Derek Hudson and Kenneth W. Luckhurst, *The Royal Society of Arts 1754–1954* (London, 1954); Bennett, *King without a Crown*, pp. 198–211; and Hermione Hobhouse, *Prince Albert: His Life and Work* (London, 1983), chapter 7.

144. RA VIC/HH 1/24. See also Prochaska, *Royal Bounty: The Making of a Welfare Monarchy*, pp. 94–6.

145. Hobhouse, *Prince Albert: His Life and Work*, p. 57.

146. Quoted in Martin, *The Life of His Royal Highness The Prince Consort*, vol. 2, p. 213.

147. R. V. Comerford, *The Fenians in Context: Irish Politics and Society 1848–82* (Dublin, 1985), p. 18.

148. Martin, *The Life of His Royal Highness The Prince Consort*, vol. 2, pp. 401–2.

149. *Ibid.*, vol. 1, p. 335.

150. See Elisabeth Darby and Nicola Smith, *The Cult of the Prince Consort* (London, 1984); Prochaska, *Royal Bounty: The Making of a Welfare Monarchy*, p. 97.

151. *The Times* (1 February 1850), p. 2.

152. See *Monarcho-Republicanism*. For a critique of this position see the *Republican*, vol. 1 (1848), p. 158.

153. *Your Dear Letter. Private Correspondence of Queen Victoria and the Crown Princess of Prussia 1865–1871*, ed. Roger Fulford (London, 1971), p. 120.

154. *Ibid.*, p. 165.

155. Longford, *Victoria R.I.*, pp. 351–2.

4. The Anti-Monarchical Moment and its Aftermath

1. 'The English Constitution', *The Collected Works of Walter Bagehot*, ed. Norman St John Stevas, 15 vols. (London, 1974–86), vol. 5, pp. 237, 240.

2. Brian Harrison, *The Transformation of British Politics, 1860–1995* (Oxford, 1996), p. 49; Giles St Aubyn, *Queen Victoria. A Portrait* (London, 1991), pp. 600–601.

3. 'The English Constitution', *The Collected Works of Walter Bagehot*, ed. St John Stevas, vol. 5, pp. 239, 244.

4. William M. Kuhn, *Democratic Royalism: The Transformation of the British Monarchy, 1861–1914* (Basingstoke, Hampshire, 1996), p. 137.

5. Frank Prochaska, *Royal Bounty: The Making of a Welfare Monarchy* (New Haven and London, 1995), pp. 122–3.

6. *Ibid.*, p. 103.

7. Royal Archives VIC/PP Vic Ledger, 1867–70.

8. Prochaska, *Royal Bounty: The Making of a Welfare Monarchy*, p. 77.

9. *Further Letters of Queen Victoria*, ed. Hector Bolitho (London, 1938), p. 155.

10. *Disraeli, Derby and the Conservative Party: The Journals and Memoirs of Edward Henry, Lord Stanley 1849–1869*, ed. John Vincent (Hassocks, Sussex, 1978), p. 210.

11. *The Times* (6 April 1864), p. 9.

12. *Punch* (23 September 1865), p. 215.

13. *Disraeli, Derby and the Conservative Party*, ed. Vincent, pp. 210–11.

14. St Aubyn, *Queen Victoria. A Portrait*, pp. 361–2. See also Richard Williams, *The Contentious Crown: Public Discussion of the British Monarchy in the Reign of Queen Victoria* (Aldershot, 1997), p. 34.

15. On the origins of republicanism in the late 1860s see Royden Harrison, *Before the Socialists. Studies in Labour and Politics 1861–1881* (London, 1965), p. 215; Edward Royle, *Radicals, Secularists and Republicans: Popular Freethought in Britain, 1866–1915* (Manchester, 1980), pp. 198–206; and Williams, *The Contentious Crown, p. 37*.

16. Fergus A. D'Arcy, 'Charles Bradlaugh and the English Republican Movement, 1868–1878', *Historical Journal*, 25, no. 2 (1982), p. 370.

17. Gathorne Hardy to Queen Victoria, 22 December 1867, RA VIC/D 22/101.

18. Prince of Wales to Queen Victoria, 24 October 1869, RA VIC/Add. A3/151. For a description of the Hyde Park demonstation see *The Times* (25 October 1869), p. 5.

19. D'Arcy, 'Charles Bradlaugh and the English Republican Movement, 1868–1878', p. 369.

20. Prochaska, *Royal Bounty: The Making of a Welfare Monarchy*, p. 109.

21. Quoted in Philip Magnus, *King Edward the Seventh* (London, 1964), p. 108.

22. *Ibid.*, pp. 108–9.

23. Quoted in Williams, *The Contentious Crown*, p. 34.

24. Philip Guedalla, *The Queen and Mr. Gladstone*, 2 vols. (London, 1933), vol. 1, p. 321.

25. *National Reformer* (1 September 1870).

26. E. S. Beesly, *A Word for France. Addressed to the London Working Men* (London, 1870), p. 13.

27. Algernon Charles Swinburne, 'Ode on the Proclamation of the French Republic, September 4th' (London, 1870), p. 23.

28. *The Times* (23 September 1870), p. 5; (26 September), p. 12; *The Bee-Hive* (24 September 1870), p. 502. See also, S. Maccoby, *English Radicalism 1853–1886* (London, 1938), p. 165.

29. Quoted in E. G. Collieu, 'The Radical Attitude towards the Monarchy and the House of Lords', B.Lit. thesis, Oxford University (1936), p. 77.

30. Elizabeth Longford, *Victoria R.I.* (London, 1964), p. 387.

31. *The Republican: A Monthly Advocate and Record of Republican and Democratic Principles and Movements* (October 1870), p. 7; (1 February 1872),

p. 2. See also Harrison, *Before the Socialists. Studies in Labour and Politics 1861–1881*, chapter 5.

32. Royle, *Radicals, Secularists and Republicans*, p. 7.

33. Quoted in D'Arcy, 'Charles Bradlaugh and the English Republican Movement, 1868–1878', p. 373.

34. *Ibid.*, pp. 380–81.

35. Hypatia Bradlaugh Bonner, *Charles Bradlaugh*, 2 vols. (London, 1895), vol. 1, p. 310.

36. Charles Bradlaugh, *The Impeachment of the House of Brunswick* (London, 1873), pp. 6–10.

37. Charles Bradlaugh, *London Republican Club. The Inaugural Address* (London, 1871), p. 7.

38. *Parliamentary Debates*, vol. 204 (16 February 1871), cols. 359–71.

39. *Autobiography of John McAdam (1806–1883)*, ed. Janet Fyfe (Edinburgh, 1980), p. 179.

40. *Parliamentary Debates*, vol. 208 (31 July 1871), col. 571.

41. *Ibid.*, col. 576.

42. *Ibid.*, cols. 583–5, 590.

43. Royle, *Radicals, Secularists and Republicans*, p. 199.

44. Collieu, 'The Radical Attitude towards the Monarchy and the House of Lords', p. 148, lists 85 republican clubs founded between 1871 and 1873. Collieu's figures are drawn from the *National Reformer* and *Reynolds's Newspaper*. He does not give a round figure for overall membership numbers, but says that 'many thousands of the working class' joined. It may be useful to compare his list with the list of provincial freethought societies provided by Royle, *Radicals, Secularists and Republicans*, Appendix C, pp. 337–42.

45. Norbert J. Gossman, 'Republicanism in Nineteenth Century England', *International Review of Social History*, vol. vii (1962), p. 59.

46. Antony Taylor, 'Republicanism reappraised: anti-monarchism and the English radical tradition, 1850–1872', *Re-reading the constitution. New narratives in the political history of England's long nineteenth century*, ed. James Vernon (Cambridge, 1996), p. 170.

47. Bonner, *Charles Bradlaugh*, vol. 1., p. 167.

48. For a wry description of a meeting in the Hole-in-the-Wall Tavern, London, see *The Times* (23 November 1871), p. 6.

49. David Tribe, *President Charles Bradlaugh, M.P.* (London, 1971), p. 127.

50. F. W. Hirst, *Early Life & Letters of John Morley*, 2 vols. (London, 1927), vol. 1, p. 217.

51. Leslie Stephen, *Life of Henry Fawcett* (London, 1885), p. 286.

52. *Ibid.*, p. 287.

53. Royle, *Radicals, Secularists and Republicans*, p. 199.

54. Charles R. Mackay, *Life of Charles Bradlaugh* (London, 1888), p. 194. On this issue see also Tribe, *President Charles Bradlaugh, M.P.*, pp. 154, 349.

55. *Republican* (February 1872), p. 2. See also Tribe, *President Charles Bradlaugh, M.P.*, p. 132.

56. Harrison, *Before the Socialists. Studies in Labour and Politics 1861–1881*, pp. 212–14; Williams, *The Contentious Crown*, pp. 31–2; Royle, *Radicals, Secularists and Republicans*, p. 199.

57. Austin Holyoake, *Would a Republican form of Government be suitable to England?* (London, 1873), p. 3.

58. For the monarchy as capitalist scarecrow see the *Republican*, vol. v, no. 10 (January 1880), p. 175.

59. Quoted in Tom Nairn, *The Enchanted Glass. Britain and its Monarchy* (London, 1988), pp. 204–5.

60. Karl Marx, *The Civil War in France*, with an introduction by Frederick Engels (London, 1933), p. 43.

61. The Queen never read Marx, but in later years may have heard of him through Princess Victoria, Empress Frederick, who read Marx's works and received first-hand reports about his views on revolution from the expert on foreign affairs, Sir Mountstuart Grant Duff. The Royal Archives has copies of two letters from Duff to Empress Frederick, dated 1 February 1879 and 21 March 1881, RA VIC/Add. A1/17; VIC/Add. U33/813. The originals were found in the papers of Empress Frederick at her home near Frankfurt in August 1945.

62. D'Arcy, 'Charles Bradlaugh and the English Republican Movement, 1868–1878', pp. 375–6.

63. Holyoake, *Would a Republican form of Government be suitable to England?*, pp. 3–4.

64. Bradlaugh, *London Republican Club. The Inaugural Address*, p. 1

65. Bradlaugh, *The Impeachment of the House of Brunswick*, p. 102.

66. *Ibid.*, pp. 8–10.

67. Holyoake, *Would a Republican form of Government be suitable to England?*, p. 3.

68. Charles Watts, *Republicanism: A reply to Mr John Bright's Letter to the Birmingham Conference* (London [1873]), p. 1.

69. J. Morrison Davidson, *The New Book of Kings* (London, 1884), p. 11.

70. RA VIC/B 26/19 and 20.

71. RA VIC/B 26/21.

72. RA VIC/D 27/75.

73. 'Solomon Temple', *What does she do with it?* (London, 1871); St Aubyn, *Queen Victoria. A Portrait*, pp. 385–6.

74. See William Kuhn, 'Queen Victoria's Civil List: What did she Do with it?', *Historical Journal*, 36, no. 3 (1993); Longford, *Victoria R.I.*, p. 387; Prochaska, *Royal Bounty: The Making of a Welfare Monarchy*, p. 77.

75. Arthur Ponsonby, *Henry Ponsonby, Queen Victoria's Private Secretary: His Life from his Letters* (London, 1942), p. 71.

76. Longford, *Victoria R.I.*, pp. 379, 387.

77. For a discussion of Gladstone and the monarchy see Kuhn, *Democratic Royalism: The Transformation of the British Monarchy, 1861–1914*, chapter 2.

78. Quoted in St Aubyn, *Queen Victoria. A Portrait*, p. 386.

79. Longford, *Victoria R.I.*, p. 388.

80. 'The Monarchy and the People', *The Collected Works of Walter Bagehot*, ed. St John Stevas, vol. 5, p. 433.

81. *The Times* (22 June 1871), p. 12; E. M. McInness, *St Thomas' Hospital* (London, 1963), p. 113.

82. *The Letters of Queen Victoria*, ed. George Earle Buckle, 2nd series, 3 vols. (London, 1926–8), vol. 2, p. 159.

83. Prince of Wales to Queen Victoria, 10 April 1871, RA VIC/T 5/43.

84. David Nicholls, *The Lost Prime Minister: A Life of Charles Dilke* (London, 1995), p. 50.

85. British Library, Dilke Papers, Add. MSS 43931, fol. 193.

86. Kingsley Martin, *The Crown and the Establishment* (London, 1962), p. 46.

87. *Sir Charles Dilke on the Cost of the Crown* (London, 1871), pp. 9, 23.

88. *The Times* (9 November 1871), p. 9.

89. Quoted in *The Times* (17 November 1871), p. 5.

90. RA VIC/B 26/67, news cutting from the *Globe* (December 1871).

91. *Ibid.*

92. Quoted in *The Times* (25 December 1871), p. 4.

93. RA VIC/A 77/36, newspaper cutting (late November 1871), author and paper unknown.

94. Ponsonby, *Henry Ponsonby, Queen Victoria's Private Secretary. His Life from his Letters*, p. 266.

95. Sir Thomas Biddulph to the Queen, 12 November 1871, RA VIC/B 26/59.

96. RA VIC/Add. A36/385.

97. RA VIC/Add. A36/386.

98. RA VIC/Add. A36/389.

99. Quoted in Longford, *Victoria R.I.*, pp. 391–2.

100. RA VIC/A 42/72.

101. *The Letters of Queen Victoria*, ed. Buckle, 2nd series, vol. 2, p. 167.

102. *Annual Register* (new series, 1871), pp. 122–3.

103. Tribe, *President Charles Bradlaugh, M.P.*, p. 132.

104. Nigel Todd, '*The Militant Democracy*': Joseph Cowen and Victorian *Radicalism* (Whitley Bay, 1991), p. 95.

105. *The Times* (17 January 1872), p. 5.

106. BL, Add. MSS 43931, fol. 185.

107. Nicholls, *The Lost Prime Minister: A Life of Charles Dilke*, p. 52.

108. Duke of Cambridge to the Duchess of Teck, 25 November 1871, RA VIC/A 8/2028.

109. BL, Add. MSS 43931, fol. 177.

110. Dilke to Seymour, 5 January 1883, RA VIC/Add. J/1495.

111. Queen Victoria to Gladstone, 4 December 1871, RA VIC/A 42/78.

112. Gladstone to Queen Victoria, 5 December 1871, RA VIC/A 42/79.

113. BL, Add. MSS 43931, fol. 179.

114. Nairn, *The Enchanted Glass. Britain and its Monarchy*, p. 329.

115. From the *Chelsea News*, 24 February 1872, quoted in Nicholls, *The Lost Prime Minister: A Life of Charles Dilke*, p. 55; see also *The Times* (20 February 1872), p. 10.

116. Quoted in Nairn, *The Enchanted Glass. Britain and its Monarchy*, p. 329.

117. 'The Illness of the Prince of Wales', *The Collected Works of Walter Bagehot*, ed. St John Stevas, vol. 5, pp. 435–6.

118. Quoted in St Aubyn, *Queen Victoria. A Portrait*, p. 388.

119. Freda Harcourt, 'Gladstone, Monarchism and the "New" Imperialism, 1868–74', *Journal of Imperial and Commonwealth History*, vol. 14 (October 1985), pp. 31–2; W. M. Kuhn, 'Ceremony and Politics: The British Monarchy, 1871–1872', *Journal of British Studies*, 26 (1987), pp. 133–62; Kuhn, *Democratic Royalism: The Transformation of the British Monarchy, 1861–1914*, pp. 39–46, 54–5.

120. Quoted in Harcourt, 'Gladstone, Monarchism and the "New" Imperialism, 1868–74', p. 31.

121. *The Bee-Hive* (2 March 1872), p. 9.

122. *The Letters of Queen Victoria*, ed. Buckle, 2nd series, vol. 2, p. 194.

123. *Ibid.*, p. 196.

124. Nicholls, *The Lost Prime Minister: A Life of Charles Dilke*, p. 55.

125. *Parliamentary Debates*, vol. 210 (19 March 1872), cols. 253–90.

126. *Ibid.*, col. 298.

127. *Ibid.*, col. 305.

128. S. Hutchinson Harris, *Auberon Herbert: Crusader for Liberty* (London, 1943), p. 141.

129. *Ibid.*, p. 130.

130. *Parliamentary Debates*, vol. 210 (19 March 1872), cols. 311–13.

131. Ponsonby to Queen Victoria, 28 April 1871, RA VIC/A 41/78.

132. *Parliamentary Debates*, vol. 210 (19 March 1872), cols. 313–17.

133. Quoted in Nicholls, *The Lost Prime Minister: A Life of Charles Dilke*, p. 56.

134. Prince Arthur to Queen Victoria, 20 March 1872, RA VIC/Add. A 15/1872.

135. RA VIC/A 43/10; VIC/A 43/32.

136. Williams, *The Contentious Crown*, pp. 49–50.

137. *The Republican Chronicle*, no. 1 (April 1875), p. 2.

138. *The Bee-Hive* (23 March 1872), pp. 1–2.

139. *Ibid.* (24 September 1870), p. 502.

140. *The Public Letters of the Right Hon. John Bright*, ed. H. J. Leech (London, 1895; reprint 1969), p. 225.

141. On the background to this article, and Harrison's companion piece titled 'The Revival of Authority', see Hirst, *Early Life & Letters of John Morley*, vol. 1, pp. 206–30.

142. *Fortnightly Review*, vol. 11 (1 June 1872), pp. 614–15, 640. In *Order and Progress* (London, 1875), pp. 118–19, Harrison saw the future of political society as 'profoundly republican', but it required 'the responsible leadership of qualified men'.

143. *Fortnightly Review*, vol. 11 (1 June 1872), pp. 613–14, 632–34.

144. *Ibid.*, pp. 616, 640.

145. Hirst, *Early Life & Letters of John Morley*, vol. 1, pp. 214, 216.

146. Lord Rosebery wanted Harrison to receive the Order of Merit, but the King thought him too old. In 1920, the Prime Minister put Harrison up for the Companion of Honour, which the King approved, but Harrison turned it down. See RA PS/GV/J 1679/2–5.

147. 'The Illness of the Prince of Wales', *Collected Works of Walter Bagehot*, ed. St John Stevas, vol. 5, p. 437.

148. *Parliamentary Debates*, vol. 217 (31 July 1873), cols. 1352–8.

149. *The Times* (12 May 1873), p. 12.

150. *Fortnightly Review*, vol. 11 (1 June 1872), p. 634.

151. James Aytoun, *Constitutional Monarchy and Republicanism* (London, 1873), pp. 5–8.

152. *The Bee-Hive* (17 May 1873), p. 9.

153. *The Times* (12 May 1873), p. 12; (13 May), p. 7.

154. Tribe, *President Charles Bradlaugh, M.P.*, p. 145; see also D'Arcy, 'Charles Bradlaugh and the English Republican Movement, 1868–1878', pp. 378–9.

155. *Speeches by Joseph Cowen, esq., M.P.* (Newcastle, 1874), pp. 77–8, 121; see also the article on Cowen in the *Biographical Dictionary of Modern British Radicals*, eds. Joseph O. Baylen and Norbert J. Gossman (Hassocks, Sussex, 1984), vol. 2, p. 161.

156. Todd, *'The Militant Democracy': Joseph Cowen and Victorian Radicalism*, p. 126.

157. This unidentifiable quotation comes from p. 5 of a fragmentary tract in the BL, 4017 e.1.

158. *Republican Chronicle*, no. 2 (May 1875), p. 12.; *Radical*, vol. 12, no. 6 (August 1886), p. 36; Royle, *Radicals, Secularists and Republicans*, pp. 203–4.

159. *Republican*, vol. 5, no. 2 (January 1880), p. 12.

160. Brian Harrison, *Drink and the Victorians. The Temperance Question in England 1815–1872* (London, 1971), p. 317.

161. Virginia Berridge, 'Popular Sunday Papers and Mid-Victorian Society', *Newspaper History from the 17th Century to the Present Day*, eds. G. Boyce, P. Wingate and J. Curran (London, 1978), pp. 252–64. For circulation figures of Victorian newspapers see Williams, *The Contentious Crown*, pp. 3–4.

162. *Republican*, vol. 5, no. 10 (January 1880), p. 169.

163. Bradlaugh, *The Impeachment of the House of Brunswick*, p. iii.

164. Quoted in Tribe, *President Charles Bradlaugh, M.P.*, p. 156. The popular 'Chant de Depart' proclaimed 'Republicans are men full-grown, Slaves are but children'. See Pamela Pilbeam, *Republicanism in Nineteenth-Century France, 1814–1871* (London, 1995), p. 1.

165. Quoted in Tribe, *President Charles Bradlaugh, M.P.*, p. 147.

166. *Ibid.*, p. 146.

167. 28 January 1874, RA VIC L 13/159.

168. 'The Illness of the Prince of Wales', *The Collected Works of Walter Bagehot*, ed. St John Stevas, vol. 5, pp. 436–7.

169. This point was made by William Henry Martin, *The Social Crisis in England. A Letter addressed by permission to the Rt. Hon. The Earl of Shaftesbury* (Birmingham, 1873), pp. 17–18.

170. On this issue see Philip Nord, *The Republican Moment. The Struggle for Democracy in Nineteenth-Century France* (Cambridge, Mass., 1995).

171. Nairn, *The Enchanted Glass. Britain and its Monarchy*, pp. 330–32.

172. Prochaska, *Royal Bounty: The Making of a Welfare Monarchy*, chapter 4.

173. Henry C. Burdett, *Prince, Princess and People. An Account of the Public*

*Life and Work of their Royal Highnesses the Prince and Princess of Wales,
1863–1889* (London, 1889), p. 306.

174. Prochaska, *Royal Bounty: The Making of a Welfare Monarchy*,
pp. 120–21. For a discussion of anti-monarchism in the colonies see Antony
Taylor, '*Down with the Crown': British Anti-Monarchism and Debates about
Royalty since 1790* (London, 1999), chapter 5.

175. George Jacob Holyoake, *Sixty Years of an Agitator's Life*, 2 vols. (London,
1893), vol. 1, pp. 270–71.

176. Longford, *Victoria R.I.*, pp. 428–9.

177. Queen Victoria to Ponsonby, 8 April 1880, *The Letters of Queen Victoria*,
ed. Buckle, 2nd series, vol. 3, pp. 75–6.

178. Queen Victoria to Gladstone, 7 August 1881, RA VIC/A 54/23.

179. Gladstone to Queen Victoria, 21 May 1880, RA VIC/C 35/101; Ponsonby
to Gladstone, 24 May 1880, RA VIC/A 52/3.

180. George Macaulay Trevelyan, *The Life of John Bright* (London, 1913),
pp. 396, 400–402; Queen Victoria's Journal, 7 February 1878, RA; RA VIC/C
50/75.

181. RA VIC/C 34/8.

182. Queen Victoria's Journal, 27 April 1880, RA.

183. Queen Victoria to Gladstone, 27 April 1880, RA VIC/C 34/138.

184. RA VIC/C 34/145. Queen Victoria's Journal, 28 April 1880, RA. See also
Frank Hardie, *The Political Influence of Queen Victoria 1861–1901* (London,
1963), p. 212.

185. Lord Granville to Ponsonby, 30 April 1880, RA VIC/C 35/23.

186. Queen Victoria to the Prince of Wales, 27 May 1882, *The Letters of Queen
Victoria*, ed. Buckle, 2nd series, vol. 3, pp. 298–9.

187. Queen Victoria's Journal, 9 October 1882, RA fol. 164.

188. RA VIC/A 56/69a.

189. Queen Victoria to Gladstone, 26 March 1882, quoted in Guedalla, *The
Queen and Mr. Gladstone*, vol. 2, p. 183.

190. Queen Victoria to Gladstone, 28 December 1882, RA VIC/Add. J1485.
For further information on this episode see Nicholls, *The Lost Prime Minister:
A Life of Charles Dilke*, chapter 7.

191. Ponsonby to Seymour, 2 January 1883, RA VIC/Add. J1489.

192. Sir Charles Dilke to Seymour, 5 January 1883, RA VIC/Add. J1495.

193. RA VIC/Add. J1493.

194. *Ibid.*, press cuttings.

195. See St Aubyn, *Queen Victoria. A Portrait*, p. 600.

196. Nicholls, *The Lost Prime Minister: A Life of Charles Dilke*, pp. 109–10.

197. Peter T. Marsh, *Joseph Chamberlain. Entrepreneur in Politics* (New Haven and London, 1994), pp. 59–60, 87–8.

198. Magnus, *King Edward the Seventh*, p. 131.

199. Queen Victoria to Gladstone, 27 April 1880, RA VIC/C 34/138.

200. RA VIC/C 34/145.

201. *The Times* (14 June 1883), p. 6.

202. Queen Victoria to Ponsonby, June 1883, RA VIC/L 15/11.

203. Queen Victoria to Gladstone, 27 July 1883, RA VIC/A 58/25.

204. *The Times* (2 July 1883), pp. 6, 9; Marsh, *Joseph Chamberlain. Entrepreneur in Politics*, p. 166.

205. Gladstone to Chamberlain, 2 July 1883, RA VIC/A 58/35.

206. Chamberlain to Gladstone, 2 July 1883, RA VIC/A 58/36.

207. Gladstone to Queen Victoria, 3 July 1883, RA VIC/A 58/38.

208. Taylor, *'Down with the Crown': British Anti-Monarchism and Debates about Royalty since 1790*, p. 96, includes a lampoon from the Birmingham magazine *Dart* (1 May 1880).

209. Queen Victoria to Gladstone, 25 July 1884, *The Letters of Queen Victoria*, ed. Buckle, 2nd series, vol. 3, p. 523.

210. Queen Victoria to Gladstone, 29 July 1884, RA VIC/A 77/63.

211. Queen Victoria to Gladstone, 22 October 1884, RA VIC/C 50/18.

212. RA VIC/B 36/4.

213. Queen Victoria to Earl Granville, 3 February 1885, RA VIC/B 36/7.

214. *Parliamentary Debates*, vol. 338 (26 July 1889), col. 1522. Lawson did not speak in the debate in 1872, but he believed that Dilke's motion 'deserved consideration'. W. B. Luke, *Sir Wilfrid Lawson* (London, 1900), p. 73.

215. *Parliamentary Debates*, vol. 339 (5 August 1889), col. 337. Algar Labouchere Thorold, *The Life of Henry Labouchere* (London, 1913), pp. 220–21.

216. *Parliamentary Debates*, vol. 338 (29 July 1889), col. 1610.

217. *Ibid.*, col. 1588.

218. On Morley's relations with Edward VII see RA VIC/W 63/19; VIC/W 64/40; VIC/W 5/39.

219. *Parliamentary Debates*, vol. 338 (26 July 1889), col. 1449.

220. *Ibid.* (25 July 1889), cols. 1340–41.

221. RA VIC/L 24/28; VIC/L 24/39; and further information from the Royal Archives.

222. *Parliamentary Debates*, vol. 339 (5 August 1889), cols. 335–6.

223. *Ibid.*, vol. 93 (9 May 1901), col. 1226. John Sainty, former Clerk of Parliament, informs me that three whips were paid for by the Civil List at the end of the nineteenth century.

224. RA VIC/Add. A12/1882. Longford, *Victoria R.I.*, p. 567.

225. *Parliamentary Debates*, vol. 298 (14 May 1885), p. 504; Thorold, *The Life of Henry Labouchere*, pp. 220–21.

226. Thorold, *The Life of Henry Labouchere*, p. 221.

227. Ponsonby to Gladstone, 22 August 1892, RA VIC/C 39/119. See also Longford, *Victoria R.I.*, p. 519.

228. RA VIC/C 39/122; VIC/C 39/137.

229. *The Times* (13 September 1892), p. 5.

230. *Ibid.*; *Truth* (1 September 1892).

231. *Parliamentary Debates*, vol. 267 (23 March 1882), cols. 1686–7.

232. George Standring, *Court Flunkeys, their Work and Wages* (London [1879]), pp. 8–12.

233. Annie Besant, *English Republicanism* (London [1878]), p. 2.

234. Royle, *Radicals, Secularists and Republicans*, p. 205.

235. *Republican*, vol. 12 (August 1886), p. 36.

236. On the birth of the future King Edward VIII in 1894 see, for example, the *Clarion* (30 June 1894), p. 1; *Labour Leader* (30 June 1894), p. 8.

237. See Antony Taylor, 'Reynolds's Newspaper, Opposition to Monarchy and the Radical Anti-Jubilee: Britain's Anti-Monarchist Tradition Reconsidered', *Historical Research*, vol. lxviii, no. 167 (October 1995), pp. 318–37.

238. Quoted in S. Maccoby, *English Radicalism, 1886–1914* (London, 1953), p. 37.

239. Quoted in Taylor, 'Reynolds's Newspaper, Opposition to Monarchy and the Radical Anti-Jubilee: Britain's Anti-Monarchist Tradition Reconsidered', p. 318. For further information on Australian republicanism see Antony Taylor and Luke Trainor, 'Monarchism and anti-monarchism: Anglo-Australian comparisons c. 1870–1901', *Social History*, vol. 24, no. 2 (May 1999), pp. 158–73. See also Taylor, *'Down with the Crown': British Anti-Monarchism and Debates about Royalty since 1790*, chapter 5.

240. *Labour Leader* (19 June 1897), p. 203.

241. Taylor, 'Reynolds's Newspaper, Opposition to Monarchy and the Radical Anti-Jubilee: Britain's Anti-Monarchist Tradition Reconsidered', p. 327.

242. *Labour Leader* (19 June 1897), p. 205.

243. Davidson, *The New Book of Kings*, pp. 7, 15, 100, 107.

244. [Daniel Chatterton], *Chatterton's Letter to the Prince of Wales and all other Aristocratic and Royal Paupers* (London [1882?]), pp. 1–6.

245. Daniel Chatterton, *The Impeachment of the Queen, Cabinet, Parliament, & People* (London, 1886), pp. 1, 8. See also the *Dictionary of Labour Biography*,

eds. Joyce M. Bellamy and John Saville, 9 vols. (London, 1972–93), vol. 8, pp. 32–5.

246. The quote is from the journalist Alfred Gardiner. See Martin, *The Crown and the Establishment*, p. 56.

247. *Labour Leader* (30 June 1894), p. 8. See also Kenneth O. Morgan, *Keir Hardie, Radical and Socialist* (London, 1975), p. 71.

248. *Standard* (29 June 1894).

249. RA VIC/Add. A/20/687.

250. *Labour Leader* (19 June 1897), p. 203.

251. *Ibid.*

252. *Daily News* (9 February 1917), RA GV/O 1056/7.

253. *Fortnightly Review*, vol. 11 (1 June 1872), p. 634.

254. *Daily News* (15 January 1917), RA GV/O 1056/7.

255. The socialist paper *Justice* (26 January 1901), p. 4, was unusual in seeing Queen Victoria's direct power to be much greater than her subjects assumed.

256. *The Letters of Sidney and Beatrice Webb*, ed. Norman MacKenzie, 3 vols. (London, 1978), vol. 2, p. 134.

257. *Justice* (26 January 1901), p. 4; H. M. Hyndman, *A Commune for London* (London [1887]), p. 16.

258. *Reynolds's Newspaper* (5 February 1901), p. 4, quoted in Williams, *The Contentious Crown*, p. 71.

5. The Advent of Socialism and the Crowned Republic

1. *Labour Leader* (19 June 1897), p. 203.

2. A. V. Dicey argued that America and France were disappointing models of democratic republicanism, for they did 'nothing to gratify the imagination or kindle the enthusiasm of mankind'. See A. V. Dicey, *Lectures on the Relation between Law and Public Opinion in England during the Nineteenth Century* (London, 1905), p. 443.

3. *The Autobiography of Margot Asquith*, 2 vols. (London, 1920, 1922), vol. 2, p. 115.

4. *The Diary of Beatrice Webb*, eds. Norman and Jeanne MacKenzie, 4 vols. (London, 1982–5), vol. 2, p. 108.

5. Philip Magnus, *King Edward the Seventh* (London, 1964), pp. 276–7. For a recent reassessment of Edward VII's political influence see Simon Heffer, *Power and Place: The Political Consequences of King Edward VII* (London,

1998). See also Frank Hardie, *The Political Influence of the British Monarchy* (London, 1970), chapter 4.

6. See, for example, the resolution of the Edinburgh branch of the Social Democratic Federation, *Justice* (2 February 1901), p. 3.

7. *Parliamentary Debates*, vol. 93 (9 May 1901), cols. 1218–32, 1251–2. For a discussion of Edward VII's Civil List see Phillip Hall, *Royal Fortune: Tax, Money and the Monarchy* (London, 1992), pp. 20–32.

8. *Justice* (28 June 1902), p. 4.

9. *Ibid.* (21 June 1902), p. 4.

10. *Labour Leader* (10 May 1902), p. 148; (21 June 1902), p. 193.

11. *Ibid.* (19 April 1902), p. 134.

12. See Canon Hensley Henson's sermon at Westminster Abbey, 27 January 1901, quoted in C. J. Montague, *Sixty Years in Waifdom; or, The Ragged School Movement in English History* (London, 1904), p. 8.

13. See, for example, *Justice* (18 November 1905), p. 1.

14. Public Record Office, HO/144 contains the files of innumerable applicants for royal patronage between 1879 and 1920. See also Arnold Sorsby, *Royal Eye Hospital, 1857–1957* (London, 1957), p. 19.

15. Frank Prochaska, *Royal Bounty: The Making of a Welfare Monarchy* (New Haven and London, 1995), p. 151.

16. See F. K. Prochaska, *Philanthropy and the Hospitals of London: The King's Fund 1897–1990* (Oxford, 1992).

17. Revd Archer Gurney, *Loyalty and Church and State: A Sermon Preached . . . on the occasion of the National Thanksgiving for the Recovery of the H.R.H. The Prince of Wales* (London, 1872), p. 6.

18. José Harris, *Private Lives, Public Spirit: Britain 1870–1914* (Harmondsworth, 1994), p. 16.

19. Viscount Esher, 'The Voluntary Principle', *The Influence of King Edward* (London, 1915), pp. 114–17. For a recent assessment of Esher see William M. Kuhn, *Democratic Royalism: The Transformation of the British Monarchy, 1861–1914* (Basingstoke, Hampshire, 1996), chapter 3.

20. Esher, 'The Voluntary Principle', *The Influence of King Edward*, p. 116.

21. Viscount Esher, *To-day and Tomorrow and Other Essays* (London, 1910), p. 227.

22. Prochaska, *Philanthropy and the Hospitals of London: The King's Fund 1897–1990*, pp. 32–6.

23. Prochaska, *Royal Bounty: The Making of a Welfare Monarchy*, p. 142.

24. Quoted in Magnus, *King Edward the Seventh*, p. 282.

25. Esher to Knollys, 1 December 1907, Royal Archives VIC/W 41/11.

26. *The Autobiography of Margot Asquith*, vol. 2, p. 115.

27. Henry Pelling and Alastair J. Reid, *A Short History of the Labour Party* (11th edn; Basingstoke, Hampshire, 1996), pp. 197, 200.

28. Quoted in Harold Nicolson, *King George the Fifth: His Life and Reign* (London, 1952), p. 94.

29. Brian Harrison, *The Transformation of British Politics, 1860–1995* (Oxford, 1996), p. 344.

30. On this issue see Paul Ward, *Red Flag and Union Jack: Englishness, Patriotism and the British Left, 1881–1924* (Woodbridge, Suffolk, 1998).

31. J. Ramsay MacDonald, *Socialism and Government*, 2 vols. (London, 1910), vol. 2, p. 41.

32. RA VIC/W 66/28.

33. See *Labour Leader*, passim, June and July 1909.

34. British Library, Add. MSS 41207, fol. 22. See also RA VIC/R 27/13.

35. BL, Add. MSS 41207, fol. 152–3. See also RA VIC/R 27/114.

36. BL, Add. MSS 41208, fol. 119.

37. Magnus, *King Edward the Seventh*, p. 441.

38. H. G. Wells believed that both apologists for the monarchy and people of republican sentiments were attracted by the phrase 'crowned republic'. See *Penny Pictorial* (19 May 1917), p. 339.

39. See, for example, *Justice* (13 May 1911), p. 5; (10 June 1911), p. 5.

40. *Parliamentary Debates*, vol. 19 (22 July 1910), cols. 1631–2, 1676.

41. Quoted in James Pope-Hennessy, *Queen Mary, 1867–1953* (London, 1959), p. 469.

42. Esher to Queen Mary, 12 January 1912, RA GV/CC 47/288.

43. George V to Queen Mary, 23 August 1911, RA GV/CC 4/74.

44. Kenneth O. Morgan, *Keir Hardie, Radical and Socialist* (London, 1975), pp. 71–3; Edgar Wilson, *The Myth of the British Monarchy* (London, 1989), p. 45.

45. This was the celebrated writer Hall Caine, a friend of Queen Alexandra. See RA PP/GV/A 1119.

46. RA GV/Q 724/6.

47. Pope-Hennessy, *Queen Mary, 1867–1953*, p. 470.

48. *The Times* (15 June 1912), p. 10.

49. Quoted in Pope-Hennessy, *Queen Mary, 1867–1953*, p. 470.

50. See Prochaska, *Royal Bounty: The Making of a Welfare Monarchy*, pp. 170–75.

51. RA GV/CC 26/22.

52. Prochaska, *Royal Bounty: The Making of a Welfare Monarchy*, pp. 174–5.

53. See, for example, Stamfordham to Asquith, 6 August 1915, RA GV/B 742/49.

54. Nicolson, *King George the Fifth*, p. 248. On the royal family's war work see Prochaska, *Royal Bounty: The Making of a Welfare Monarchy*, pp. 175–82.

55. RA GV/Q 1104/13. See also Arthur Marwick, *The Deluge: British Society and the First World War* (London, 1991), p. 105.

56. Pope-Hennessy, *Queen Mary, 1867–1953*, p. 505.

57. *War Memoirs of David Lloyd George*, 2 vols. (London, 1938), vol. 2, pp. 1162–3.

58. See the article by John Grigg in *The Times* (6 November 1998), p. 24.

59. John Stevenson, *British Society 1914–45* (Harmondsworth, 1984), p. 197.

60. RA GV/P 476/60.

61. Kenneth Rose, *King George V* (London, 1983), pp. 200–201.

62. Stamfordham to Lord Revelstoke, 13 June 1917, RA GV/O 1106/40. This letter is quoted in Nicolson, *King George the Fifth*, p. 309.

63. Stamfordham to Lloyd George, 25 August 1918, RA GV/K 1348/7.

64. Quoted in Nicolson, *King George the Fifth*, p. 64.

65. RA GV/O 1106/9 and 10.

66. *Justice* (5 April 1917), RA GV/O 1106/1.

67. Andrei Maylunas and Sergei Mironenko, *A Lifelong Passion: Nicholas and Alexandra, their own Story* (London, 1996), pp. 569–70. See RA GV/M 1067/61; Nicolson, *King George the Fifth*, pp. 301–2; Mark D. Steinberg and Vladimir M. Kaustalev, *The Fall of the Romanovs* (New Haven, 1995), pp. 120–21.

68. George V's Diary, 17 January 1914, RA.

69. Stamfordham to Lloyd George, 25 August 1918, RA GV/K 1348/7.

70. Lloyd George to Stamfordham, 22 August 1918, RA GV/K 1348/6.

71. Bishop of Chelmsford to Stamfordham, 5 April 1917, RA GV/O 1106/3.

72. *Ibid.*

73. RA GV/O 1106/29 and 30.

74. Unsworth to Stamfordham, 5 April 1917, RA GV/O 1106/2.

75. Stamfordham to Unsworth, 9 April 1917, RA GV/O 1106/7.

76. *Dictionary of Labour Biography*, eds. Joyce M. Bellamy and John Saville (London, 1972), vol. 1, pp. 317–18. See also Will Thorne, *My Life's Battles* (London, 1925), p. 213.

77. RA GV/O 1106/8.

78. G. G. Whiskard to Stamfordham, 9 April 1917, RA GV/O 1106/6.

79. *Justice* (5 April 1917), RA GV/O 1106/1.

80. *Daily Herald* (28 April 1917), RA GV/O 1106/27.

81. *The Times* (21 April 1917), p. 7; (23 April 1917), p. 9, RA GV/O 1106/16 and 19.

82. H. G. Wells, 'The Future of the Monarchy', *Penny Pictorial* (19 May 1917), pp. 337–41, RA GV/O 1106/52.

83. See, for example, the *National News* (20 May 1917), RA GV/O 1106/45.

84. RA GV/O 1106/33 and 35.

85. *The Times* (21 April 1917), RA GV/O 1106/16.

86. Nicolson, *King George the Fifth*, pp. 308–9.

87. Strachey to Stamfordham, 27 April 1917, RA GV/Q 1104/1. For more information on Strachey see Amy Strachey, *St. Loe Strachey: His Life and His Paper* (London, 1930).

88. Stamfordham to Strachey, 30 April 1917, RA GV/Q 1104/8.

89. Strachey to Stamfordham, 2 May 1917, RA GV/Q 1104/10.

90. Stamfordham to Strachey, 3 May 1917, RA GV/Q 1104/12.

91. Information from the Royal Archives.

92. Quoted in Nicolson, *King George the Fifth*, p. 310.

93. Geordie Greig, *Louis and the Prince: A Story of Politics, Intrigue and Royal Friendship* (London, 1999), p. 120.

94. RA GV/O 1130/33. Much of the information in the Cabinet Office report could have been gleaned from the *Daily Herald*, which ran a special issue on the Leeds Conference on 9 June 1917.

95. *Clarion* (29 June 1917), RA GV/O 1106/45.

96. *Ibid.*

97. Stamfordham to King George V, 3 July 1917, RA GV/K 1135/1.

98. RA GV/B 1173/5.

99. Bishop of Chelmsford to Stamfordham, 6 July 1917, RA GV/O 1106/49.

100. Unsworth to Stamfordham, 18 July 1917, RA GV/O 1106/57.

101. *Thatched with Gold: The Memoirs of Mabell, Countess of Airlie*, ed. Jennifer Ellis (London, 1962), p. 131.

102. Nicolson, *King George the Fifth*, p. 252.

103. *Ibid.*, p. 336.

104. Rose, *King George V*, p. 257.

105. See Prochaska, *Royal Bounty: The Making of a Welfare Monarchy*, p. 178.

106. There were 25,000 recipients of the OBE by the end of 1919 according to John Walker, *The Queen has been Pleased: The British Honours System at Work* (London, 1986), p. 12.

107. Stamfordham to the Bishop of Chelmsford, 15 June 1918, RA GV/O 908/10.

108. A. J. P. Taylor, *English History, 1914–1945* (Oxford, 1965), p. 175.

109. Extract of a letter from the Archbishop of Canterbury to Stamfordham [1918], RA GV/O 1341/1.
110. Quoted in *ibid*.
111. Esher to Stamfordham, 22 January 1918, RA GV/Q 724/100.
112. Esher to Stamfordham, 15 April 1918, RA GV/Q 724/104.
113. Esher to Stamfordham, 28 July 1918, RA GV/Q 724/108.
114. Esher to Stamfordham, 26 October 1918, RA GV/Q 724/109.
115. RA GV/O 1361/2.
116. John W. Wheeler-Bennett, *King George VI* (London, 1958), p. 159.
117. *Nation* (26 October 1918), RA GV/O 1106/61.
118. Born in 1878, Clifford Salisbury Woodward had a steady rise: a curate in Bermondsey, he became Canon of Southwark, King's Chaplain (1919–33), Canon of Westminster (1926–33) and Bishop of Bristol from 1933.
119. Woodward to Stamfordham, 8 October 1918, RA GV/O 1341/6.
120. *Ibid*.
121. *Ibid*.
122. Stamfordham to Woodward, 21 October 1918, RA GV/O 1341/8.
123. Woodward to Stamfordham, 26 October 1918, RA GV/O 1341/9.
124. Woodward to Stamfordham, 19 November 1918, RA GV/O 1341/10.
125. Esher to Stamfordham, 4 November 1918, RA GV/Q 724/110.
126. Bishop of Chelmsford to Stamfordham, 11 November 1918, RA GV/O 1106/64.
127. Esher to King George, 12 November 1918, RA GV/Q 724/111.
128. No record of George V's view of the Representation of the People Act has been found in the Royal Archives and Harold Nicolson does not even mention the subject.
129. *The Times* (15 November 1918), p. 8. See also Frank Owen, *Tempestuous Journey: Lloyd George, his Life and Times* (London, 1954), pp. 498–9.
130. RA GV/O 1220/31.
131. For a description of their reception see *The Times* (14 November 1918), p. 8; (15 November), p. 9; (16 November), p. 8.
132. *The Autobiography of Margot Asquith*, vol. 2, p. 287.
133. Quoted in Nicolson, *King George the Fifth*, p. 327.
134. Esher to Stamfordham, 26 November 1918, RA GV/Q 724/113. It is likely that Esher would have seen *The Times* article of 15 November 1918, which reported on the Labour Party election meeting of 14 November. It noted the cries of 'release John Maclean'. But some days before Esher wrote to the King, the government had taken a decision about Maclean, and he was released on 3 December 1918. See Nan Milton, *John Maclean* (London, 1973), p. 180.

135. Stamfordham to the Bishop of Chelmsford, 25 November 1918, RA GV/O 1106/65.

136. *Parliamentary Debates*, vol. 110 (18 November 1918), cols. 3237–8.

137. Bishop of Chelmsford to Stamfordham, 5 April 1919, RA GV/O 1106/66.

138. Bishop of Chelmsford to Stamfordham, 18 August 1919, RA GV/O 1106/68.

139. See, for example, RA GV/O 1220/39.

140. Thornton had served as a general during the war, supervising the Allied railways. See D'Arcy Marsh, *The Tragedy of Henry Thornton* (Toronto, 1935).

141. RA GV/O 1220/53; 1220/66.

142. Wigram to Thornton, 21 January 1921, RA GV/O 1220/81.

143. RA GV/O 1220/80.

144. Quoted in Keith Laybourn and Dylan Murphy, *Under the Red Flag: A History of Communism in Britain, c. 1849–1991* (Stroud, 1999), pp. xv, xix.

145. RA GV/O 1220/78; 1220/148.

146. RA GV/O 1220/97.

147. RA GV/O 1220/64.

148. RA GV/O 1220/88.

149. RA GV/K 1740/1.

150. RA GV/K 1740/4.

151. RA GV/K 1740/5.

152. RA GV/K 1740/3.

153. RA GV/K 1740/9.

154. RA GV/K 1740/8.

155. RA GV/O 1220/132.

156. RA GV/O 1220/140; 1220/141; 1220/146; 1220/147.

157. For a discussion of this trend see Bruce P. Lenman, *The Eclipse of Parliament: Appearance and Reality in British Politics since 1914* (London, 1992). For an alternative reading of the transformation of government, which emphasizes legal administration, see Joseph M. Jacob, *The Republican Crown: Lawyers and the Making of the State in Twentieth-Century Britain* (Aldershot, Hampshire, 1996).

158. For a more thorough discussion of the monarchy's social policy in the reign of George V see Prochaska, *Royal Bounty: The Making of a Welfare Monarchy*, chapter 6.

159. Sarah Bradford, *George VI* (London, 1991), p. 103.

160. *A King's Story. The Memoirs of the Duke of Windsor* (New York, 1951), p. 217.

161. Quoted in Philip Ziegler, *King Edward VIII* (London, 1990), p. 111.

162. Henry Hector Bolitho, *A Century of British Monarchy* (London, 1951), p. 206.

163. See Prochaska, *Royal Bounty: The Making of a Welfare Monarchy*, pp. 194–201.

164. RA GV/CC 47/672.

165. RA PS/GVI/PS 1627.

166. Nicolson, *King George the Fifth*, p. 121.

167. Quoted in *ibid.*, p. 384.

168. *Ibid.*

169. Taylor, *English History, 1914–1945*, p. 209

170. Quoted in Nicolson, *King George the Fifth*, p. 389.

171. Memorandum by Sir Frederick Ponsonby, 3 January 1924, RA GV/K 1918/104.

172. Nicolson, *King George the Fifth*, pp. 390–91.

173. Russell Galbraith, *Without Quarter. A Biography of Tom Johnston, 'The Uncrowned King of Scotland'* (Edinburgh and London, 1995), p. 83. Willie Hamilton, *My Queen and I* (London, 1975), p. 103.

174. William Gallacher, *The Last Memoirs of William Gallacher* (London, 1966), p. 69. MacDonald, who had a fondness for ceremonial, did not wish to offend the King and took issue with purists like Gallacher. See David Marquand, *Ramsay MacDonald* (London, 1977), p. 313.

175. RA GV/K 1918/208, cited in Nicolson, pp. 391–2.

176. In his memoirs, Shinwell excised the republicanism of his youth, see *Shinwell Talking* (London, 1984). On Shinwell's republicanism see *Parliamentary Debates*, vol. 311 (5 May 1936), col. 1605.

177. Hamilton, *My Queen and I*, pp. 103–4.

178. RA GV/K 1940/1.

179. Memorandum by Stamfordham, 28 June 1924, RA GV/K 1940/3.

180. RA GV/K 1940/4.

181. RA GV/K 1940/17.

182. RA GV/K 1940/6.

183. RA GV/K 1940/10. On communists and the army see also RA GV/K 1940/14, 15.

184. Ethel Snowden to Stamfordham, 12 October 1925, RA GV/O 2016/4.

185. Ethel Snowden to Stamfordham, 19 November 1925, RA GV/O 2016/12.

186. RA GV/O 2016/24.

187. For a discussion of the contribution of the Communist Party to the General Strike see *The General Strike*, ed. Jeffrey Skelley (London, 1976).

188. RA GV/B 2052/14. See also Nicolson, *King George the Fifth*, p. 418.

189. Stamfordham to Ethel Snowden, 8 September 1926, RA GV/O 2016/28.

190. Quoted in Nicolson, *King George the Fifth*, p. 421.

191. Stamfordham to Ethel Snowden, 1 April 1927, RA GV/O 2016/42.

192. John Hodge, *Workman's Cottage to Windsor Castle* (London, 1931), pp. 190–91.

193. Philip Viscount Snowden, *An Autobiography*, 2 vols. (London, 1934), vol. 2, pp. 829–30.

194. *The Diary of Beatrice Webb*, vol. 4, p. 193.

195. In the 1931 crisis, the King took advice from the three party leaders, but, according to Clive Wigram, he found the Liberal leader, Sir Herbert Samuel, the most persuasive. Samuel told the King, in Harold Nicolson's words: 'in view of the fact that the necessary economies would prove most unpalatable to the working class, it would be to the general interest if they could be imposed by a Labour Government. The best solution would be if Mr Ramsay MacDonald, either with his present, or with a reconstituted Labour Cabinet, could propose the economies required', *King George the Fifth*, p. 461.

196. Herbert Morrison, *Government and Parliament: A Survey from the Inside* (Oxford, 1954), pp. 77–80.

197. Vernon Bogdanor, *The Monarchy and the Constitution* (Oxford, 1995), p. 112.

198. See, for example, *Parliamentary Debates*, vol. 318 (11 December 1936), col. 2210.

199. Hamilton, *My Queen and I*, p. 106.

200. Marquand, *Ramsay MacDonald*, pp. 774–5. For a glimpse of the demonstration of loyalty at the time see *The Official Index to The Times*, April–June 1935.

201. Raymond Postgate, *The Life of George Lansbury* (London, 1951), p. 251.

202. *Parliamentary Debates*, vol. 301 (8 May 1935), col. 981.

203. *Ibid.* (9 May 1935), cols. 1109–11.

204. Quoted in Nicolson, *King George the Fifth*, p. 524.

205. *The Collected Essays, Journals and Letters of George Orwell*, eds. Sonia Orwell and Ian Angus, 4 vols. (Harmondsworth, 1970), vol. 3, p. 33.

206. Antony Taylor, *'Down with the Crown': British Anti-Monarchism and Debates about Royalty since 1790* (London, 1999), pp. 223–4.

207. *The Times* (11 June 1935), p. 17.

208. From the *Morning Post* (7 May 1935), quoted in *Politics in Review*, vol. 2, no. 2 (April–June 1935), pp. 17–18.

209. *Parliamentary Debates*, vol. 319 (26 January 1937), col. 1458.

210. See Vernon Bogdanor, 'How we carried on regardless', *Times Literary Supplement* (3 January 1997), p. 6.

211. Stamfordham to Woodward, 21 October 1918, RA GV/O 1341/8.

212. Tom Nairn, *The Enchanted Glass. Britain and its Monarchy* (London, 1988), p. 213.

213. *Parliamentary Debates*, vol. 311 (5 May 1936), col. 1605.

214. From *Forward* (1 February 1936), quoted in *Politics in Review*, vol. 3, no. 1 (January–March 1936), p. 50.

215. *Railway Review* (31 January 1936), quoted in *Politics in Review* (see note above).

216. *Parliamentary Debates*, vol. 324 (27 May 1937), col. 457.

217. *Ibid.* (24 May 1937), col. 41.

218. Leonard Woolf, *Quack, Quack!* (London, 1935), pp. 34–5.

219. *Parliamentary Debates*, vol. 311 (5 May 1936), cols. 1607, 1610.

220. *Ibid.*, col. 1623.

221. *Ibid.* (7 May 1936), col. 2003.

222. *Morning Post* (21 September 1937); Colin Cooke, *The Life of Richard Stafford Cripps* (London, 1957), p. 160; *The Times* (15 January 1934), p. 14.

223. *Clarion* (29 June 1917), RA GV/O 1106/45.

224. Fred Simpson, MP for Ashton-under-Lyne, was paraphrasing a remark by Dicey. See *Parliamentary Debates*, vol. 311 (7 May 1936), col. 2000. Dicey's precise remark was 'Republicanism . . . has ceased to be a heresy, but it has also ceased to be a faith'. He, in turn, was quoting a French saying. See *Lectures on the Relation between Law and Public Opinion in England during the Nineteenth Century*, p. 443.

225. *Parliamentary Debates*, vol. 318 (11 December 1936), cols. 2204–5; vol. 324 (24 May 1937), col. 40.

226. *Ibid.*, vol. 318, col. 2217.

227. *Forward* (19 December 1936). See also Galbraith, *Without Quarter. A Biography of Tom Johnston, 'The Uncrowned King of Scotland'*, pp. 206–7.

228. Ziegler, *King Edward VIII*, p. 304.

229. This was the view, not entirely detached, of Willie Hamilton, who claimed to be an eyewitness. See *My Queen and I*, pp. 107–8.

230. Clement Attlee, *As It Happened* (London, 1954), p. 86.

231. *The Times* (7 December 1936), p. 8.

232. Quoted in Ziegler, *King Edward VIII*, p. 321.

233. Taylor, *English History, 1914–1945*, pp. 401–2.

234. At least two writers sought to use the abdication crisis to stir up republican sentiment. See An American Resident, *The Twilight of the British Monarchy:*

Reflections on the Abdication and Coronation (London, 1937); Kingsley Martin, *The Magic of Monarchy* (London, 1937).

235. Harrison, *The Transformation of British Politics, 1860–1995*, p. 343.

236. Quoted in *The Times* (11 December 1936), p. 8.

237. *Parliamentary Debates*, vol. 318 (11 December 1936), cols. 2205–8.

6. The Crowned Republic and its Enemies

1. *Parliamentary Debates*, vol. 324 (27 May 1937), col. 463.

2. *Ibid.* (1 June 1937), cols. 933–54.

3. For a recent biography which plays up the King's political importance see Robert Rhodes James, *A Spirit Undaunted: The Political Role of George VI* (London, 1998). For a more general biography see Sarah Bradford, *George VI* (London, 1991). For a discussion of George VI's charitable work see Frank Prochaska, *Royal Bounty: The Making of a Welfare Monarchy* (New Haven and London, 1995), chapter 7.

4. Harold Nicolson, *Diaries and Letters, 1945–1962*, ed. Nigel Nicolson (London, 1971), p. 327.

5. *The Diary of Beatrice Webb*, eds. Norman and Jeanne MacKenzie, 4 vols. (London, 1982–85), vol. 4, p. 435.

6. *The Times* (28 December 1937), p. 12.

7. Marion Yass, *This is your War: Home Front Propaganda in the Second World War* (London, 1983), p. 58.

8. *New Statesman and Nation* (23 December 1944), p. 421.

9. Willie Hamilton, *My Queen and I* (London, 1975), p. 108.

10. Marion Crawford, *The Little Princesses* (New York, 1950), p. 226.

11. *The Diaries of Sir Henry Channon*, ed. Robert Rhodes James (London, 1967), p. 463.

12. Sir John W. Wheeler-Bennett, *King George VI: His Life and Reign* (London, 1958), pp. 650, 653; Kingsley Martin, *The Crown and the Establishment* (London, 1962), p. 116.

13. *Forward* (19 December 1936). See also Russell Galbraith, *Without Quarter. A Biography of Tom Johnston, 'The Uncrowned King of Scotland'* (Edinburgh and London, 1995), pp. 206–7.

14. Ben Pimlott, *The Queen: A Biography of Elizabeth II* (London, 1996), p. 82.

15. For a more detailed discussion of the royal family and the NHS see Prochaska, *Royal Bounty: The Making of a Welfare Monarchy*, pp. 232–8.

16. H. A. Strutt to Ulick Alexander, 22 January 1947, Royal Archives PP/GVI 3892.

17. Pimlott, *The Queen*, pp. 132–3.

18. *Parliamentary Debates*, vol. 445 (17 December 1947), cols. 1734, 1749, 1752–3.

19. From a saving of £200,000 during the war, the King donated £100,000 to the Treasury in consideration of the annuity to his daughter. See Phillip Hall, *Royal Fortune: Tax, Money and the Monarchy* (London, 1992), pp. 85–8.

20. *Parliamentary Debates*, vol. 445 (17 December 1947), col. 1746.

21. *Ibid.*, cols. 1745–7.

22. *Ibid.*, cols. 1748–9.

23. *Ibid.*, col. 1725.

24. *Ibid.*, col. 1728.

25. Vernon Bogdanor, *The Monarchy and the Constitution* (Oxford, 1995), p. 270.

26. See Prochaska, *Royal Bounty: The Making of a Welfare Monarchy*, p. 246.

27. *Parliamentary Debates*, vol. 504 (23 July 1952), col. 670.

28. *Ibid.*, vol. 503 (9 July 1952), col. 1365.

29. *Ibid.*, vol. 504 (23 July 1952), col. 699.

30. Hamilton, *My Queen and I*, p. 110.

31. *Parliamentary Debates*, vol. 503 (9 July 1952), cols. 1342–3, 1411–12.

32. *Ibid.*, vol. 504 (23 July 1952), col. 670.

33. See David Low's 'The Morning After', *Manchester Guardian* (3 June 1953), reproduced in Kenneth Baker, *The Kings and Queens: An Irreverent Cartoon History of the British Monarchy* (London, 1996), p. 168.

34. Pimlott, *The Queen*, p. 217. See also E. Shils and M. Young, 'The Meaning of the Coronation', *Sociological Review*, vol. 1, no. 2 (December 1953), pp. 63–70.

35. David Cannadine, 'The Context, Performance and Meaning of Ritual: The British Monarchy and the "Invention of Tradition"', c. 1820–1977', *The Invention of Tradition*, eds. Eric Hobsbawm and Terence Ranger (Cambridge, 1984), pp. 153–4.

36. Herbert Morrison, *Government and Parliament: A Survey from the Inside* (Oxford, 1954), pp. 91–2.

37. Pimlott, *The Queen*, p. 207.

38. Hamilton, *My Queen and I*, p. 14.

39. *Ibid.*, p. 111.

40. *Ibid.*, p. 118.

41. *New Statesman and Nation* (22 October 1955), pp. 499–500.

42. *Saturday Evening Post* (19 October 1957).

43. *National and English Review* (August 1957); see also Lord Altrincham and others, *Is the Monarchy Perfect?* (London, 1958), chapter 1.

44. Geoffrey Bocca, *The Uneasy Heads. A Report on European Monarchy* (London, 1959), pp. 213–14.

45. Cannadine, 'The Context, Performance, and Meaning of Ritual: The British Monarchy and the "Invention of Tradition"', c. 1820–1977', pp. 156–8.

46. See Bogdanor, *The Monarchy and the Constitution*, pp. 95–9.

47. Leonard Harris, *Long to Reign over us? The Status of the Royal Family in the Sixties* (London, 1966), pp. 37–8, 43, 78.

48. *Ibid.*, pp. 69, 72–3.

49. See Philip Ziegler, *Crown and People* (London, 1978), p. 127.

50. R. Rose and D. Kavanagh, 'The Monarchy in Contemporary Political Culture', *Comparative Politics*, vol. 8 (July 1976), pp. 548–76. See also Pimlott, *The Queen*, p. 370.

51. Pimlott, *The Queen*, pp. 322–3.

52. *Fortnightly Review*, vol. 11 (June 1872), p. 632. See also Brian Harrison, *The Transformation of British Politics, 1860–1995* (Oxford, 1996), p. 346.

53. Martin, *The Crown and the Establishment*, p. 176.

54. Hamilton, *My Queen and I*, pp. 3, 126.

55. *Ibid.*, pp. 1–2.

56. See Hall, *Royal Fortune: Tax, Money and the Monarchy*, p. 63, passim. Hamilton, who died on 23 January 2000, lived to have the satisfaction of seeing his arguments about taxing royal income adopted.

57. *Parliamentary Debates*, vol. 887 (26 February 1975), cols. 601–4.

58. Harold Wilson, *Final Term. The Labour Government 1974–1976* (London, 1979), p. 132.

59. *Times Literary Supplement* (31 January 1975), p. 108.

60. *Parliamentary Debates*, vol. 887 (26 February 1975), cols. 575–632.

61. *New Statesman* (3 June 1977), pp. 738–9.

62. Pimlott, *The Queen*, p. 446.

63. Antony Taylor, *'Down with the Crown': British Anti-Monarchism and Debates about Royalty since 1790* (London, 1999), p. 231.

64. *The Times* (24 October 1978), p. 4.

65. Ben Pimlott, 'Monarchy and the Message', *Politics and the Media: Harlots and Prerogatives at the Turn of the Millennium*, ed. Jean Seaton (Oxford, 1998), p. 91.

66. *Sunday Times* (21 June 1987), quoted in Pimlott, *The Queen*, p. 527.

67. See, for example, Julia Atkinson, 'The Monarchy Show', *Freethinker*, vol. 102 (August 1982), pp. 118–19.

68. *Republic*, vol. 2, no. 3 (spring 1985), pp. 16–19. The Bishopsgate Institute has copies of the *Republic* and other materials on the association.

69. Piers Brendon, *Our Own Dear Queen* (London, 1986), p. 228.

70. Christopher Hitchens, *The Monarchy* (London, 1990), pp. 11, 19.

71. Tom Nairn, *The Enchanted Glass. Britain and its Monarchy* (London, 1988), pp. 13, 52, 54. See also his earlier article 'The House of Windsor', *New Left Review*, no. 127 (May/June 1981), pp. 96–100.

72. Nairn, *The Enchanted Glass. Britain and its Monarchy*, pp. 53–4, 155.

73. *Ibid.*, p. 126.

74. Tom Nairn, 'A Story's End', *Power and the Throne: The Monarchy Debate*, ed. Anthony Barnett (London, 1994), p. 154. This volume was a compendium based on the 'Monarchy Debate', held at the Queen Elizabeth Centre, London, in 1993.

75. For a good survey see Pimlott, *The Queen*.

76. See Tony Benn's The Commonwealth of Britain Bill, included in Tony Benn and Andrew Hood, *Common Sense: A New Constitution for Britain* (London, 1993), Appendix 1.

77. *Punch* (29 January–4 February 1992).

78. See, for example, 'Monarchy: The Nation Decides', at the Birmingham Amphitheatre in January 1997, reported in *The Times* (8 January 1997), p. 2; (9 January 1997), p. 6.

79. David Hare, 'Guts or Garters', *Power and the Throne*, p. 210.

80. Martin Amis, 'My Imagination and I', *Power and the Throne*, pp. 79–80.

81. A Mori poll in September 1994 put the level of republicanism in the population at 20 per cent. See *The Economist* (10 December 1994), p. 34. For the series of Mori polls on the monarchy between April 1993 and June 1999 see *British Public Opinion*, vol. xxii, no. 6 (August 1999), p. 4.

82. For a critique of the republican threat, with historical comparisons, see the *Independent* (27 November 1992), p. 23.

83. *Daily Telegraph* (1 May 1998), p. 5. The Queen Mother and the Duke of Edinburgh continued to receive annuities.

84. Nairn, 'The House of Windsor', *New Left Review*, no. 127 (May/June 1981), p. 100.

85. On royal finances see Vernon Bogdanor, *The Monarchy and the Constitution*, chapter 7. For a critical appraisal see Hall, *Royal Fortune: Tax, Money and the Monarchy*.

86. Frank Vibert, Deputy Director of the Institute of Economic Affairs, con-

sidered the abolition of the monarchy in a paper, which he later altered for publication. For the modified version see 'Constitutional Reform in the United Kingdom – An Incremental Agenda', *Britain's Constitutional Future*, ed. Frank Vibert (IEA, 1991), pp. 15–36.

87. Brian Micklethwait, 'Privatise the Royal Family?, *Economic Affairs*, vol. 5, no. 2 (March 1990).

88. Jonathan Freedland, *Bring Home the Revolution: The Case for a British Republic* (London, 1999), p. 190. When first published in 1998, this work had the title *Bring Home the Revolution: How Britain can Live the American Dream*.

89. Stephen Haseler, 'Monarchy is Feudal', *Power and the Throne*, pp. 65–71. See also Stephen Haseler, *The End of the House of Windsor* (London, 1993).

90. Freedland, *Bring Home the Revolution: The Case for a British Republic*, pp. 191, 194.

91. See Ferdinand Mount, *The British Constitution Now: Recovery or Decline?* (London, 1992), p. 100.

92. Daniel T. Rodgers, 'Republicanism: the Career of a Concept', *Journal of American History*, 79 (June 1992), p. 37.

93. Philip Pettit, *Republicanism: A Theory of Freedom and Government* (Oxford, 1997), chapter 5.

94. Jeremy D. Mayer and Lee Sigelman, 'Zog for Albania, Edward for Estonia, and Monarchs for all the Rest? The Royal Road to Prosperity, Democracy, and World Peace', *PS: Political Science and Politics*, December 1998, p. 773.

95. See, for example, Haseler, 'Monarchy is Feudal', *Power and the Throne*, p. 70.

96. See Charles Moore, 'The Importance of the Monarchy', *Power and the Throne*, pp. 54–9.

97. Peter Hennessy believes the 'reserve powers' of the sovereign are more important than is commonly assumed, though he accepts that the Queen does not materially affect the content of political life, see *The Hidden Wiring: Unearthing the British Constitution* (London, 1995), p. 53. For a reformer's view see Jack Straw, 'Abolish the Royal Prerogative', *Power and the Throne*, pp. 125–9. For further discussion of the constitutional issues raised by the royal prerogative see Bogdanor, *The Monarchy and the Constitution*, chapter 3; Christopher Vincenzi, *Crown Powers, Subjects and Citizens* (London, 1998), pp. 74–6.

98. Mount, *The British Constitution Now: Recovery or Decline?*, p. 102.

99. For a discussion of scepticism and the republican tradition see Michael Oakeshott, *The Politics of Faith and the Politics of Scepticism*, ed. Timothy Fuller (New Haven and London, 1996), pp. 83–4.

100. Caroline Ellis, 'A Right Little Royalist', *Power and the Throne*, p. 146. Another republican, Hilary Wainwright, conceded that 'the abolition . . . of the monarchy would only create an opportunity for democratic republicanism. It would not mark its achievement', see 'Across to London', *Power and the Throne*, p. 147.

101. *Fortnightly Review*, vol. 11 (1 June 1872), p. 634.

102. Charles Bradlaugh, *London Republican Club. The Inaugural Address* (London, 1871), p. 7.

103. Quoted in the *Times Literary Supplement* (5 March 1999), p. 30.

104. See R. W. K. Hinton, 'The Prime Minister as an Elected Monarch', *Parliamentary Affairs*, vol. xiii (1959–60), pp. 297–303.

105. Harrison, *The Transformation of British Politics, 1860–1995*, pp. 324–5.

106. *Labour Leader* (19 June 1897), p. 203.

107. Anthony Barnett, 'The Empire State', *Power and the Throne*, pp. 40–41.

108. Paul Richards, *Long to reign over us?* (Fabian pamphlet, 1996), p. 7.

109. Bogdanor, *The Monarchy and the Constitution*, pp. 300–301.

110. Haseler, *The End of the House of Windsor*, pp. 56–7; Freedland, *Bring Home the Revolution: The Case for a British Republic*, p. 220.

111. Richard Hoggart, 'Rank Attitudes', *Power and the Throne*, p. 131.

112. Christopher Hitchens, 'The People and the Monarchy', *Power and the Throne*, p. 76.

113. Decca Aitkenhead, 'Time to let them go', *Guardian* (12 July 1999), p. 17.

114. *Red Pepper* (October 1997).

115. Richards, *Long to reign over us?*; Tim Hames and Mark Leonard, *Modernising the Monarchy* (Demos, 1998). For a critique of the Demos proposals see *The Times* (8 September 1998), p. 22.

116. See Barnett, 'The Empire State', *Power and the Throne*, pp. 1–2.

117. See, for example, the *Independent* (8 September 1997), p. 15; the *Guardian* (17 September 1997), p. 17. Two years later, republicans still sought to capitalize on the death of the Princess of Wales. See, for example, Beatrix Campbell, 'Comment', *Independent on Sunday* (29 August 1999). For a republican perspective on the constitutional implications of the death of the Princess see Anthony Barnett, *This Time Our Constitutional Revolution* (London, 1997), chapter 5. See also Taylor, *'Down with the Crown': British Anti-Monarchism and Debates about Royalty since 1790*, pp. 235–6.

118. *Red Pepper* (October 1997).

119. See, for example, the poll in *The Times* (27 August 1998), pp. 1–2. A survey of children aged 15 to 16 published in the *Sunday Times* (7 February 1999), put the Prince of Wales second after Sir Bobby Charlton as 'the best

moral and spiritual leader in Britain today'. For more polling information on the Prince of Wales see *British Public Opinion*, vol. xxii, no. 6 (August 1999), p. 4.

120. *The Times* (27 August 1998). A *Sunday Times* poll published on 14 September 1997, weeks after the death of the Princess of Wales, showed that only 13 per cent of the sample wanted the monarchy abolished, though 73 per cent thought the Queen was out of step with public feelings. Another poll in *The Times* taken soon after the death of the Princess of Wales found that 18 per cent wanted the monarchy abolished. A series of Mori polls put the level of support for the monarchy at over 70 per cent for most of the 1990s. See *British Public Opinion*, vol. xxii, no. 6 (August 1999), p. 4.

121. See the leaflet distributed by the Movement against the Monarchy. Their newsletter, the *Guillotine*, vol. 2, issue 3, claimed that 1,000 people paraded through central London with a mobile guillotine but were prevented from reaching the Palace by the police.

122. *Observer* (25 May 1997), p. 20. Anthony Holden, a member of the constitutional reform club, Common Sense, thought 90 per cent of Labour back-benchers were republicans. *Red Pepper* (October 1997).

123. Bogdanor, *The Monarchy and the Constitution*, p. 301.

124. See, for example, Will Self, 'Comment', *Independent on Sunday* (8 August 1999).

125. *Guillotine*, vol. 2, issue 3. I am grateful to the Movement against the Monarchy for providing me with information and for permission to reproduce one of their leaflets.

126. See Nairn, 'A Story's End', *Power and the Throne*, p. 154.

127. See *The Times* (8 July 1999), p. 22.

128. For recent statements of 'republican virtues' see Haseler, *The End of the House of Windsor*, pp. 179–84; Freedland, *Bring Home the Revolution: The Case for a British Republic*, passim.

129. A. J. P. Taylor, *English History, 1914–1945* (Oxford, 1965), p. 175.

130. David Cannadine, *History In Our Time* (New Haven and London, 1998), p. 30.

131. For details of the workload of the royal family in 1997, see *The Times* (2 January 1998), p. 17. See also Prochaska, *Royal Bounty: The Making of a Welfare Monarchy*, p. 275, passim.

132. James Morton, *Prince Charles: Breaking the Cycle* (London, 1998), p. 11. See also *The Times* (27 December 1996), p. 16.

133. See, for example, the views expressed on civil society by Freedland, *Bring Home the Revolution: The Case for a British Republic*, pp. 219–23.

134. See, for example, Revd Archer Gurney, *Loyalty and Church and State: A Sermon Preached ... on the occasion of the National Thanksgiving for the Recovery of H.R.H. The Prince of Wales* (London, 1872), p. 6.

135. *The Times* (26 December 1991), p. 19. For Paine's views, see 'Of Society and Civilization', *Rights of Man*, part 2, chapter 1.

136. Bogdanor, *The Monarchy and the Constitution*, p. 308.

137. The quote is from Tom Shebbeare, Director of the Prince's Trust. See the *Sunday Times* (12 January 1997), p. 15.

138. *The Big Issue* (13–17 December 1999), pp. 14–15. Of those sampled in a Mori poll of June 1999, 85 per cent thought the Prince of Wales 'caring', see *British Public Opinion*, vol. xxii, no. 6 (August 1999), p. 4.

139. See, for example, Prince Charles's address to the conference to launch the 'Volunteers' programme at St James's Palace in 1990.

140. *Red Republican* (22 June 1850), pp. 4–5.

141. *Parliamentary Debates*, vol. 39 (20 December 1837), col. 1369.

142. Harold Nicolson, *King George the Fifth: His Life and Reign* (London, 1952), p. 106. See also Bogdanor, *The Monarchy and the Constitution*, pp. 298–9.

143. On America see Rodgers, 'Republicanism: the Career of a Concept', *Journal of American History*, 79 (June 1992).

144. See the discussion of the 'neo-Roman theory of free states' in Quentin Skinner, *Liberty before Liberalism* (Cambridge, 1998), pp. 54–5, passim.

145. *The Times* (25 November 1992), p. 3.

146. Herbert Spencer, 'The Americans', *Essays*, 3 vols. (London, 1891), vol. 3, pp. 478–9.

Index